RELATED TITLES FOR COLLEGE-BOUND STUDENTS

Titles for the New SAT starting March 12, 2005

The NEW SAT

The NEW SAT with CD-ROM

NEW SAT 2400

The NEW SAT Critical Reading Workbook

The NEW SAT Math Workbook

The NEW SAT Writing Workbook

SAT II

SAT II Biology E/M

SAT II Chemistry

SAT II Literature

SAT II Math IC and IIC

SAT II Physics

SAT II Spanish

SAT II U.S. History

SAT II World History

Vocabulary-Building for the SAT

Extreme SAT Vocabulary Flashcards Flip-O-Matic

SAT Vocabulary Flashcards Flip-O-Matic

SAT Vocab Velocity

Frankenstein: A Kaplan SAT Score-Raising Classic

The Ring of McAllister: A Score-Raising Mystery Featuring 1,046 Must-Know SAT Vocabulary Words

SAT for Native Spanish Speakers

Domina el SAT: Prepárate para Tomar el Examen para Ingresar a la Universidad

Test Prep and Admissions

The NEW PSAT®

2005 Edition

By the Staff of Kaplan Test Prep and Admissions

Simon & Schuster

NEW YORK · LONDON · SYDNEY · TORONTO

Kaplan Publishing
Published by Simon & Schuster
1230 Avenue of the Americas
New York, NY 10020

Contributing Editors: Jon Zeitlin and Seppy Basili
Project Editor: Charli Engelhorn
Cover Design: Cheung Tai
Interior Page Layout and Production: Jan Gladish
Managing Editor: Déa Alessandro
Production Manager: Michael Shevlin
Executive Editor: Jennifer Farthing
Senior Managing Editor: Eileen Mager

July 2004
10 9 8 7 6 5 4 3 2 1

Manufactured in the United States of America
Published simultaneously in Canada

ISBN 0-7432-5175-X

Table of Contents

kaptest.com/publishing

The material in this book is up-to-date at the time of publication. However, since the new PSAT does not debut until October 2004, certain details are not yet public. The College Entrance Examination Board may institute changes in the test after this book goes to print. For any important late-breaking developments—or changes or corrections to the Kaplan test preparation materials in this book—we will post that information online at **kaptest.com/publishing**. Check to see if there is any information posted there regarding this book.

kaplansurveys.com/books

What did you think of this book? We'd love to hear your comments and suggestions. We invite you to fill out our online survey form at **kaplansurveys.com/books**. Your feedback is extremely helpful as we continue to develop high-quality resources to meet your needs.

Get with the Program

The PSAT is an important test for students who want to get a head start on their college paths because it serves two basic and important functions:

- It can earn you cash for college.
- It can prepare you to take the SAT.

For these two reasons alone, getting the highest score possible is essential. Our Kaplan PSAT Program is designed to help you do just that.

KAPLAN'S PSAT PROGRAM

The Kaplan PSAT Program is your detailed plan for getting your highest score possible on the PSAT. The Program is organized into five chapters. Each chapter maximizes your performance on the PSAT, so each chapter is an integral part of your preparation.

Chapter One

Chapter one tells you about the PSAT and teaches you time-tested strategies for managing everything it throws at you. By becoming an expert—like us—in what the PSAT tests, how it tests, and how you should approach the exam, you *will* improve your score.

Chapters Two, Three, and Four

The next three chapters take on the PSAT's Critical Reading, Math, and Writing components. Kaplan is the largest test-prep company in the world. Our unbeatable resources mean that we can put more time, money, and effort into finding out what makes the PSAT sections tick, including the new question types in Critical Reading and Math.

We share with you everything we have compiled on the new PSAT and then give you specific strategies for earning your best score on each section.

Chapter Five

Knowing how to plan for and succeed on the day of the test is almost as important as knowing what's on the test. In chapter five, we break down your count down to the test day by day, hour by hour, so the minute the test proctor says *Ready?*—you are.

But wait, there's more!

Practice PSATs

An essential feature of the Kaplan PSAT Program is the **three practice PSATs** you will find at the back of the book. The tests are written and designed to be as close to the actual PSAT as possible. You can use one as a diagnostic exam to determine your strengths and weaknesses and then take the other tests to practice your test-taking skills and measure your improvement.

Important Appendices

The PSAT Program also includes six (count 'em, *six*) important appendices that cover a preview of the new essay section on the SAT (Appendix One), figuring out hard words and improving your writing skills (Appendices Two–Four), vocabulary words that the PSAT tests over and over again (Appendix Five), and math concepts that the PSAT tests over and over again (Appendix Six). We suggest that you try to build these appendices into your study plan to optimize and further improve your score.

PSAT Vitals

We have also created a one-page reference sheet filled with short review notes on the most important things from each chapter of this book, as well as important details about the PSAT test and test-day prep. This page is meant to be a quick access from your purse, wallet, or glove compartment. Cut it out and keep it on you all the way to test day.

Ready? Let's begin.

How to Use this Book

The Kaplan PSAT Program can be used in several different ways, depending on your schedule, time constraints, and strengths and weaknesses. Perhaps it would be easier to think of this book not as a massive paperweight, but as a multi-featured DVD containing the standard theatrical release and the film trailer.

THE TEN-WEEK PROGRAM (THEATRICAL RELEASE)

To avoid cramming and to give yourself ample time to study and review, we suggest you complete the Kaplan Program over 8–10 weeks. That way, you will have plenty of time to:

- Read and understand every part of the book
- Do every practice question and read every answer explanation
- Focus and improve upon any of your PSAT weaknesses
- Take all three practice exams

With this program, you could do one section every week or two. (Chapter one doesn't take long to work through, but you'll want to use what you learn in that section for the entire study period.) Get a good grasp of the material in chapter one before moving on. It will help guide your focus as you work through the other chapters. We also suggest that you take time off from your PSAT preparation when you need to. Nobody should consume such a heavy load of information day in and day out for weeks at a time without a break.

We believe that 8–10 weeks is the most advantageous time frame because if you do the Kaplan Program over a much longer period of time, you may forget some of the material you learned *waaay* back when you started. If you go through the book over a much shorter period of time, you will basically be prepping for the PSAT every spare minute and have no life (see our two-week plans for more on this). Also, cramming has a tendency to cause increased levels of stress and poor memory retention, which are two things that will only hinder your success on test day.

Here are the steps in our Ten-Week Program along with a suggested time frame for each step:

- Take a timed Practice Test: Score it, and review the answers and explanations to the questions you got wrong and the questions you got right. Use this diagnostic test to determine how much time to spend on each section of the PSAT. (Week 1)
- Work through chapters one–five in order or in an order that you feel comfortable with. (Weeks 1–6)
- Review the chapters on the PSAT sections you need to improve upon. (Week 7)
- Take the other two timed Practice Tests: Score them. (Week 8)
- Re-read chapter five. Try to live the life it recommends until test day. (Week 8)

THE ADJUSTED TWO-WEEK PROGRAM (FAST FORWARD)

Don't have a couple of months to prepare? If you go through one or two chapters every day, you can work through every page in this book in 1–2 weeks. So, try adjusting our Ten-Week Program to your accelerated schedule, but take two practice tests, rather than all of them as we previously suggested. Give yourself a day before the test to rest and allow everything you have learned to sink in. You will be able to focus better if you allow your brain some down time, and you will deserve it.

THE TWO-WEEK PROGRAM (FILM TRAILER)

If you have limited time to prepare for the PSAT, we suggest you do the following abbreviated prep program:

- Review chapter one. This is our overview of the PSAT and our must-know PSAT strategies.

- Take one timed practice test. This will help you use the knowledge you have gained. Review your results, with special attention to the questions you missed.

- Memorize the directions. By memorizing the PSAT directions, you save valuable time reading them on test day. You are going to need it!

Again, try to make sure to give yourself the day before the test off. Your brain will be running on overdrive and will need some space from the content to help it sink in.

PSAT Strategies

Almost everyone prepares for the SAT. The same cannot be said for the PSAT. This is great news for you. Because you are one of the students who *is* preparing, you have a really good chance of scoring higher than the kids who don't.

Think about it. If you prep for the PSAT, *you have an advantage*. You will be the one running downhill, the one swimming downstream, and the one with the wind at your back.

Chapter One: **Be the PSAT**

CHAPTER ONE OVERVIEW

Chapter one of the Kaplan PSAT Program is an overview of the PSAT and Kaplan's strategies for doing your absolute best on the exam. The following chapters on Critical Reading, Math, and Writing build upon the materials in this chapter, so read chapter one slowly and methodically. Be sure you understand the information it presents before you move on to chapters two–four.

BASICS

If you don't have much time to prep for the PSAT, spend what time you do have reading this chapter. It covers the basic information on the PSAT and Kaplan's overall strategies for approaching the test—the fundamentals you need to be ready for the exam and to feel confident about improving your score.

Like we said, the PSAT can only help. A good PSAT score *could* earn you a nice scholarship, making your college experience a little cheaper and a lot more fun. Furthermore, by prepping for the PSAT, you are familiarizing yourself with the same kinds of questions the SAT uses.

Where and When to Take the PSAT

The PSAT is offered once a year every mid-October. It is administered at your high school, not at a testing center. Home-schooled students can sign up at the nearest local high school. Most high schools administer the exam on a Saturday; some offer it on Tuesday.

Some high schools recommend that their students take the test for additional practice as sophomores. Sophomores who take the PSAT are not eligible to qualify for the National Merit Scholarship unless they are in an accelerated program and are preparing to graduate the following year. However, some schools will administer the test to their students only once, in the beginning of their junior year; thus, students wanting to take it as sophomores would have to get permission from their guidance counselors.

Why Take the PSAT

The PSAT/NMSQT stands for the Preliminary SAT/National Merit Scholarship Qualifying Test. It has two main functions.

Function 1

The first is to give you practice for the SAT. Although shorter than the SAT (2 hours 10 minutes compared to 3 hours 45 minutes), it contains the same types of math, reading, and writing questions, except for a written essay, as those found on the SAT. It also measures your score against your classmates across the country, just like the SAT does.

Function 2

Taking the PSAT also gives you a chance to qualify for several scholarship programs, most notably the National Merit Scholarship Program. Aside from the possibility of receiving tuition for college, recognition by the National Merit Scholarship program is an impressive addition to your college applications.

The top 50,000 scorers on the PSAT are recognized by the National Merit Program and sent letters of commendation. More than 10,000 of these students share more than $47 million in National Merit Scholarship money.

SCHOLARSHIPS OFFERED

The most well-known scholarship offered, of course, is the National Merit Scholarship. As noted, only juniors who take the PSAT are eligible for National Merit Scholarships. The top 50,000 scorers are recognized by the National Merit Scholarship Program and sent letters of commendation. The top 16,000 scorers become semi-finalists, and approximately 14,000 semi-finalists become finalists. Finally, almost 8,500 National Merit finalists actually receive National Merit Scholarships, which award up to $2,500 a year toward a college education. Many high scorers who don't receive National Merit Scholarships may still be awarded merit scholarships from the schools to which they apply on the basis of their high scores. Whether you qualify as a Commended Student, a Semi-Finalist, a Finalist, or a full-fledged National Merit Scholar, it's definitely worth noting this achievement on your college applications.

Note, also, that if you do receive a letter of commendation but do not qualify to become a National Merit finalist, you could still be eligible for a Special Scholarship. To be considered for Special Scholarships, students who meet a corporate or business sponsor's criteria must file entry forms directly with that organization, which then forwards the entry forms back to the National Merit Scholarship Corporation. A list of corporate organizations that sponsor Special Scholarships is given in the PSAT/NMSQT Student Bulletin. The NMSC subsequently contacts high scoring candidates through their high schools, and the students and their school officials then submit detailed scholarship applications. Finally, these applications are evaluated, and 1,700 students are awarded Special Scholarships.

For more information on the National Merit Scholarships and Special Scholarships, visit www.nationalmerit.org or write to:

National Merit Scholarship Corporation
1560 Sherman Avenue, Suite 200
Evanston, IL 60201-4897

The National Hispanic Scholar Recognition Program

Hispanic students may qualify for aid from this program, which sends the names of 4,000 high-scoring students to colleges to promote recruitment efforts and offers of financial aid.

For more information, write to:
National Hispanic Scholar Recognition Program
c/o The College Board
1233 20th Street, NW
Washington, DC 20036

National Scholarship Service and Fund for Negro Students

African American students who plan to attend two- or four-year colleges may qualify for this program. This program offers a college advisory and recruitment service at no charge. For more information, email nhrp@collegeboard.org or write to:

National Scholarship Service and Fund for Negro Students
250 Auburn Avenue NE, Suite 500
Atlanta, GA 30303

KAPLAN
Test Prep and Admissions

The Telluride Association

This association offers scholarships to gifted juniors for summer seminars in the humanities and social sciences.

For more information, email telluride@cornell.edu, visit www.tellurideassociation.org, or write to:

Telluride Association
217 West Avenue
Ithaca, NY 14850

STRUCTURE

The PSAT is 2 hours and 10 minutes long and is made up of mostly multiple-choice questions testing three subject areas. Those areas are Critical Reading, Math, and Writing, and they are broken down into five sections on the exam.

Sections 1 and 3—Critical Reading	
Length	Content
25 minutes each	13 Sentence Completion and 35 Reading Comprehension multiple-choice questions (short and long passages)

Sections 2 and 4—Math	
Length	Content
25 minutes each	28 Regular math multiple-choice questions and 10 Grid-in questions

Section 5—Writing Skills	
Length	Content
30 minutes	14 Usage, 20 Sentence Correction, and 5 Revision-in-Context questions

You get a five-minute break between Sections 2 and 3 and a one-minute break between Sections 4 and 5.

SCORING

Here's how the PSAT is scored:

Correct answer	1 point
Unanswered question	0 points
Incorrect answer to a Math grid-in	0 points
Incorrect answer to a multiple-choice question	−1/4 point

You gain one point for each correct answer on the PSAT and lose a fraction of a point (1/4) for every wrong answer. The exception is Math Grid-ins, where you lose nothing for a wrong answer. You do not lose any points for questions you leave blank. This is important, so we'll repeat it: you do not lose *any* points for questions you leave blank.

Raw Scores

The totals for the Critical Reading, Math, and Writing sections are added up to produce three separate raw scores. These raw scores equal the number you got right minus a fraction of the number you got wrong.

Raw score = number right minus 1/4 of the number wrong

These scores are converted into scaled scores from 20 to 80. A table providing a rough translation of how raw scores convert into scaled scores (the conversion formula changes slightly from test to test) appears in Section Two.

Selection Index

Add the three scores together and you get your *Selection Index*. At the time of printing, the Selection Index ranges from 60 to 240. The average raw score on the Critical Reading, Math, and Writing components is approximately 49. The average Selection Index is approximately 147.

Percentile

The PSAT also gives you a percentile, which allows you to compare your scores with those of other juniors applying to college. A student with a percentile of 63 has earned a score better than 63 of every 100 college-bound juniors who took the test.

BASIC STRATEGIES

Now that you know *why* to take the test and *what* it is all about, let's get into *how*, as in, *how* to attack the PSAT.

The PSAT is different from the tests you are used to taking in school. The good news is you can use the PSAT's particular structure to your scoring advantage.

Here's an example. On a school test, you probably go through the problems in order. You spend more time on the hard questions than on the easy ones because harder questions are usually worth more points. You probably often show your work because the teacher tells you that *how* you approach a problem is as important as getting the answer right.

None of this works on the PSAT. If you use the same approach on the PSAT, your score will suffer. On the PSAT, you benefit from moving around within a section if you come across hard questions because the hard questions are worth the same as the easy ones. It doesn't matter how you answer the questions—only that you get them right.

The PSAT is *special*. To succeed on the PSAT, you need to know its quirks and how to use them to your advantage. Once you fully understand the PSAT's personality, you may even find yourself wishing tests at school were more like it.

Basic Strategy 1

Know the Enemy

The key to success on the PSAT is knowing what to expect. The PSAT format—that is, the directions, the types of questions, and the traps that the test makers put in the questions— is almost identical from test to test. The only thing the test makers change are the questions themselves.

That means one of the easiest things you can do to improve your performance on the PSAT is to know its format *before* you take the test. For example, if you learn the PSAT directions as you read this book, you can spend all of your time during the test answering the questions and getting your highest score possible instead of reading the directions, which you already know, because they never change. Get it? Great.

Basic Strategy 2

Use Order of Difficulty to Your Advantage

Many of the PSAT sections arrange their questions so they get more difficult as you work through a question set. In a question set that goes from 1 to 9, question 2 would be fairly easy, question 5 would be moderately more difficult, and question 9 would be really hard.

This is true of both Math question types (regular math and Grid-ins) and the Sentence Completion questions in the Critical Reading sections. The Reading Comprehension portion of the Critical Reading sections and the Writing Skills section questions are NOT arranged in any particular order of difficulty.

You can use this knowledge to your scoring advantage. As you work, always be aware of where you are in the set. When working on the easy problems, you can generally trust your first impulse—the obvious answer is likely to be right. As you get to the end of the set, you need to become more suspicious. The answers probably *shouldn't* come easily. If they do, look at the problem again because the obvious answer is likely to be wrong. Watch out for the answer that just *looks right*. It might be a distractor, or a trap—a wrong answer choice meant to entice you. (We'll go into detail on the PSAT's favorite kinds of distractors later.)

Basic Strategy 3

Don't Get Stuck. Move On

You're not allowed to work on other sections during the test, but you are allowed to skip around within each section of the PSAT. High scorers know this. They move through the test efficiently. They don't dwell on any one question, even a hard one, until they've tried every question at least once.

The key is to be systematic. When you run into questions that look tough, circle them in your test booklet and skip them. Go back and try again after you have answered the easier ones. Remember, you don't get more points for answering hard questions. If you get two easy ones right in the time it would have taken you to get one hard one right, you just gained points.

There's another benefit for coming back to hard ones later. On their second look, troublesome questions can turn out to be simple. By answering some easier questions first, you can come back to a harder question with fresh eyes, a fresh perspective, and more confidence.

Basic Strategy 4

Know When to Guess

There is no penalty for guessing on the PSAT. There is only a penalty for getting a *wrong answer*. If you can determine that one or more answers are definitely wrong, then you should probably guess from the remaining choices. Even if you aren't sure which one of them is absolutely correct, you've at least increased your chances of success by paring the selection down.

Here's why. If you get an answer wrong on any multiple-choice question on the PSAT, you lose 1/4 point. These fractional points you lose are supposed to offset the points you might earn accidentally by guessing the correct answer, and here's where our techniques really help you out. By learning Kaplan's techniques, you can eliminate wrong answer choices on almost all PSAT questions, even if you have no idea what the actual right answer is. By eliminating wrong answer choices, you are creating a *guessing advantage*.

The PSAT has one question type that is not affected by this strategy. Remember, if you get an answer wrong on a Grid-in math question, for which you write in your own answers, you lose nothing. So you should write in an answer for every Grid-in. The worst that can happen is that you get zero points for the questions you guessed on.

Basic Strategy 5

Respect Your Answer Sheet

It sounds simple, but it's extremely important: Don't make mistakes filling out your answer grid. When time is short, it's easy to get confused going back and forth between your test book and your grid. If you know the answer, but misgrid, you won't get the points. To avoid mistakes on the answer grid, you could try some of the methods below.

Circle the Questions You Skip

Perhaps the most common PSAT disaster is filling in all of the questions with the right answers in the wrong spots. Every time you skip a question, put a big circle in your test booklet around questions you skip to help you locate these questions when you are ready to go back to them. Also, if you accidentally skip a box on the grid, you can always check your grid against your book to see where you went wrong.

Circle the Answers You Choose

Circling your answers in the test book makes it easier to check your grid against your book. It also makes the next grid strategy possible.

Grid Five or More Answers at Once

Time is of the essence on this exam. To save time and make sure you are marking your answers in the correct bubbles, transfer your answers after every five questions or at the end of each reading passage, rather than after every question. That way, you won't keep breaking your concentration to mark the grid. You'll end up with more time and fewer chances to make a mistake on your answer sheet.

Basic Strategy 6

Think About the Question Before You Check the Answer Choices

The people who make the test love to put distractors among the answer choices. Distractors are answer choices that look right but aren't, and they are easy to choose if you haven't read the question carefully. If you jump right into the answer choices without thinking first about exactly what you're looking for, you're much more likely to fall for these traps.

Basic Strategy 7

Use Shortcuts if You Have To

There are usually a number of ways to get to the right answer on a PSAT question. Most of the questions on the PSAT are multiple choice. That means the answer is right in front of you—you just have to find it. This makes PSAT questions open to several different ways of finding the answer.

If you can't figure out the answer the straightforward way, try other techniques. We'll explore these approaches in detail in the following chapters.

Basic Strategy 8

Pay Attention to Where You Are in a Question Set

As we noted earlier, many of the question sets (except for Reading Comprehension and the Writing Skills section) start out easy and gradually get harder. So if an early question seems hard, make sure to take a second look; you're bound to be missing something obvious. If a hard question seems easy, watch out! You may be falling into a trap.

Finally, don't be upset if you have to skip a couple of the hard questions altogether; by spending your time elsewhere, you'll probably do better on the questions you did answer. You don't have to answer every single question, even if you're aiming for a National Merit Scholarship.

Basic Strategy 9

Look for Quick Points When You're Running Out of Time

Some questions can be done quickly. For instance, some Critical Reading questions will ask you to identify the meaning of a particular word in the passage. These can be done at the last minute, even if you haven't read the passage. When you start to run out of time, try to locate and answer the questions that can earn you quick points. When you take the PSAT, you should have one clear objective in mind—to score as many points as you can. It's that simple. The rest of this book will help you do that.

CHAPTER ONE SUMMARY

○ The PSAT can help you in two ways: 1) getting scholarship money, and 2) getting SAT practice.

○ There are five sections on the PSAT. They appear in the following order

Critical Reading	25 min.
Math	25 min.
Critical Reading	25 min.
Math	25 min.
Writing	30 min.

○ You get one point for every right answer, and you lose 1/4 point for every wrong answer (except for Grid-ins, where you lose nothing for a wrong answer).

○ Know when a question set is arranged easiest to hardest and approach it accordingly.

○ Don't spend too much time on any single question. Move around in a section, answering the questions you know you can do easily and saving the hard ones for last.

○ If you can eliminate at least one wrong answer choice, you should guess.

○ Be careful transferring your answers from your booklet to your answer sheet.

○ Think about the question before you look at the answers.

○ Look for quick points when you are running out of time.

Chapter Two: **How to Attack the Critical Reading Sections**

The two PSAT Critical Reading sections are pretty predictable. They don't test your knowledge of Shakespeare or Hemingway. They don't test your grammar knowledge, either. (The Writing section takes care of that.) Instead, they test a fixed set of skills in three areas: reading, reasoning, and vocabulary.

So no matter what kind of English student you are, we can help you improve your skills and score on the PSAT's Critical Reading section.

CHAPTER TWO OVERVIEW

The PSAT's Critical Reading section is pretty straightforward. Chapter two explains the Critical Reading question types (Sentence Completion and Reading Comprehension) and gives you specific strategies for approaching each. Once you feel comfortable with the material, work through the practice set at the end of the section.

CRITICAL READING BASICS

There are two scored sections comprising the Critical Reading section on the PSAT. Each lasts 25 minutes and is made up of two question types:

- 13 Sentence Completion questions
- 35 Reading Comprehension questions (short and long passages)

Sentence Completion

Sentence Completion questions can be answered fairly quickly, leaving you time to concentrate on the more demanding Reading Comprehension questions. The Sentence Completion question sets start off easy and increase in difficulty. So it's important to always pay attention to where you are in a Sentence Completion set. Early and late questions call for different approaches: early questions in a set should be straightforward and easier to handle, whereas later questions contain more traps and trickier vocabulary.

Reading Comprehension

Reading Comprehension question sets follow no particular order. The first question could be the hardest, or the last could be the easiest. Like many things in life, the questions in this area are random and unpredictable.

The PSAT includes both long and short passages. Although the subject matter for reading comprehension varies widely, expect to see one science passage and one passage in the form of a first-person narrative, which could be either fiction or nonfiction. Other common PSAT passage topics include history, literature, and art. You'll also see one or two paired-passage sets that present two different passages on the same topic.

Long Reading Comprehension passages begin with italicized introductions. Read these carefully—they provide helpful information for understanding the passage: where it comes from, what it's about, when it was written, and so on.

VOCABULARY AND CONTEXT

The PSAT Critical Reading section, as we've noted, tests your reading and thinking skills, and, to a smaller extent, your vocabulary. In this book, we will help you to develop a good PSAT-friendly vocabulary between now and test day. It's simply a matter of knowing how to make the most of your time so you can learn words quickly and achieve the score you're looking for.

Just as important as a good vocabulary is the ability to decipher the meaning of unfamiliar words. When you come across a strange word in a book you are reading, do you look it up? Most times, probably not. Often, you don't really need to look up the meaning because the manner in which it is used clues you into the meaning of the word.

This is called understanding vocabulary through context, and it's an essential Critical Reading skill. The PSAT Critical Reading section always provides some sort of context for tough vocabulary words. Our strategies show you how to squeeze the most out of these context clues.

Boosting Your Vocabulary

There are two distinct types of tough PSAT vocabulary words:

- Unfamiliar words
- Familiar words with unfamiliar secondary meanings

Some words will be hard simply because you have never seen them before. There's a good chance you've never come across words like *redoubtable* or *expiate*, but these words could easily appear on the PSAT.

Other common words, such as *appropriate* and *flag*, could also pose some problems because the test makers will most likely be testing their secondary, less familiar definitions. Watch for this, especially on Reading Comprehension questions; this section almost always contains questions that will test your knowledge of unfamiliar meanings to familiar words.

To get a sense of your vocabulary strength, take a few minutes to go through the following list of typical PSAT vocabulary words and see how many you know. Write your definition to the right of each word, and then score yourself. Give yourself one point for every word you know. (You'll find answers and study advice based on your score following the quiz.)

chafe _____

veracity _____

vanquish _____

ardor _____

lethargic _____

eradicate _____

pensive _____

legible _____

vex _____

stoic (adj.) _____

adept (adj.) _____

exculpate _____

guile _____

disinterested _____

pine (v.) _____

din _____

covert _____

wag (n.) _____

censure (n.) _____

loquacious _____

temper (v.) _____

acumen _____

diffident _____

lachrymose _____

toady _____

lumber (v.) _____

latent _____

admonish _____

foible _____

specious _____

Here are the definitions:

chafe	to wear away or irritate by rubbing
veracity	truthfulness
vanquish	to defeat or conquer in battle
ardor	fiery intensity; zeal
lethargic	sluggish, inactive, apathetic
eradicate	to remove; tear up by the roots
pensive	thoughtful
legible	possible to read or decipher
vex	to irritate or annoy
stoic (adj.)	indifferent; impassive
adept (adj.)	skilled
exculpate	to remove guilt or blame
guile	skillful deceit; treacherous cunning
disinterested	impartial; unbiased
pine (v.)	to long for
din	loud noise; clamor
covert	not openly shown; secret
wag (n.)	a humorous person, a wit
censure	strong disapproval or harsh criticism
loquacious	extremely talkative
temper (v.)	to moderate
acumen	accuracy and keenness of judgment or insight
diffident	shy and timid
lachrymose	tearful
toady	a flatterer; a sycophant
lumber (v.)	to walk with heavy clumsiness
latent	present but inactive; dormant
admonish	to scold or reprove gently
foible	minor weakness or failing of character
specious	seemingly true but actually fallacious

If you got 10 definitions or fewer right, you should start working on building your vocabulary. The techniques and tools in this chapter will teach you ways to improve your word base and make the most out of what you do know about words.

If you got between 11 and 20 correct, your vocabulary is about average. If you're willing to put in the time, using these techniques and tools can help you improve your vocabulary and your score on the exam.

If you knew the definitions to more than 20 words, your vocabulary is in great shape. You can polish it further, particularly if you are aiming for a National Merit Scholarship, but you don't have to. If your time is short, learn the strategies in the "Decoding Tough Vocabulary" part of this chapter first, and concentrate on other aspects of the PSAT that you find difficult.

A VOCABULARY-BUILDING PLAN

A great vocabulary can't be built overnight, but you can develop a better PSAT vocabulary in a relatively short period of time with a minimum amount of pain. But you need to study wisely. Be strategic. How well you use your time between now and the day of the test is just as important as how much time you spend prepping.

Learn Words Strategically

The best words to learn are words that have appeared often on the PSAT and SAT. Fortunately, the test makers are not very creative in their choice of words for each test, so words that have appeared frequently are likely bets to show up again.

Start with the PSAT Word List in the PSAT Study Aids appendices at the back of this book. This list contains words that have been seen on previous PSATs (and SATs). You probably already know a lot of the words on this list. We suggest you learn 10 words a day from this list by using the techniques discussed in this chapter. You'll want to continue to review those words until you know their definitions as well as you know the class schedule of the intriguing new transfer student!

Study Word Roots

Most PSAT words are made up of prefixes and roots that can get you at least partway to a definition. Thankfully, on the PSAT, partway is often far enough to get you points. (Remember what we said in chapter one about guessing?)

For instance, if you know that the prefix *circum* means *around* or that *locution* means *talk* or *speech*, you might be able to decode the definition of *circumlocution*, which means talking around, as when someone avoids talking about a particular subject. Use the Root List in the PSAT Study Aids appendices to pick up the most valuable PSAT roots. Target these words in your vocabulary review. For some, many of these word roots—including *circum* and *locution* in this case—may already be familiar if you've studied a foreign language, particularly a romance language such as French, Spanish, or Latin.

Personalize Your Vocabulary Study

There's not just one right way to study vocabulary. Figure out a study method that works best for you, and stick to it. Here are some of our proven strategies:

- Use flashcards. Write down new words or word groups on one side of a 3 x 5 index card and a short definition on the back. Run through the flashcards whenever you have some spare time.

- Create a vocabulary notebook. List words in one column and their meaning in another. Cover up the meanings or fold the page to test yourself, and see what words you can define from memory. Make a sample sentence using each word in context.

- Make a vocabulary tape. Record the unfamiliar words and their definitions. Pause for a moment before you read the definition. This will give you time to define the word in your head when you play the tape back. Quiz yourself. Listen to your tape in your portable cassette player. Play it when you're in the car, on the bus, or whenever you have some free time.

- Try to come up with hooks to lodge a new word in your mind: Create visual images of words to build associations between them and their definitions.

- Use rhymes and other devices that help you remember the words. For example, you might remember that a *verbose* person uses a lot of verbs.

It doesn't matter which techniques you use, as long as you learn words steadily and methodically. Doing so over several months with regular reviews is ideal.

DECODING TOUGH VOCABULARY

No matter how much time you spend with flashcards, tapes, or word lists, you're bound to face some mystery words on your PSAT. No big deal. Fortunately, there are ways of dealing with unfamiliar vocabulary on the PSAT.

Trust Your Hunches

Vocabulary knowledge is not an all-or-nothing proposition. Don't write off a word you see on the PSAT just because you can't recite its definition. If you feel like you've seen or heard the word before but are not sure what the exact definition is, look through the answer choices, and trust your gut. Don't be afraid to take a risk.

Try to Recall Where You've Heard the Word Before

If you can recall a phrase in which the word appears, that may be enough to get you to the correct answer. Take a look at the following example. Remember that you don't need to know the dictionary definition to solve a question like this one. A sense of where you've heard a word before may be all you need.

> After the military government banned the opposing
> political party, its members continued to meet in
> ---- groups.
>
> (A) amicable
> (B) elaborate
> (C) clandestine
> (D) auspicious
> (E) sanctioned

Looking through the answer choices, you may not know the definition of *clandestine*, but you may have heard the word used in phrases like "clandestine operations" or "clandestine meetings" on the news or in spy movies. If you remembered clandestine in this context, you could have gleaned the meaning of the word. *Clandestine* means *done in secret.* Choice (C) is correct.

Think Positive/Negative

Sometimes just knowing the charge of a word—that is, whether a word has a positive or negative sense—is enough to get a question correct. Take the word *auspicious*. Let's assume you don't know its dictionary definition. Ask yourself: Does auspicious sound positive or negative? How about *vituperative*? Negative words sometimes have ugly or harsh sounds that enhance their sense of negativity, whereas positive words often sound more friendly. If you thought *auspicious* sounded positive, you're right. It means *favorable or hopeful.* Likewise, if you thought *vituperative* sounded negative, you're right again. *Vituperative* means *critical and abusive.*

You can also use prefixes to help determine a word's charge. *Pro-*, *ben-*, *magn-*, and *eu-* often indicate a positive, whereas *mal-*, *de-*, *dis-*, *dys-*, *un-*, *in-*, *im-*, and *mis-* are often negative words. In the example below, begin by getting a sense of the charges of the words that will appear in the blanks. Then look for the pair of words whose charges match your prediction.

> I did not set out to ---- my colleague; I meant well,
> but my words came across as ----.
>
> (A) irk . . affable
> (B) impress . . confused
> (C) ostracize . . sincere
> (D) appease . . belligerent
> (E) offend . . gauche

You should get the sense from the sentence that things did not go so well between the writer of the sentence and her colleague. This means you're looking for negatively charged words for both the first and second blanks. For the first blank, neither *impress* nor *appease* has the negative charge you are looking for, so you can eliminate choices (B) and (D). Looking at the second blank, *affable* and *sincere* are both positively charged, so you can eliminate (A) and (C). All that's left is choice (E), the correct answer, because it is the only one with two negatively charged words.

That's it for vocabulary. Now it's time for strategies that help you master each of the PSAT's Critical Reading question types.

SENTENCE COMPLETION QUESTIONS

Sentence Completion questions test your knowledge of PSAT vocabulary and your ability to follow the logical flow of a sentence. Lots of students like Sentence Completion questions because you can work through them faster and gain points more quickly than with Reading Comprehension questions. Also, unlike Reading Comprehension questions, you only have to deal with one sentence at a time. With practice, you should be able to handle this question type with speed and confidence.

It's important to remember that Sentence Completion question sets are arranged in increasing order of difficulty. The first few Sentence Completion questions in a set should be the easiest, and the last few should be the hardest. By becoming an expert with this question type, you'll be well on your way to a great Critical Reading score.

Let's take a look at the Sentence Completion directions and a sample question.

Directions: Select the lettered word or set of words that best completes the sentence.

> Rain is traditionally viewed as an ---- sign; many
> believe that if it rains on the day of your wedding, you
> will enjoy financial prosperity.
>
> (A) unfortunate
> (B) oblique
> (C) auspicious
> (D) original
> (E) indifferent

So, you're looking for the answer that fits the meaning of the rest of the sentence. In this example, the second half of the sentence states many people believe that rain can predict financial prosperity. This is considered a good thing, so rain must be viewed as a positive sign. Thus, (C), *auspicious*, meaning favorable, is correct.

As you can see, the key to answering a Sentence Completion question is to locate clues in the rest of the sentence that will allow you to predict the meaning of the missing word. Let's take a look at our strategy for Sentence Completion questions.

KAPLAN'S FOUR-STEP METHOD

Step 1. Read the sentence for clues.

Step 2. Predict an answer.

Step 3. Scan the answer choices for a match.

Step 4. Read your selected answer choice back into the sentence.

Step 1. Read the Sentence for Clues

Don't look at the answer choices before you've read through and thought about the sentence. Each Sentence Completion question contains clues that lead you directly to the correct answer. With practice, and with our help, you'll learn to spot these clues.

Step 2. Predict an Answer

Once you've spotted the clues within the sentence, think up a word that would fit in the blank. This will save you valuable time when you go through the answer choices. You generally don't have to make an exact prediction. Sometimes it's enough simply to predict whether the word is positive or negative.

Step 3. Scan the Answer Choices for a Match

Quickly eliminate choices that do not match your prediction, and zero in on the answer choice that is the closest to your word. Make sure to read *every answer choice* before deciding.

Step 4. Read Your Selected Answer Choice Back into the Sentence

Confirm your answer choice by reading it back into the sentence. Learn to trust your ear on Sentence Completion questions. If something doesn't sound right, it probably isn't.

Okay, buckle up. Let's take the strategy for a test drive.

> Although some of the revelations in the movie
> star's memoirs will surprise even his most ardent
> fans, much of his story is quite ----.
>
> (A) significant
> (B) familiar
> (C) impressive
> (D) explicit
> (E) thorough

Read the sentence carefully, looking for clues. The word *although* is a major clue here. It tells you that the sentence switches direction midstream. Another clue is *some . . . revelations . . . will surprise*. So, although some revelations will surprise the fans, the rest of his story must be the opposite of surprising.

You're ready to predict an answer. Here you might predict something like *unsurprising*. Scan the answer choices for a match. The only answer choice that comes close to our prediction is (B), *familiar*. Something that is familiar is not surprising at all.

You still want to check your answer by reading the selected choice back into the sentence: *Although some of the revelations in the movie star's memoirs will surprise even his most ardent fans, much of his story is quite familiar*. That sounds fine, so (B) is the correct answer.

Let's work through another example.

> As different schools of thought on child rearing go
> in and out of vogue, parents who at one time were
> esteemed for imposing strict rules and strong disci-
> pline upon their children may find themselves mar-
> ginalized, decried for being ----.
>
> (A) despotic
> (B) controversial
> (C) effective
> (D) pragmatic
> (E) erratic

There are no obvious structural clues in this sentence, but there are clues to tell you that the sentence contains a contrast. Given that attitudes *go in and out of vogue*, if the parents were at one time seen as good disciplinarians, they were later seen as bad examples of how to discipline children. Clearly you can predict that a negative word will fill in the blank. From that alone you can get rid of *effective* (C) and *pragmatic* (D), which are positive in charge.

You're looking for a negative take on *imposing strict rules and strong discipline*. A good prediction would be *overly disciplinarian* (you don't have to come up with a perfect one-word prediction). The best match for this prediction is (A), *despotic*, which means repressive and authoritarian.

Even if you didn't know the meaning of *despotic*, by the process of elimination, you would still get the correct answer; neither *controversial* (B) nor *erratic* (E) matches our prediction. Once again, if you read answer choice (A) back into the sentence, it sounds right, which means you're done.

Get a Clue

Structural clues help you to get a fix on whether the sentence will continue along in the same line or shift directions and contrast with the rest of the sentence. Be on the look-out for structural clues such as the following:

Continuations:
- ; (a semicolon)
- and
- because
- also
- consequently

Contrasts:
- but
- however
- although
- despite
- yet

TWO-BLANK SENTENCE COMPLETION QUESTIONS

Think two-blank Sentence Completion questions must be twice as hard as one-blank questions? Think again. With two-blank Sentence Completion questions, you have twice as many opportunities to zero in on the correct answer, so these questions can actually be easier than those with just one blank. However, to handle two-blank questions in the most efficient manner possible, we have to alter our approach ever so slightly.

Step 1. Read the sentence for clues.

Step 2. Decide which blank is easier to predict. Predict an answer for that blank.

Step 3. Scan the answer choices, and eliminate those that don't match the prediction.

Step 4. Read the remaining answer choices back into the sentence. Keep the one that works for both blanks.

Notice that with this type of question, you need to decide which blank will be easier to make a prediction for. By focusing on one blank at a time and eliminating answer choices based on that blank, your job becomes much easier. Take a look:

> Jazz developed as a style of music that was uniquely characterized by its heavy reliance on improvisation and on ---- musical boundaries, yet today, a lot of jazz has become so ---- that many listeners cannot stand to hear one of their favorite "jazz standards" played in a novel manner.
>
> (A) respecting . . fixed
> (B) expanding . . ambiguous
> (C) expanding . . standardized
> (D) sustaining . . particularized
> (E) transgressing . . universal

The structural clue *yet* lets you know that there is a contrast in this sentence. The first half discusses the origins of jazz, which are based in improvisation. The second half discusses its current state, which avoids anything *novel* or original.

It might be easier to predict the second blank here. We want a word that means the opposite of *original*; a good prediction might be *rigid* or *formulaic*.

The only answer choices that match this prediction for the second blank are *fixed* (A) and *standardized* (C). We could go ahead and try to make a prediction for the first blank now, but we've narrowed down the field so much that we can also just try out the remaining choices. First try (A).

> Jazz developed as a style of music that was uniquely characterized by its heavy reliance on improvisation and on *respecting* musical boundaries, yet today, a lot of jazz has become so *fixed* that many listeners cannot stand to hear one of their favorite "jazz standards" played in a novel manner.

Respecting musical boundaries? That doesn't sound right—the early musicians were innovators. Trust your ear, eliminate, and move on. But we should make sure that (C) works before we start to celebrate.

> Jazz developed as a style of music that was uniquely characterized by its heavy reliance on improvisation and on *expanding* musical boundaries, yet today, a lot of jazz has become so *standardized* that many listeners cannot stand to hear one of their favorite "jazz standards" played in a novel manner.

Now that makes sense. (C) is the correct answer.

Guessing Tips

If a Sentence Completion question on the PSAT has you stumped—you don't know a lot of the words in the sentence or in the answer choices—do not freak out. You should almost always be able to eliminate a few wrong-sounding answer choices, and then guess. Here are a few things to remember about eliminating and guessing on Sentence Completion questions:

- Don't forget to use our strategies for decoding unfamiliar words on the test. Try to recall where you've seen the word before; see if you can break the word apart, and try to get a sense of the word's charge.

- If an answer sounds wrong to your ear for any reason, trust your instincts, and get rid of that clunker. Your ear often does know best on Sentence Completion questions.

- If you're completely stumped on the very last Sentence Completion question (the toughest question in the set), try picking the answer choice that contains the very weirdest and toughest vocabulary word. Use this strategy only if you otherwise don't have a clue.

Sometimes it can be very difficult to make a prediction for either blank on a two-blank Sentence Completion question. Take a stab at the tough question below.

> Sanders was blind to his own double standards,
> which were so apparent to all those who knew him;
> he was unable to tolerate even the slightest hint of
> ---- in others, and yet he regularly offended his col-
> leagues with his own ---- conduct.
>
> (A) snobbery . . boorish
> (B) timidity . . impudent
> (C) conceit . . supercilious
> (D) impropriety . . prudish
> (E) duplicity . . moralistic

You probably figured out that we're looking for negative words here. But that doesn't help much because all the words in the answer choices are somewhat negative. So what kind of negative behavior are we looking for? Unfortunately, the sentence doesn't contain any solid clues. When you find that none of your question-busting techniques is working, try the following *if-all-else-fails* technique.

If you can't make exact predictions on a two-blank Sentence Completion question, determine the relationship between the blanks. Are the missing words opposites? Are they very similar in meaning?

You know that Sanders operates with a double standard. Therefore, you can predict that he engages in the very behavior that he cannot tolerate in others. You don't know what the missing words are, but you know that they should be practically synonymous. Now let's check out the answer choices.

(A) Is *snobbery* a synonym for *boorish*? No, boorish means crude or unrefined, which is nothing like being a snob.

(B) Is *timidity* a synonym for *impudent*? No, someone who is timid is shy, whereas someone who is impudent is offensively bold—in other words, they are antonyms.

(C) Is *conceit* a synonym for *supercilious*? Why yes, it is! Both mean arrogance. Let's keep checking the other choices to be sure, though.

(D) Is *impropriety* a synonym for *prudish*? No, impropriety is the state of being improper, whereas prudish means overly proper— here's another case of antonyms.

(E) Is *duplicity* a synonym for *moralistic*? No, duplicity means deceit, whereas moralistic means self-righteous.

So (C) is, in fact, the answer.

If you thought that the vocabulary was starting to get a bit tough on the last example, you haven't seen anything yet. Some of the Sentence Completion questions in the practice set at the end of the chapter reach the PSAT's maximum level of difficulty. Sentence Completion questions definitely make serious demands on your vocabulary skills. So if you want to do well on this question type, it really pays to study the PSAT word lists in the back of this book.

Speed Tip

On two-blank Sentence Completion questions, the second blank is usually the easier one to predict.

READING COMPREHENSION QUESTIONS

The Reading Comprehension question sets combine to make up 35 of the 48 Critical Reading section questions. Just like with all of the other question types, we have several strategies for maximizing your points on Reading Comprehension questions. Let's get right to them.

Know the Directions

The same directions apply to each passage, with a few important differences with paired passages. There are a couple of things to notice about these directions.

First, note that every question is based strictly on the content of the passage. This means that you should be careful not to apply outside knowledge when answering the questions. This is actually good news. No matter how unfamiliar the subject matter may be to you, the information to answer the question is right there in front of you.

Next, notice the italicized introduction to the long passages. (Short passages don't have these introductions.) These introductions provide helpful *and important* context about the author and the passage.

Long Versus Short Passages

We mentioned at the beginning of this chapter that the Reading Comprehension sections are composed of two types: long and short passages. What's the difference? The short passages are single paragraphs, approximately 100 words long. The longer passages usually have several paragraphs and range from 450 to 800 words.

The passages and questions are predictable because the test makers use a formula to write them. The topics are drawn from the arts, humanities, social sciences, natural sciences, and fiction. Both passage types use the same kinds of questions that test the same skills. When we get to our strategy for Reading Comprehension questions, you'll see that the method works for short *and* long Reading Comprehension passages.

What Do Reading Comprehension Questions Test?

Reading Comprehension questions do not test your ability to read thoroughly and understand every facet of what you just read. They do not test your ability to relate what you read to outside knowledge. They also do not test your ability to offer a creative or original interpretation of what you just read.

In the Reading Comprehension section, you'll be asked about the overall tone and content of a passage, specific details from the text, and what the author suggests or implies in the passage. The paired passages we've mentioned will consist of two related excerpts with questions that ask you to compare and contrast the texts.

Reading Strategically

Many students have trouble approaching a Reading Comprehension passage with confidence. They may ask themselves, "How am I ever going to get through this long passage and get to all those questions in such a short period of time?" Good question.

Time management is critical on the PSAT Reading Comprehension section. Students often spend too much time meticulously reading the passage. They should instead:

- Read through the passage once.
- Attack the answer choices, returning to the passage later to answer specific questions.
- Choose the best response.

As you read through a passage, you don't want to get bogged down by details. Focusing on details can hurt your score. Why? Most of the passage's details *will not* be referenced in the questions, so reading and remembering useless details will waste your valuable time.

We're going to teach you how to read these passages strategically. You will focus on getting a sense of the passage as a whole. The main ideas of the passages offer the most bang for the buck—often these ideas relate to the most questions and, therefore, give you the most points.

Making a Passage Map

Longer passages cover many different aspects of a topic. For example, the first paragraph might introduce the subject, the second paragraph might present one viewpoint, and the third paragraph might argue for a different viewpoint. Within each of these paragraphs, there are several details that help the author convey a message.

Because there is a lot to keep track of, you need to mark up long passages as follows:

- Write simple notes in the margin as you read.
- Write down the purpose of each paragraph.
- Underline key points.
- Concentrate especially on places where the author expresses an opinion. Most Reading Comprehension questions hinge on opinions and viewpoints, not facts.

These notes are your *passage map*. The passage map helps you find the part of the passage that contains the information you need. The process of creating your passage map also forces you to read actively. Because you are constantly trying to identify the author's viewpoint and the purpose of each sentence and paragraph, you will be working hard to understand what's happening in the passage. This translates into points on the test.

Passage Map

A good passage map should:

- Contain short words or phrases, not whole sentences (e.g., "what author now believes")
- Include markings in the passage like underlined and circled words
- Concentrate on viewpoints and opinions
- Note places where opinions other than the author's are expressed
- Avoid specific details

Strategic Reading Practice

Try out your passage map skills on the passage below. Remember to read for the main idea, and identify the author's point of view. After you read, fill out the questions about the main idea and the purpose of each paragraph.

This passage is from a book on classical art and architecture.

Some places are so beautiful that it's hard to believe they are real, and not some glimpse into another world or paradise. Lying on the bank of the Yamuna River in northern India is one such place, one of the world's most famous
(5) and beautiful buildings. The Taj Mahal was built by the Mughal emperor Shah Jahan as a mausoleum for his favorite consort, Arjumand Banu Bagam. She was known as Mumtaz Mahal, "the Elect of the Palace." Construction began soon after her death in 1631. The mausoleum was
(10) completed by about 1643, and the surrounding complex of buildings and gardens was completed about ten years later.

The Taj Mahal is much more than an expression of love and loss, though. Its architect employed centuries of Iranian and Central Asian mausoleum design to construct a
(15) breathtakingly symmetrical representation of heaven. The mausoleum is set within a square garden 1,002 feet on each side. The garden is bounded by red sandstone walls. Canals divide the garden into four smaller squares, each of which contains fountains, flower beds, and cypress trees—Mughal
(20) symbols of death. The canals converge on a large, rectangular pool in which the white marble mausoleum appears to float. Flanking the mausoleum are two identical red sandstone buildings.

One of these buildings is a mosque; the other is a replica
(25) (Jawab, or, "answer") of the mosque placed there to preserve the complex's unearthly proportionality. One can see this proportionality in the design of the mausoleum's exterior. The mausoleum is essentially a cube set upon a raised, marble platform of approximately 313 square feet. Minarets
(30) (towers) jut skyward from the platform's corners. The mausoleum has four identical façades, each of which contains a large, recessed, pointed arch 108 feet in height. On top of the cube rests a 240-foot-high onion dome. Four smaller domes lie next to this dome. They are situated along the
(35) diagonal axes formed by the top square face of the mausoleum, thus mirroring the placement of the minarets on the square platform. A sense of serene majesty pervades the mausoleum's interior. Sunlight enters the octagonal hall through delicately carved, jewel-studded marble screens.

(40) Mumtaz Mahal's gem-encrusted tomb lies in the center. Her beloved's equally opulent crypt lies at its side.

The Taj Mahal complex is one of the supreme human achievements. As an architectural representation of the afterlife, it is unmatched. The heaven it portrays is one of
(45) serenity and symmetry. A perfect balance is struck between the mausoleum's curves and straight lines, between its bulges and recesses—even between the solidity of its marble and the form that marble gives to the empty space around it. This equilibrium pervades the surrounding gar-
(50) dens, where the constant, gentle flow of water mixes with the aroma of flowers to produce the sense of peace after death yearned for by all cultures.

What's the topic of the passage? _____

Passage Map:

Paragraph 1 (in 2–6 words):_____

Paragraph 2 (in 2–6 words):_____

Paragraph 3 (in 2–6 words):_____

Paragraph 4 (in 2–6 words):_____

What's the main idea of the passage (in no more than 15 words)?_____

_____

TYPES OF READING COMPREHENSION QUESTIONS

When you read passages on the PSAT, you're reading for a specific purpose: to be able to correctly answer as many questions as possible. Fortunately, the PSAT tends to use the same kinds of Reading Comprehension questions over and over again, so whatever the passage is about and however long it may be, you can expect the same four basic question types:

- Big Picture
- Little Picture
- Inference
- Vocabulary-in-Context

You can expect slightly more than half of the questions to be Little Picture and Inference questions; fewer (approximately 30%–40%) will be Big Picture questions and Vocabulary-in-Context questions.

Big Picture Questions

Big Picture questions test how well you understand the passage as a whole. They ask about:

- The main point or purpose of a passage or individual paragraphs
- The author's overall attitude or tone
- The logic underlying the author's argument
- How ideas relate to each other in the passage

If you're still stumped on a Big Picture question after reading the passage, do the Little Picture questions first. They can help you fill in the Big Picture. Big Picture questions will usually be at the end of the question set anyway, so you can often use the question order to help you get a deeper understanding of the whole passage.

Here's a Big Picture question based on the long passage you read earlier.

The author's primary purpose in the passage is to describe

(A) the Taj Mahal as an expression of love and loss

(B) the relationship between Shah Jahan and Mumtaz Mahal

(C) the Taj Mahal as an architectural representation of heaven

(D) the balance between the mosque and the mausoleum in the Taj Mahal complex

(E) the size and dimensions of the Taj Mahal complex

This is a little tricky because the main idea is in the first third of the passage but not in the first paragraph. If you identified the big idea and thought about the passage before looking at the question, this shouldn't have been too hard. The first paragraph gives you a hint at the main idea and describes one reason for the Taj Mahal's construction. The rest of the passage—as indicated by the first two sentences of the second paragraph— shows that the main idea is that *the Taj Mahal is an architectural representation of heaven*, choice (C).

Of the wrong answers, (A) and (B) say more or less the same thing, and both are directly contradicted by the first sentence of paragraph 2. Many wrong answers to Big Picture questions can be eliminated because they are too specific, referring to only one part of the passage. In this case, (D) and (E) are also just details from the passage.

Little Picture Questions

About a third of Reading Comprehension questions are Little Picture questions that ask about localized bits of information—usually specific facts or details from the passage. These questions usually give you a line reference—a clue to where in the passage you'll find your answer. Beware of answer choices that provide a reasonable answer to the stem but don't make sense in the context of the passage or that are true but refer to a different section of the text.

Little Picture questions often test:

- Whether you understand significant information that's stated in the passage
- Your ability to locate information within a text
- Your ability to differentiate between main ideas and specific details

Sometimes the answer to a Little Picture question will be directly in the line or lines that are referenced. Other times, you might need to read a few sentences before or after the referenced line(s) to find the correct answer. When in doubt, use the context (surrounding sentences) to confirm the right choice.

Answer the following Little Picture question, still based on the previous passage.

According to the passage, the Jawab (line 25) was placed across from the mosque in order to

(A) provide more white marble to complement the red sandstone walls

(B) maintain the perfect balance among the various architectural elements in the complex

(C) introduce an element of disproportion to the complex

(D) divide the garden into four equal squares

(E) provide support for the onion dome

Go directly to line 25. The passage states that the Jawab was placed across from the mosque for proportion's sake. (B) is a paraphrase of this thought.

(A) is wrong because the Jawab was made of red sandstone. (C) contradicts the passage. (D) is a distortion—the canals divide the garden into four equal squares. (E) is also a distortion. The Jawab is a freestanding building—it can't support the mausoleum's onion dome. Notice how the correct answer to this question is consistent with the answer to the Big Picture we looked at earlier.

Inference Questions

If you've done any practice exams, you probably noticed that many Reading Comprehension questions begin as follows: "It can be inferred that the author...." To *infer* is to draw a conclusion based on reasoning or evidence. For example, if you wake up in the morning and there's three feet of fresh snow on the ground, you can safely infer that school will be canceled.

Often, writers will use suggestion or inference rather than stating ideas directly. But they will also leave you plenty of clues so you can figure out just what they are trying to convey. Inference clues include word choice (diction), tone, and specific details. For example, say a passage states that a particular idea "was perceived as revolutionary." You might infer from the use of the word *perceived* that the author believes the idea was not truly revolutionary but only *perceived* that way.

Thus, Inference questions test your ability to use the information in the passage to come to a logical conclusion. The key to Inference questions is to stick to the evidence in the text. Most Inference questions have pretty strong clues, so avoid any answer choices that seem far fetched. If you can't find any evidence in the passage, then it probably isn't the right answer.

Take a shot at the Inference question below. Like the previous questions, it refers to the passage you read earlier.

What does the passage suggest about the long history of Iranian and Central Asian mausoleum design?

(A) It had little to do with the design of the Taj Mahal complex.

(B) It stipulated that only white marble be used for mausoleums.

(C) It was the proper architectural tradition to use to express the loss of a loved one.

(D) It constituted the architectural tradition of which the Taj Mahal was the culmination.

(E) It emphasized a balance between curves and straight lines.

Scan the passage for *Iranian*. You'll find it in the sentence at the beginning of paragraph 2, which states that the architect *employed centuries of Iranian and Central Asian design*, so you can definitely eliminate (A). You can also eliminate any choice that refers to any paragraph other than the second one, so (E) is out. *White marble* and *love and loss* are in the second paragraph, but both are wrong—the *white marble* reference, (B), is a distortion; the *love and loss* choice, (C), goes against the main idea of the passage. Only choice (D) is consistent with the passage as a whole and the language of paragraph 2 in particular.

Vocabulary-in-Context Questions

Vocabulary-in-Context questions ask about the usage of a single word. These questions do not test your ability to define hard words like *archipelago* and *garrulous*. Instead, they test your ability to infer the meaning of a word from the context in which it is used.

The words tested on the PSAT will probably be familiar to you—they are usually fairly common words with more than one definition. But that's the trick! Many of the answer choices will be different definitions of the tested word, but only one will work in context. Vocabulary-in-Context questions almost always have a line reference, and you should always use it!

Sometimes one of the answer choices will jump out at you. It'll be the most common meaning of the word in question—but it's RARELY right. You can think of this as the *obvious* choice. For example, say *curious* is the word being tested. The obvious choice is *inquisitive*. But curious also means *odd*, and that's more likely to be the answer.

Using context to find the answer will help prevent you from falling for this trap. But you can also use these obvious choices to your advantage. If you get stuck on a Vocabulary-in-Context question, you can eliminate the *obvious* choice and guess from the remaining answers.

Here's our strategy for Vocabulary-in-Context questions: Once you find the tested word in the passage, treat the question like a Sentence Completion question. Pretend the word is a blank in the sentence. Read a line or two around the imaginary blank if you need to. Then predict a word for that blank. Check the answer choices for a word that comes close to your prediction. Now, use this knowledge to work through the following Vocabulary-in-Context question, which refers to the Taj Mahal passage

> As used in the passage, "unmatched" (line 44) most nearly means?
>
> (A) uneven
> (B) solitary
> (C) outmoded
> (D) noncompeting
> (E) supreme

Go to line 44 and read the sentence, *As an architectural representation of the afterlife, it is unmatched.* This sentence refers to the Taj Mahal, so even if you were unsure of the meaning of unmatched, you should be able to tell from this sentence, as well as from the passage as a whole, that its meaning must be positive. Thus, the only answer that makes sense is (E), supreme. When you read this choice back into the sentence, it still makes sense.

KAPLAN'S FIVE-STEP METHOD

Once you've read a passage strategically and created a passage map, you're ready to attack the questions. Here's Kaplan's Five-Step Method for Reading Comprehension questions:

Step 1. Read the question stem.

Step 2. Locate the material you need.

Step 3. Predict the answer.

Step 4. Scan the answer choices.

Step 5. Select your answer.

Step 1. Read the Question Stem

This is the place to really read carefully. Make sure you understand exactly what the question is asking. Is it a Big Picture question? Little Picture? Inference? Vocabulary? Are you looking for an overall main idea or a specific piece of information? Are you trying to determine the author's attitude or the meaning of a particular word?

Step 2. Locate the Material You Need

If you are given a line reference, read the material surrounding the line mentioned. It will clarify exactly what the question is asking and provide you with the context you need to answer the question correctly.

If you're not given a line reference, scan the text to find the place where the question applies, and quickly reread those few sentences. Keep the main point of the passage in mind.

Step 3. Predict the Answer

Don't spend time making up a precise answer. You need only a general sense of what you're after so you can recognize the correct answer quickly when you read the choices.

Step 4. Scan the Answer Choices

Scan the choices, looking for one that fits your idea of the right answer. If you don't find an ideal answer, quickly eliminate wrong choices by checking back to the passage. Rule out choices that are too extreme or go against common sense. Get rid of answers that sound reasonable but don't make sense in the context of the passage or the question. Don't pick farfetched inferences, and make sure there is evidence for your inference in the passage. Remember, PSAT inferences tend to be strongly implied in the passage.

Step 5. Select Your Answer

You've eliminated the obvious wrong answers. One of the remaining should fit your ideal. If you're left with more than one contender, consider the passage's main idea, and make an educated guess.

The Five-Step Method in Action

Let's see how the method works on a typical short Reading Comprehension passage.

>   I cannot remember my first train ride, but by the time I
> was six, trains were a serious hobby. Not for me were the
> swept-back fins of gas-guzzling 1950s sedans. No, my vision
> of the ultimate was the rise and fall of a train's melancholy
> (5) whistle. The very names of long-distance trains resonated
> with adventure: the *Yankee Clipper*, the *Silver Meteor*, and
> the *Twentieth-Century Limited*. By my tenth birthday, my
> collection of railroad timetables filled three large scrapbooks.
> I knew the stops on entire routes by heart, and my after-
> (10) school playground was Grand Central Station in New York.

For the author, the names of his favorite long-distance trains served to

(A) aid in locating the schedules of particular
      trains in the timetables

(B) indicate the originating points and destina-
      tions of the trains

(C) create an aura of adventure and excitement

(D) remind the author of exciting train journeys
      he had taken

(E) make the trains more compelling than auto-
      mobiles for the author

Step 1. Read the question stem

This question has a very narrow focus—the names of the trains.

Step 2. Locate the material you need

Here's the sentence you need: "The very names of long-distance trains resonated with adventure: the *Yankee Clipper*, the *Silver Meteor*, and the *Twentieth-Century Limited*."

Step 3. Predict the answer

The author seems very fond of the names. He also notes that they *resonated with adventure*. Look for an answer choice that talks about this sense of adventure.

Step 4. Scan the answer choices

(C) and (D) both mention adventure. (A) and (B) are too mundane and functional—they don't allude to the excitement from your prediction. (E) is a distortion of ideas from the passage; the author does prefer trains to cars but not simply because of the train's names.

Step 5. Select your answer

Choose between (C) and (D). On closer inspection, (D) doesn't quite work—the author never says that train names remind him of trips. In fact, he hardly mentions actually getting on a train at all. (C), however, works well.

CHAPTER TWO SUMMARY

○ The two Critical Reading sections each have the following types of questions: Sentence Completion questions and Reading Comprehension questions. They test reading, reasoning, and vocabulary.

○ Tough vocabulary on the PSAT can be broken down into plain old hard words and words you know with unfamiliar secondary meanings.

○ You can decode tough words by trusting your hunches, remembering where you have heard the word before, and *listening* for positive and negative charges.

○ Sentence Completion questions are faster reads than Reading Comprehension questions. Kaplan has a strategy for approaching Sentence Completion questions:

—Step 1. Read the sentence for clues.

—Step 2. Predict an answer.

—Step 3. Scan the answer choices for a match.

—Step 4. Read your selected answer choice back into the sentence.

○ It's important to read the passages strategically—especially the long passages. Make a passage map as you read.

○ Reading Comprehension questions can be divided into four categories:

—Big Picture questions

—Little Picture questions

—Inference questions

—Vocabulary-in-Context questions

○ Reading Comprehension questions include both short and long passages. The strategy for each passage is the same:

—Step 1. Read the question stem.

—Step 2. Locate the material you need.

—Step 3. Predict the answer.

—Step 4. Scan the answer choices.

—Step 5. Select your answer.

PRACTICE

The following practice set should give you some sense of your areas of strength and weakness on the PSAT Critical Reading sections. Be sure to keep in mind the strategies you have learned in this chapter.

When you finish the practice set, take time to thoroughly review the answers, *even for the questions you got right*. You may find that you got the right answer for the wrong reason or that you missed a more efficient way to tackle the problem.

Finally, be sure to take advantage of the Study Aids at the end of this book to help you build your vocabulary and Critical Reading skills for test day.

1. Except for specific, solitary life stages, wolves act as ---- animals, generally living in packs with strong bonds and clear hierarchies.

   (A) carnivorous
   (B) fearsome
   (C) social
   (D) singular
   (E) wild

2. Psychologists disagree about whether multiple personality is ---- disease or a shield behind which some criminals hide in order to ---- prosecution.

   (A) a fallacious . . forestall
   (B) an authentic . . ensure
   (C) a genuine . . evade
   (D) an invalid . . elude
   (E) a diagnosable . . guarantee

3. Despite its stated goals of fostering productivity and hard work, the company promotes many unproductive and ---- employees.

   (A) creative
   (B) discontented
   (C) independent
   (D) lackadaisical
   (E) meritorious

4. Despite his ---- beginnings as the son of a minor tribal chieftain, the conqueror Tamerlane became one of the greatest ---- in Asia.

   (A) impoverished . . nuisances
   (B) auspicious . . failures
   (C) famed . . enigmas
   (D) obscure . . rulers
   (E) luxuriant . . monarchs

5. Winston Churchill's ---- speeches boosted British morale during World War II.

   (A) stolid
   (B) ignoble
   (C) farcical
   (D) resolute
   (E) tremulous

6. Because of her ----, Elizabeth Bishop was not a ---- writer, but she won critical acclaim for the hundred or so poems she allowed to be published during her lifetime.

    (A) notoriety . . creative

    (B) perfectionism . . prolific

    (C) affluence . . renowned

    (D) allusiveness . . poetic

    (E) aphasia . . contemplative

7. President Calvin Coolidge was notoriously ----, usually saying no more than was absolutely necessary.

    (A) abstemious

    (B) clairvoyant

    (C) nefarious

    (D) parsimonious

    (E) taciturn

Questions 8–9 refer to the following passage.

In the early 1990s, commuter railroads expanded greatly, effectively doubling in number in the United States. This incredible expansion was largely in response to a complex, inter-related set
(5) of factors: suburban population growth, increasing traffic on crowded roads and highways caused by a growing work force, governmental and private concern over air pollution, and escalating fuel costs. Many state governments saw in commuter
(10) rails a remedy to these growth pains, and established programs to finance and manage commuter railroads to service metropolitan areas. Despite the great expense involved, most governments also chose to partially subsidize the cost of the tickets,
(15) rather than transfer the entire burden of the cost of the system to its users.

8. The author gives all of the following as reasons for the expansion of commuter railroads in the United States EXCEPT

    (A) growing congestion and traffic due to automobiles

    (B) an increase of population in suburbs

    (C) the extreme expense involved in such an expansion

    (D) the rise in the price of fuel

    (E) concerns about unclean air due to cars

9. The information in the passage suggests that government funding of commuter railroads

    (A) was seen primarily as a response to environmental pollution

    (B) failed to achieve its primary goals

    (C) was an effective alternative to subsidizing rapidly-rising fuel costs

    (D) succeeded in reducing traffic congestions and air pollution

    (E) was chosen as an alternative to relying solely on ticket prices to provide funding

Question 10 refers to the following passage.

While studying Sanskrit, linguist Sir William Jones made a surprising discovery. He found that this ancient language of India bore some striking similarities to Latin and Greek. This caused schol-
(5) ars to posit that both Sanskrit and Latin had a common source, which likely originated in north-central Europe. The scientist further hypothesized that this root language then developed into dozens of different languages, leaving traces of common
(10) lineage. For example, we see that the English word "three" is quite similar to "tre" in Albanian, "tri" in Russian, "trois" in French, "drei" in German, and even "tri" in Sanskrit.

10. The many versions of the English word "three" from other languages listed in lines 11–13 serve as

(A) an illustration of the development of an ancient central European root language

(B) a citation of the similarities of Greek and Latin

(C) proof that Greek and Latin evolved into the cited modern languages

(D) evidence that several different languages likely originated from a common source

(E) partial proof that modern languages influence one another to at least a minor extent

Questions 11–17 are based on the following passage.

The following passage analyzes one of the best known works of Younghill Kang (1903–1972), a Korean writer who came to the United States as an immigrant in 1921.

East Goes West, published in 1937, is one of two important books written by Younghill Kang over a period of seven years. It has been described as a travelogue, a record of an Asian immigrant's

(5) experiences in America during the early decades of this century. But it is much more than a mere catalogue of experiences. It chronicles a journey of disillusionment and despair, for Kang discovered that the utopian image of America which he had

(10) constructed in his own mind before departing his native Korea bore little resemblance to the actual conditions he found upon arriving at America's shores.

East Goes West is written in the form of an

(15) autobiographical novel. It is the fervent personal expression of an immigrant who longed to be accepted into American society. The protagonist Chungpa Han, a slightly fictionalized representation of Kang, comes to America from Korea not

(20) for a temporary sojourn but to establish a new life. Han's attempts to find a doorway into American society prove to be largely futile, however. Searching for the Western civilization to which he has been introduced in his reading of Shakespeare,

(25) he receives an education of another sort altogether as he is ridiculed and exploited by employers and rejected by those he would befriend. Han's hopes and expectations clash continually with the loneliness and alienation with which he must contend.

(30) He is gradually forced to give up his dream of finding the place for himself in America that he had envisioned.

No doubt because it painted a less than flattering picture of life in America for Asian immi-

(35) grants, *East Goes West* was not well received by contemporary literary critics. According to them, the novel displayed a curious lack of insight regarding the American effort to accommodate those who had come over from Korea. The facet of

(40) the novel the reviewers did find praiseworthy was

Han's perseverance and sustained optimism in the face of adversity. This was, in their opinion, a model that Asian Americans should use in overcoming the obstacles of racism and discrimination.

(45) *East Goes West* is a precious part of America's cultural heritage. It has given subsequent generations of Asian Americans a rare glimpse into the trials and tribulations undergone by their immigrant ancestors. Although Kang cannot be consid-

(50) ered representative of the Korean American community of his time, whose members generally were not concerned with immersing themselves in American life, his novel contains many bits and pieces of their collective experience.

(55) Furthermore, *East Goes West* was an important literary event because Kang broke new ground in his description of his experiences in America. One finds neither the superficial commentary of the casual tourist nor the polite observations of the

(60) visiting dignitary, both of which were characteristic of the works of Asian authors prior to Kang. Kang differed from those who had come to America before him in that he did not consider himself to be a guest in someone else's country; he

(65) wanted to forge an American identity for himself.

11. The primary focus of the passage is on the

(A) terrible plight of Asian immigrants in the early decades of last century

(B) failure of Chungpa Han to assimilate into American society

(C) significance that *East Goes West* had as an innovative literary form

(D) literary expression of an Asian immigrant's effort to create an American identity

(E) response of the critics to Younghill Kang's depiction of America in *East Goes West*

12. The statement " . . . he receives an education of another sort altogether . . . " (line 25) conveys a sense of

    (A) irony regarding the difference between Han's expectations and reality

    (B) disdain for Han's hopelessly idealistic aspirations

    (C) dismay that Han was the victim of such horrible treatment

    (D) amusement that Han was so misinformed about life in America

    (E) surprise that Han did not find what he was looking for

13. In line 29, "contend" most likely means

    (A) argue

    (B) believe

    (C) discuss

    (D) struggle

    (E) accept

14. In line 37, the word "curious" most nearly means

    (A) engrossed

    (B) inquisitive

    (C) odd

    (D) unfamiliar

    (E) interested

15. Paragraph 3 indicates that the response of critics to the publication of *East Goes West* was one of

    (A) outright rejection of the novel as a one-sided account of historical events

    (B) admiration of the courage and creativity Kang showed in breaking from literary tradition

    (C) confusion about the motivation of the protagonist

    (D) qualified disapproval of Kang's perception of his adopted homeland

    (E) anger that Kang had so viciously attacked American society

16. The author indicates that Kang "cannot be considered representative of the Korean American community of his time" (lines 49–51) primarily because

    (A) few Korean Americans wrote novels about their experiences

    (B) most Korean Americans were involved in diplomatic relations

    (C) few Korean Americans tried to assimilate into the American way of life

    (D) only part of Kang's novel relates to the immigrant experience

    (E) few Korean Americans were knowledgeable about Western civilization

17. The casual tourist and the visiting dignitary are presented primarily as examples of people who

    (A) became disillusioned with America

    (B) struggled against racism and discrimination

    (C) wrote about America as outsiders

    (D) influenced Kang in his work

    (E) tried to forge American identities

Questions 18–19 refer to the following passage.

Today, it's a widely-held belief that James
Watson and Francis Crick "discovered" DNA—
deoxyribonucleic acid, the transmitter of genetic
information from parent to offspring. However, it
(5) would be more accurate to consider their discovery of DNA's structure as a single milestone in a
long history leading up to and continuing after
the breakthrough. For example, in 1869 Johann
Friedrich Miescher identified an acidic substance
(10) (later named DNA) in the nuclei of human cells,
though its function remained obscure. In 1949, a
biochemist named Erwin Chargaff found that the
amount of DNA in a cell varies from one species
to another, marking it as a likely carrier of genetic
(15) information.

18. The author would most likely describe the belief
    cited in line 1 as a

    (A) dangerously incomplete notion
    (B) vitally important milestone
    (C) somewhat inaccurate simplification
    (D) sound, though complex, impression
    (E) simplistic and naive conception

19. In line 14, the word "marking" most nearly means

    (A) indicating
    (B) transmitting
    (C) writing
    (D) commemorating
    (E) assessing

Questions 20–27 are based on the following passages.

The following passages present two views of the current state of professions in America. Passage 1 discusses professions from a historical point of view. Passage 2 presents a defense of the legal profession.

Passage 1

Despite the honor accorded them by society and the usually substantial monetary rewards they enjoy for their work, many modern professionals complain that they feel demoralized. They don't
(5) command the respect of the public or enjoy special privileges as members of exclusive groups to the extent that professionals once did. This decline in the status of the professions is difficult for them to bear because, they vehemently maintain, the
(10) knowledge and unique skills of professionals are as vital and indispensable to society as they have ever been.

Originally, being a professional meant practicing in one of the "learned professions," a category
(15) that included only law, theology, university scholarship, and (eventually) medicine. Members of these groups distinguished themselves from the rest of society by their possession of certain special knowledge that brought with it power and abilities
(20) most others could not even fully fathom. Aspirants to a profession were required not only to devote themselves to a demanding life of learning but also to adhere to a specifically tailored system of ethics in order to prevent the misuse of profes-
(25) sional powers. The special deference and privileges these professionals received were their reward for using their knowledge in the service of others rather than of themselves.

Although many of today's professionals would
(30) argue that this description still applies to them, the truth of the matter is that the professional scene has changed quite a bit since the days of the "learned professions." When the members of the professions began to organize themselves in the
(35) nineteenth century, establishing work standards and policing themselves in order to prevent the government from cleaning house for them, they proclaimed that they were doing this for the good of the public. The professional associations that
(40) emerged from this structuring proved to be, how-ever, far more advantageous for the professionals than for the general populace, because the associations began to function as lobbies and interest groups.

(45) A further consequence of this organizing was that the elevated position of the professional gradually eroded as members of other occupations jumped on the bandwagon. When just about any group could organize itself and call itself a profes-
(50) sion, the concept of the professional as the possessor of special knowledge and abilities didn't seem to be as valid. Thus, many professions have had to struggle to sustain the notion that their members provide a critical service to society that no one else can.

Passage 2

In the past few years, numerous editorials and speeches have decried a real as well as perceived lack of ethics in various professions, often zeroing in on the profession everyone now seems to love
(5) to hate. Not a lawyer myself, I feel no personal defensiveness at the charges levied against this group in the last decade. As someone who earns a living and derives a tremendous amount of job satisfaction by working with lawyers, however,
(10) I find the repeated attacks quite troubling.

Certainly the legal world in general and lawyers as practitioners in it are subject to charges of inequality, inefficiency, and ineffectiveness. Examples abound. We all know the accounts of
(15) high legal fees, prolonged, acrimonious conflicts, underfunded legal services for the poor, inaccessible legal services for the middle class and an overburdened system of justice for all. The backlog in civil and criminal courts, the proliferation of nui-
(20) sance suits and abuses within the profession's financial base have been cited as examples of an elite group run amok.

The ills are obvious, but the maladies are frequently symptoms of more pervasive societal
(25) frailty than peculiar to the body—or profession—associated with the remedy. There is reason for suspicion from without and malaise, even demoralization, from within the legal profession. But this very fact argues for attentiveness to and support of
(30) the profession's efforts at healing the body politic,

rather than a continued obsession with the profession's ill health.

A refreshing look at ways to achieve that health is evident in the recently published work of
(35) an American Bar Association Council task force. Established by the council's section of legal education and admissions to the bar, the task force devoted three years to a review of the legal profession. Its recommendations review the practice set-
(40) tings for which lawyers must prepare, reaffirm the principles of organization and self regulation that must govern any profession, and provide an inventory of behaviors and attitudes—labeled "skills and values"—with which any individual in
(45) the legal profession should be equipped.

The contribution such values and skills make to a society in which they are disseminated is immeasurable. Certainly, many individuals, many "professionals"—both lawyers and otherwise—fall
(50) short of the marks set out in such reports. That doesn't mean that professional credos are not worth articulating. Neither does it mean that the individuals who enter a profession, but fail to embody the ideal of skills and values, are hateful,
(55) nor the profession itself dispensable.

20. Passage 1 indicates that the response of professionals to the "decline in the status of the professions" (lines 7–8) has been one of

(A) understanding that this is due to the rise of professional organizations

(B) denial that the professions command less respect from the public than in the past

(C) insistence that their monetary rewards should be greater

(D) dejection over the lack of appreciation of their work

(E) urgent desire to regain public respect by reorganizing the professions

21. In Passage 1, line 17, the word "distinguished" most nearly means

(A) isolated

(B) differentiated

(C) recognized

(D) honored

(E) discerned

22. In lines 5–10 of Passage 2, the author most likely describes herself in order to

(A) emphasize that she cannot be accused of a lack of ethics

(B) indicate that people should empathize with the plight of lawyers

(C) admit that she cannot offer an expert opinion on law matters

(D) state her impartiality toward the issue discussed

(E) explain the position from which she will argue

23. The author of Passage 2 uses the example of the work of the American Bar Association Council task force (lines 35–39) primarily to illustrate the

(A) number of areas in which the legal profession needs improvement

(B) difficulty encountered when reform of a profession is undertaken

(C) endeavor on the part of the legal profession to improve its condition

(D) result of the legal profession's obsession with its failings

(E) changes that have been effected in the legal profession

24. The tone the author uses when describing the recommended "behaviors and attitudes" (Passage 2,
line 43) of lawyers is

    (A) laudatory

    (B) disparaging

    (C) indifferent

    (D) cynical

    (E) hesitant

25. In the last paragraph of Passage 2, the author
acknowledges which flaw in the legal profession?

    (A) the ineffectiveness of professional credos

    (B) the poor quality of most aspiring lawyers

    (C) the lack of respect for the task force's work

    (D) the presence of professionals with inadequate
    skills

    (E) the rigidity of the code of skills and values

26. How would the author of Passage 1 respond to the
affirmation of the American Bar Association task
force that "principles of organization and self regulation must govern any profession" (Passage 2,
lines 41–42)?

    (A) A group's ability to organize and regulate
    itself develops as its members acquire
    knowledge.

    (B) Only a few of the professions should be
    organized and regulated.

    (C) The government should regulate the profes-
    sions in order to prevent abuses.

    (D) The American Bar Association is merely
    seeking to extend its political influence.

    (E) The professions have been hurt as well as
    helped by organization and self regulation.

27. The view expressed in lines 26–32 shows the
author of Passage 2 to be different from the
author of Passage 1 in that she

    (A) considers the possibility of future improve-
    ment in the professions

    (B) refuses to admit that professionals are
    demoralized

    (C) maintains that professionals are at odds with
    the rest of society

    (D) investigates the relationship between profes-
    sionals and the public

    (E) believes there are legitimate reasons for
    professionals to be demoralized

ANSWERS AND EXPLANATIONS

1. C

The phrase "generally living in packs with strong bonds and clear hierarchies" virtually defines the missing word. Animals like wolves that live in such groups are (C), *social* animals, in contrast to the "lone wolf" stereotype alluded to in the sentence's opening phrase. While wolves are (A) *carnivorous*, or meat eating, the topic of the sentence is their social habits, not their eating habits. The words *wild* (E) and *singular* (D) both miss the sentence's point—that wolves live in packs. *Fearsome* (B) can have two nearly opposite meanings: "frightening" or "timid."

2. C

The sentence sets up a contrast between two differing views of multiple personality; either *it's a —- disease* or *it's a shield that some criminals use to —- prosecution*. Since it's a safe bet that criminals don't want to be prosecuted, or tried for their crimes, the second blank should be filled by a word like "escape." To provide the necessary contrast, the first word must be something like "genuine." *Genuine . . . evade* is the best match for this prediction. *Authentic* (genuine) and *diagnosable* (capable of having its cause determined) might fit in the first blank, but the second words in (B) and (E)—*ensure and guarantee*, respectively— contrast sharply with our prediction for the second blank. In (A) and (D), the second words are possibilities, but the first words don't fit. In (A), *forestall* means "prevent," but *fallacious* means "false," just the opposite of what's needed in the first blank. Likewise, in (D), *elude* fits the second blank, but *invalid* (not legitimate) doesn't work in the first blank.

3. D

The sentence sets up a contrast between the company's goal of "fostering (encouraging) productivity and hard work" and the fact it "promotes . . . unproductive and —- workers." *Unproductive* obviously contrasts with *productivity*, so it's logical to assume that the correct answer should be something that contrasts with *hard work*— perhaps something like "lazy." *Lackadaisical*, which means "indifferent, lazy, or apathetic," comes closest to this prediction. The workers may well be *discontented* (B), but discontented doesn't complete the sentence's implied contrast with hard work. *Meritorious* (E) means "deserving of praise or reward."

4. D

The clue word, *despite*, sets up a contrast between the conqueror Tamerlane's beginnings and his later life. A word like "humble" would fit the first blank, and something like "general" or "conqueror" would fit logically in the second. *Obscure . . rulers* is the best match; *obscure* means "not well-known." In (A), impoverished, which means "very poor," might work for the first blank, but *nuisances* doesn't create the necessary contrast or enhance the idea of a conqueror. *Auspicious* (B) means "promising" or "having good prospects." *Enigmas* (C) means "puzzles." In (E), *luxuriant* means "lush, profuse, or prolific," not necessarily "luxurious."

5. D

To boost morale or make people feel better during a war, you'd want speeches that were "courageous," "emotionally stirring," "fiercely determined," or something along those lines. *Resolute* fits best—it means "resolved and determined, with a strong sense of purpose." None of the other choices fits the meaning of the sentence. *Stolid* means "having or showing little emotion," but you'd want an emotional speech to boost morale. *Ignoble* means "dishonorable." *Farcical*, which comes from the noun *farce*, means "laughably absurd." And *tremulous* means "timid and fearful" or "shaking or quivering"—certainly not a quality that would make people feel better in times of war.

6. B

You have to inspect the structure of this sentence carefully in order to infer anything about what belongs in the blanks. You're told something about the quantity of Elizabeth Bishop's output (a hundred or so of her poems were published during her lifetime) and something about the quality of these poems (they received critical acclaim, that is, high praise from literary critics). The words that fill the blanks must also relate to the quantity and/or quality of her output. *Perfectionism . . prolific* is the best answer. A *prolific* writer is one who produces a great amount of work. *Perfectionism* is a trait that could lead a poet to spend more time rewriting existing poems than starting new ones; it could easily keep a writer from being prolific. (A) is wrong, both because a writer who was not *creative* would be unlikely to receive critical acclaim, and because notoriety, that is, "unfavorable fame or celebrity," wouldn't prevent a writer from being creative. If Bishop won critical acclaim, she was renowned, so (C) won't work. (*Affluence* is wealth or financial ease.) The two words in choice (D), *allusiveness . . poetic*, relate to the subject of poetry; *allusiveness* means "the habit of making indirect literary references" (allusions). But how could allusiveness make a writer not poetic? In (E), *contemplative* means "thoughtful;" *aphasia* is an inability to use or understand words in speech or writing.

7.   E

You don't have to know that Coolidge was nicknamed "Silent Cal" to answer this vocabulary question correctly. But you do have to see that the missing word is defined by the phrase *usually saying no more than was absolutely necessary*. The only choice that fits is *taciturn*, which means "uncommunicative" or "not inclined to speak much." A writer might describe a taciturn person as being "parsimonious with words," but by itself, *parsimonious* means "miserly," "stingy," or ungenerous with money, not with words. *Abstemious* means "moderate in appetite." *Clairvoyant* means "able to see the future." And *nefarious* means "evil."

8.   C

The list of factors is contained in a single sentence, and you can rule out four of the five answer choices just by reading carefully: "This incredible growth was largely in response to … suburban population growth [that's (B)], increasing traffic on crowded roads and highways caused by a growing work force [rules out (A)], governmental and private concern over air pollution [(E)], and escalating fuel costs [and finally (D)]." That leaves only (C). The expansion of railroads was expensive, but that's not a cause, it's a result.

9.   E

The last sentence indicates that the burden of paying for the railroads was not transferred entirely to the railroad users. Instead, the state governments subsidized ticket prices. That matches choice (E). (A) is too extreme, since there were many factors besides pollution that lead to the railroad expansion. (B), (C), and (D) all deal with the success of the program. Since the passage never says whether the railroads actually dealt with the problems listed, you can rule out all three of these answer choices.

10.   D

Why would the author bother to list the number 3 in five other languages? In order to show that apparently different languages actually have a lot in common. Why is this important? To help prove that these languages came from the same root language (D). The author doesn't spend too much time talking about the root language itself (A), or the specifics of Greek and Latin (B). (C) is a tempting distortion—it was the root language that evolved into so many languages, not Greek and Latin. (E) would be a feasible explanation for the similarities, but it's not an explanation that the author endorses.

11.   D

This is a Big Picture question. The right answer will cover the entire passage, not just a paragraph or two. Step back for a second and you'll see that the passage focuses primarily on the book *East Goes West*; in fact, you knew that it would before you read the passage because you wisely read the introduction. (D) states the correct answer, "Kang's book," in a slightly fancy way. All of the other choices are wrong because they home in on various details of the passage rather than taking in the big picture.

12.   A

When you go back and reread the line in which this reference appears as well as a couple of lines before and after it, you get a feel for the author's tone. It is the difference between what Han expects (the world of Shakespeare) and what Han experiences (ridicule and rejection) that creates the cruel irony of the statement "he receives an education of another sort altogether." (A) captures the tone nicely. The author is definitely not expressing disdain for Han (B); if anything, we feel sorry for him. In (C), however, "dismay" is much too strong a word to be the correct answer. Neither the author nor anyone else is very likely to be amused by what happens to Han, so (D) is wrong, but you also aren't surprised that he doesn't find the world of Shakespeare, so (E) can be eliminated as well.

13.   D

Depending on the context, the word "contend" can mean a variety of things. Here, the author's using it in a sense that means "combat" or (D), *struggle*—the character discussed has to contend with "loneliness and alienation" in a foreign country. Wrong choices (A) through (C) are possible definitions of "contend" that don't fit here—you can't *argue, believe,* or *discuss* with loneliness. Choice (E), *accept,* isn't a possible definition, and it doesn't fit the passage either—there's no indication that Kang's hero has to accept his fate.

14. C

The most familiar and therefore attractive definitions of "curious" are *inquisitive* (B) and *interested* (E), but neither works in the context of the passage. Tackling Vocabulary-in-Context questions means figuring out how the word is used in the context of the passage, so never choose an answer without checking back to the indicated line. In the sentence referred to by the question stem, critics think Kang's lack of insight is curious, that is, strange or *odd* (C). All of the other answer choices are synonyms of or words related to "curious," but don't make sense in the context of the passage.

15. D

According to paragraph 3, the critics thought that *East Goes West* gave too negative a portrayal of America, but they regarded Han as a worthy model for Asian Americans due to his perseverance and optimism. This makes (D) the right answer. Both (A) and (E) are too extreme to be the right answer: the critics did not reject the book outright, nor did they see the book as an "attack" of American society. (B) is misleading because it is not the critics but the author of the passage who admires Kang for breaking from literary tradition. (C) is wrong simply because the passage never mentions "confusion" on the part of the critics.

16. C

Lines 49–54 explain why Kang's novel wasn't "representative" of the Korean American community as a whole. Unlike Kang's hero, we're told, most Korean Americans of Kang's generation were not interested in "immersing themselves in American life." Choice (C), *assimilating,* paraphrases this idea nicely. Choice (A)—that few Korean Americans wrote novels about their experiences—seems like a true statement looking at the passage as a whole, but it's not the specific reason that the author describes Kang as "not representative". Similarly, choice (E) hits on a unique aspect of Kang's own experience, which isn't mentioned in paragraph 4. (B) distorts paragraph 5's reference to visiting dignitaries—there's no indication that the majority

of Korean Americans were diplomats. Finally, (D) is wrong because most of Kang's novel is about the immigrant experience.

17. C

This question tests your understanding of the author's logic in mentioning tourists and dignitaries in the passage. The reference appears in the fifth paragraph, so go back and skim the sentences there in order to pick up the surrounding context. Kang's literary contribution was that he wrote not as a guest in America, as had the tourists and dignitaries, but as someone trying to be American. (C) is therefore correct: the author is using the tourist and the dignitaries as examples of Asians who wrote about America as outsiders. (E) directly contradicts (C). There is no reason to think tourists and dignitaries ever became disillusioned with America (A) as Kang did, or that they struggled against racism and discrimination (B). (You may know this is true, but the author doesn't mention tourists and dignitaries to make this point.) Finally, it's clear that Kang was not influenced by the writing of tourists and dignitaries (D), because the author stresses the fact that Kang wrote from an entirely new perspective.

18. C

The author says that it would be more accurate to think of Crick and Watson's discovery as "a single milestone in a long history," and then goes on to describe a few other discoveries that helped pave the way for Watson and Crick's work. So, thinking that Watson and Crick did all the work is a "somewhat inaccurate simplification" (C). (A) is too strong—there's nothing particularly *dangerous* going on here. (B) might describe the discovery itself, but doesn't cover beliefs about the discovery. The word *sound* lets you rule out (D)—the author doesn't think that the belief is sound at all. Like (A), (E) is too extreme. There's a very negative tone to the words *simplistic* and *naïve,* and the author hasn't shown this negative attitude toward people who have this mistaken belief.

19. A

A scientist found that DNA depends on the species, thus "marking [DNA] as a likely carrier of genetic information." The discovery made DNA look like such a carrier, so "marking" here means *indicating* (A). The DNA does plenty of *transmitting* (B), but the discovery about DNA did not. (C), *writing*, is a common meaning of marking, but it doesn't fit here. *Commemorating* (D) means memorializing, so that doesn't work. (E) is also out, since it was the scientists, not the discoveries, that did the *assessing*.

20. D

When you read the sentence to which the line reference directs you as well as the two sentences that precede it, you know that professionals are feeling "demoralized" because they don't get the respect they deserve for the knowledge and skills they have. Take a second to get this clear in your mind and then go back to the answer choices; choice (D) gives you just what you're looking for. Nowhere does the author indicate that professionals see the rise of professional organizations as the cause of the decline, so (A) is out. Contrary to (B), professionals do think they command less respect than past professionals. Desire for "monetary rewards" (C) or "to regain public respect" (E) isn't mentioned in the passage at all.

21. B

As with all Vocabulary-in-Context questions, you should resist the impulse to pick an answer without checking to see how the word is used in the passage. The author is using "distinguished" here to say that members of the "learned professions" set themselves apart, or (B) *differentiated* themselves, from others by acquiring knowledge and abilities most people didn't have. All of the other choices are possible meanings of "distinguished," but they don't make sense in the context of the passage.

22. E

In the cited lines of Passage 2, the author declares that she is not a lawyer but that she likes working with them and finds the attacks on lawyers "troubling." She's describing herself in order to let the reader know what axe she's grinding here; in other words, she's "explaining the position from which she will argue" (E). The author is definitely not impartial on the subject of lawyers, so (D) is wrong. (A) and (C) distort the author's motivation for stating that she is not a lawyer. (B) may have been a tempting answer choice because the author seems to empathize with lawyers, but she does not describe herself in order to try to persuade the reader to feel the same way.

23. C

The author's purpose in bringing up the work of the ABA task force is pretty clear from a rereading of the sentence containing the line reference and the preceding sentence. She's showing how the legal profession is attempting to heal itself, or "improve its condition" (C). She talks about areas of the legal profession that need improvement primarily in the second paragraph, not the fourth, so (A) is wrong. You should have been able to eliminate (B) pretty quickly because the author doesn't discuss the difficulty of reform at all. Obsession with the legal profession's failings is just what the author wants to discourage, and she views the work of the ABA task force positively, so (D) is out. Finally, (E) is wrong because the work of the task force consisted of a review and recommendations, not changes.

24. A

The fact that the author has a high opinion of the behaviors and attitudes—the "skills and values"—of lawyers is hard to mistake: she declares that the contribution they make to society is "immeasurable." The trick here is knowing that the word *laudatory* (A) has to do with praise. If you didn't know this, you could reach the correct choice by eliminating the others. *Disparaging* (B) means critical or derogatory, which the author definitely is not. The other choices don't come close to matching the author's tone.

25. D

Go back and reread the rest of the final paragraph quickly (you already reread the first sentence in answering the last question). A quick summary: It's true that some professionals, including lawyers, don't meet ABA standards, but it's still useful to have standards. Also, the author says, just because some members of a profession are below par, this doesn't mean we should do away with the whole profession. Now take a second to think. What flaw in the legal profession did the author just acknowledge? "The presence of lawyers with inadequate skills" (D). (A) directly contradicts what the author says about the worth of professional credos. Furthermore, she never says anything about the quality of aspiring lawyers (B), lack of respect for the task force's work (C), or rigidity in the ABA's standards (E).

26. E

The remaining two questions involve relating the two passages to each other. This one requires you to figure out what the author of Passage 1 thinks about professions organizing and regulating themselves. According to his historical sketch, professions organized themselves to prevent government intervention and in so doing gained political influence, but they lost their "elevated position" at the same time. It's safe to conclude he would think that "professions have been hurt as well as helped by organization and self regulation" (E). There is nothing in Passage 1 to indicate he would think that organization has anything to do with acquiring knowledge (A), that only a few professions should be organized (B), or that the government should regulate professions (C)—he only states that the government was on the verge of doing so in the 19th century. Nothing in the passage supports (D).

27. A

A quick reread of the third paragraph of Passage 2 reminds you that the author thinks that the problems within the legal profession indicate problems in society and that there is reason for lawyers to be demoralized but that we should support the profession's attempt to heal rather than continually criticizing it. It's the last part that sticks out the most as being different from the views of the first author. He never "considers the possibility of future improvement" (A) in any profession. (B) is wrong because the author of Passage 2 does admit that professionals are demoralized. She does not, however, say that professionals are "at odds with the rest of society" (C); the wording of this choice is much more extreme than her statement that "there is reason for suspicion" from outside the legal profession. (D) and (E) point out similarities, not differences, between the two authors.

Chapter Three: **How to Attack the Math Sections**

Not very good at math? Join the club. You're great at math? Good for you. Whoever you are, pay attention to this chapter because being successful at math in school is not the same as being successful at math on the PSAT. The skills you will learn in this chapter will translate into success on the PSAT. So for you, math-challenged reader, there is hope. And for you, math genius, there is always more to learn.

CHAPTER THREE SUMMARY

The PSAT tests a lot of math. Some of it is basic, and some of it is tough. Chapter three starts out by showing you Kaplan's strategies for approaching the two types of PSAT Math questions: multiple choice and Grid-ins. After that, we go through the math concepts—easy and hard—the PSAT is likely to test. We cap it off with a practice quiz so you can see what skills you still need to work on when it comes to PSAT Math.

MATH BASICS

On math tests you take in your school classes, solving a problem by working it out and showing all of your work reaps many rewards. However, on the PSAT, solving problems in that way will get you into trouble. Also, your teachers will probably still give you partial credit if you do the work properly but accidentally miss a step. On the PSAT, you will get nothing.

With all of this in mind, Kaplan has developed some score-raising strategies for approaching the PSAT Math section. We'll show you how to take advantage of the PSAT's question style. Turning a good PSAT Math score into a great PSAT Math score requires learning to avoid the traps built into the questions by the PSAT writers.

One more word to those of you not crazy about math: Keep an open mind. Our strategies will show you how to do the least amount of math required to still answer the questions correctly and quickly. By following our advice and by taking advantage of the PSAT standardized test format, you can get a very good score on PSAT Math, even if you're not that great at math.

The PSAT Math questions are divided into two 25-minute-long sections. There are two question types tested in the Math sections:

1. Multiple-choice questions that have five answer choices, which we call *regular math*.
2. Questions where you write your answer into a grid. We call those *Grid-ins*.

The first Math section contains 18 multiple-choice questions, and the second section is composed of 10 more multiple-choice questions as well as 10 Grid-in questions.

MULTIPLE-CHOICE QUESTIONS

The directions for multiple-choice Math questions are written below for your benefit. Learn these directions now so you won't waist time reading them on test day. That time could be spent answering one or two more questions.

<u>Directions:</u> Solve each of the following problems, decide which is the best answer choice, and darken the corresponding oval on the answer sheet.

Here is an example of what a multiple-choice question might look like.

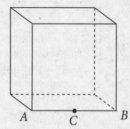

If the surface area of the cube above is 96, and C is the midpoint of AB, what is the length of AC?

(A) 1
(B) 2
(C) 2.5
(D) 3
(E) 4

Don't worry about trying to answer it—you'll get plenty of practice later!

GRID-INS

The 10 Grid-in questions on the PSAT are *more* like the math questions you are used to answering in math class. You don't get five answer choices to choose from. Instead, you're simply given a question and asked to figure out the answer yourself. The directions for Grid-ins appear on the following page.

DIRECTIONS FOR STUDENT-PRODUCED RESPONSE QUESTIONS

For each of the questions below (29–38), solve the problem and indicate your answer by darkening the ovals in the special grid. For example:

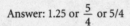

Answer: 1.25 or $\frac{5}{4}$ or 5/4

Write answer in → boxes.

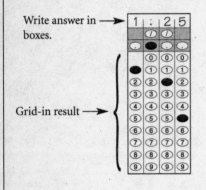

Grid-in result →

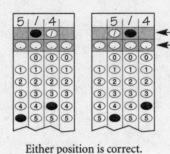

Fraction line
Decimal point

Either position is correct.

You may start your answers in any column, space permitting. Columns not needed should be left blank.

• It is recommended, though not required, that you write your answer in the boxes at the top of the columns. However, you will receive credit only for darkening the ovals correctly.

• Grid only one answer to a question, even though some problems have more than one correct answer.

• Darken no more than one oval in a column.

• No answers are negative.

• Mixed numbers cannot be gridded. For example: the number $1\frac{1}{4}$ must be gridded as 1.25 or 5/4.

(If [1 | 1 | / | 4] is gridded, it will be interpreted as $\frac{11}{4}$ not $1\frac{1}{4}$.)

• Decimal Accuracy: Decimal answers must be entered as accurately as possible. For example, if you obtain an answer such as 0.1666..., you should record the result as .166 or .167. **Less accurate values such as .16 or .17 are not acceptable.**

Acceptable ways to grid $\frac{1}{6}$ = .1666...

When you come to a Grid-in on the PSAT test, you'll just see a question without any answer choices. Your task is to answer the question and come up with the solution yourself. Here's the catch, just finding the correct answer is not enough. You then have to write the answer into the special grid, which seems easy enough, but if you don't fill out the grid correctly, your correct answer won't be counted. Read the following discussion about filling in the grid carefully. It will be one less thing to worry about on test day.

Filling in the Grid

Here's all you need to know about filling in Grid-in grids. First of all, none of the follow-ing formats or number types will work as answers for Grid-in questions.

- Negative answers
- Answers with variables
- Answers greater than 9,999
- Answers with commas
- Mixed numbers
- Fractions with more than four digits

These restrictions sound complicated, but knowing what you can't do is just as important as knowing what you can with Grid-ins. If you come up with an answer that you deter-mine cannot be gridded based on these restrictions, you will know your answer is wrong. For instance, if you come up with a mixed number or a fraction that won't fit, you should be able to convert it into a decimal or a fraction that does fit.

Let's say you came up with an answer of $1\frac{1}{2}$. If you tried to fill this answer into the grid without converting it, your answer would be read as the fraction $\frac{11}{2}$. Two ways to con-vert it are to turn the mixed number into the fraction $\frac{3}{2}$ or into its decimal equivalent 1.5. Either option, so long as you fill it in properly, is acceptable.

More Than One Right Answer

There can be several right ways to grid in an answer, and there may be several possible correct answers to a Grid-in question. When you get an answer in decimal form, you have to grid your answer as fully as possible, but you don't have to bother rounding up. For instance, if you wanted to fill in the decimal equivalent of $\frac{7}{9}$, which is the repeating decimal $.\overline{7}$, either .777 or .778 would be acceptable, but .77 or .78 would not.

Because you need to fill in numbers as fully as possible, we have a recommendation.

Do this even if your answer has only one or two numbers. Technically, you can start in any column, but by following this rule you'll avoid mistakes. If you always start with the first column, your answers will always fit.

Of course, there is an exception to this rule: the answer 0. Because there is no oval for 0 in the first column, grid an answer of 0 in the second column.

> **HINT**: Always start your Grid-in answer in the first column box

Difficulty Level: Easiest to Hardest

Both PSAT Math question types are grouped into sets. These question sets start off with easy questions and gradually get harder. One of the keys for doing well on the PSAT Math section is to always know where you are in a question set. This is so important that we're going to repeat it, and we're going to add an exclamation point.

Always know where you are in a question set!

There's another important point about difficulty level. Sometimes the questions at the end of each set are hard, not because the math is a lot more complicated, but because they involve more steps and are filled with traps. We'll talk a lot about these math traps later. But first, we're going to set you up with our best strategy for attacking PSAT Math questions.

KAPLAN'S THREE-STEP METHOD

Now that you are familiar with the two questions types and understand order of difficulty, it's time to learn Kaplan's Three-Step Method for attacking PSAT Math:

> **Step 1.** Read through the question.
> **Step 2.** Decide whether to do it now or later.
> **Step 3.** Look for the fastest way to answer the question.

To get your best possible math score, you need to use your time efficiently. You need to learn how to pace yourself so that you don't get bogged down and waste too much time on a single problem. That's what this strategy is all about. Here's how it works. Read the following Math question. It's the 12th question in a 18-question set.

> At Fast Burger, two hamburgers and five orders of French fries cost the same as four hamburgers and two orders of French fries. If Fast Burger charges $1.50 for a single order of French fries, how much does it charge for two hamburgers?
>
> (A) $2.25
> (B) $3.00
> (C) $4.50
> (D) $5.00
> (E) $6.00

Step 1. Read Through the Question

We suggest you never try to solve a problem before reading it all the way through. If you jump the gun, you may end up doing unnecessary work. Ask yourself: Is this question easy, medium, or hard? Because this example is question 12 from a 18-question set, you know that the test makers consider this a moderately difficult word problem.

If this was question 17, you would definitely want to watch out for math traps (more on those later on in the chapter). But even here, there's a slight twist. Notice that you're being asked to find the cost of two hamburgers, not one. Many students will get this question wrong by finding the price for one hamburger and then forgetting to double it. That's why you always have to make sure you know what's being asked.

Step 2. Decide Whether to Do It Now or Later

Before you try to solve the problem, decide whether you want to do it now or later. If you have no idea how to solve the problem, or if you think the problem will take a long time to solve, you should skip it and circle the question in your test booklet. Spend your time on the problems you can solve quickly, and then return to ones that give you trouble after you've finished the rest of the section.

Step 3: Look For the Fastest Way to Answer the Question

Once you decide to tackle the question, it's time to look for shortcuts. Sometimes the obvious way to solve the problem is the long way. For instance, the obvious way here for many students would be to turn this word problem into two algebraic equations: $2H + 5F = 4H + 2F$, and $F = 1.50$. From there you could substitute 1.50 for F in the first equation, solve for H, and then multiply your answer by 2.

But if you think carefully, there's often an easier approach. If two hamburgers and five orders of fries cost the same as four hamburgers and two orders of fries, take away all the items that are the same in the two orders, and you're left with three orders of fries costing the same as two hamburgers. Because one order of fries costs $1.50, three orders cost $4.50, so $4.50 must also be the cost of two hamburgers. The correct answer is (C), and you didn't even have to set up any algebraic equations.

MATH SHORTCUTS: KID-TESTED, KAPLAN APPROVED

Because saving time is a big part of doing well on the PSAT, shortcuts can be a really big help. Now, sometimes the textbook approach will be the best way to the answer on the PSAT. However, other times, as we've just seen, shortcuts will get you to the correct answer more quickly and easily. The key is to be open to creative approaches to problem-solving.

On regular math questions, the answer is right in front of you—you just have to decide which answer of five is the correct one. We have three shortcuts that are extremely useful when you don't see—or would rather not use—the textbook approach to solving the question. They are as follows:

- Picking numbers
- Backsolving
- Eyeballing

Keep in mind that these shortcuts aren't *always* faster than using textbook methods, but they are always a great way to make confusing problems more concrete. If you know how to apply these shortcuts, you will get the correct answer every time you use them. Let's take a look.

Picking Numbers

Here's what we mean by picking numbers to make an abstract problem concrete.

> If a, b, and c are all odd integers, which of the following must be even?
>
> I. $ab + c$
>
> II. $c(ab + 3)$
>
> III. $2a + bc$
>
> (A) I only
> (B) I and II
> (C) I and III
> (D) II and III
> (E) I, II, and III

Rather than try to think this one through abstractly, it's easier for most students to pick numbers for a, b, and c. Because a, b, and c are all odd, you could pick $a = 1$, $b = 3$, and $c = 5$. There are rules for adding, subtracting, and multiplying odd and even integers, but there's no need to memorize the rules if you pick numbers. Let's see what happens when we plug these numbers into the equations.

> I. $1 \times 3 + 5 = 8$ Even
> II. $5(1 \times 3 + 3) = 30$ Even
> III. $2 \times 1 + 3 \times 5 = 17$ Odd

So the correct answer must be (B).

Here's another abstract question that can be made concrete by picking numbers. It's the classic *remainder* question. Take a look:

When n is divided by 14, the remainder is 10.
What is the remainder when n is divided by 7?

(A) 2

(B) 3

(C) 4

(D) 5

(E) 6

You first have to pick a number for n. The easiest strategy is to pick $n = 24$ (because $14 + 10 = 24$). Now, try your number out: $24 \div 7 = 3r3$. Thus, the answer is (B).

Picking Numbers: Word Problems with Variables

Picking numbers works great not only on odd/even and remainder problems, but also on word problems that contain variables. This is great news because these problems can be especially confusing on the PSAT. Give the following question a try.

Four years from now, Ray will be twice as old as his sister will be then. If Ray is now R years old, how many years old is his sister now?

(A) $\dfrac{R-4}{2}$

(B) $R - 4$

(C) $\dfrac{R+4}{2}$

(D) $R - 2$

(E) $2R - 4$

If you *love* to translate word problems into algebra equations, fine, do it your way. But picking numbers is so much easier here—and safer. Here's how you do it. Begin by picking a number for R, Ray's age now. Let's make it a nice and simple round number such as $R = 10$. Now substitute 10 for R in the question and the answer choices, and you're left with the following, much simpler problem:

Four years from now, Ray will be twice as old as his sister will be then. If Ray is now 10 years old, how many years old is his sister now?

(A) $\dfrac{10-4}{2}$, or 3

(B) $10 - 4$, or 6

(C) $\dfrac{10+4}{2}$, or 7

(D) $10 - 2$, or 8

(E) $2 \times 10 - 4$, or 16

Now let's see. Ray is 10 years old, so in four years, he'll be 14, which means his sister will be seven years old then. Because she'll be seven in four years, that means she must be three years old now. The correct answer must be (A).

As we've just seen, picking numbers on word problems containing variables involves the following the steps:

Three-Step Picking Numbers Method

Step 1. Pick nice, easy numbers for the variables in your question.

Step 2. Answer the question using the numbers you've picked. This answer is your target number.

Step 3. Substitute the numbers you picked for the variables in the answer choices. See which answer gives you your target number.

To be safe, you should always try out all the answer choices. If more than one answer choice gives you your target number, pick different numbers to eliminate the remaining wrong answers. Don't worry. This rarely happens, and it doesn't take much time to pick numbers twice.

Not only does picking numbers make problems such as the previous one easier to understand, but when you solve a problem by picking numbers, you can be sure you got the right answer; thus, there's no need to double check your work.

Picking Numbers: Word Problems with Unknown Values + Percents or Fractions

The problems we've just looked at all contain variables in the answer choices, but there are two other types of questions where picking numbers comes in handy. These are word problems that contain unknown values and either *percents* or *fractions* in the answer choices. The key to solving these problems quickly lies in knowing how to pick good numbers. Let's take a look.

> The value of a certain stock rose by 30 percent from March to April and then decreased by 20 percent from April to May. The stock's value in May was what percent of its value in March?
>
> (A) 90%
>
> (B) 100%
>
> (C) 104%
>
> (D) 110%
>
> (E) 124%

Notice that even though the question involves the value of a certain stock, that value is never given. If we pick a number for the value of the stock, we can see much more easily what is going on. On percent problems, you're almost always better off picking 100 for the unknown value. Let's say the stock originally cost $100. If it rose by 30 percent from March to April, its value in April would have been $130. If the value then decreased by 20 percent in May, 20 percent of $130 is $26, so the value drops to $104 in May. Because $104 is 104 percent of $100, the correct answer is (C).

Did you follow? Let's look at another word problem, although this time the answers are fractions.

Keiko spent $\frac{1}{4}$ of her monthly salary on a television and spent half of what was left to pay her rent and utility bills. If she spent $\frac{2}{3}$ of her remaining salary on other expenses and put what was left into her savings account, what fraction of her monthly salary went into her savings account?

(A) $\frac{1}{6}$

(B) $\frac{1}{8}$

(C) $\frac{1}{12}$

(D) $\frac{1}{24}$

(E) $\frac{1}{36}$

ur general rule for picking numbers on fraction problems is to pick the largest number from among the denominators in the answer choices. But sometimes when you start with the largest denominator in the answer choices, you quickly see that this isn't the best number. If you assume that Keiko starts with $36, she spends $\frac{1}{4}$ of that, or $9, on a television. That leaves her with $27. She is supposed to spend half of that on rent and utilities, but 27 divided by 2 does not equal a whole number. As soon as the numbers start to get ugly, you know it's time to try the next highest denominator.

Let's say that Keiko starts with $24. She spends $\frac{1}{4}$ of that, or $6, on a television. That leaves her with $18. She spends half of that on rent and utilities, so she's left with $9. She spends $\frac{2}{3}$ of that on other expenses, leaving her with $3. She puts that into her savings account, so she puts $\frac{3}{24} = \frac{1}{8}$ of her monthly salary into her savings account. The correct answer must be (B).

Backsolving

In the picking numbers problems, the answer choices contained variables, percents, or fractions. But some of the nastier PSAT Math problems have numbers in the answer choices, so picking numbers won't work. On these questions, try backsolving instead.

When you backsolve, you simply plug the answers back into the question until you find one that works. If you do it systematically, it shouldn't take you too much time. Here's the system.

Three-Step Backsolving Method

Step 1. Start with choice (C).

Step 2. Eliminate choices you know are too big or too small.

Step 3. Keep going until you find the choice that works.

Watch and learn.

> In a certain school, the ratio of boys to girls is 3:7. If there are 84 more girls than boys, how many boys are there?
>
> (A) 36
>
> (B) 48
>
> (C) 63
>
> (D) 84
>
> (E) 147

The correct answer should yield a ratio of boys to girls of 3:7, so try out choice (C).

If there are 63 boys, there are $63 + 84 = 147$ girls, so the ratio of boys to girls is $\frac{63}{147} = \frac{9}{21} = \frac{3}{7}$, which is just what we are looking for. That means we're done.

Okay, so that was kind of easy. The answer isn't *always* (C). But usually, when you start with (C) and it doesn't work, you'll know which direction to go. Either (C) will be too big or too small, leaving you with only two answers that could possibly be correct. Let's try the example from earlier in the chapter.

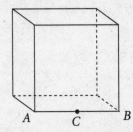

A　C　B

If the surface area of the cube above is 96, and C is the midpoint of AB, what is the length of AC?

(A) 1

(B) 2

(C) 2.5

(D) 3

(E) 4

For some reason, when the problem involves geometry, many students completely forget that there are shortcuts to the answer. On a confusing geometry problem with numbers in the answer choices, backsolving is definitely the way to go.

Start with (C): If $AC = 2.5$, the edge length of the cube is 5, so each face of the cube is $5^2 = 25$ square inches. There are 6 faces to a cube, so the entire surface area would be $25 \times 6 = 150$ square inches. This is too large, so (C), (D), and (E) are all out.

Try (B): If $AC = 2$, the edge length of the cube is 4, so each face of the cube is 4^2 square inches. There are 6 faces to a cube, so the entire surface area would be 96 square inches. The answer is (B).

Now let's take a look at one last shortcut that can help you out in a pinch on tough geometry problems.

Eyeballing

One of the nice things about PSAT geometry problems is that, according to the test maker's own rules, the figure will always be drawn to scale unless you are told it is not: "Note: Figure not drawn to scale."

Why is this such a nice thing? It means when you're in doubt, you can always trust your eyes. On about half of all diagram questions, you can get a reasonable answer without solving anything. This technique works especially well on difficult geometry problems.

Here's a tough one that you might just want to answer by eyeballing:

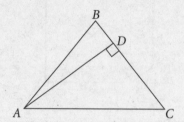

If $AB = 5$, $BC = 5$, and $AC = 6$, what is the length of AD?

(A) $4\sqrt{3}$

(B) $4\dfrac{4}{5}$

(C) 4

(D) $2\sqrt{3}$

(E) $2\dfrac{2}{5}$

You can eliminate at least three of the five answer choices by estimating roughly. Eyeballing should tell you that AD is slightly smaller than AB, so it's just slightly less than 5. Going to the answer choices:

(A) $4\sqrt{3} \approx 6.93$. This is too big. Eliminate.

(B) $4\dfrac{4}{5}$

(C) 4

(D) $2\sqrt{3} \approx 3.46$. This is too small. Eliminate.

(E) $2\dfrac{2}{5}$ is too small. Eliminate.

But you can do even better than that. If you take the edge of a piece of paper and mark it to make a ruler, you'll see that AB is only very slightly longer than AD. Choice (B) is therefore the best answer.

Okay, you have been very patient. We know you have been reading through this stage with one question gnawing at your gut:

What about calculators?

Here you go.

CALCULATORS AND THE PSAT

On the PSAT, just like on the SAT, students are allowed to use calculators on the math sections. Does this mean a perfect score is now within your grasp? Probably not, unless you were really close to begin with.

The best calculator in the world is not going to improve your PSAT Math score dramatically. In fact, since students were first allowed to use calculators on the PSAT, the test makers have made it their mission to write math problems that offer no advantage to using a calculator. The nerve! In fact, you can easily be tempted to waste a lot of time using the calculator on questions that don't actually require lengthy computations. Remember, you don't *need* to use a calculator to answer any math question on the PSAT.

The more familiar you become with the PSAT Math problems and the best way to solve them, the less tempted you'll be to automatically pull out your calculator on every question. We do not, however, recommend that you avoid using a calculator altogether. Research has shown that students who use calculators on the PSAT perform slightly better than students who do not.

It's just that you have to know how to use a calculator, when to use a calculator, and when not to use a calculator. That's where we come in.

When to Use One

Calculators are most helpful on Grid-ins. Grid-ins require you to be especially careful with your calculations because there are no answer choices to help you out. But you still have to know how to use your calculator selectively. Consider this problem.

> If a gallon of fertilizer covers an area of 300 square feet and costs $4.75, what is the cost in dollars to fertilize a level rectangular field that measures 160 feet by 750 feet? (Disregard $ sign when gridding in your answer.)

This word problem has two steps. First you have to set up a proportion:

$$\frac{\$4.75}{300 \text{ sq. ft}} = \frac{x}{160 \text{ ft.} \times 750 \text{ ft}}.$$

After a bit of manipulating, you're ready to whip out the calculator:

$$\frac{4.75 \times 160 \times 750}{300} = x, \text{ so } x = 1,900$$

When Not to Use One

The rule is pretty simple. Any time a question involves a ton of calculating, there's bound to be an easier approach. For instance, try the following:

$$2(9 - 6)^2 + 56 \div 4 =$$

(A) 18.5

(B) 32

(C) 50

(D) 95

(E) 158

Simply plugging the numbers and operations into the calculator will just create trouble. You must follow PEMDAS: $2(9 - 6)^2 + 56 \div 4 = 2(3)^2 + 56 \div 4 = 18 + 14 = 32$. The correct answer is (B).

If you don't know the order of operations PEMDAS (or its helpful mnemonic: Please Excuse My Dear Aunt Sally), the calculator will do you no good. What PEMDAS means is: first you do all the stuff inside Parentheses, then all the Exponents, then all the Multiplication and Division (together, going from left to right), and then all the Addition and Subtraction (likewise). So, with the calculator, do not make these following steps your first:

- Grab calculator.
- Punch in all the numbers.
- Put down an answer and hope you didn't screw up.

Instead, try this approach:

- Think first.
- Decide on the best way to solve it.
- Then—and only then—use your calculator.

BASIC MATH AND HOW TO ATTACK IT

It's impossible to cover every problem-solving technique that can help you on the PSAT Math section. If you find yourself struggling with the practice set at the end of the chapter or on any of the practice tests in this book, you should spend some time studying the "Math in a Nutshell" appendix at the back of this book. It reviews the recommended approaches to almost any kind of math question that could appear on the PSAT.

That said, there are some problems that appear on just about every PSAT and deserve special mention. It's time now to take a look at them, along with Kaplan's techniques for solving them.

Symbols

You can count on having at least one symbol question on the PSAT. Symbol questions can be scary because they contain weird-looking symbols that you've never seen before. Take a look:

> If $a \star b = a^2b + a - b$ for all integers a and b, then
> $4 \star 3 =$
>
> (A) 12
> (B) 16
> (C) 37
> (D) 49
> (E) 111

No, they did not teach the star symbol on that day you were absent from algebra class. The PSAT writers like to put strange symbols in questions to confuse or unnerve you. Don't let them. Symbol questions really just test your ability to understand and follow directions.

For the above question, you just have to plug in 4 for a and 3 for b into the expression $a^2b + a - b$. You should get $4 \star 3 = (4)^2(3) + 4 - 3 = 16 \times 3 + 4 - 3 = 48 + 4 - 3 = 49$. So (D) is the correct answer. It also deserves mention that sometimes symbol questions come in pairs. When this happens, the second question is almost always more difficult than the first, requiring more steps to solve it. But we still think you can handle it.

> If $a \star b = a^2b + a - b$ for all integers a and b, then
> $5 \star 3 =$
>
> (A) $3 \star 5$
> (B) $6 \star 2$
> (C) $15 \star 1$
> (D) $4 \star 4$
> (E) $2 \star 25$

First you have to figure out the value of 5 ★ 3.

$$5 ★ 3 = (5)^2(3) + 5 - 3 = 25 \times 3 + 5 - 3 = 75 + 5 - 3 = 77$$

Now you have to go to the answer choices and find one that equals 77. You're likely to save time if you realize that answer choices with numbers that remind you of the original numbers in the question are usually traps:

(A) 3 ★ 5. Probable trap, so ignore for now.

(B) $6 ★ 2 = 6^2 2 + 6 - 2 = 36 \times 2 + 6 - 2 = 72 + 6 - 2 = 76$. Eliminate.

(C) 15 ★ 1. Possible trap, so ignore for now.

(D) $4 ★ 4 = 4^2 4 + 4 - 4 = 16 \times 4 + 4 - 4 = 64 + 4 - 4 = 64$. Eliminate.

(E) $2 ★ 25 = 2^2 25 + 2 - 25 = 4 \times 25 + 2 - 25 = 100 + 2 - 25 = 77$. Bingo!

> Symbol answer choices that remind you too much of the *numbers* you're given (ignoring the *equation* you're given) are often traps. If you have to check out the answer choices, try those answer choices last.

Averages

You're bound to see at least one average problem on the PSAT. There's not much to fear here because you just have to know the formula for solving average questions, i.e.,

$$\text{Average} = \frac{\text{Sum of terms}}{\text{Number of terms}}.$$

Of course, PSAT average problems often put a slight spin on the formula. Take a look:

> The average age of the members in a five-person choir is 34. If the ages of four of the members are 47, 31, 27, and 36, what is the fifth member's age?
>
> (A) 29
>
> (B) 32
>
> (C) 34
>
> (D) 37
>
> (E) 41

HINT: Work with the sum.

Note that the average formula involves three elements: the average, the sum, and the number of terms. Thus, any time you are given two of the elements in the formula, you can automatically calculate the third element.

For instance, here you're told that the average age of the members in a five-person choir is 34. So that means you can calculate the sum of their ages: $34 = \frac{\text{Sum}}{5}$; therefore, the sum of their ages is 170. If we call the fifth member's age x, then $47 + 31 + 27 + 36 + x = 170$, so $x = 170 - 141 = 29$. The answer is (A).

Sometimes you may be asked to find the average of a large group of evenly spaced numbers. These questions would seem to require a lot of calculating.

But as you know, whenever it seems that you need to pull out a calculator and start punching away, there's got to be an easier approach. Try this one.

> What is the average (arithmetic mean) of all the even integers greater than 25 and less than 347?
>
> (A) 167
> (B) 175
> (C) 186
> (D) 206
> (E) 212

In case you never learned it, here's the trick. Whenever you're dealing with evenly spaced numbers, the average is equal to the average of the two outer numbers.

So in this case: Average $= \dfrac{26 + 346}{2} = \dfrac{372}{2} = 186$

Rates

A rate is simply a word fraction. A rate compares *distance* over *time* or *amount* over *time* or *cost* over *units*. In other words:

$$\text{Rate} = \frac{\text{Distance}}{\text{Time}} \text{ or } \frac{\text{Amount}}{\text{Time}} \text{ or } \frac{\text{Cost}}{\text{Units}}$$

To solve a rate problem, you just have to set up a proportion, convert units if necessary, and solve. Try the following out for size:

> It takes Cameron 1 hour and 30 minutes to drive to work at an average speed of 40 miles per hour. If she returns home along the same route at an average speed of 45 miles per hour, how long, in minutes, does the return trip take?
>
> (A) 75
> (B) 80
> (C) 85
> (D) 90
> (E) 95

If you use common sense, you can often ballpark the answer to an averages problem. If most of the given terms are more than the given average, then the unknown term must be less than the average to balance them out. Likewise, if adding a new term increases the average of a group, then the new term must be larger than the original average.

It takes Cameron 1 hour and 30 minutes (i.e., 1.5 hours) to travel at a rate of 40 miles per hour, so first figure out the distance from Cameron's home to work:

$$\frac{40 \text{ miles}}{1 \text{ hour}} = \frac{\text{Distance}}{1.5 \text{ hours}},$$ so the distance is $40 \times 1.5 = 60$ miles.

Furthermore, if she travels at a new rate of 45 mph, her new traveling time would be:

$$\frac{45 \text{ miles}}{1 \text{ hour}} = \frac{60 \text{ miles}}{x \text{ hours}},$$ so $x = \frac{60}{45} = \frac{4}{3}$ hours, which equals $\frac{4}{3} \times 60 = 80$ minutes.

(B) is the correct answer.

> Many rate problems on the PSAT use variables rather than numbers. On these, we strongly recommend that you pick numbers!

Special Triangles

Take it from people who've spent *way* too much time looking at PSAT: If there's one thing the PSAT Math test makers love, it's a triangle. And if there's one kind of triangle they really can't get enough of, it's a *special* triangle.

Just what are these special, special triangles? Take a look.

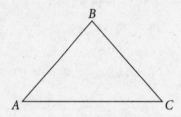

Note: Figure not drawn to scale.

In $\triangle ABC$ above, $AB = 5$ and $AC = 8$. If $\triangle ABC$ is isosceles and $BC < AC$, what is the area of this triangle?

(A) 10
(B) 12
(C) 16
(D) 18
(E) 24

Special triangles are triangles that convey a lot of information. For instance, if you know the length of one side of a 30-60-90 triangle, you can easily work out the lengths of the other sides.

Special triangles allow you to transfer one piece of information around the whole figure. Before we solve the above problem, here are all the special triangles that you should look out for on the PSAT. It's a good idea to memorize the ratios, although many of them are listed in the instructions. But even more important, you should be sufficiently familiar enough with the triangles to recognize them when you see them.

Equilateral Triangle

All interior angles are 60°, and all the sides are the same length. You may want to memorize the area formula for an equilateral triangle, which is $area = \frac{1}{2}(side)^2$.

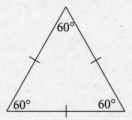

Isosceles Triangle

Two sides are the same length, and the angles opposite these sides are equal.

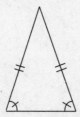

Right Triangles

These contain a 90° angle. The sides are related by the Pythagorean theorem: $a^2 + b^2 = c^2$, where a and b are the legs and c is the hypotenuse.

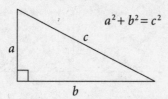

The *Special* Right Triangles

Many triangle problems contain *special* right triangles whose lengths always come in predefined ratios. If you recognize them, you won't have to use the Pythagorean theorem to find the value of a missing side.

The Isosceles Right Triangle

Note the side ratio: 1 to 1 to $\sqrt{2}$. Also note that this triangle is half a square divided diagonally.

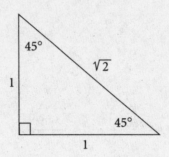

The 30-60-90 Right Triangle

Note the side ratio: 1 to $\sqrt{3}$ to 2. Also note that this triangle is half an equilateral triangle divided along its height.

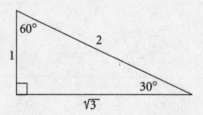

The 3-4-5 and 5-12-13 Right Triangles

Be on the lookout for multiples of 3-4-5 and 5-12-13 as well.

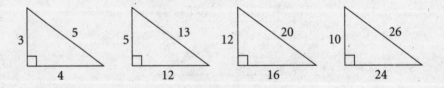

Now let's get back to our previous example. If you drop a vertical line from *B* to line *AC*, the triangle divides into two 3-4-5 right triangles. Now it's easy to find the area.

$Area = \frac{1}{2}bh$.

The base is 8, and the height is 3, so $Area = \frac{1}{2}(8 \times 3) = \frac{1}{2}(24) = 12$.

The correct answer is (B).

ADVANCED MATH AND HOW TO ATTACK IT

Every year up until 2004, this is where the PSAT Math chapter ended. Not anymore. In 2004, the PSAT (and SAT) writers decided that your life was way too easy. They decided the best way to make it harder was to put harder math on the PSAT. So they did. Here is some of the harder math that is now tested on the PSAT.

Sets

The things in a set are called *elements*, or *members*. The PSAT will likely ask a question about the union or intersection of two sets. The union of Set A and Set B, sometimes expressed as A∪B, is the set of elements that are in either or both of Set A and Set B. If Set A = {1, 2} and Set B = {3, 4}, then A∪B = {1, 2, 3, 4}. The intersection of Set A and Set B, sometimes expressed as A∩B, is the set of elements common to both Set A and Set B. If Set A = {1, 2, 3} and Set B = {3, 4, 5}, then A∩B = {3}. Here's a sample question:

> Set A consists of all the even integers greater than 5.
> Set B consists of all the numbers greater than 2 and
> less than 7. Which of the following numbers is in
> the union, but not the intersection, of Sets A and B?
>
> (A) 1
> (B) 2
> (C) 4
> (D) 6
> (E) 9

The union of two sets consists of all the elements that are in either set. The intersection consists of all the elements that are in *both* sets. You need to find a number that is in one set but not in both sets. (A), (B), and (E) are not in either set. (D) is in both sets. So (C) is the answer. Let's do another.

> Set K consists of all the negative integers greater
> than or equal to −100. Set L consists of all the num-
> bers which have an absolute value equal to or less
> than 5. How many elements are in the intersection
> of sets K and L?
>
> (A) 5
> (B) 6
> (C) 10
> (D) 12
> (E) infinitely many

(A) is the answer. The intersection of two sets consists of the elements found in both sets. How many numbers are in both set K and set L? Set L consists of all numbers between −5 and 5, including the endpoints. Set K contains 5 of these numbers: −5, −4, −3, −2, and −1. Thus, (A) is the correct answer.

Sequences Involving Exponential Growth

In a geometric sequence, if r is the ratio between consecutive terms, a_1 is the first term, and a_n is the nth term, then $a_n = a_1 r^{n-1}$. Here's an example:

> If the fourth term in a geometric sequence is 81, and $r = 3$, what is the first term?
>
> (A)   3
> (B)   6
> (C)   9
> (D) 18
> (E) 27

Use $a_n = a_1 r^{n-1}$ to solve for the first term:

$$81 = a_1 3^3$$
$$81 = a_1 27$$
$$a_1 = 3$$

So the answer is (A).

Absolute Value

The absolute value of a number is the distance of the number from zero on the number line. Because absolute value is a distance, *it is always positive*. If there's ever a negative answer choice in an absolute value question, that answer is wrong and should be eliminated immediately. So the absolute value of 7 is 7; this is expressed $|7| = 7$. Similarly, the absolute value of -7 is 7: $|-7| = 7$. Every positive number (like 7) is the absolute value of two numbers: itself (7) and its negative (-7).

> If $|b - 7| = 0$, which of the following must be true?
>
> (A) $|b^2 - 7| = 0$
> (B) $|b + 7| = 0$
> (C) $b = 7$
> (D) $b = -7$
> (E) $|b + 7| = 7$

If $|b - 7| = 0$, that means the distance on the number line between b and 7 is 0. Therefore, b must equal 7. None of the answer choices other than (C) is true when $b = 7$.

Ready for another one? Wonderful.

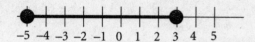

Which of the following inequalities best describes
the indicated values on the number line above?

(A) $|x + 5| \leq 3$

(B) $|x - 3| \leq 5$

(C) $|x - 3| \leq 0$

(D) $|x + 1| \leq 3$

(E) $|x + 1| \leq 4$

(E) is the answer. The easiest way to solve this problem is probably to plug the largest and smallest values given into the answer choices to see if they fit. For example, $|3 + 5| = 8$, which is not less than or equal to 3, so (A) is incorrect. You could also note that the center of the highlighted values is −1. The endpoints are each 4 units away. Therefore, the difference between any highlighted value x and −1 must be less than or equal to 4. This can be written as $|x - (-1)| = |x + 1| \leq 4$.

Rational Equations

Your first goal when solving for a variable is to isolate that variable on one side of the

equation. If you have a quadratic equation, try to factor it. If it can't be factored easily,

you can use the quadratic formula $\left(x = \dfrac{-b \pm \sqrt{b^2 - 4ac}}{2a} \right)$, but most quadratic equa-

tions on the PSAT can be factored. Try one:

If $\dfrac{x^2 - 4x + 4}{x - 2} = 2$, what is the value of x?

(A) −4

(B) −2

(C) 0

(D) 2

(E) 4

The quadratic equation in the numerator can be factored, which allows you to simplify the problem considerably:

$\dfrac{x^2 - 4x + 4}{x - 2} = \dfrac{(x - 2)(x - 2)}{x - 2} = x - 2$. Since $x - 2 = 2$, $x = 4$.

(E) is your answer. Let's try another.

If $\dfrac{a+4}{a^2+a+3}=1$, what are the possible values of a?

(A) -1 and 0

(B) -1 and 1

(C) 0 and 1

(D) 0 and 3

(E) 1 and 2

(B) is the answer. Here's how we got it.

$$\frac{a+4}{a^2+a+3}=1$$

$$a+4=a^2+a+3$$

$$0=a^2-1$$

$$0=(a+1)(a-1)$$

$$a=1 \text{ or } a=-1$$

Radical Equations

A radical equation contains at least one radical expression. Solve radical equations by using standard rules of algebra. If $5\sqrt{x}-2=13$, then $5\sqrt{x}=15$ and $\sqrt{x}=3$, so $x=9$.

If $2\sqrt{x}+3=9$, what is the value of x?

(A) 1

(B) $\sqrt{3}$

(C) 3

(D) $\sqrt{6}$

(E) 9

Isolate $\sqrt{x}$ on one side of the equation, then square both sides:

$$2\sqrt{x}+3=9$$

$$2\sqrt{x}=6$$

$$\sqrt{x}=3$$

$$x=9$$

(E) is the correct answer.

Okay, again.

> If $4p = 8\sqrt{p}$ and $p \neq 0$, what is the value of p?
>
> (A) 8
>
> (B) 4
>
> (C) 2
>
> (D) $\sqrt{2}$
>
> (E) $\dfrac{1}{\sqrt{2}}$

Again, isolate the variable first, then square both sides of the equation:

$$4p = 8\sqrt{p}$$
$$p = 2\sqrt{p}$$
$$(p)^2 = (2\sqrt{p})^2$$
$$p^2 = 4p$$
$$p^2 - 4p = 0$$
$$p(p - 4) = 0$$
$$p = 0 \text{ or } p = 4$$

Eliminate $p = 0$, because you're given that $p \neq 0$; you're then left with $p = 4$.

(B) is the correct answer.

Manipulation with Integer and Rational Exponents

To find the value of a number raised to a negative power, simply rewrite the number, without the negative sign, as the bottom of a fraction with 1 as the numerator of the fraction:

$3^{-2} = \dfrac{1}{3^2} = \dfrac{1}{9}$. If x is a positive real number and a is a nonzero integer, then $x^{\frac{1}{a}} = \sqrt[a]{n}$.

so $4^{\frac{1}{2}} = \sqrt[2]{4} = 2$. If p and q are integers, then $x^{\frac{p}{q}} = \sqrt[q]{x^p}$. So $4^{\frac{3}{2}} = \sqrt[2]{4^3} = 64 = 8$.

> If $m^{\frac{3}{2}}$ and $n^{\frac{4}{3}}$ are both greater than zero, which of the following must be true?
>
> I. $m > 0$
>
> II. $n > 0$
>
> III. $n \neq 0$
>
> (A) I only
>
> (B) III only
>
> (C) I and III only
>
> (D) II and III only
>
> (E) I, II, and III

If you have trouble remembering the rules of exponents, try picking numbers for m and n to see which of the answer choices could be correct. Because $m^{\frac{3}{2}}$ is positive, m must also be positive. You can think of $m^{\frac{3}{2}}$ as $(\sqrt{m})^3$. $\sqrt{m}$ must be positive, since $\sqrt{m}$ raised to an odd power is positive. $(\sqrt{m})^2 = m$ must also be positive. No such condition holds for n, however—whether n is positive or negative, $n^{\frac{4}{3}}$ will be positive. However, you can see that n cannot equal zero, because if $n = 0$, $n^{\frac{4}{3}}$ will also equal zero. So options I and III must be correct, but option II is not necessarily true. (C) is the answer. Let's try another one:

If $q^{\frac{-1}{2}} > 1$, $q > 0$, and $r^2 < 1$, what is one possible value of $q + r$?

[grid-in answer box]

$0 \le q + r < 2$

Find the range of possible values for q and r, and then add them together:

$q^{\frac{-1}{2}} > 1$

$\dfrac{1}{\sqrt{q}} > 1$

$1 > \sqrt{q}$

$1 > q$

So $0 < q < 1$

$r^2 < 1$

$-1 < r < 1$

$-1 < q + r < 2$, but you can't grid negative numbers, so grid 0 or a number between 0 and 2.

Direct and Inverse Variation

In direct variation, $y = kx$, where k is a nonzero constant. In direct variation, the variable y changes directly as x does. For example, if a unit of Currency A is worth 2 units of Currency B, then $A = 2B$. If the number of units of B were to double, the number of units of A would double, and so on for halving, tripling, etc. In inverse variation, $xy = k$, where x and y are variables and k is a constant. A famous inverse relationship is *rate* × *time* = *distance*. Imagine having to cover a distance of 24 miles. If you were to travel at 12 miles per hour, you'd need 2 hours. But if you were to halve your rate, you would have to double your time. This is just another way of saying that rate and time vary inversely. Try this Grid-in:

> The number of pigeons and squirrels in Davies Park is described by the equation $ps = 1{,}000$, where p is the number of pigeons and s is the number of squirrels. If there are 100 pigeons in the park, how many squirrels are there?

This is really just a simple substitution problem—plug the given value of p into the equation and solve for s:

$100s = 1{,}000$

$s = 10$

Now let's do a multiple-choice question.

> The time Dave spends working on homework each
> week is directly proportional to the number of
> pages his teachers assign. One week, Dave's teachers
> assigned ten pages of homework, and he spent two
> hours working on it. Another week, Dave spent
> four hours and 24 minutes working on homework.
> How many pages did his teachers assign that week?
>
> (A) 10
> (B) 20
> (C) 22
> (D) 24
> (E) 26

If the time Dave spends on homework is directly proportional to the number of pages assigned, the relationship between time spent (t) and pages assigned (n) can be expressed as $t = kn$, where k is a constant. You can use the first week's data to find k, then plug that in with the time spent in the second week to find the number of pages assigned that week.

$$120 \text{ minutes} = k(10 \text{ pages})$$

$$\frac{12 \text{ minutes}}{\text{page}} = k$$

$$264 \text{ minutes} = \frac{12 \text{ minutes}}{\text{page}}(n)$$

$$22 \text{ pages} = n$$

The answer is (C).

Functions as Models

The PSAT will likely ask you to glean and use information from tables like these.

Number of plants			
	Bushes	Pine trees	Maple trees
Smith family	2	2	1
Jones family	3	2	4
Harris family	1	3	3

Fertilizer needed each year (in liters)			
	Bush	Pine tree	Maple tree
In good soil	.1	0	.7
In poor soil	.2	.5	1.2

The tables above show the number of plants each of three families has around their houses and the amount of fertilizer each plant requires each year. The amount of fertilizer needed depends on whether the plant is in good soil or poor soil. If all the plants around the Jones family's house are in good soil, how much fertilizer does the Jones family need to apply each year?

(A) 1.4 L

(B) 2.2 L

(C) 3.1 L

(D) 5.2 L

(E) 6.4 L

You only need to use one line from each table. In this case, you need to know how many plants of each type the Jones family has and how much fertilizer each of those plants will need in good soil:

$3(.1) + 2(0) + 4(.7) = .3 + 2.8 = 3.1$

The answer is (C).

If all the plants around the Harris family's house are in poor soil, how much fertilizer will the Harris family have to apply each year?

(A) 1.2 L

(B) 2.4 L

(C) 3.1 L

(D) 5.3 L

(E) 6.4 L

Now you need to know how many plants of each type the Harris family has and how much fertilizer they need in poor soil:

$1(.2) + 3(.5) + 3(1.2) = .2 + 1.5 + 3.6 = 5.3$

(D) is the answer.

The amount of time it takes for a company to produce a new software product can be represented by the equation $t = 140 - 6\sqrt{p}$, where t is the number of days it takes to produce the software and p is the number of programmers working on the project. This relationship holds as long as there is at least one programmer working on the project. How many programmers would the company need to complete a new product in 80 days?

(A)   2

(B)   5

(C)   10

(D)   100

(E) 1,000

The answer is (D). This problem looks a little complicated, but all you have to do is solve the equation $t = 140 - 6\sqrt{p}$ when t equals 80:

$$80 = 140 - 6\sqrt{p}$$
$$6\sqrt{p} = 60$$
$$\sqrt{p} = 10$$
$$p = 100$$

(Backsolving would also work well here.)

Linear Functions—Equations and Graphs

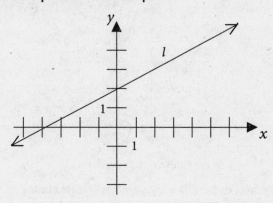

Which of the following equations represents a line parallel to line l above?

(A) $y = \frac{1}{2}x + 5$

(B) $y = \frac{2}{3}x + 2$

(C) $y = x - 2$

(D) $y = \frac{3}{2}x + 2$

(E) $y = 2x - 4$

Parallel lines have the same slope. First, calculate the slope of line l, then find the answer choice with that slope. Recall that slope is change in y over change in x: Use the points $(-4, 0)$ and $(0, 2)$ on the line and the slope formula.

$$\frac{2 - 0}{0 - (-4)} = \frac{2}{4} = \frac{1}{2}$$

So the answer is (A). Let's do another.

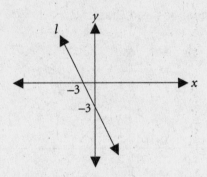

Note: Figure not drawn to scale.

Which of the following points is on line *l* in the graph above?

(A) $(-2, -5)$

(B) $(-1, -4)$

(C) $(-4, 5)$

(D) $(2, -5)$

(E) $(5, -2)$

When in doubt, use logic and eliminate answer choices that are obviously wrong. This makes your odds increase of guessing the right answer.

Use the given points to determine the equation of line *l*:

$$y = mx + b$$
$$(-3) = m(0) + b$$
$$-3 = b$$
$$(0) = m(-3) + (-3)$$
$$3 = m(-3)$$
$$m = -1$$

So, the equation of our line is $y = -x - 3$. Now we just plug in the points in the answer choices and see which one works:

$$y = -x - 3$$
$$(-5) = -(-2) - 3$$
$$-5 = -1 \text{—choice (A) does not work.}$$

$$y = -x - 3$$
$$(-4) = -(-1) - 3$$
$$-4 = -2 \text{—choice (B) does not work.}$$

$$y = -x - 3$$
$$(5) = -(-4) - 3$$
$$5 = 1-\text{choice (C) does not work.}$$

$$y = -x - 3$$
$$(-5) = -(2) - 3$$
$$-5 = -5-\text{choice (D) works!}$$

Properties of Tangent Lines

When a line is tangent to a circle, the radius of the circle is perpendicular to the line at the point of contact. Don't forget!

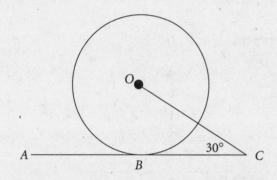

In the figure above, the center of the circle is O. $\overline{AC}$ is tangent to the circle at its midpoint, B. If $OC = 4\sqrt{3}$, what is the length of $\overline{AC}$?

(A) $2\sqrt{3}$

(B) 4

(C) 6

(D) $6\sqrt{3}$

(E) 12

What did we tell you not to forget? That's right—a line tangent to a circle is perpendicular to the radius of the circle. You can use this to sketch in a radius between O and B, creating a 30-60-90 special triangle. Then you can find BC, and from that AC. Like this:

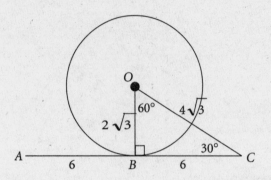

$6 + 6 = 12$

That would be answer (E).

Coordinate Geometry

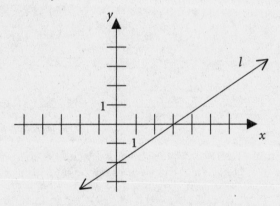

The figure above shows line *l*. Which of the following equations describes a line perpendicular to line *l*?

(A) $y = \dfrac{-3}{2}x + 1$

(B) $y = -3x + 2$

(C) $y = \dfrac{-2}{3}x + 4$

(D) $y = \dfrac{2}{3}x - 2$

(E) $y = \dfrac{3}{2}x + 3$

This problem is actually a little simpler than it looks. All you need to do is find the slope of line *l*, then find the slope of a line perpendicular to *l*. The slope of a line is equal to the change in *y* over the change in *x*. You can use two points from the graph, say

(0, −2) and (3, 0), to find this. The slope of a perpendicular line will be the negative reciprocal of the slope of the other line.

Slope of *l*:

$$\frac{0 - (-2)}{3 - 0} = \frac{2}{3}$$

Slope of perpendicular line:

$$\frac{-3}{2}$$

Only Choice (A) has this slope. Let's try another one.

> $\overline{PQ}$ extends from $(1, 0)$ to $(5, 4)$. Which of the following equations describes a line that intersects $\overline{PQ}$ at its midpoint and is perpendicular to $\overline{PQ}$?
>
> (A) $y = -3x + 2$
> (B) $y = -2x + 3$
> (C) $y = -x$
> (D) $y = -x + 5$
> (E) $y = x + 5$

You will need to find the midpoint of $\overline{PQ}$, as well as its slope. You can then use the slope to find the slope of a line perpendicular to $\overline{PQ}$, and plug in the midpoint to find the *y*-intercept of the line using the equation $y = mx + b$.

Midpoint:

$$\frac{5 + 1}{2} = \frac{6}{2} = 3$$

$$\frac{4 + 0}{2} = 2$$

So the midpoint of $\overline{PQ}$ is (3, 2)

Slope:

$$\frac{4 - 0}{5 - 1} = \frac{4}{4} = 1$$

So the slope of the perpendicular line is −1.

$y = -1x + b$

$2 = -3 + b$

$5 = b$

So the equation of the perpendicular line is $y = -x + 5$. Answer (D) is correct.

Data Interpretation, Including Scatterplots

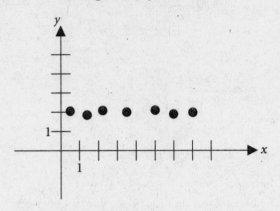

Which of the lines described by the following equations best fits these points?

(A) $y = 2x + 2$

(B) $y = 2x$

(C) $y = x + 2$

(D) $y = -x + 2$

(E) $y = 2$

Try to figure out what sort of line would fit these points. What should the slope be? What should the y-intercept be? If you think visually, you might want to try sketching the line described by each answer choice to see which one most nearly fits the points on the graph. A horizontal line has slope 0. These points are more or less horizontal, so we need to find an equation with a slope near or equal to 0. The only equation that has a slope of 0 is $y = 2$. That would be (E). Ready for another one?

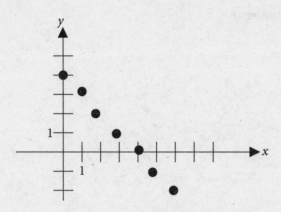

Which of the lines described by the following equations best fits these points?

(A) $y = -4x$

(B) $y = -4x + 4$

(C) $y = -x - 4$

(D) $y = -x + 4$

(E) $y = x - 4$

Find the slope and y-intercept from the graph. Since each point is about as far below the previous point as it is to the right, the slope of this line should be around -1. The y-intercept is near 4. The equation that fits those criteria is $y = -x + 4$. In other words, (D).

Geometric Probability

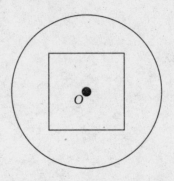

Note: Figure not drawn to scale.

In the figure above, the radius of the circle centered at O and each side of the square has a length of one unit. What is the probability that a point selected randomly from inside the circle will lie outside the square?

(A) $\dfrac{1}{\pi}$

(B) $\dfrac{\pi-1}{\pi}$

(C) $\dfrac{\pi}{2}$

(D) $\pi-1$

(E) π^2-1

The answer is (B), and there are two ways to get to it. First, the probability of selecting a point outside the square will equal 1 minus the probability of selecting a point inside the square, which you calculated in the last problem. Second, you could find the area of the part of the circle that is outside the square, and then divide that by the total area of the circle.

Total area of circle:

$\pi(1)^2 = \pi$

Area of square:

$(1)^2 = 1$

Area of circle outside of square:

$\pi - 1$

Probability:

$\dfrac{\pi - 1}{\pi}$

Let's try another one using the same figure above.

If a point is selected at random from the interior of the circle, what is the probability that it will lie within the square?

(A) $\dfrac{1}{\pi}$

(B) $\dfrac{1}{\pi^2}$

(C) $\dfrac{1}{2\pi}$

(D) $\dfrac{2}{\pi}$

(E) 2π

You'll need to find the area of the circle and the area of the square. The probability that a randomly selected point will lie within the square is the area of the square divided by the area of the circle.

Area of circle:

$\pi(1)^2 = \pi$

Area of square:

$(1)^2 = 1$

Probability:

$\dfrac{1}{\pi}$

The answer is (A).

Median and Mode

In a set of numbers, the median divides the set into an upper and lower half. The median of $\{1, 2, 3, 4, 5\}$ is 3. The median of $\{-4, 0, \frac{1}{2}, \pi, 479\}$ is $\frac{1}{2}$. Note that in these two examples, the sets contained an odd number of elements. To find the median of a set with an even number of elements, simply take the average of the two middle numbers. For example, the median of $\{3, 4, 5, 6\}$ is 4.5, the average of 4 and 5. In a set of evenly spaced numbers, the median equals the average. For example, the median of $\{10, 30, 50, 70, 90\}$ is 50—the average of 10, 30, 50, 70, and 90. (For that matter, it is also the average of 90 and 10 only, as well as of 70 and 30 only.) The mode is the element that appears most frequently in a set. The mode of $\{0, 0, 1, 1, 1, 2\}$ is 1, because it appears three times—more than any other element.

What is the positive difference between the median
and mode of the set $\{-1, -1, 0, 0, 0, 4, 7, 7, 7, 7, 7\}$?

[grid-in answer box]

The median of the set is 4: five elements are smaller than it, and five are greater than it. The mode of the set is 7—the number that appears more than any other in the set. The positive difference between 4 and 7 is 3.

CHAPTER THREE SUMMARY

○ The PSAT uses multiple-choice and Grid-In questions in its math sections. Kaplan strategies work for both question types.

○ With Grid-ins, always start in the far left box, and remember, there can be more than one right answer to some questions.

○ Both Math sections are arranged easiest to hardest.

○ Kaplan has a strategy for attacking math questions:

  —Step 1. Read through the question.

  —Step 2. Decide whether to do it now or later.

  —Step 3. Look for the fastest way to answer the question.

○ Sometimes shortcuts can save you a lot of time on a Math question. Kaplan has three good shortcuts: picking numbers, backsolving, and eyeballing.

○ A calculator is allowed on the PSAT, but you have to be careful how use you it.

○ The PSAT tests several basic and advanced math concepts. They include:

  —Symbols

  —Averages

  —Rates

  —Special Triangles

- –Sets

- –Sequences Involving Exponential Growth

- –Absolute Value

- –Rational Equations

- –Radical Equations

- –Manipulation with Integer and Rational Exponents

- –Direct and Inverse Variation

- –Functions as Models

- –Linear Functions–Equations and Graphs

- –Properties of Tangent Lines

- –Coordinate Geometry

- –Data Interpretation

- –Geometric Probability

- –Median and Mode

PRACTICE

Ready for a little quiz? Great, let's go.

1. If $c \neq 0$, then $\dfrac{c^5}{c^4} - \dfrac{c^3}{c^2} =$

   (A) $2c$
   (B) c
   (C) 2
   (D) 1
   (E) 0

2. The ratio of girls to boys in a class is 3:5. If there are 15 girls, how many boys must there be in the class?

   (A) 10
   (B) 18
   (C) 21
   (D) 25
   (E) 30

3. If $a^2 - 1 = (a - 1)^2$, what is the value of a?

   (A) −1
   (B) 0
   (C) 1
   (D) 2
   (E) 3

4. In a plane, lines r and s are drawn such that $r \parallel s$. If a third line t is drawn such that $t \perp s$, and a fourth line u is drawn such that $u \parallel t$, which of the following statements must be true?

   I. $t \perp r$
   II. $s \perp u$
   III. $r \parallel u$

   (A) I only
   (B) II only
   (C) III only
   (D) I and II
   (E) I and III

5. If 9 is x percent of 90, what is 50 percent of x?

   (A) 5
   (B) 9
   (C) 10
   (D) 15
   (E) 18

RANGE OF TEMPERATURES IN SELECTED CITIES IN 1992 (IN DEGREES CELSIUS)

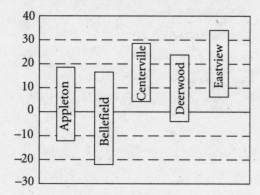

6. Which city had the greatest difference between highest and lowest temperatures in 1992?

   (A) Appleton
   (B) Bellefield
   (C) Centerville
   (D) Deerwood
   (E) Eastview

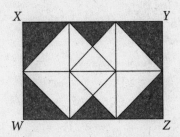

7. In the figure above, rectangle *WXYZ* is divided into six squares. If the area of each square is 2, what is the area of the shaded region?

   (A) 2.5
   (B) 3
   (C) 4.5
   (D) 5
   (E) 6

8. If the average (arithmetic mean) of 20, 37, 40, and *y* is *y* – 2, what is the value of *y*?

   (A) 33
   (B) 34
   (C) 35
   (D) 36
   (E) 37

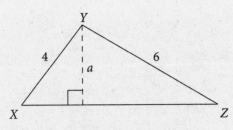

Note: Figure not drawn to scale.

9. In the figure above, if the area of triangle *XYZ* is 4*a*, what is the perimeter of triangle *XYZ*?

   (A) 14
   (B) 16
   (C) 18
   (D) 20
   (E) 24

10. The cost of a taxi ride in a certain city is $1.25 for the first half-mile and $0.25 for each additional $\frac{1}{8}$ of a mile. If a taxi ride costs $7.75, which of the following could be the length of the ride in miles?

    (A) $3\frac{3}{8}$

    (B) $3\frac{1}{2}$

    (C) $3\frac{3}{4}$

    (D) $3\frac{7}{8}$

    (E) 4

11. Circle *A* has a circumference of 4π and circle *B* has a circumference of 36π. If the circles intersect at exactly one point, which of the following could be the distance from the center of circle *A* to the center of circle *B*?

    (A) 10
    (B) 12
    (C) 14
    (D) 16
    (E) 18

12. A broken watch loses 15 minutes per hour. If this watch is set to the correct time at 6 o'clock, what is the least number of hours that it would take this watch to show the correct time again?

    (A) 12
    (B) 24
    (C) 36
    (D) 48
    (E) 60

13. If $|b-3| = 6$, what are the two possible values of b?

    (A) -9 and 3

    (B) -9 and 9

    (C) -6 and 6

    (D) -3 and 3

    (E) -3 and 9

14. Which of the following lines is parallel to the line $y = 4x - 6$?

    (A) $y = \dfrac{1}{4}x - 6$

    (B) $y = \dfrac{1}{2}x + 3$

    (C) $y = 2x - 6$

    (D) $y = 2x - 3$

    (E) $y = 4x + 6$

15. If $\dfrac{3}{x-6} = 3$, what is the value of x?

    (A) 3

    (B) 6

    (C) 7

    (D) 12

    (E) 14

16. If $x = \dfrac{1}{5}$, $x^{-3} =$

    (A) -25

    (B) $-\dfrac{1}{125}$

    (C) 5

    (D) $\dfrac{1}{25}$

    (E) 125

17. If $xy = k$, where k is a constant, what happens to the value of x if the value of y is halved?

    (A) It doubles.

    (B) It halves.

    (C) It increases $\sqrt{2}$ times.

    (D) It squares.

    (E) It remains the same.

Note: Figure not drawn to scale.

18. In $\overline{PS}$ above, $PQ = 3$, $RS = 10$, and $PS = 19$. What is the measure of QR?

    (A) 2

    (B) 3

    (C) 6

    (D) 9

    (E) 10

19. If P is the set of all numbers between −5.5 and 5.5, inclusive, Q is the set of all prime numbers, and R is the set of all positive integers, then the intersection of P, Q, and R contains how many elements?

    (A) 0
    (B) 1
    (C) 2
    (D) 3
    (E) 5

20. The initial number of elements in a certain set is p, where $p > 0$. If the number of elements in the set doubles every hour, which of the following represents the total number of elements in the set after exactly 48 hours?

    (A) $24p$
    (B) $48p$
    (C) $2p^{24}$
    (D) $(2^{48})p$
    (E) $(2p)^{48}$

21. If the price of one grapefruit is $0.45 and the price of one orange is $0.20, how many oranges are equal in cost to 16 grapefruit?

22. The integer p is divisible by 3, and when p is divided by 10, the remainder is 2. If p is greater than 100 and less than 200, what is one possible value of p?

23. The perimeter of a rectangle is 14. If the length of the rectangle is greater than 6, what is one possible value for the width?

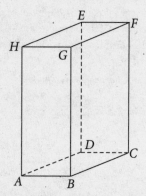

24. In the rectangular solid above, $AB = 3$, $BC = 4$, and $FC = 12$. What is the area of triangle ACF?

25. At a certain company, the number of production employees was increased from 300 to 390. The number of clerical employees was increased by twice the percent increase of the production employees. If the final number of clerical employees was 192, what was the original number of clerical employees?

ANSWERS AND EXPLANATIONS

1. E

Simplify each term using rules of exponents. When dividing like bases, subtract the exponents:

$\frac{c^5}{c^4} = c^{5-4} = c^1$ which equals c;

$\frac{c^3}{c^2} = c^{3-2}$ or c^1 which also equals c.

Since $c - c = 0$, answer choice (E) is correct.

2. D

A ratio can also be written as a fraction. If the ratio of girls to boys is 3:5, then $\frac{\text{girls}}{\text{boys}} = \frac{3}{5}$. You're given that there are 15 girls, so set up a proportion to find the number of boys: Let b be the number of boys. So, $\frac{3}{5} = \frac{15}{b}$. Cross-multiply and solve for b: $3b = 5 \times 15$, or 75. Divide both sides by 3 to get $b = 25$, so choice (D) is correct.

3. C

Using the FOIL method to expand $(a - 1)^2$, or $(a - 1)(a - 1)$, we get $a^2 - a - a + 1$, or $a^2 - 2a + 1$. So $a^2 - 1 = a^2 - 2a + 1$. Subtract a^2 from both sides: $-1 = -2a + 1$. Now subtract 1 from both sides, which gives you $-2 = -2a$, or $1 = a$. So answer choice (C) is correct.

4. D

Draw a diagram. Draw r and s parallel to each other. Then draw t perpendicular to s. Notice that t is also perpendicular to r, so (I) is true. Now draw u parallel to t. Notice that u is perpendicular to r and s, so (II) is true.

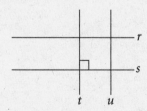

Since r is perpendicular to u, the lines cannot be parallel, so (III) is false. Therefore, choice (D) is the correct answer.

5. A

If 9 is x percent of 90, then $9 = \frac{x}{10} \times 90$, or $9 = \frac{9x}{10}$.

Multiply both sides by the reciprocal of $\frac{9}{10}$ to get $\frac{10}{9} \times 9$

$= \frac{10}{9} \times \frac{9x}{10}$ or $10 = x$. So 50% of x is 50% of 10. That is

$\frac{1}{2} \times 10$, or 5. Therefore, choice (A) is correct.

6. B

The highest temperature in a particular town is the value corresponding to the top of that town's bar, and the lowest temperature is the value corresponding to the bottom of that bar. So the town with the longest bar will have the greatest difference in temperatures. Looking at the graph, you can see that the longest bar corresponds to Bellefield. Therefore, Bellefield has the greatest difference in temperature, so choice (B) is correct.

7. D

Looking at the diagram, you can see that there are 4 shaded half squares and 2 shaded quarter squares. So 4 half squares equal 2 whole squares, and 2 quarter squares equal a half square. So the shaded part is 2.5 squares. If the area of each square is 2, then the area of the shaded part is 2.5×2, or 5. So answer choice (D) is correct.

8. C

The average formula tells us that the average $=$

$\frac{\text{the sum of the terms}}{\text{the number of the terms}}$. In this case

$\frac{20 + 37 + 40 + y}{4} = y - 2$. Multiplying both sides by 4

gives you $97 + y = 4y - 8$. Adding 8 and subtracting y

from both sides gives you $105 = 3y$, or $y = 35$. Answer

choice (C) is correct.

9. C

To find the perimeter of triangle *XYZ*, you need to find the length of the base *XZ*. You can use the area to find the base. The formula for the area of a triangle is area $\frac{1}{2}bh$, where *b* is the base and *h* is the height. The area of triangle *XYZ* is 4*a*, and the height equals *a*. Therefore, $4a = \frac{1}{2}ba$. Solve for *b*: divide both sides by *a*, which gives you $4 = \frac{1}{2}b$; multiply both sides by 2 (the reciprocal of $\frac{1}{2}$), which gives you $8 = b$. So *XZ* = 8, and the perimeter of the triangle is 4 + 6 + 8 = 18. Choice (C) is correct.

10. C

The first $\frac{1}{2}$ mile costs $1.25. Subtract 1.25 from 7.75 to find the cost of the remaining distance: 7.75 − 1.25 = 6.50. Each $\frac{1}{8}$ additional mile costs $0.25. Divide 6.50 by .25 to find how many eighths of a mile were traveled: $\frac{6.50}{.25} = 26$ eighths of a mile or $\frac{26}{8}$ miles, which simplifies to $\frac{13}{4}$ miles or $3\frac{1}{4}$ miles. Now add the first $\frac{1}{2}$ mile to get the total distance; $3\frac{1}{4} + \frac{1}{2} = 3\frac{3}{4}$, which is answer choice (C).

11. D

If circles *A* and *B* intersect at exactly one point, then the circles are tangent to each other. Draw a diagram. There are two ways that the circles can be drawn:

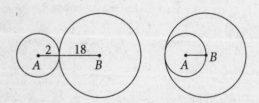

Circumference of a circle equals $2\pi r$. The circumference of circle *A* = 4π, so its radius equals 2. The circumference of circle *B* = 36π, so its radius equals 18. Look at diagram #1. The distance between the centers of the two circles is

2 + 18 = 20. That's not one of the choices, so look at diagram #2. The distance between the centers of the two circles is 18 − 2 = 16. So answer choice (D) is correct.

12. D

A watch shows the same time every 12 hours. So the watch will show the correct time again when it has lost 12 hours. If the watch loses 15 minutes per hour, then it loses 1 hour every 4 hours (or the watch loses $\frac{1}{4}$ of the time elapsed). Let *h* be the least number of hours it would take the watch to be correct again. Therefore, $\frac{h}{4} = 12$, or *h* = 48. So answer choice (D) is correct.

13. E

Remember that there are two possibilities whenever you see part of an equation inside absolute value signs: $|b - 3| = 6$, so either *b* − 3 = 6 and *b* = 9, or −(*b* − 3) = 6, in which case −*b* + 3 = 6 and −*b* = 3, so *b* = −3.

14. E

Lines are parallel if they have the same slope. Remember that when an equation for a line is given in the form *y* = *mx* + *b*, *m* represents the slope. In this case, only *y* = 4*x* + 6 has the same slope as *y* = 4*x* − 6.

15. C

This is a good problem to backsolve, but it can also be solved algebraically. Whichever method you choose, remember to work carefully. Here's the algebraic solution:

$$\frac{3}{x - 6} = 3$$
$$3 = 3(x - 6)$$
$$3 = 3x - 18$$
$$21 = 3x$$
$$7 = x$$

16. E

Be very careful when substituting given values for variables. Be sure to keep track of the sign and to write every step down as you proceed with the operation.

$$x^{-3} = \frac{1}{x^3} = \frac{1}{(\frac{1}{5})^3} = \frac{1}{(\frac{1}{125})} = 125$$

17. A

Pick numbers. Say $x = 4$ and $y = 6$. Then $xy = k = 24$. When y is halved to 3, x becomes 8—it doubles.

18. C

If $PS = 19$ and $PQ = 3$, then $PS - PQ = QS = 19 - 3 = 16$. Using $QS = 16$ and $RS = 10$, we can say that $QS - RS = QR$, or $16 - 10 = 6$.

19. D

The things in a set are called elements or members. The union of sets is the set of elements in one or more of the sets being united. Think of the union set as what you get when you merge sets. The symbol for union set is ∪. The intersection of sets is the set of common elements of the sets being intersected. Think of the intersection as the overlap of sets. The symbol for the intersection of sets is ∩. To be in $P \cap Q \cap R$—that is, the intersection of P, Q, and R—a number would have to be: between −5.5 and 5.5, inclusive; prime; and positive. Given the sets in question, the only such numbers are 2, 3, and 5—that's three elements.

20. D

Think about the question in common sense terms. To double is to multiply by two. The question calls for this doubling to occur 48 times. The mathematical way of expressing "doubling to occur 48 times" is 2^{48}. The answer is the total growth that occurs times the original population. Again, total growth is 2^{48}. The original population is p.

21. 36

To find out how many oranges are equal in cost to 16 grapefruit, you need to figure out how much 16 grapefruit would cost and then divide that amount by the price of one orange. If each grapefruit sells for $0.45, then 16

would cost $0.45 \times 16 = $7.20. If each orange costs $0.20, you could buy $\frac{\$7.20}{\$0.20} = 36$ oranges.

22. 102, 132, 162, 192

If a number is divisible by 3, the sum of its digits must be divisible by 3. If a number is divisible by 10, its units' digit is 0—the last digit of a number represents the remainder that results when that number is divided by 10. So you need to find a number whose last digit is 2 and the sum of whose digits is divisible by 3. There are only ten numbers between 100 and 200 that end in 2, (102, 112, 122, 132, 142, 152, 162, 172, 182, and 192). The hundreds' digit of each is 1, while the units' digit is of course 2—since these digits sum to 3, in order for the entire number to be divisible by 3, the tens' digit must be divisible by 3. 102, 132, 162, and 192 are the only numbers that meet both tests.

23. 0 < width < 1

The perimeter of a rectangle is equal to 2(length + width), so $14 = 2(\ell + w)$ or $7 = \ell + w$. You are told that $\ell > 6$, so for $\ell + w$ to equal 7, w must be less than 1. If this isn't clear, manipulate the equation for perimeter to get $\ell = 7 - w$, and then substitute $7 - w$ into the inequality for ℓ. So $7 - w > 6$; adding w and subtracting 6 from both sides shows that $1 > w$. Since width must be a positive measurement, you could grid in any decimal or fraction between 0 and 1 for the width.

24. 30

This is a pretty tough visualization problem. It is helpful to label each segment with the appropriate measure. Since triangle ACF isn't clearly visible, draw in line segments AC and AF. Triangle ACF is inside this rectangular solid. One thing you need to remember about rectangular solids is that the faces, or planes, are either perpendicular or parallel to each other. For example, plane ABC is perpendicular to plane EFC. Therefore, line segment AC, which is on plane ABC, is perpendicular to line segment FC, which is on plane EFC. This means that triangle ACF is a right triangle, where the right angle is angle *ACF*. To find the area of triangle *ACF*, we need the length of the base, *AC*, and the height, *FC*. *FC* is given as 12; to find *AC*, we need to look at triangle *ABC*. Although it may not look like it in the diagram, triangle *ABC* is a right triangle with a right angle at angle *ABC*, since each face of a rectangular solid is a rectangle and has right angles at the corners. So, for right triangle *ABC*, leg *AB* is 3 and the other leg, *BC*, is 4. Right away that tells us that *AC*, the hypotenuse, is 5 because right triangle *ABC* is a 3-4-5 Pythagorean triplet. Now, the area of triangle *ACF* is $\frac{1}{2}$ (base)(height), or $\frac{1}{2}(AC)(CF)$, or $\frac{1}{2}(5)(12)$, or 30.

25. 120

If the number of production employees increases from 300 to 390, that's an increase of $\frac{90}{300} = \frac{30}{100} = 30\%$. The number of clerical workers increases by twice that percent, or $2 \times 30\% = 60\%$, resulting in a total of 192 clerical workers. The question asks you to solve for the original number of clerical workers, which you can call *x*. You aren't told how many of the 192 are new employees, but you know that this total of 192 is equal to the original number plus 60% of the original number. Since percent × whole = part, then $160\% \times x = 192$, or $1.6 \times x = 192$. So $x = 120$.

Chapter Four: **How to Attack the Writing Section**

If you've ever read a sentence and thought "Hmm . . . that doesn't look right," you've used the skills that will get you a good score on the Writing section of the PSAT. The Writing section is all about one thing—spotting grammar mistakes and sentence construction. After you're finished working through chapter four, you'll be able to recognize grammatical errors with the zeal and acuteness of your English teacher and will score higher on the PSAT.

CHAPTER FOUR SUMMARY

You probably haven't seen questions like the ones on the Writing section before because most of your high school classes don't teach grammar this way. We'll spend a lot of time in chapter four on the three question types used in the Writing section. We'll also show you the grammar and sentence construction errors that are most often tested on the PSAT, so you know what to look for on test day.

WRITING BASICS

On the PSAT Writing section, you are not required to write anything. You won't have to identify words as adverbs or prepositions or past participles. You'll never see the words *ambiguous pronoun reference* or *subordinate clause*. You also won't be tested on spelling or capitalization.

What you will be required to do is demonstrate your ability to recognize the elements of good writing, including basic grammar, sentence structure, word choice, and paragraph construction.

In the days, weeks, or months that precede the PSAT, read everything—and we mean everything—with an eye toward sentence structure. Look for fragments in advertisements. Find run-on sentences in emails from your friends. Weed out misplaced modifiers in your school newspaper. Become a reader who looks for *mistakes*.

While you're training your eyes to look for writing errors, also train on your ears to listen for them. Listen to how people talk. Does the English language sound different on the nightly news than it does on *Friends* reruns? Why might that be? What word choices do your friends and teachers use? Are they different? How? We're not suggesting that you start correcting people. Just listen with a more critical ear than usual. Learning to trust your ear is the best way to prepare for the PSAT Writing section.

Question Types

Unlike the Math sections, the PSAT Writing section questions have never been designed to increase in difficulty as the section progresses. Easy, medium, and hard questions are all jumbled up. Knowing how each question type works and being familiar with the other quirks of the PSAT Writing section will save you lots of time on test day. Following is a detailed summary of the three question types:

- 14 Usage questions
- 20 Sentence Correction questions
- 5 Revision-in-Context questions

Usage Questions

The directions for Usage questions look like this.

<u>Directions:</u> The following sentences test your knowledge of grammar, usage, diction (choice of words), and idiom.

Some sentences are correct.

No sentence contains more than one error.

Several parts of the sentence will be underlined and lettered. You will find that the error, if there is one, is underlined and lettered. Elements of the sentence that are not underlined will not be changed. In choosing answers, follow the requirements of standard written English.

If there is an error, select the <u>one underlined part</u> that must be changed to make the sentence correct and fill in the corresponding oval on your answer sheet.

If there is no error, fill in answer oval (E).

Here's an example:

<u>Even though</u> he <u>had to</u> supervise a large staff, his
   A   B

salary <u>was no greater</u> than <u>a clerk</u>. <u>No error</u>
        C   D   E

Spot the Mistake!

All Usage questions are *spot-the-mistake* type questions. You're given a sentence with four words and phrases underlined. The underlined parts are labeled (A) through (D). One of the underlined pieces may contain a usage error. Your task is to spot the error and fill in the corresponding oval on your grid. If the sentence is error-free, the correct answer is (E), No error. Also, you should assume that the parts of the sentence not underlined are correct.

Usage questions test your ability to catch words or phrases that high school students often use incorrectly. If you can spot these types of errors, the test makers assume that you can use the right words and phrases in your own writing.

In this example, the correct answer is (D). The current wording makes it sound as though the size of the subject's salary is being compared to the size of a clerk; in fact, the subject's salary should be compared to the size of a clerk's *salary*.

Sentence Correction Questions

The Sentence Correction section begins with directions that look like this:

<u>**Directions:**</u> The following sentences test correctness and effectiveness of expression. In choosing answers, follow the requirements of standard written English; that is, pay attention to grammar, choice of words, sentence construction, and punctuation.

In each of the following sentences, part of the sentence or the entire sentence is underlined. Beneath each sentence you will find five ways of phrasing the underlined part. Choice (A) repeats the original; the other four are different.

Choose the answer that best expresses the meaning of the original sentence. If you think the original is better than any of the alternatives, choose it; otherwise, choose one of the others. Your choice should produce the most effective sentence—clear and precise, without awkwardness or ambiguity.

Here's an example:

> To the surprise of the school's staff, the new freshman class at Ravenswood High <u>being larger than last year's</u>.

(A) being larger than last year's

(B) is large more so than last year

(C) which is larger than the one last year

(D) is larger than last year's

(E) by far larger than the last

In Sentence Correction questions, there's just one underlined section. Your task is to decide whether the underlined section is grammatically correct. If the sentence is correct, pick answer choice (A), which is always identical to the original sentence. If the sentence is flawed, pick the answer choice that *best* corrects the error.

Fix the Mistake!

Sentence Correction questions test your ability to identify and correct problems with sentence structure that often appear in students' essays. The test makers assume that if you can spot poorly constructed sentences and correct the errors, then you can probably write good sentences on your own. In this question above, the correct answer is choice (D). The verb *being* is in the wrong form, thus creating a run-on sentence. (D) corrects the error in a straightforward fashion.

In this question, the correct answer is (D). The verb *being* is in the wrong form, thus creating a run-on sentence. (D) corrects the error in a straightforward fashion.

Revision-in-Context Questions

Just when you're getting great at picking apart sentences, Revision-in-Context (Paragraph Corrections) questions come along. In this question type, your task is to correct sentences in the context of an entire paragraph! But don't worry; these may be the easiest questions in the Writing section.

In this section, questions follow short paragraphs that can be about any topic. You do not have to know anything about the topic to answer the questions correctly. The sentences in each paragraph will be numbered. You will probably notice as you read through the passage that it is riddled with errors. Don't bother to mark them because the questions will tell you where the mistakes are located.

Most Paragraph Correction questions ask you to clean up awkward and ambiguous sentences. The most important thing with these questions is their *context*. You can't determine the best way to repair poor or unclear sentences without knowing what comes before and after them.

A few Paragraph Correction questions will also ask you about the overall organization of the essay. Again, context is critical. You can't, for example, decide which of five sentences best concludes an essay without knowing what the essay is all about.

There's only one Revision-in-Context passage on the PSAT. The directions on your test will look like this:

Directions: The passage below is an early draft of an essay. Parts of the passage need to be rewritten.

Read the passage and answer the questions that follow. Some questions are about individual sentences or parts of sentences; in these questions, you are asked to select the choice that will improve sentence structure and word choice. Other questions refer to parts of the essay or the entire essay and ask you to consider the organization and development of the essay. You should follow the conventions of standard written English in answering the questions. After you have chosen your answer, fill in the corresponding oval on your answer sheet.

(1) *I agree with the school board's recent decision to require high school students to complete a community service requirement before graduating.* (2) *As a student who has both worked and volunteered, my volunteer experience has truly enriched me as a person.* (3) *When I worked at a hamburger joint, all I was caring about was the money.* (4) *Tutoring disadvantaged children taught me to appreciate how much I have.*

Which of the following is the best way to revise the underlined portion of sentence 2 (reproduced below)?

As a student who has both worked and volunteered, <u>my volunteer experience has truly enriched me as a person</u>.

(A) my experience as a volunteer has been the
thing that has truly enriched me as a person

(B) I have been truly enriched by my volunteer
experience

(C) it is by volunteering that I have truly become
an enriched person

(D) I will have been truly enriched by my volunteer experience

(E) that which has truly enriched me as a person is
my volunteer experience

Revision-in-Context questions test your ability to spot and correct logical flaws in a passage that contains errors often found in student essays. If you can fix the sample passage, the test makers assume you can probably do the same thing to your own writing.

In the above question, the correct answer is (B) because it clarifies that *I* and *a student*
are the same person. The original wording is awkward; it sounds as though *my volunteer
experience* and *a student* are the same person, which they can't be. Choice (D) uses
the incorrect verb tense, and choices (C) and (E) are unnecessarily complicated.

KAPLAN'S THREE-STEP METHOD

Now that you know what kinds of questions you'll be facing on the Writing section, we'll
show you how to attack each question type to achieve the highest score possible. Our
search-and-repair tactics work wonders on PSAT Writing questions. Our score-raising
techniques are as follows:

Step 1. Read the sentence, *listening* for a mistake.

Step 2. Identify the error.

Step 3. Check the answer choices.

This basic, time-tested strategy works for all three question types on the Writing section.
We'll show you how to refine it for each specific question type.

USAGE QUESTIONS

Usage questions are a great place for the Writing skills test to begin because you don't have to correct the answer yourself. You simply have to point out what word or phrase is incorrect.

Let's try the Three-Step Method on the following question. First, read the sentence, *listening* for a mistake. Read silently, and listen to the voice in your head.

> The <u>club members</u> are so busy <u>studying</u> for exams
>   A   B
>
> that attendance is <u>rare</u> more <u>than fifty percent</u>.
>   C   D
>
> <u>No error</u>
>   E

Did you hear the mistake? If so, your work is done. Fill in the appropriate oval, and move on. If you didn't hear a mistake on the first reading, go back, read each underlined part, and start eliminating underlined parts that are right. There's no problem with the phrase *club members*. *Studying* seems fine in this context. How about *rare*? Something doesn't sound right about it. *"Rarely* more than fifty percent" would be the correct construction here. Choice (C) contains the error and is the correct answer.

This is a classic example of an adjective/adverb error. There are several different usage errors the PSAT tests over and over again. You'll learn more about the most common errors in the following pages, which offer a quick reference to the most frequently made and tested grammatical mistakes. It's so much easier to spot errors when you know what to look for.

Verb Tense Errors

The verb is the action part of the sentence. The verb's tense tells you in what time frame the action is taking place. You won't need to identify verb tenses by name on the test, but you will need to recognize the difference between correct and incorrect usage of verb tenses. Here's an example:

> When David was in Holland, he was seeing many windmills.

You don't need to know the rules about proper use of the past tense to know that something's wrong here. Your ear should have told you that the verbs don't sound right. Try this instead:

> When David was in Holland, he saw many windmills.

That sounds better, and it's correct. Now let's look at a question with a verb tense error.

<u>Unsatisfied</u> with the ending, the director <u>considering</u>
A   B
<u>reshooting</u> <u>the entire film</u>. <u>No error</u>
C   D   E

Did this sentence make sense to you? If not, where did the confusion come in? We don't know when the director's action took place because *considering* isn't a complete verb. You could substitute *is considering* or *was considering* or even *considered*. Because choice (B) contains the error in this sentence, it's the right answer.

For a detailed explanation of the different verb tenses and how they are used, check out Appendix Four, "Writing Skills," in the Study Aids appendices in the back of this book.

Subject-Verb Agreement Errors

Grammar textbooks tell you that the subject and the verb of a sentence must agree in number. Put simply, this means that a singular subject takes a singular verb and a plural subject takes a plural verb. Subject and verb also have to agree in person. This means that you need to use the right form of the verb depending on whether the subject is in the first person, second person, or third person.

You most likely do this correctly a million times a day without even noticing it, and it's not as tricky as it sounds. Take a look at these sentences:

> The 4:05 train to Boston leave from the north platform.
>
> Henry's dog are brown with a white tail.
>
> The ballerinas practices for eight hours a day.
>
> You spends too much time thinking about subject-verb agreement.

Did you find the agreement errors? These are fairly basic examples of subject-verb agreement errors, and the sentences on the PSAT won't be quite this easy. But with a little practice, you'll be able to spot agreement errors in any sentence. Be on the lookout for these three classic subject-verb agreement traps:

- Collective nouns
- Intervening phrases
- Subject after the verb

Trap 1: Collective Nouns

A very common trap that appears on the PSAT Writing section uses collective nouns (singular nouns describing multiple persons) to trick you. Words such as *group*, *audience*, or *committee* require a singular verb.

> The group has decided to plan a trip to a chocolate factory.
>
> The audience was moved to throw rotten vegetables at the mime.
>
> The committee votes to clean up the waterfront every year.

All of these sentences are correct. Let's try a sample question.

> That <u>particular</u> gang of pirates <u>were</u> often <u>referred to</u>
>   A   B   C
> as the <u>scourge of</u> the seven seas. <u>No error</u>
>   D   E

Even with advance warning, this one is tricky. The correct answer here is (B) because the subject being modified (described) is the collective singular noun *gang*. The error was harder to spot in this case because the prepositional phrase *of pirates* insinuated that the modifying verb should be plural. That phrase was thrown in the sentence just to confuse you, so be careful when deciding what the subject of a sentence is. This brings us to Trap 2.

Trap 2: Intervening Phrases

The test makers will often try to confuse the issue of subject-verb agreement by inserting an intervening phrase between the subject and verb. The following question is an example of this.

> Tax evasion, <u>a crime</u> that <u>has been documented</u> in
>   A   B
> many modern novels and films, <u>remain</u> a relatively
>   C
> <u>uncommon offense</u>. <u>No error</u>
>   D   E

Did you pick choice (C)? You're right. The verb *remain* goes with *evasion*, a singular word, which requires the verb form *remains*. Don't be fooled by the plural nouns *novels and films*, which are part of the intervening phrase.

Trap 3: Subject After the Verb

Another way the test makers try to confuse you is by placing the subject after the verb. Take a look at this example.

<u>Although</u> nutritionists have <u>criticized pizza</u> for
A B

being too high in fat, there <u>is</u> many people <u>who</u>
C D

continue to enjoy it. <u>No error</u>
E

People is the subject of the verb *to be*, and it requires a plural subject. *There are many people* is the correct form of this sentence. . . . Choice (C) is correct.

Pronoun Errors: Case and Number

You will see a few questions on the PSAT that test pronoun use. The key thing about pronouns is that they must agree with their antecedents in case and number. What does this mean?

Case is the form the word takes in the sentence. If the pronoun refers to the subject, it has a different case than if it refers to an object.

Sally dances, and <u>she</u> also sings.

Bob praised Sally, and he also applauded <u>her</u>.

These sentences are correct.

The **number** of a pronoun is just what it sounds like: singular or plural.

Give this question a try:

A student <u>who</u> applies for a part-time job assisting
A

Dr. Frankenstein <u>may get</u> more than <u>they</u> were
B C

<u>expecting</u>. <u>No error</u>
D E

Did you see the error here? The antecedent here is *a student* and the pronoun is *they*. To make the plural pronoun agree with its singular antecedent, you would have to use *he* or *she*, or even possibly *he or she*. This example demonstrates a common grammatical mistake. Many people use *they* in spoken English to refer to a single person of unknown sex. However, this is not grammatically correct in standard written English because *they* is plural. Watch out for this every time you see *they* and *them* on test day.

Pronoun Errors: Ambiguous Reference

Another common pronoun error on the PSAT Writing section is the ambiguous reference. As we previously stated, every pronoun must have a clear antecedent.

Give this question a try:

> To expand the newspaper's <u>coverage</u> of local poli-
>   A
>
> tics, <u>they</u> transferred a <u>popular</u> columnist <u>to</u> the
>   B   C   D
>
> City desk. <u>No error</u>
>   E

This one may have been easy because you knew what you were looking for. Choice (B), *they*, is a pronoun without a clear antecedent. Who transferred the columnist? The sentence doesn't tell us. Choice (B) is correct.

Questions like this one can be tricky, because they read smoothly and do not grab the attention of your well-trained ear. Keep an eye out for ambiguous references in sentences that seem too good to be true.

Idioms

Idioms are hard on non-native speakers of English because idioms are the hardest thing to learn in any foreign language. The reason for this is that idioms are simply word combinations that have become part of a language. They are correct, but there's no particular rhyme or reason for why they're correct. Most—although certainly not all—native speakers will know the proper idiom to use simply because they've heard them a thousand times. This is not so for non-native speakers.

Prepositions are the, often times, short words—such as *by*, *at*, *among*, and *before*—that link prepositional phrases to the rest of the sentence. Most preposition questions tested on the PSAT are idiomatic. This means that you'll be listening for word combinations that often go together. Use your ear to catch prepositions that just don't sound right.

Give the following question a try. Be sure to use Kaplan's Three-Step Method.

> Many people are <u>desensitized to</u> violence on TV
>   A
>
> shows, <u>but</u> this does not mean that they are not
>   B
>
> sensitive <u>of</u> the real-life violence around <u>them</u>.
>   C   D
>
> <u>No error</u>
>   E

There are two idiomatic uses of prepositions in this sentence. Did you spot them? *Desensitized to* and *sensitive of* are choices (A) and (C). *Sensitive of* simply isn't idiomatic. The proper idiomatic phrase is *sensitive to*. Choice (C) is the correct answer.

Comparison Errors

Another error that frequently shows up on the PSAT Writing section involves comparisons. This one can be sneaky because some of these sentences will sound normal to your ear. Our Three-Step Method relies on you having a good ear. So approach comparisons slightly differently.

When you compare two or more parts of speech, like nouns or verb phrases, the parts of speech must be in the same form. Take a look at this example.

> The producer agreed that casting a drama series is
> harder than comedy.

If you heard this sentence, you'd probably understand what it means, although it's not grammatically correct. *Casting a drama series* is harder than . . . what exactly? The sentence would be clearer if it were written as follows:

> The producer agreed that casting a drama series is
> harder than casting a comedy series.

Both parts of the comparison are in the same form, making the sentence easier to understand and grammatically correct. See if you can spot the mistake in the next question.

> Even though <u>he</u> is a Nobel Laureate,
>   A
>
> <u>Elie Wiesel's name</u> is still <u>less well known</u> than
>   B   C
>
> <u>last year's</u> Heisman Trophy winner. <u>No error</u>
>   D   E

Did you spot the faulty comparison? The sentence compares *Elie Wiesel's name* with the *Heisman Trophy winner*. If we change choice (B) to read simply *Elie Wiesel*, the comparison is parallel and easier to understand.

Adjective and Adverb Errors

You probably haven't thought about adjectives and adverbs since those junior high sentence diagrams. The good news is that you probably use adjectives and adverbs correctly all the time.

> That painting is beautiful.

> The artist painted it skillfully.

In the first sentence, *beautiful* is an adjective modifying *painting*, a noun. In the second sentence, *skillfully* is an adverb modifying *painted,* a verb form. Now take a look at how adjectives and adverbs are often tested in the Usage section.

<u>Since the onset</u> of <u>his</u> blindness, the artist
    A   B

<u>has sculpted</u> more <u>slow</u> than before. <u>No error</u>
    C   D   E

Did you hear it? Choice (D) is the correct answer because the adverb *slowly* is required to modify the verb form *has sculpted*.

Double Negatives

In standard written English, it's incorrect to use two negatives in a row. Just as in math, two negatives added together create a positive.

I don't want none of that pizza, thank you!

This sentence, if you cancel the negatives, translates to:

I'll have that pizza, thank you!

You'll find the occasional double negative in the Usage section, although the sentences will be more difficult than the one above. Give the next example a try.

The town hasn't <u>hardly any</u> money left in <u>its</u> budget
            A   B

<u>because of</u> the unexpected snowplow <u>costs</u>.
   C   D

<u>No error</u>
 E

The words *hasn't* and *hardly any* are both negative and cancel each other out, making it sound as if the town doesn't have money problems. We can figure out from the rest of the sentence that the author's trying to tell us that the town does have money problems because of the unexpected costs. Changing choice (A), *hardly any*, to *much* would help to eliminate one of the negatives, clearing up the meaning of the sentence.

The town hasn't much money left in its budget
because of the unexpected snowplow costs.

Now that you have learned what sort of grammatical errors to look for in the Usage section, keep those rules in mind as you move into sentence corrections.

SENTENCE CORRECTION QUESTIONS

Sentence Correction questions test the same skills as Usage questions. You'll still be using your eyes and ears to spot errors and oddities in sentences. Here's the difference: with this question type, you will be asked to correct the mistakes you find.

Each Sentence Correction question has an underlined phrase. You will be asked to decide whether the sentence is okay as is, in which case you would pick choice (A), or whether the underlined portion should be replaced by one of the four other answer choices.

Take a look at Kaplan's Three-Step Method for Sentence Corrections. It has been slightly modified from the general Three-Step Method.

> **Step 1.** Read the sentence, *listening* for a mistake.
> **Step 2.** Predict a correction.
> **Step 3.** Select the answer choice that matches your prediction while eliminating clearly wrong answer choices.

Now apply the Three-Step Method to this question.

> Hoping to receive a promotion, <u>the letter he received instead informed Burt</u> that he had been fired.
>
> (A) the letter he received instead informed Burt
> (B) the letter having been received, instead informed Burt
> (C) Burt instead received a letter informing him
> (D) information from the received letter instead told Burt
> (E) Burt, instead informed by the letter he received

First, read the sentence, *listening* for a mistake. Something sounds wrong. Burt hoped to receive the promotion, but this makes it sounds as if the letter hoped to receive the promotion. Next, predict a correction. Putting *Burt* at the beginning of the second phrase seems to make the sentence sound better. Now select the choice that fits your prediction, eliminating the wrong choices. Choices (C) and (E) both put Burt at the beginning of the phrase. Choice (C) is the clearest and most concise choice, so it is the correct answer.

Any of the grammatical rules discussed in the Usage section could also appear in the Sentence Correction question set. But with this question type, there are additional errors that need to be taken into consideration. We review those on the following pages.

Sentence Fragments

Sentence fragments are incomplete sentences. To be complete, a sentence requires a main subject and a main verb. Some sentences are fragments because they lack the necessary elements to make logical sense. Here are some fragments. How would you repair them?

> Stereo equipment on sale at the mall today!

Repair:_____

> The busload of tourists that wandered curiously around the ancient ruins.

Repair:_____

> Because Myrna likes the Adirondacks, frequently taking photos of them.

Repair:_____

Do you get an empty feeling when you read these fragments? Watch for that feeling on test day, and you'll be able to spot the fragments. Here are suggested repairs on each of the sample sentences above.

> Stereo equipment on sale at the mall today!

Repair: Stereo equipment <u>is</u> on sale at the mall today!

> The busload of tourists that wandered curiously around the ancient ruins.

Repair: The busload of <u>curious tourists wandered</u> around the ancient ruins.

> Because Myrna likes the Adirondacks, frequently taking photos of them.

Repair: Myrna likes the Adirondacks, <u>so she frequently takes</u> photos of them.

Give this example a try. Use Kaplan's Three-Step Method.

> Last of the world's leaders to do so, the prime minister admits that terrorist threats <u>credible enough to warrant</u> the imposition of stringent security measures.
>
> (A) credible enough to warrant
> (B) credible enough warrant
> (C) are credible enough to warrant
> (D) credible enough, warranting
> (E) are credible enough to be warranted

That empty feeling sets in right in the middle of the sentence. *Terrorist threats* are the subject, but where's the verb? *Credible* is the adjective modifying *terrorist threats*, so adding *are*, as choices (C) and (E) do, repairs the fragment. Choice (E), however, introduces a new problem with the phrase *to be warranted*, which is confusing. Choice (C) clearly fixes the fragment and is correct.

Run-On Sentences

A run-on sentence occurs when two complete sentences that should be separate are joined together. Here is an example.

> Jane was the preeminent scientist in her class her experiments were discussed across campus.

You can tell that this is a run-on sentence because it sounds like it should be two separate sentences. There are three ways to fix a run-on sentence.

1. Use a period.

> Jane was the preeminent scientist in her class. Her experiments were discussed across campus.

2. Use a conjunction, making one sentence dependent.

> Because Jane was the preeminent scientist in her class, her experiments were discussed across campus.

3. Use a semicolon.

> Jane was the preeminent scientist in her class; her experiments were discussed across campus.

Use the Three-Step Method and the information you just learned to fix the next sentence.

> Jonas Salk was born in East Harlem, New York, the developer of the polio vaccine.

(A) Jonas Salk was born in East Harlem, New York, the developer of the polio vaccine.

(B) Jonas Salk being the developer of the polio vaccine and was born in East Harlem, New York.

(C) Being the developer of the polio vaccine, Jonas Salk was born in East Harlem, New York.

(D) Jonas Salk was the developer of the polio vaccine, having been born in East Harlem, New York.

(E) Jonas Salk, who was born in East Harlem, New York, was the developer of the polio vaccine.

Because the entire sentence is underlined, you know that either it's correct or there's a better rewrite among the choices. What's wrong with the sentence? Well, it's clearly a run-on because there are two independent thoughts that are not joined in any way. It's also a bit confusing because it sounds as if Salk was born the developer of the vaccine. (He probably had to grow up and go to school for a while before he developed the vaccine.) Choice (E) fixes the problem by making the facts about Salk's birthplace dependent, thus clearing up the meaning and fixing the run-on problem.

Coordination and Subordination Errors

Sometimes a sentence won't make sense because it contains clauses that aren't logically joined. There are two types of errors involving the improper joining of clauses in a sentence: coordination and subordination errors.

Proper **coordination** expresses the logical relationship between two clauses. Misused conjunctions can bring about faulty coordination and make a sentence confusing or just plain nonsensical.

> Because he was very thirsty, he refused to drink the
> water.

This sentence doesn't make much sense (unless we're dealing with a very stubborn and confused person). What would be a better conjunction?

> Although he was very thirsty, he refused to drink
> the water.

This is better. We still don't know why he won't drink the water, but the conjunction *although* sets up the contrast between the two clauses that helps the sentence make sense.

Problems with **subordination** occur when a group of words contains two or more subordinate clauses (also known as dependent clauses) but no independent clause.

> Since the advent of inexpensive portable stereos,
> because of a boom in the manufacture of head-
> phones has resulted.

Connective words like *since, because, so that, if,* and *although* introduce subordinate clauses. As it stands, this sentence consists of two dependent clauses, with no independent clause. We can eliminate *because of* in order to make this a grammatically correct sentence.

> Since the advent of inexpensive portable stereos, a
> boom in the manufacture of headphones has
> resulted.

Try the following two questions, using Kaplan's Three-Step Method.

> New restaurants appeared on the <u>waterfront, however merchants</u> were finally able to convince diners of the area's safety.
>
> (A) waterfront, however merchants
> (B) waterfront; merchants
> (C) waterfront, yet merchants
> (D) waterfront, because merchants
> (E) waterfront, although merchants

However is a conjunction that indicates contrast. This sentence is about cause-and-effect. Choice (D) is correct because the use of the conjunction *because* shows the relationship between the appearance of the new restaurants and the merchants' ability to convince diners that the area was safe.

> Because Megan was unable to finish her tax forms before April 15, <u>so she filed</u> for an extension.
>
> (A) so she filed
> (B) but she was filing
> (C) she filed
> (D) and this led to her filing
> (E) and she filed

This question tests subordination. The sentence contains two dependent clauses, each beginning with a linking word. Choice (C) eliminates the linking word and fixes the problem by creating an independent clause.

Misplaced Modifiers

Modifiers are phrases that provide information about nouns and verbs in a sentence. A modifier must appear next to the word or words that it's modifying. Otherwise, things can get a bit confusing (not to mention ungrammatical).

Take a look at this example.

> Dripping on his shirt, Harvey was so eager to eat his hamburger that he didn't notice the ketchup.

As it's written, it sounds as if Harvey was dripping on his shirt, which isn't a very pleasant image. In fact, it's the ketchup that's dripping on his shirt. Misplaced modifiers are easy to fix. As long as you can spot them, these questions are usually quite easy to answer.

> Harvey was so eager to eat his hamburger that he didn't notice the ketchup dripping on his shirt.

This clears up the confusion and is a logical sentence. Now let's look at a test-like question that tests misplaced modifiers.

> Flying for the first time, the roar of the jet engines
> intimidated the elderly man as the plane sped
> down the runway.

(A) Flying for the first time, the roar of the jet
   engines intimidated the elderly man as the
   plane sped down the runway.

(B) The roar of the jet engines intimidated the elderly man as the plane, flying for the first
   time, sped down the runway.

(C) Flying for the first time, the elderly man was
   intimidated by the roar of the jet engines as
   the plane sped down the runway.

(D) The plane sped down the runway as, flying for
   the first time, the roar of the jet engines
   intimidated the elderly man.

(E) As the plane sped down the runway, flying for
   the first time, the elderly man was intimidated by the roar of the jet engines.

We need a choice that makes it clear that the elderly man is the one who is flying for the first time, not the roar. Choice (C) accomplishes this by placing the modifier *flying for the first time* next to *the elderly man*. Note that choice (E) also places the two phrases next to each other, but the modifier is sandwiched between two phrases, making it unclear which phrase it is meant to modify. Choice (C) is correct.

Bad Parallelism

Parallelism is very much like comparison, which we covered earlier. Essentially, whenever you list items, they must be in the same form. Take a look at the following sentence:

> On Saturday, Ingrid cleaned her apartment, bought
> her plane tickets for France, and was deciding to go
> out to dinner.

The first two verbs are parallel in the past tense, but the third verb is in a different form, thus not parallel.

> On Saturday, Ingrid cleaned her apartment, bought
> her plane tickets for France, and decided to go out
> to dinner.

In this corrected sentence, *cleaned, bought,* and *decided* are all in the past tense form, so the parallel structure is correct.

Test Prep and Admissions

Try the next question, and see how you do.

> Changing over from a military to a peacetime economy means producing tractors rather than tanks, radios rather than rifles, and <u>producing running shoes rather than combat boots</u>.
>
> (A) producing running shoes rather than combat boots
>
> (B) the production of running shoes rather than combat boots
>
> (C) running shoes rather than combat boots
>
> (D) replacing combat boots with running shoes
>
> (E) running shoes instead of combat boots

Choice (C) does the trick by maintaining the parallel structure of the sentence: *tractors rather than tanks, radios rather than rifles, and running shoes rather than combat boots.*

Getting the hang of it? Good. Let's move on to the final question type in the Writing section.

REVISION-IN-CONTEXT QUESTIONS

Revision-in-Context questions look a little scary because you have to read a whole paragraph. However, many students find them to be the easiest question type in the PSAT Writing section and there are only five questions of this type tested. The reason this type of question is tested is because test makers want to make sure you can recognize (and, in theory, write) a concise, logical, and stylistically smooth essay. The questions in this section are designed to test your skills in this area.

Lucky for you, Kaplan's Three-Step Method for Revision-in-Context questions make these kinds of questions a breeze.

Step 1. Read the essay.

This first read-through can be a quick skim that will give you a sense of the essay's main idea.

Step 2. Read the question stem, identifying the error.

At this point, you should understand what the question wants you to do. Often you can predict an answer at this point.

Step 3. Reread the relevant portion of the essay.

Reread the lines around the significant portion of the essay. This will help you get the context of the sentence and choose the correct answer.

Try using Step 1 on the following essay. Keep your eye out for obvious errors, but don't spend time trying to repair them now. For now, just get acquainted with the passage.

> (1) *School administrators don't respect the rights of students.* (2) *They don't understand that many students are vegetarians.* (3) *I think that eating meat is unnecessary.* (4) *There are many delicious vegetarian dishes that all students could enjoy for lunch.* (5) *Students all across America have fought with administrators about this issue.* (6) *They may think that it's too expensive to provide a vegetarian alternative every day.* (7) *Many dishes can be made either with meat or meat-free.* (8) *For example, burritos and pizza.* (9) *At my school, there was a survey about whether students would like vegetarian meals or not.* (10) *I believe that schools should show that they respect students' needs by providing vegetarian options for lunch.*

This is a fairly typical Revision-in-Context passage. It contains a number of errors in sentence structure and overall logic and structure. Now let's tackle Step 2 and look over the various Revision-in-Context question types.

Sentence Revision

Step 2 is to read the question stem. Take a look at this typical sentence revision question.

> In context, which is the best revision of the underlined portion of sentence 6 (reproduced below)?
>
> <u>They may think</u> that it's too expensive to provide a vegetarian alternative every day.
>
> (A) (As it is now)
> (B) The administration may think
> (C) The students may think
> (D) The administration may have been thinking
> (E) They may have thought

This question asks you to revise a sentence in the passage. Notice that the sentence is reprinted below the question. You're given the option to keep the sentence as is, choice (A). This is sometimes, *but not always*, an option on revision questions.

After you've read the stem, you should go back and reread the surrounding sentences to get a sense of the sentence's context. In sentence 6, the pronoun *they* doesn't have a clear antecedent. The sentences leading up to the sentence in question discussed the struggle between students and administration on the topic of vegetarian meals. From the preceding sentences, it's clear that students are pro-vegetarian meals, and the administration is con, so we can assume that the writer would substitute *the administration* for *they* in this sentence.

Choice (D) changes the verb tense, which is unnecessary. Choice (B) improves the sentence and is correct.

Did this remind you of a Sentence Correction or Usage question? It should have because the same skills are tested in Revision-in-Context questions, with the added twist of the rest of the paragraph being included.

Sentence Combination

Give the next question a try.

Which of the following is the best way to combine sentences 7 and 8 (reproduced below)?

Many dishes can be made with or without meat.
For example, burritos and pizza.

(A) Many dishes, such as burritos and pizza, can be made with or without meat.

(B) With or without meat, many dishes such as burritos and pizza can be made.

(C) For example, burritos and pizza are many dishes that can be made with or without meat.

(D) Burritos and pizza, for example, are among many dishes that can be made with or without meat.

(E) Many dishes can be made with or without meat, for example, burritos and pizza.

This question asks you to combine two sentences together. Can you see why? The second sentence is a fragment. Choice (E) attempts to join the sentences with a simple comma, which won't do the trick. Choices (B), (C), and (D) are all awkward constructions that don't make sense of the sentence combination. Choice (A) smoothly combines the sentences and preserves the author's meaning, which makes it the correct answer.

Remember that the test makers don't like wordiness, awkwardness, and redundancy. The correct answer will always be clear, concise, and grammatically correct.

KAPLAN
Test Prep and Admissions

Logic and Clarity

The third type of Revision-in-Context question asks you to find and repair gaps in the author's logic and clarity.

Take a look at following question.

> The writer of the passage could best improve sentence 9 (reproduced below) by
>
> *At my school, there was a survey about whether students would like vegetarian meals or not.*
>
> (A) providing data from the survey showing that students want vegetarian meals.
>
> (B) profiling an individual vegetarian student
>
> (C) including vegetarian recipes
>
> (D) weakening the administration's arguments
>
> (E) providing a dictionary definition of the term "respect"

Start by rereading sentence 9. What's the problem here? Well, this sentence doesn't help the author's case very much because we know only that there was a survey. We don't know what the results of the survey showed.

Choice (A) is correct. Whereas all of the other choices provide ideas that may help the author's argument, none specifically pertains to sentence 9, which is the focus of this question.

CHAPTER FOUR SUMMARY

○ The Writing section does not involve doing any writing.

○ Prepare for it every day by reading for mistakes.

○ The Writing questions are NOT ordered easiest to hardest.

○ There are three Writing question types:

   –Usage questions

   –Sentence Correction questions

   –Revision-in-Context questions

○ You can attack all three question types with the following strategy:

   –Step 1. Read the sentence.

   –Step 2. Identify the error.

   –Step 3. Check answer choices.

○ Common Usage errors to look out for are:

   –Verb tense errors

   –Subject-verb agreement errors

   –Pronoun errors: case and number

   –Pronoun errors: ambiguous reference

   –Idioms

   –Comparison errors

   –Adjective and adverb errors

   –Double negatives

○ Common Sentence Correction errors to look out for are:

   –Sentence fragments

   –Run-on sentences

   –Coordination and subordination errors

   –Misplaced modifiers

   –Bad parallelisim

○ There are three basic Revision-in-Context question types:

   –Sentence revision

   –Sentence combination

   –Logic and clarity

PRACTICE

If you found the questions in this chapter to be relatively easy, you should be in pretty good shape for the Writing Skills section. If you're feeling unsure, go back and review the different question types, then try this quiz. From now until test day, remember to use your eyes and ears whenever you read. Remember to search and repair, and you'll be in good shape for the test!

1. In <u>recently</u> constructed concert halls, there <u>is</u> usu-
       A   B

   ally at least two <u>sets</u> <u>of</u> stairs at the rear of the bal-
                    C D

   cony. <u>No error</u>
          E

2. Whenever we <u>travel</u> abroad, a <u>sense</u> of excitement
               A   B

   and an anticipation of being in a foreign land

   <u>overtake</u> <u>you</u>. <u>No error</u>
      C   D   E

3. Many foreign electronics <u>companies</u> have learned
                            A

   <u>to build</u> machines at a lower cost by using
     B

   <u>inexpensive</u> produced <u>components</u>. <u>No error</u>
       C   D   E

4. The chairwoman felt that she <u>could not</u> give in
                            A

   <u>with</u> his demands, <u>which</u> she thought were
    B   C

   <u>completely</u> unreasonable. <u>No error</u>
      D   E

5. <u>One</u> can learn more <u>about</u> new computers by
     A   B

   actually working with <u>them</u> than one can by <u>merely</u>
                   C   D

   reading the instruction manual. <u>No error</u>
                             E

6. The police officer <u>noticed</u> the wanted suspect only
                   A

   after <u>he</u> <u>removed</u> his sunglasses and <u>sat down</u> at
        B   C   D

   the counter. <u>No error</u>
           E

7. The triathlete <u>had swam</u> three miles <u>before</u> leg
                A   B

   cramps <u>caused</u> her to <u>withdraw from</u> the competi-
        C   D

   tion. <u>No error</u>
       E

8. The speaker <u>whom</u> the graduating class <u>chose</u>
          A   B

   <u>to deliver</u> their commencement address was an
     C

   <u>imminent</u> authority on international diplomacy.
     D

   <u>No error</u>
     E

9. The jazz band <u>was forced</u> <u>to return</u> the gate
                A   B

   receipts after <u>they</u> had arrived at the arena one
              C

   hour <u>late</u>. <u>No error</u>
       D   E

10. The Soviet Union had <u>not hardly</u> developed a
                           A

    spaceship <u>suitable</u> for lunar <u>travel</u> when the first
               B   C

    U.S. astronaut <u>landed on</u> the moon in 1969.
                D

    <u>No error</u>
      E

11. This group of artists, masters of the short brush stroke developed by the Impressionists in the nineteenth century, did not believe in selling works of art; however, <u>some giving paintings away</u>.

    (A) some giving paintings away

    (B) giving some paintings away

    (C) paintings were given away by some of them

    (D) some having given paintings away

    (E) some gave paintings away

12. <u>Credulous people believe</u> in the existence of extra-terrestrial beings, most scientists and other informed students of nature do not.

    (A) Credulous people believe

    (B) While credulous people believe

    (C) Credulous people are always believing

    (D) Since credulous people believe

    (E) Credulous people tend to believe

13. Exposed to the extremely long and severe cold spell, <u>frost soon killed the buds of the citrus trees and they did not produce fruit that season</u>.

    (A) frost soon killed the buds of the citrus trees and they did not produce fruit that season

    (B) soon the buds of the citrus trees were killed by frost, and therefore not producing fruit that season

    (C) the buds of the citrus trees were soon killed by frost, they did not produce fruit that season

    (D) fruit was not produced by the citrus trees that season because their buds had been killed by frost

    (E) the buds of the citrus trees were soon killed by frost, and the trees did not produce fruit that season

14. In the closing decades of the eighteenth century, it was believed that young women should not only <u>be obedient and soft-spoken but also master</u> such skills as needlepoint.

    (A) be obedient and soft-spoken but also master

    (B) being obedient and soft-spoken but also mastering

    (C) obey and speak softly but also to master

    (D) be obedient and soft-spoken but also to master

    (E) obeying and speaking softly but also mastering

15. Initiated in 1975, <u>sandhill cranes must unwittingly cooperate in the conservationists' project to raise</u> endangered whooping crane chicks.

    (A) sandhill cranes must unwittingly cooperate in the conservationists' project to raise

    (B) sandhill cranes' unwitting cooperation is required in the conservationists' project to raise

    (C) the conservationists require that sandhill cranes unwittingly cooperate in their project of raising

    (D) the conservationists require sandhill cranes to cooperate unwittingly in their project to raise

    (E) the conservationists' project requires the unwitting cooperation of sandhill cranes in raising

16. Environmental scientists are very concerned <u>about dangerous fluorocarbons found in pressurized aerosol cans which quicken the erosion of the ozone layer when emitted</u>.

    (A) about dangerous fluorocarbons found in pressurized aerosol cans which quicken the erosion of the ozone layer when emitted

    (B) that, while emitting dangerous fluorocarbons, pressurized aerosol cans quicken the erosion of the ozone layer

    (C) about the erosion of the ozone layer caused by pressurized aerosol cans emitting dangerous fluorocarbons

    (D) that pressurized aerosol cans emitting dangerous fluorocarbons which quicken the erosion of the ozone layer

    (E) when, quickening the erosion of the ozone layer, pressurized aerosol cans emit dangerous fluorocarbons

17. The characteristics of a typical Avery canvas are a purposely limited palette, a distinctive use of color for perspective, <u>and it employs obvious brushstrokes for effect</u>.

    (A) and it employs obvious brushstrokes for effect

    (B) and an employment of obvious brushstrokes for effect

    (C) but it employs obvious brushstrokes for effect

    (D) whereby, for effect, it employs obvious brushstrokes

    (E) it employs obvious brushstrokes for effect

Questions 18–20 are based on the following essay, which is a response to an assignment to write about an economic issue facing the United States.

(1) *Recently a report came out in a science magazine that claimed the earth's protective ozone layer was being steadily depleted.* (2) *It named several companies that produced chemicals responsible for this situation, and consumers were advised by it to boycott these businesses.*

(3) *An editorial in a business magazine insisted that this report was faulty.* (4) *It stated that there could be other, less dangerous reasons for the changes in climate that we have been experiencing.* (5) *However, I believe that the scientists are right, we should all consider the effect we can have on making sure the ozone layer is not harmed more than it already has been.* (6) *The depletion of the ozone layer means that harmful ultraviolet rays get through to our atmosphere.* (7) *People who do these bad things, which contribute to this situation, should know that their actions could harm future generations.*

18. Considering the essay as a whole, which is the best edit for the underlined section of sentence 2 (reproduced below)?

    It named several companies that produced chemicals responsible for this situation, and consumers were advised by it to boycott these businesses.

    (A) (As it is now)
    (B) It names several companies that produced chemicals responsible for this situation and advises consumers
    (C) Naming several companies that produce chemicals responsible for this situation, consumers are advised by the report
    (D) It is naming several companies that produce chemicals responsible for this situation and advising consumers
    (E) The report named several companies that produced chemicals responsible for this situation, and advised consumers

19. Considering the essay as a whole, which is the best way to edit and link the underlined portions of sentences 3 and 4 (reproduced below)?

    An editorial in a business magazine insisted that this report was faulty. It stated that there could be other, less dangerous reasons for the changes in climate that we've been experiencing.

    (A) The report was faulty, an editorial in a business magazine insisted, it stated
    (B) An editorial in a business magazine insisted that this report was faulty, stating
    (C) In an editorial in a business magazine was the insistence that the report was faulty and
    (D) The editorial in a business magazine insists that the consumers were faulty,
    (E) Insisting that the report was faulty, an editorial in a business magazine states

20. Sentence 7 would read more clearly in the context of the essay if the phrase "do these bad things" were replaced by which of the following?

    People who do these bad things which contribute to this situation should know that their actions could harm future generations.

    (A) exacerbate the situations
    (B) don't participate in events
    (C) are in need of services
    (D) use the types of chemicals
    (E) consider options

ANSWERS AND EXPLANATIONS

1. B

The only verb in the sentence is the singular *is*. The subject of the sentence is *sets*, a plural noun. The word *there* preceding *is* serves to delay the subject *sets*. The subject is no longer in the position where we expect to find it: before the verb. Nevertheless, the verb should be plural—*are*—to agree with the plural subject.

2. D

We and *you* are not interchangeable in this sentence, although either one could be grammatical. But when two pronouns within one sentence refer to the same performer of actions, the pronouns should be consistent. Here, because it's underlined, *you* can change to match *we*.

3. C

Inexpensive seems to modify the word *produced* and to describe how the components were produced. But adverbs describe how an action is done, so the adjective *inexpensive* needs an adverbial ending. The word needed at (C) is the adverb *inexpensively*.

4. B

The idiomatic verb-preposition combination *give in to* means *submit to*, and that is the meaning of the verb in this sentence. The preposition *with* is simply unidiomatic in this usage.

5. E

There is no error in this sentence. The parallel construction in this sentence balances perfectly.

6. B

It is unclear to whom the pronoun *he* refers. Because the singular pronoun *he* could agree with either noun, *officer* or *suspect*, the pronoun's reference is unclear, and the noun should be restated.

7. A

Swam is the simple past tense of the verb *to swim*. But the required verb tense in this sentence is the past perfect because the triathlete *had swum* before *cramps caused her to withdraw*. The past perfect is formed with an auxiliary verb, *had*, and the past participle, *swum*, not *swam*.

8. D

The words *imminent* and *eminent* are easily confused. *Imminent* means *likely to occur at any moment*; it is familiar and appropriate in the phrase *imminent disaster*. But *eminent*, the word this sentence needs, means *highly regarded*.

9. C

They seems to refer to the first subject, *jazz band*. But *jazz band* is a singular noun, although a band is made up of several musicians. The band must be singular because it acts as a unit, arriving late and disappointing the audience together. The pronoun referring to the band should be *it*.

10. A

Hardly is a modifier that negates the word it modifies. In this sentence, it negates *developed*. *Not* also negates *developed* and creates a double-negative construction where only one negation is intended. Such double negatives are substandard usage in modern English.

11. E

The underlined portion of the sentence follows a semicolon that seems to signal an independent clause, but what follows the semicolon is only a phrase. Choice (C) is an independent clause, but the passive verb, *were given (away)*, makes it wordy and roundabout. Only choice (E) gives the proper grammatical structure in a compact way.

12. B

The given sentence is a run-on; two independent clauses are joined only by a comma, with no proper conjunction. The run-on can be corrected by turning the first clause into a dependent clause. Only choice (B) creates a clause that solves the run-on problem and expresses the logical relation of the two clauses.

13. E

This sentence contains a misplaced modifier. The introductory phrase should modify the noun immediately following the comma, but it does not in this sentence. In choices (E) and (C), the modified noun, *the buds*, is in the correct position following the introductory modifying phrase. But notice that choice (C) introduces a new error when it links the second clause to the first with only a comma. Only choice (E) corrects the original problem without adding a new one. Of course, the modifying phrase itself cannot be rearranged in this case because it isn't underlined.

14. A

The sentence is correct as given. Word order is parallel after the correlative words *not only . . . but also.*

15. E

An introductory modifying phrase must modify the subject of the sentence. Since the introductory phrase isn't underlined, the subject must be changed. It's the *project*, not the *cranes* or the *conservationists*, that was initiated in 1975. (E) gets it right.

16. C

This sentence contains a misplaced modifier, *which quicken the erosion of the ozone layer*. Choice (C) corrects the problem and connects the facts in a logical manner.

17. B

The phrase following the comma should be a second clause with word order that is parallel to that of the first clause. Choice (B) correctly supplies a main or indicative verb, *fear,* for the subject, *most of us,* and converts the phrase to a clause. The word order and active verb of this second clause also follow the active construction of the first clause.

18. E

The word *It* does not clearly refer to the report, so choices (A), (B), and (D) are incorrect. Only choice (E) includes the phrase *The report;* furthermore, the rest of this sentence is grammatically consistent with the paragraph as a whole.

19. B

Choices (B) and (E) are the only ones that clearly maintain that the *editorial,* as opposed to the magazine itself, was *stating that there could be other, less dangerous reasons for the changes in climate that we've been experiencing.* However, choice (E) is in the present tense, whereas the rest of the information surrounding the discussion of the report and the editorial is in the past tense. Therefore, choice (B) is correct.

20. D

The types of products that contribute to the destruction of the ozone layer are certain types of *chemicals;* therefore, choice (D) is the most logical and specific answer.

Chapter Five: **How to Prepare for Test Day**

As we noted in the beginning of the book, the PSAT can only help you, so there's no real reason for you to get stressed out as your test date approaches. Plus, if you've read through this book and have practiced the strategies we've outlined, you should be in great shape to achieve your best score on the exam.

However, some students will still get nervous before a test, whether it counts or not and whether they are prepared or not. That's understandable. For others, having to use your brain for any extended period of time is reason enough to worry. With that in mind, chapter five provides a game plan for the week heading into the test and arms you with strategies for stifling any pretest jitters.

CHAPTER FIVE OVERVIEW

This final chapter in the PSAT Program is all about getting your head on straight. It goes over what you can do before the test to make sure you are as ready as you can be and what you can do during the test to make sure you perform as well as possible.

THE DAY BEFORE

Our first piece of advice: do not cram! The best test takers do less and less as the test approaches. Taper off your study schedule, and take it easy on yourself. You should feel relaxed and ready on the day of the test. Besides, cramming only causes undue stress and doesn't allow the information you are taking in to settle and take shape.

Give yourself the night off the evening before the exam. By that time, if you've studied well, everything you need to know will be firmly stored in your memory banks. If you haven't studied well, it's kind of too late by that point anyway. What do you think is better: to be relaxed and unprepared or panicked and unprepared?

Of course the best way to achieve being relaxed *and* prepared is to get your act together sooner rather than later. That's why you bought this book. The same goes for the night before the test. Have everything (including choice of clothing) laid out in advance. Most likely you'll be taking the test on Saturday morning in your own high school. If you're not taking the test in your own high school, make sure you know how to get to where your test will be given.

Keep the upcoming test out of your consciousness the night before; go to a movie, take a long walk, play your favorite computer game, or just simply relax. Get plenty of rest the night before the test. Just don't go to bed too early. It's hard to fall asleep earlier than you're used to, and you don't want to lie there thinking about the test. In fact, don't do anything that drastically changes from your everyday behavior. You don't need any weird surprises the day of the test as a result of a change in behavior.

Note: If you're not much of a weekend-morning person and you're taking the test on Saturday, try taking a practice test at 8:00 in the morning on the Saturday before the test. Feel free to return to your unconscious weekends after you take the test.

THE DAY OF THE TEST

Not everyone feels stress when taking standardized tests, but for some students, all the test preparation in the world won't keep their food in their stomachs. If you know from experience that you are likely to feel test-day jitters, the first thing you should realize is that jitters are not necessarily a bad thing. That edgy feeling simply means that your body is pumping adrenaline into your system, and a little adrenaline can actually help you to think more quickly (and get a higher score).

Here are some strategies for managing your stress during the test.

Plow Ahead

Remember to keep moving forward. You don't have to get everything right to get a great score or a National Merit Scholarship. Don't linger on a question that is going nowhere, even if you've spent a lot of time on it, which you should never do in the first place. The best test takers skip difficult material temporarily in search of the easier material. They mark the ones that require extra time and thought, and then return to them after they have answered all of the easy questions. This strategy also builds confidence so you can handle the tough questions later.

Wear Blinders

Don't be thrown if other test takers seem to be working more busily and furiously than you are. In fact, don't even pay attention to the other students at all. Work at the pace we've told you to work at. Take the test the right way. It's going to lead to higher-quality test taking and better results. Don't mistake the intense scribbling of others for signs of progress and superiority. Cave men did a lot of scribbling. Sabre-tooth tigers didn't. Who was afraid of whom?

Breathe In, Breathe Out

Oxygen comes in, carbon dioxide goes out. It's the natural process that keeps you alive *and* helps your PSAT score. Weak test takers tend to forget to breathe properly as the test proceeds. They start holding their breath without realizing it, or they breathe erratically or arrhythmically. Improper breathing interferes with clear thinking—especially if you black out. It's really hard to fill in the right bubble if you're unconscious.

Get Funky

Don't be afraid to take a 20-second break now and then. Performing some quick isometrics during the test—especially if your concentration is wandering or energy is waning—can put you back in test-taking mode. Try this one: Put your palms together and press intensely for a few seconds. Concentrate on the tension you feel through your palms, wrists, forearms, and up into your biceps and shoulders. Then, quickly release the pressure. Feel the difference as you let go. Focus on the warm relaxation that flows through the muscles. As long as you're quiet about it and don't disturb your neighbor, no one's going to care.

Great. You're armed and ready to do your best on the test. This book and all that you have learned in school have given you the information you'll need to answer the questions. You've learned everything you need to tame your test anxiety and stress. You're going to get a great score.

DURING THE TEST

Remind yourself how well you've prepared. You know the feel and structure of the test. You don't have to waste time on the instructions. You've studied every question type. You know where to find the tough questions and what to do with a question that gives you trouble.

If something goes wrong, don't panic. The proctor is there to help you if there's a defect in your test booklet or a problem with your desk. If you accidentally misgrid your answer sheet or put the answers in the wrong section, again, don't panic. Raise your hand, and tell the proctor. He may be able to arrange for you to regrid your test after it's over, when it won't cost you any time.

AFTER THE TEST

Once the test is over, congratulate yourself and put it out of your mind. You did your best, and you should feel great about that.

When you get your score results, we hope you are pleased.

ONE WEEK TO PSAT GREATNESS

We have put together a week-before chart for you to use as the test approaches.

Seven Days Before the Test

Take a full-length PSAT. If you haven't done so already, take one of the practice tests in this book. Score your test and see where your strengths and weaknesses are.

Note: If you happen to use a sample SAT to practice on, skip the essay-writing portion. There is no essay on the PSAT. Also, keep in mind that the math tested on the SAT is more difficult than the concepts tested on the PSAT, so don't get discouraged if you do not understand everything being asked.

Three to Six Days Before the Test

Review one to two chapters from this book a day. Focus primarily on the areas where you want to improve your score, but don't overload your brain. Cramming generally doesn't help on the PSAT. Continue to solidify and expand your PSAT vocabulary knowledge by reading through the vocabulary lists in this book's appendix section.

Two Days Before the Test

Do your final studying—a few more practice problems, a few more vocabulary words, and whatever strategies you want to read one last time, and call it quits.

The Night Before the Test

Don't study. Eat a healthy dinner. Get together the following items:

- A comfortable outfit, with different layers for different temperatures
- A familiar calculator with fresh batteries
- A few sharpened No. 2 pencils
- Erasers
- A snack—there's a break between Sections 2 and 3, and you'll probably get hungry. A banana or an energy bar makes for an especially good *brain* snack.

Now relax. Read a good book, watch TV, or take a bubble bath. A little exercise may also help you to unwind. Get a good night's sleep. Get to bed at a reasonable hour, and leave yourself some extra time in the morning.

The Morning of the Test

Eat breakfast. Make it substantial, but don't veer too far from your normal breakfast eating habits. Stay away from heavy or greasy food. Also, try to not drink a lot of coffee if you're not used to it; bathroom breaks can eat into valuable test time, and the caffeine could make you jumpy.

Dress in layers so that you can adjust to the temperature of the test room. Read a newspaper or magazine article to warm up your brain. Don't let the PSAT be the first thing you read that day.

CHAPTER FIVE SUMMARY

○ Don't cram the night before the PSAT.

○ When you are taking the PSAT, plow ahead, don't pay attention to other test takers, breathe, and take time out to relax if you feel yourself getting tired or stressed.

○ The week before the PSAT you should:

  –Take a practice test

  –Review chapters one to four and any appendices you feel will help

○ Get your stuff ready the night before the test

○ Eat a good breakfast, and dress in layers.

○ Go for it.

Practice Tests and Explanations

Chapter Six: **Practice Test One**

HOW TO TAKE THIS PRACTICE TEST

Before taking this practice test, find a quiet room where you can work uninterrupted for two and a half hours. Make sure you have a comfortable desk, your calculator, and several No. 2 pencils. Use the answer sheet to record your answers. Once you start, don't stop until you've finished. Remember—you can review any questions within a section, but you may not jump from one section to another.

PSAT Practice Test One
Answer Sheet

Remove (or photocopy) this answer sheet and use it to complete the practice test. See the answer key following the test when finished. The "Compute Your Score" section at the end of Section Two will show you how to find your score.

Start with number 1 for each section. If a section has fewer questions than answer spaces, leave the extra spaces blank.

SECTION 1

1. Ⓐ Ⓑ Ⓒ Ⓓ Ⓔ
2. Ⓐ Ⓑ Ⓒ Ⓓ Ⓔ
3. Ⓐ Ⓑ Ⓒ Ⓓ Ⓔ
4. Ⓐ Ⓑ Ⓒ Ⓓ Ⓔ
5. Ⓐ Ⓑ Ⓒ Ⓓ Ⓔ
6. Ⓐ Ⓑ Ⓒ Ⓓ Ⓔ

7. Ⓐ Ⓑ Ⓒ Ⓓ Ⓔ
8. Ⓐ Ⓑ Ⓒ Ⓓ Ⓔ
9. Ⓐ Ⓑ Ⓒ Ⓓ Ⓔ
10. Ⓐ Ⓑ Ⓒ Ⓓ Ⓔ
11. Ⓐ Ⓑ Ⓒ Ⓓ Ⓔ
12. Ⓐ Ⓑ Ⓒ Ⓓ Ⓔ

13. Ⓐ Ⓑ Ⓒ Ⓓ Ⓔ
14. Ⓐ Ⓑ Ⓒ Ⓓ Ⓔ
15. Ⓐ Ⓑ Ⓒ Ⓓ Ⓔ
16. Ⓐ Ⓑ Ⓒ Ⓓ Ⓔ
17. Ⓐ Ⓑ Ⓒ Ⓓ Ⓔ
18. Ⓐ Ⓑ Ⓒ Ⓓ Ⓔ

19. Ⓐ Ⓑ Ⓒ Ⓓ Ⓔ
20. Ⓐ Ⓑ Ⓒ Ⓓ Ⓔ
21. Ⓐ Ⓑ Ⓒ Ⓓ Ⓔ
22. Ⓐ Ⓑ Ⓒ Ⓓ Ⓔ
23. Ⓐ Ⓑ Ⓒ Ⓓ Ⓔ
24. Ⓐ Ⓑ Ⓒ Ⓓ Ⓔ

☐ # right in Section 1

☐ # wrong in Section 1

SECTION 2

1. Ⓐ Ⓑ Ⓒ Ⓓ Ⓔ
2. Ⓐ Ⓑ Ⓒ Ⓓ Ⓔ
3. Ⓐ Ⓑ Ⓒ Ⓓ Ⓔ
4. Ⓐ Ⓑ Ⓒ Ⓓ Ⓔ
5. Ⓐ Ⓑ Ⓒ Ⓓ Ⓔ

6. Ⓐ Ⓑ Ⓒ Ⓓ Ⓔ
7. Ⓐ Ⓑ Ⓒ Ⓓ Ⓔ
8. Ⓐ Ⓑ Ⓒ Ⓓ Ⓔ
9. Ⓐ Ⓑ Ⓒ Ⓓ Ⓔ
10. Ⓐ Ⓑ Ⓒ Ⓓ Ⓔ

11. Ⓐ Ⓑ Ⓒ Ⓓ Ⓔ
12. Ⓐ Ⓑ Ⓒ Ⓓ Ⓔ
13. Ⓐ Ⓑ Ⓒ Ⓓ Ⓔ
14. Ⓐ Ⓑ Ⓒ Ⓓ Ⓔ
15. Ⓐ Ⓑ Ⓒ Ⓓ Ⓔ

16. Ⓐ Ⓑ Ⓒ Ⓓ Ⓔ
17. Ⓐ Ⓑ Ⓒ Ⓓ Ⓔ
18. Ⓐ Ⓑ Ⓒ Ⓓ Ⓔ

☐ # right in Section 2

☐ # wrong in Section 2

SECTION 3

25. Ⓐ Ⓑ Ⓒ Ⓓ Ⓔ
26. Ⓐ Ⓑ Ⓒ Ⓓ Ⓔ
27. Ⓐ Ⓑ Ⓒ Ⓓ Ⓔ
28. Ⓐ Ⓑ Ⓒ Ⓓ Ⓔ
29. Ⓐ Ⓑ Ⓒ Ⓓ Ⓔ
30. Ⓐ Ⓑ Ⓒ Ⓓ Ⓔ

31. Ⓐ Ⓑ Ⓒ Ⓓ Ⓔ
32. Ⓐ Ⓑ Ⓒ Ⓓ Ⓔ
33. Ⓐ Ⓑ Ⓒ Ⓓ Ⓔ
34. Ⓐ Ⓑ Ⓒ Ⓓ Ⓔ
35. Ⓐ Ⓑ Ⓒ Ⓓ Ⓔ
36. Ⓐ Ⓑ Ⓒ Ⓓ Ⓔ

37. Ⓐ Ⓑ Ⓒ Ⓓ Ⓔ
38. Ⓐ Ⓑ Ⓒ Ⓓ Ⓔ
39. Ⓐ Ⓑ Ⓒ Ⓓ Ⓔ
40. Ⓐ Ⓑ Ⓒ Ⓓ Ⓔ
41. Ⓐ Ⓑ Ⓒ Ⓓ Ⓔ
42. Ⓐ Ⓑ Ⓒ Ⓓ Ⓔ

43. Ⓐ Ⓑ Ⓒ Ⓓ Ⓔ
44. Ⓐ Ⓑ Ⓒ Ⓓ Ⓔ
45. Ⓐ Ⓑ Ⓒ Ⓓ Ⓔ
46. Ⓐ Ⓑ Ⓒ Ⓓ Ⓔ
47. Ⓐ Ⓑ Ⓒ Ⓓ Ⓔ

☐ # right in Section 3

☐ # wrong in Section 3

KAPLAN
Test Prep and Admissions

KAPLAN
Test Prep and Admissions

Practice Test One

SECTION ONE

Time—25 Minutes
24 Questions

For each of the following questions, choose the best answer and darken the
corresponding oval on the answer sheet.

Select the lettered word or set of words that best
completes the sentence.

Example:

Today's small, portable computers contrast
markedly with the earliest electronic computers,
which were ----.

(A) effective
(B) invented
(C) useful
(D) destructive
(E) enormous

1. While the musician's biography mostly reiterates
   stories that many readers will find familiar, several
   chapters about his childhood may even be ---- to
   experts.

   (A) surprising
   (B) trivial
   (C) boring
   (D) unclear
   (E) irrelevant

2. The chairman ---- the decision of the board members, describing it as a ---- of every worthwhile
   ideal that the organization stood for.

   (A) defended . . denial
   (B) lamented . . repudiation
   (C) criticized . . fulfillment
   (D) endorsed . . renunciation
   (E) applauded . . negation

3. While George Balanchine's choreography stayed
   within a classical context, he challenged convention
   by recombining the traditional idioms of ballet
   in ---- ways.

   (A) novel
   (B) familiar
   (C) redundant
   (D) naive
   (E) awkward

GO ON TO THE NEXT PAGE ⇒

4. Despite their outward resemblance, the brothers could not be more ---- temperamentally; while one is quiet and circumspect, the other is brash and ----.

   (A) inimical . . timid
   (B) passionate . . superficial
   (C) dissimilar . . audacious
   (D) different . . forgiving
   (E) alike . . respectful

5. Prior to the American entrance into World War I, President Woodrow Wilson strove to maintain the ---- of the United States, warning both sides against encroachments on American interests.

   (A) involvement
   (B) belligerence
   (C) versatility
   (D) munificence
   (E) neutrality

6. The movie star's ex-husband, increasingly bitter, wrote an intensely ---- memoir about her that was widely considered a betrayal of their years of ----.

   (A) hateful . . antipathy
   (B) laconic . . estrangement
   (C) malicious . . intimacy
   (D) adoring . . affection
   (E) doting . . antagonism

7. At one time, historians spoke of ancient Greece as though its cultural and scientific achievements were wholly ----, whereas it is now generally recognized that at least some Greek science and culture was ---- .

   (A) monolithic . . homogeneous
   (B) original . . derivative
   (C) primitive . . simple
   (D) mistaken . . dubious
   (E) successful . . significant

GO ON TO THE NEXT PAGE

Answer the questions below based on the information in the accompanying passages.

Questions 8–11 are based on the following passages.

Passage 1

During the 1840s America saw a rapid expansion of its territory into the unexplored West. Politicians of the time saw this ever-increasing westward migration and settlement as America's "Manifest
(5) Destiny." American politicians (and later American citizens) believed that it was their mission to claim all the land from the Atlantic to the Pacific. They wanted to "extend the boundaries of freedom" and bring democracy to all those who were capable of
(10) self-government. Despite unfortunate prejudices, the goal was just. Every nation needs a sense of purpose and destiny; every nation has a right and a duty to explore the limits of its geography and to extend its culture as far as possible.

Passage 2

From the vantage point of the 21st century one can only look back with dismay on the expansionist fever that gripped Americans in the 1840s. Fueled by fears of English alliances with Mexico, the aftermath
(5) of two economic depressions, and a desire to expand the slave trade, Americans, egged on by the politicians of the time, pushed westward seeking their "Manifest Destiny." And what was this destiny? The settlement of the entire country, from the
(10) Atlantic to the Pacific, by white people of European descent. The tragedy, of course, is that this came at such a high price—the decimation of Native American cultures and the despoiling of the wilderness.

8. According to Passage 1, "Manifest Destiny" is best described as

(A) the desire of Americans to settle the West

(B) a form of self-government

(C) the belief that America should extend from the Atlantic to the Pacific

(D) an unfortunate prejudice held by 19th century Americans

(E) one of the Constitutional rights to which Americans are entitled

9. The phrase "egged on" in Passage 2, line 6 most nearly means

(A) urged

(B) dismissed

(C) discouraged

(D) belittled

(E) rewarded

10. The author of Passage 2 would most likely respond to the contention of the author of Passage 1 that "the goal [of Manifest Destiny] was just" (line 11) by

(A) ridiculing the author of Passage 1 as naive

(B) commending the author's insight

(C) presenting a similar position

(D) defending the author's right to his opinion

(E) arguing for an alternative point of view

11. Both authors would probably agree that

(A) despite its drawbacks, Manifest Destiny produced good results

(B) Americans were encouraged by their political leaders to pursue Manifest Destiny

(C) Americans began the westward migration because they were suffering from the results of economic depression

(D) people have no right to impose cultural values on others

(E) Manifest Destiny was an inevitable result of the cultural climate of the time

GO ON TO THE NEXT PAGE

Questions 12–18 are based on the following passage.

The following passage is excerpted from a historian's account of the development of European classical music.

During the first half of the nineteenth century, the political and social currents in Europe in the aftermath of the French Revolution brought with them significant developments in the world of
(5) music. Patronage of the arts was no longer considered the exclusive province of the aristocracy. The increasingly prosperous middle class swelled the ranks of audiences at public concerts and music festivals. New opera houses were built to accom-
(10) modate the demand, and these in turn enabled musicians to reach a larger public. Furthermore, the elevated status of the middle-class increased the participation of women in the musical field, which had traditionally been associated with men.
(15) Bourgeois families encouraged their daughters to take advantage of the new-found leisure time by studying voice or piano, since this would improve their marriage possibilities and thus be an asset in the family's climb to social acceptance. Singing in
(20) particular became a focus of the woman's education, stemming from the traditional notion that a mother's singing was beneficial in nurturing a child. So many women became involved in amateur musical activities, in fact, that all the businesses
(25) that served music—piano-building, music publishing and music journalism—burgeoned.

Society was only beginning to enlarge its concept of appropriate musical education and activities for women, however. Female musical professionals
(30) were still very uncommon. Even the most competent could be forbidden by husbands and fathers to appear in public, to publish music under their own names, or to accept fees for their teaching if the men feared that these activities would have a
(35) negative impact on the family's social status. The advice and support of a man was still a necessity in the musical career of a woman no matter how talented she was.

The prevailing negative opinions that contin-
(40) ued to constrain women musicians during this century, especially composers, can be traced back to the previous one. Many prominent eighteenth-century writers believed that women did not possess the intellectual and emotional capacity to
(45) learn or to create as artists. The influential social and educational philosopher Jean-Jacques Rousseau, for example, asserted that "women, in general, possess no artistic sensibility ... nor genius." Furthermore, it was held to be unnecessary and
(50) even dangerous for women to acquire extensive musical knowledge, as such knowledge could only detract from the business of being a wife and mother. Johann Campe's opinion of female composers was representative of this view: "Among a
(55) hundred praiseworthy female composers hardly one can be found who fulfills simultaneously all the duties of a reasonable and good wife, an attentive and efficient housekeeper, and a concerned mother."

Most nineteenth-century men and women
(60) seemed to agree with these sentiments. Women who performed publicly or attempted creative work therefore suffered not only societal censure but internal conflicts about the propriety and sensibility of their own aspirations. Even the great
(65) Clara Schumann, who was exceptional in that she was encouraged both by her husband and by the musical public to compose, entertained doubts about her creative ability. In 1839 she wrote, "I once believed that I possessed creative talent, but I
(70) have given up this idea; a woman must not desire to compose." Standard views on proper feminine behavior were so firmly entrenched that this mother of eight could not recognize the significance of her own accomplishments.
(75) Schumann was in fact a trail-blazer—one of the very first female composers to construct a large-scale orchestral work. In the early nineteenth century, the "art song" was considered to be the "safe," appropriate genre for women composers.
(80) The art song was a type of chamber music and as such fit comfortably into a domestic environment—the woman's domain. Women composers also gravitated to the art song as a medium for musical expression because its composition did
(85) not require the intensive training (often denied to women musicians) that the more intricate sonata or symphony did. Schumann defied convention,

GO ON TO THE NEXT PAGE

however, when she composed the "masculine" orchestral piece *Piano Concerto in A Minor.*
(90) Although not among those considered her finest, the work demonstrated to the women musicians who followed Schumann that female musical creativity could slip loose from the bonds of society.

12. The first paragraph of the passage suggests that for the majority of bourgeois women, their increased participation in music in the nineteenth century was

    (A) consistent with their traditional roles in the family

    (B) burdensome since they were now obliged to become involved

    (C) ground-breaking in that women had never become professional musicians before

    (D) discouraged by men because playing as an amateur was socially inappropriate

    (E) justified, considering that women had shown talent equal to men in music

13. The statement that the "advice and support of a man was still a necessity" (line 36) for a woman musician no matter how talented she was suggests primarily that women musicians

    (A) were more emotionally fragile than their male counterparts

    (B) accepted the fact that they had little experience in making decisions

    (C) were as critical of themselves as the men in the family were of them

    (D) generally conformed to accepted norms of behavior

    (E) did not need ability so long as they were well connected

14. In the third paragraph (lines 39–58), the author presents evidence to show that

    (A) the perception of women in society can be altered

    (B) women had an indirect influence on eighteenth-century philosophy

    (C) nineteenth-century beliefs about women were long-standing and firmly rooted

    (D) chauvinism was even more rampant in the eighteenth than in later centuries

    (E) the role of great intellectuals is to point out society's faults

15. In line 48, "sensibility" most nearly means

    (A) aptitude

    (B) direction

    (C) thoughtfulness

    (D) practicality

    (E) knowledge

16. The quotation from Campe (lines 54–58) suggests that he thought women

    (A) did not have the ability to compose

    (B) had too many domestic responsibilities

    (C) could balance the demands of home and career

    (D) ought to concentrate their efforts in a single area

    (E) should not neglect domestic duties in favor of music

GO ON TO THE NEXT PAGE

17. If Schumann was a trail-blazing composer, why, according to the author, did she write in 1839 that she no longer thought she had creative talent?

    (A) She was compelled by her husband to do so in order to preserve the family's social status.

    (B) She was not receiving the praise that she once had.

    (C) She had not produced anything of significance by that time.

    (D) She had been influenced by society's view of women.

    (E) She felt she had exhausted her talent in the creation of *Piano Concerto in A Minor*.

18. All of the following questions can be explicitly answered on the basis of the passage EXCEPT

    (A) What were the advantages to the nineteenth-century bourgeois family of having a daughter educated in music?

    (B) What were the usual limitations imposed on nineteenth-century women regarding their musical aspirations?

    (C) What was the intellectual source of nineteenth-century beliefs regarding women's artistic ability?

    (D) What changes did Clara Schumann herself bring about in society's general attitude toward women as professional musicians?

    (E) What impact did the newfound prosperity of the middle class in the nineteenth century have on businesses associated with the music world?

GO ON TO THE NEXT PAGE ⇒

Questions 19–24 are based on the following passage.

The following passage about evolutionary science was excerpted from the writings of a well-known biologist.

There is something intrinsically fascinating about the idea of evolution. What principles govern the evolution of species? And what does evolution tell us about the place of Homo sapiens in the

(5) grand order of things? The writer George Bernard Shaw held that a mystical guiding force impels life to evolve toward eventual perfection. Modern scientists may not believe in this guiding force or in the possibility of perfection, but many would agree

(10) that life has been improving itself through evolution for billions of years. (Note that this conveniently makes Homo sapiens, a very recent product of evolution, one of the newest and most improved versions of life.) In the view of these scientists, con-

(15) stant competition among species is the engine that drives the process of evolution and propels life upward. In order to win one day's struggle and live to fight another day, a species always has to adapt, be a little faster, a little stronger, and a little smarter

(20) than its competitors and its predecessors.

No less an eminence than Charles Darwin put forth the idea that species were in constant competition with each other. To Darwin, nature was a surface covered with thousands of sharp wedges, all

(25) packed together and jostling for the same space. Those wedges that fared best moved toward the center of the surface, improving their position by knocking other wedges away with violent blows. The standard example that textbooks give of such

(30) competitive wedging is the interaction between the brachiopods and the clams. Clams were long held to be ancient undersea competitors with brachiopods due to the fact that the two species inhabited the same ecological niche. Clams are abundant

(35) today, whereas brachiopods (dominant in ancient times) are not. Modern clams are also physiologically more complex than brachiopods are. The standard interpretation of these facts is that the clams' physiology was an evolutionary improve-

(40) ment that gave them the ability to "knock away" the brachiopods.

In recent years, however, the prominent naturalists Stephen Jay Gould and C. Brad Calloway have challenged the validity of this example as

(45) well as the model it was meant to support. Gould and Calloway found that over most of geological time clams and brachiopods went their separate ways. Never did the population of brachiopods dip as that of the clams rose, or vice versa. In fact,

(50) the two populations often grew simultaneously, which belies the notion that they were fighting fiercely over the same narrow turf and resources. That there are so many more clams than brachiopods today seems rather to be a consequence

(55) of mass dyings that occurred in the Permian period. Whatever caused the mass dyings—some scientists theorize that either there were massive ecological or geological changes, or a comet crashed down from the heavens—clams were simply able to weather the

(60) storm much better than the brachiopods.

Out of these observations, Gould and Calloway drew a number of far-reaching conclusions. For instance, they suggested that direct competition between species was far less frequent than Darwin

(65) thought. Perhaps nature was really a very large surface on which there were very few wedges, and the wedges consequently did not bang incessantly against each other. Perhaps the problem facing these wedges was rather that the surface continually

(70) altered its shape, and they had to struggle independently to stay in a good position on the surface as it changed. In this alternate model, competition between species is not the impetus for evolutionary adaptation—changes in the environment (geologi-

(75) cal and climatic variations) are.

So where does that leave Homo sapiens if evolution is a response to sudden, unpredictable and sweeping changes in the environment rather than the result of a perpetual struggle? No longer are

(80) we the kings of the mountain who clawed our way to the top by advancing beyond other species. We are instead those who took to the mountains when floods began to rage below and then discovered that living high up has its definite advantages

(85) . . . so long as our mountain doesn't decide to turn into a volcano.

GO ON TO THE NEXT PAGE

19. The primary purpose of the passage is to

(A) discuss a new alternative to an established theory

(B) demonstrate the usefulness of metaphors in explaining biology

(C) criticize the fundamental tenets of evolutionary theory

(D) examine the nature of the interaction between two species

(E) explain a complicated theory in straightforward terms

20. The author uses the parenthetical statement in lines 11–14 to make which of the following points?

(A) Humankind is as close to perfection as life can hope to reach.

(B) Scientists may be influenced by the desire to see their own species as very advanced.

(C) Scientists often merely confirm our own common-sense views.

(D) Humankind has not had sufficient time to improve itself through evolution.

(E) Our species has evolved from lower forms of life.

21. As used in the paragraph 2, the term "wedges" refers to

(A) an organism of a particular species

(B) an underwater creature

(C) an entire species

(D) an ancient animal that has become extinct

(E) a group of humans

22. In the third paragraph (lines 42–60), the author presents evidence primarily to show that

(A) evolutionary biologists rarely agree with each other on major issues

(B) brachiopods have never experienced a decline in population

(C) the theories and data in antiquated textbooks should not be trusted

(D) the decline of the brachiopod was not the result of competition with clams

(E) two competing species can undergo simultaneous increases in population

23. A "comet" is mentioned in line 58 as an example of

(A) a possible reason that brachiopods are no longer abundant

(B) an event that could have obscured the geological record

(C) a phenomenon that is as infrequent as mass extinction

(D) an occurrence that temporarily halted inter-species competition

(E) a threat that could have had an equal impact on many different species

24. With which statement concerning Gould and Calloway's theory of evolution would the author most likely agree?

(A) It does not allow for rapid changes in individual species.

(B) It rules out the possibility that one species could cause the extinction of another.

(C) It puts the status of humans in a new perspective.

(D) It places too much importance on the effect of natural disasters.

(E) It has not yet been tested as much as the previous model.

IF YOU FINISH BEFORE TIME IS CALLED, YOU MAY CHECK YOUR WORK ON THIS SECTION ONLY. DO NOT TURN TO ANY OTHER SECTION IN THE TEST.

SECTION TWO

Time—25 Minutes
18 Questions

Solve each of the following problems, decide which is the best answer choice, and darken the corresponding oval on the answer sheet.

Notes:
(1) Calculator use is permitted.
(2) All numbers used are real numbers.
(3) Figures are provided for some problems. All figures are drawn to scale and lie in a plane UNLESS otherwise indicated.

Information

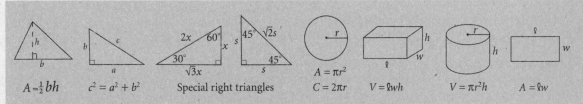

$A = \frac{1}{2}bh$ $c^2 = a^2 + b^2$ Special right triangles $A = \pi r^2$ $C = 2\pi r$ $V = \ell wh$ $V = \pi r^2 h$ $A = \ell w$

The sum of the degree measures of the angles of a triangle is 180.
The number of degrees of arc in a circle is 360.
A straight angle has a degree measure of 180.

1. What is the hundredths' digit in the number 123,456.789?

   (A) 1
   (B) 4
   (C) 5
   (D) 8
   (E) 9

2. All of the following are equal to $9x^2$ EXCEPT

   (A) $x^2 + 8x^2$
   (B) $4x + 5x$
   (C) $(9x)(x)$
   (D) $(3x)(3x)$
   (E) $(-3x)(-3x)$

3. If $\frac{1}{3}(2x) = 30$, what is the value of x?

   (A) $3\frac{1}{3}$
   (B) 45
   (C) $5\frac{1}{3}$
   (D) 6
   (E) 10

GO ON TO THE NEXT PAGE

KAPLAN
Test Prep and Admissions

4. The circle graph above represents household expenses in dollars. If $33\frac{1}{3}$ percent of expenses go toward rent, which region on the graph best represents dollars spent on rent?

(A) A

(B) B

(C) C

(D) D

(E) E

5. A rectangle is cut in half, resulting in squares each of area 25. What is the perimeter of the original rectangle?

(A) 10

(B) 20

(C) 30

(D) 40

(E) 50

6. Driving at an average rate of 48 miles per hour, John reached his destination in exactly 2 hours and 15 minutes. To drive the same route in exactly 2 hours, John would have to average what rate of speed?

(A) 50 miles per hour

(B) 54 miles per hour

(C) 55 miles per hour

(D) 60 miles per hour

(E) 64 miles per hour

7. If $x^2 = 7$, what is the value of $(x + 1)(x - 1)$?

(A) 6

(B) 8

(C) 48

(D) 50

(E) It cannot be determined from the information given.

8. If x is $66\frac{2}{3}$ percent of y, then y is what percent of x?

(A) $33\frac{1}{3}\%$

(B) 75%

(C) $133\frac{1}{3}\%$

(D) 150%

(E) $166\frac{2}{3}\%$

9. A number that is divisible by 4, 6, and 10 must be divisible by all of the following EXCEPT

(A) 8

(B) 12

(C) 15

(D) 20

(E) 30

10. If the sum $\frac{1}{2} + \frac{1}{4} + \frac{1}{8} + \frac{1}{16} + \frac{1}{32} + \frac{1}{64}$ is calculated and expressed in simplest terms, what is the numerator of the sum?

(A) 1

(B) 3

(C) 6

(D) 12

(E) 63

GO ON TO THE NEXT PAGE

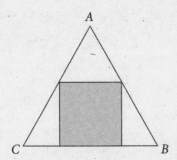

11. In the figure above, the shaded region is a square of area 3, and $\triangle ABC$ is equilateral. What is the perimeter of triangle ABC?

(A) $3\sqrt{3}$

(B) $9\sqrt{3}$

(C) $2 + \sqrt{3}$

(D) $3 + 6\sqrt{3}$

(E) $6 + 3\sqrt{3}$

12. $\sqrt{48} + \sqrt{12} + \sqrt{3} =$

(A) $\sqrt{63}$

(B) $7\sqrt{3}$

(C) $20\sqrt{3}$

(D) $4\sqrt{15} + 3$

(E) $30 + \sqrt{3}$

13. Let $x \, ¿ \, y$ be defined as $x^2 + \dfrac{y}{2}$ for all x and y.

If $3 \, ¿ \, 4 = 5 \, ¿ \, n$, what is the value of n?

(A) -28

(B) -7

(C) $\dfrac{12}{5}$

(D) 6

(E) 60

14. If the average (arithmetic mean) of three distinct positive integers is 4, what is the greatest possible value for one of those integers?

(A) 5

(B) 6

(C) 9

(D) 11

(E) 12

15. If the length of one leg of a right triangle is $x + 2$, and the length of the hypotenuse is $x + 3$, where $x > -2$, what is the length of the other leg in terms of x?

(A) x

(B) $x + 1$

(C) $x + \sqrt{5}$

(D) $\sqrt{x + 5}$

(E) $\sqrt{2x + 5}$

16. When the positive integer n is divided by 9, the remainder is 7. What is the remainder when $5n$ is divided by 9?

(A) 4

(B) 5

(C) 6

(D) 7

(E) 8

GO ON TO THE NEXT PAGE

17. Box *A* contains 4 black marbles and 1 white marble. Box *B* contains 4 black marbles and 3 white marbles. What is the minimum number of marbles that must be moved from Box *A* to Box *B* so that the ratio of black marbles to white marbles is the same in the two boxes?

(A) 1

(B) 2

(C) 3

(D) 4

(E) It cannot be done.

18. In the equation $V = \frac{4}{3}\pi r^3$, if the value of r is multiplied by $\frac{1}{2}$, then the value of V is multiplied by

(A) $\frac{1}{8}$

(B) $\frac{1}{6}$

(C) $\frac{1}{4}$

(D) $\frac{1}{2}$

(E) $\frac{2}{3}$

SECTION THREE

Time—25 Minutes
24 Questions

For each of the following questions, choose the best answer and darken the corresponding oval on the answer sheet.

Select the lettered word or set of words that best completes the sentence.

Example:

Today's small, portable computers contrast markedly with the earliest electronic computers, which were ----.

(A) effective

(B) invented

(C) useful

(D) destructive

(E) enormous

25. The pollution caused by mining and smelting the lead for electric car batteries may ---- the environmental benefits offered by the cars themselves.

(A) create

(B) outweigh

(C) reinforce

(D) eliminate

(E) overcome

26. The discovery of the Dead Sea Scrolls in the 1940s quickly ---- the popular imagination, but the precise significance of the scrolls is still ---- by scholars.

(A) impressed . . understood

(B) alarmed . . obscured

(C) troubled . . perceived

(D) fired . . disputed

(E) eluded . . debated

27. Dietitians warn of the dangers of anorexia, an illness that can cause people with relatively normal physiques to starve themselves until they are too ---- to survive.

(A) glutted

(B) lachrymose

(C) emaciated

(D) superfluous

(E) satiated

28. Since the mid-eighteenth century, there has been much ---- between the cultures of France and Germany despite the frequent ---- between those two countries.

(A communication . . alliances

(B) hatred . . opposition

(C) interaction . . enmity

(D) antagonism . . misunderstandings

(E) hostility . . alienation

29. The downsizing of American corporations is probably not an ---- phase; it is becoming a permanent feature of American corporate management.

(A) arbitrary

(B) anticipated

(C) ephemeral

(D) administrative

(E) equivocal

30. One theory contends that patriarchy is not ---- part of human nature, but rather it is a cultural institution that dominates in most societies because of the political and social forces that ---- it.

(A) a continuous . . trivialize

(B) an analogous . . effect

(C) an inherent . . discourage

(D) an instinctive . . promote

(E) a learned . . underwrite

GO ON TO THE NEXT PAGE

Answer the questions below based on the information in the accompanying passages.

Questions 31–32 are based on the following passage.

Are they mammals or reptiles? This was the dilemma scientists faced when they tried to classify three animals—the platypus, the short-nosed echidna, and the long-nosed echidna—that are
(5) found only in Australia and New Guinea. Scientists were perplexed since these animals have some things in common with reptiles and some things in common with mammals. For example, they lay eggs like reptiles, but they nurse their young with
(10) milk excreted from special glands, like mammals. Their eye structure is similar to that of reptiles, while their ear structure is like a mammal's. In the end, scientists, understanding that there was no perfect solution to the predicament, decided to
(15) classify them as mammals and to place them in their own order—Monotremata.

31. The opening sentence ("Are they. . . reptiles?") serves primarily as

(A) a summary of the information in the paragraph

(B) an indication that the question is ultimately unanswerable

(C) a challenge to prevailing scientific opinion

(D) an introduction of the paragraph's topic

(E) an attempt to rebut criticism

32. In lines 11–12, the author most likely discusses the eye and ear structure of the animals in question in order to

(A) provide an in-depth discussion of their anatomy

(B) demonstrate that the animals are more like mammals than reptiles

(C) justify the foundation of the Monotremata order

(D) illustrate that the animals cannot be easily classified

(E) question the wisdom of the scientists' eventual decision

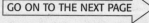

GO ON TO THE NEXT PAGE

KAPLAN
Test Prep and Admissions

Questions 33–38 are based on the following passage.

The following is adapted from a short story first published in 1921. The author was a Native American woman.

It was summer on the western plains, and fields of golden sunflowers, facing eastward, greet-ed the rising sun. Blue-Star Woman, with wind-shorn braids of white hair over each ear, sat in the

(5) shade of her log hut before an open fire. Lonely but unmolested, she dwelt here like the ground squirrel that took its abode nearby—both through the easy tolerance of the landowner. As the Indian woman held a skillet over the burning embers, a

(10) large round cake, with long slashes in its center, baked and crowded the capacity of the frying pan.

In deep abstraction, Blue-Star Woman pre-pared her morning meal. "Who am I?" had become the obsessing riddle of her life. She was

(15) no longer a young woman, being in her fifty-third year; yet now it was required of her, in the eyes of the white man's law, to give proof of her member-ship in the Sioux tribe in order to get her share of tribal land. The unwritten law of heart prompted

(20) her naturally to say, "I am a being. I am Blue-Star Woman. A piece of earth is my birthright."

It was taught for reasons now forgotten that an Indian should never pronounce his or her name in answer to any inquiry. It was probably a

(25) means of protection in the days of black magic; be that as it may, Blue-Star Woman lived in times when this teaching was disregarded. It gained her nothing, however, to pronounce her name to the government official to whom she applied for her

(30) share of tribal land. His persistent question was always, "Who are your parents?" Blue-Star Woman was left an orphan at a tender age, so she did not remember them. They were long-gone to the spir-it-land—and she could not understand why they

(35) should be recalled to earth on her account. It was another one of the old, old teachings of her race that the names of the dead should not be idly spo-ken—in fact, it was considered a sacrilege to men-tion carelessly the name of any departed one,

(40) especially in disputes over worldly possessions. The unfortunate circumstances of her early child-hood, together with the lack of written records of a roving people, placed a formidable barrier

between her and her heritage. The fact was, events

(45) of far greater importance to the tribe than her reincarnation had passed unrecorded in books. The verbal reports of the old-time men and women of the tribe were varied—some were con-tradictory. Blue-Star Woman was unable to find

(50) even a twig of her family tree . . .

Blue-Star Woman was her individual name. For untold ages the Indian race had not used fam-ily names—a new-born child was given a brand-new name. Blue-Star Woman was proud to write

(55) her name for which she would not be required to substitute another's upon her marriage, as is the custom of civilized peoples. "The times are changed now," she muttered under her breath. "My individual name seems to mean nothing."

(60) Looking out into space, she saw the nodding sun-flowers, and they acquiesced with her . . . With fried bread and black coffee she regaled herself, and once again her mind reverted to her riddle. "This also puzzles me," thought she to herself.

(65) "Once a wise leader of our people, addressing a president of this country, said: 'I am a man. You are another. The Great Spirit is our witness!' This is simple and easy to understand, but the times are changed—the white man's laws are strange."

33. The major purpose of the passage is to

(A) highlight the differences between the laws of two cultures

(B) describe the impact of a changing world on a woman

(C) illustrate the danger of living apart from society

(D) show the futility of preserving ancient myths in modern times

(E) explore the challenge of establishing tribal membership

GO ON TO THE NEXT PAGE

34. The author most likely mentions the "ground squirrel" (lines 6–7) in order to

    (A) suggest Blue-Star Woman's profound understanding of nature

    (B) demonstrate Blue-Star Woman's keen observation of her surroundings

    (C) show Blue-Star Woman's adaptability to squalid living conditions

    (D) indicate Blue-Star Woman's overwhelming loneliness

    (E) reveal Blue-Star Woman's use of a stranger's land

35. In line 8, "tolerance" most nearly means

    (A) neglect

    (B) fortitude

    (C) permission

    (D) open-mindedness

    (E) limitation

36. The second paragraph suggests that the white man's law differs from the "unwritten law of heart" (lines 19–20) in that the latter

    (A) suggests that every person deserves land of his or her own

    (B) has practical consequences for Blue-Star Woman

    (C) considers each human being to be different

    (D) places restrictions on who can and cannot own land

    (E) can be explained in straightforward language

37. In the third paragraph the author conveys a feeling of tension by juxtaposing which two of the following elements?

    (A) The woman's desire for land versus her pronouncement of her name.

    (B) The assertion that the woman was an orphan versus her speculation about her parents.

    (C) The official's demand versus the woman's belief about uttering the names of the dead.

    (D) The woman's dominant presence versus the official's show of authority.

    (E) The woman's reluctance to answer questions versus her willingness to disregard beliefs.

38. In line 59, "My individual name seems to mean nothing" most nearly reflects Blue-Star Woman's

    (A) gradual acceptance of the fact that she now has to change her name

    (B) devastating loss of prestige and good reputation among her people

    (C) sad comprehension that cherished old customs are losing their relevance

    (D) great dismay that she has no children to carry on the family name

    (E) unsettling realization that no member of the tribe remembers her

GO ON TO THE NEXT PAGE

Questions 39–40 are based on the following passage.

Rowan couldn't believe his luck. He had pro-
posed to Miss Ashley and she had accepted.
She was such a reserved little person that he
wasn't sure that she would. To be sure, they had
(5) been stepping out for the past year, but their con-
versations had been rather one-sided. He would
recount his day or explain how his superiors could
better run their business. She would nod and
smile, offer a word of encouragement here, ask for
(10) clarification there. Really, she was perfect. Her
father, when Rowan asked for Miss Ashley's hand,
was reluctant, but when Rowan hinted that, after
all, Miss Ashley was almost thirty and there
wouldn't be too many other offers, Major Ashley
(15) consented. Now began the long period of
engagement.

39. In the context of the passage, "stepping out for the past year" (line 5) most likely means that Rowan and Miss Ashley

(A) spent all their time together taking walks

(B) were planning to be married in a year

(C) enjoyed the sport of hiking

(D) had been dating for a year

(E) waited too long to get engaged

40. The sentence in line 10 ("Really . . . perfect") indi-cates that Rowan most likely preferred women who

(A) listened to him rather than speaking themselves

(B) were almost thirty years old

(C) enjoyed walking with him

(D) discussed business with him

(E) shared his dreams

GO ON TO THE NEXT PAGE

Questions 41–48 are based on the following passages.

The two passages, excerpted from the writings of two of America's greatest black leaders, were published just two years apart, in 1901 and 1903, respectively. Booker T. Washington, the author of Passage 1, founded Tuskegee Institute in Alabama and was an adviser to presidents. W.E.B. Du Bois, the author of Passage 2, was a pioneer in sociology and historiography.

Passage 1

My own belief is, although I have never before said so in so many words, that the time will come when the Negro in the South will be accorded all the political rights which his ability, character and
(5) material possessions entitle him to. I think, though, that the opportunity to freely exercise such political rights will not come in any large degree through outside or artificial forcing, but will be accorded to the Negro by the white people
(10) themselves, and that they will protect him in the exercise of those rights. Just as soon as the South gets over the old feeling that it is being forced by "foreigners," or "aliens", to do something which it does not want to do, I believe that the change in
(15) the direction that I have indicated is going to begin. In fact, there are indications that it is already beginning in a slight degree.

Let me illustrate my meaning. Suppose that some months before the opening of the Atlanta
(20) Exposition* there had been a general demand from the press and public platform outside the South that a Negro be given a place on the opening pro-gramme, and that a Negro be placed upon the board of jurors of award. Would any such recogni-
(25) tion of the race have taken place? I do not think so. The Atlanta officials went as far as they did because they felt it to be a pleasure, as well as a duty, to reward what they considered merit in the Negro race. Say what we will, there is something in
(30) human nature which we cannot blot out, which makes one man, in the end, recognize and reward merit in another, regardless of colour or race.

I believe it is the duty of the Negro—as the greater part of the race is already doing—to

(35) deport himself modestly in regard to political claims, depending upon the slow but sure influ-ences that proceed from the possession of property, intelligence, and high character for the full recog-nition of his political rights. I think that the
(40) according of political rights is going to be a matter of natural, slow growth, not an over-night, gourd-vine affair. . .

Washington was an invited speaker at the Atlanta Exposition in September of 1895.

Passage 2

. . . Mr. Washington represents in Negro thought the old attitude of adjustment and sub-mission . . . [I]n our own land, the reaction from the sentiment of war-time has given impetus to
(5) race-prejudice against Negroes, and Mr. Washington withdraws many of the high demands of Negroes as men and American citizens. In other periods of intensified prejudice all the Negro's tendency to self-assertion has been called forth; at
(10) this period a policy of submission is advocated. In the history of nearly all other races and peoples the doctrines preached at such crises has been that manly self-respect is worth more than lands and houses, and that a people who voluntarily surren-
(15) der such respect, or cease striving for it, are not worth civilizing.

In answer to this it has been claimed that the Negro can survive only through submission. Mr. Washington distinctly asks that black people give
(20) up, at least for the present, three things—First, political power; Second, insistence on civil rights; Third, higher education of Negro youth—and con-centrate all their energies on industrial education, and accumulation of wealth, and the conciliation
(25) of the South. This policy has been courageously and insistently advocated for over fifteen years, and has been triumphant for perhaps ten years. As a result of this tender of the palm-branch, what has been the return? In these years there have occurred:
(30)   1. The disfranchisement* of the Negro.
    2. The legal creation of a distinct status of civil inferiority of the Negro.

GO ON TO THE NEXT PAGE

3. The steady withdrawal of aid from institutions for the higher training of the Negro.

(35)   These movements are not, to be sure, direct results of Mr. Washington's teachings; but his propaganda has, without a shadow of a doubt, helped their speedier accomplishment. The question then comes: Is it possible, and probable, that

(40) nine millions of men can make effective progress in economic lines if they are deprived of political rights, made a servile caste, and allowed only the most meagre chance for developing their exceptional men? If history and reason give any distinct

(45) answer to these questions, it is an emphatic No.

     . . . They [who disagree with Mr. Washington] do not expect that the free right to vote, to enjoy civil rights and to be educated, will come in a moment. They do not expect to see the bias and

(50) prejudice of years disappear at the blast of a trumpet. But they are absolutely certain that the way for a people to gain their reasonable rights is clear. Negroes must insist continually. . . that voting is necessary to modern [citizenship], that color dis-

(55) crimination is barbarism, and that black boys need education as well as white boys.

disfranchisement: deprivation of the right to vote

41. In Passage 1, the author's attitude toward white people in the South in his time is primarily one of

(A) empathy for their stoic resistance to change

(B) distrust of all but the most openly humanitarian individuals in power

(C) confidence that they cannot help but eventually act responsibly

(D) exasperation that their behavior so resembles that of foreign citizens

(E) respect for the fact that they are so willing to heed criticism

42. The second paragraph of Passage 1 suggests that the author believes that his being invited to speak at the Atlanta Exposition was

(A) a move calculated to improve the South's image

(B) a result of pressure from outside the South

(C) an indication that the South has overcome old-fashioned views

(D) an example of the influence already wielded by blacks in the South

(E) a reflection not just on himself but on his race

43. The phrase "slow but sure influences" (Passage 1, lines 36–37) most likely refers to the

(A) good impressions made by wealth and accomplishments

(B) Southern blacks' growing belief in the political system

(C) gradual and unnoticed usurpation of power

(D) option to move out of the South

(E) South's adoption of Northern ways of thinking

44. The author of Passage 2 mentions "the history of nearly all other races and peoples" (line 11) in order to

(A) suggest that material possessions are an important part in a race's struggle for respect

(B) suggest that blacks should seek equality as individuals rather than as a community

(C) suggest that a policy of submission will never improve the status of blacks

(D) illustrate that blacks have been the victims of prejudice throughout the world

(E) illustrate that racism is not a problem unique to America

GO ON TO THE NEXT PAGE

45. The author's tone in describing the "result of this tender of the palm-branch" (Passage 2, line 28) is

    (A) analytical and distanced
    (B) mournful and full of regret
    (C) ironic and critical
    (D) both surprised and disillusioned
    (E) alternately outraged and apathetic

46. Passage 2 suggests that Passage 1's view of "human nature" (line 30)

    (A) is naive and optimistic
    (B) may be borne out by future events
    (C) reflects the experience of an entire race
    (D) is only partially accurate
    (E) applies only to educated individuals

47. The authors of both passages would most probably agree that

    (A) the best way to gain the respect of others is to use force
    (B) accumulation of wealth does not automatically bring political power
    (C) long-standing prejudice cannot be conquered overnight
    (D) education is not as important as the possession of political rights
    (E) one should not use speculation to support an argument

48. If these 2 passages were found in one chapter in a collection of historical writings, the title of the chapter would most likely be

    (A) Twentieth-century Leaders
    (B) Historical Perspectives
    (C) Conflicting Points of View
    (D) The History of the South
    (E) Viewpoints of Twentieth-century Black Leaders

IF YOU FINISH BEFORE TIME IS CALLED, YOU MAY CHECK YOUR WORK ON THIS SECTION ONLY. DO NOT TURN TO ANY OTHER SECTION IN THE TEST.

SECTION FOUR

Time—25 Minutes
20 Questions

Solve each of the following problems, decide which is the best answer choice, and darken the corresponding oval on the answer sheet.

Notes:

(1) Calculator use is permitted.

(2) All numbers used are real numbers.

(3) Figures are provided for some problems. All figures are drawn to scale and lie in a plane UNLESS otherwise indicated.

Information

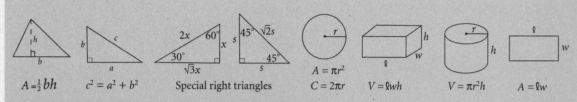

$A = \frac{1}{2}bh$ $c^2 = a^2 + b^2$ Special right triangles $A = \pi r^2$ $V = \ell wh$ $V = \pi r^2 h$ $A = \ell w$
                                                                        $C = 2\pi r$

The sum of the degree measures of the angles of a triangle is 180.
The number of degrees of arc in a circle is 360.
A straight angle has a degree measure of 180.

19. If $x - y = 6$, $y = 5z$, and $z = 4$, what is the value of x?

   (A) −26
   (B) −14
   (C) 14
   (D) 15
   (E) 26

20. The sum of 9a and the square root of 2b is equal to the square of the sum of 3a and 3b.

   Which of the following is an expression for the statement above?

   (A) $9a + (2b)^2 = \sqrt{3a + 3b}$
   (B) $9a + \sqrt{2b} = (3a + 3b)^2$
   (C) $(9a + 2b)^2 = \sqrt{3a + 3b}$
   (D) $\sqrt{9a + 2b} = 3a^2 + 3b^2$
   (E) $\sqrt{9a} + \sqrt{2b} = (3a + 3b)^2$

21. One pound of spaghetti serves either 7 adults or 9 children. Of the following, which best approximates how many pounds of spaghetti are needed to serve 75 people, 15 of whom are children?

   (A) 7
   (B) 8
   (C) 9
   (D) 11
   (E) 13

GO ON TO THE NEXT PAGE

22. $3^{-3} + \left(\frac{1}{3}\right)^3 =$

    (A) -9

    (B) $-\frac{2}{27}$

    (C) 0

    (D) $\frac{2}{27}$

    (E) 1

23. If $x = \frac{1}{2}$, what is the value of $\frac{2}{x} + \frac{2}{(x-1)}$?

    (A) -2

    (B) -1

    (C) 0

    (D) 1

    (E) 2

24. If 20 percent of J is 1,500, what is 15 percent of J?

    (A) 1,125

    (B) 3,000

    (C) 5,125

    (D) 6,000

    (E) 7,500

25. Which of the following is an integer greater than 1 that has <u>only</u> itself, its square root, and 1 as its three positive integer factors?

    (A) 49

    (B) 81

    (C) 100

    (D) 144

    (E) 225

26. When an integer is multiplied by itself, it can end in all of the following EXCEPT

    (A) 1

    (B) 3

    (C) 5

    (D) 6

    (E) 9

27. $(-3x^5y^4)^4 =$

    (A) $-3x^9y^8$

    (B) $-3x^{20}y^{16}$

    (C) $-81x^{20}y^{16}$

    (D) $81x^9y^8$

    (E) $81x^{20}y^{16}$

28. If $j, k, l,$ and m are four nonzero numbers, all of the following proportions are equivalent EXCEPT

    (A) $\frac{j}{k} = \frac{l}{m}$

    (B) $\frac{k}{m} = \frac{l}{j}$

    (C) $\frac{m}{l} = \frac{k}{j}$

    (D) $\frac{jm}{kl} = 1$

    (E) $\frac{l}{j} = \frac{m}{k}$

GO ON TO THE NEXT PAGE

DIRECTIONS FOR STUDENT-PRODUCED RESPONSE QUESTIONS

For each of the questions below (29–38), solve the problem and indicate your answer by darkening the ovals in the special grid. For example:

Answer: 1.25 or $\frac{5}{4}$ or 5/4

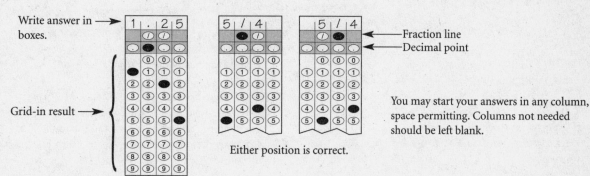

Write answer in boxes.

Grid-in result

Fraction line
Decimal point

Either position is correct.

You may start your answers in any column, space permitting. Columns not needed should be left blank.

- It is recommended, though not required, that you write your answer in the boxes at the top of the columns. However, you will receive credit only for darkening the ovals correctly.

- Grid only one answer to a question, even though some problems have more than one correct answer.

- Darken no more than one oval in a column.

- No answers are negative.

- Mixed numbers cannot be gridded. For example: the number $1\frac{1}{4}$ must be gridded as 1.25 or 5/4.

(If $\boxed{1 \cdot 1 \mid / \mid 4}$ is gridded, it will be interpreted as $\frac{11}{4}$ not $1\frac{1}{4}$.)

- <u>Decimal Accuracy:</u> Decimal answers must be entered as accurately as possible. For example, if you obtain an answer such as 0.1666..., you should record the result as .166 or .167. **Less accurate values such as .16 or .17 are not acceptable.**

Acceptable ways to grid $\frac{1}{6}$ = .1666...

KAPLAN
Test Prep and Admissions

29. If A is the set of digits and B is the set of even numbers, then the intersection of A and B contains how many elements?

30. If $\sqrt{2-x} - 1 = 0$, what is the value of x?

31. Half the product of 8 and 9 is the square root of what number?

32. What is the average (arithmetic mean) of $\frac{1}{4}$ and $\frac{1}{6}$?

$$
\begin{array}{r}
AA \\
+BA \\
\hline
1B8
\end{array}
$$

33. If A and B represent distinct digits in the correctly worked addition problem above, what is the value of A?

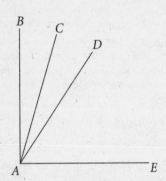

34. In the figure above, AB is perpendicular to AE. If the measure of $\angle BAD$ is 53 degrees, and the measure of $\angle CAE$ is 73 degrees, what is the degree measure of $\angle CAD$?

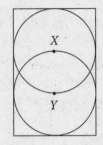

35. In the figure above, X and Y are the centers of the two circles. If each circle has circumference 9π, what is the perimeter of the rectangle?

36. Nuala baked 64 cookies for a party. After each party guest ate n cookies, there were 9 cookies left uneaten. If there were more than 9 guests at the party, and if n is an integer greater than 1, what is the value of n?

37. Boxes of candy were sold for a school fund-raiser. Small boxes cost $2 each and large boxes cost $5 each. If 150 boxes were sold for a total of $444, how many large boxes were sold?

38. What is the maximum possible area of a rectangle with perimeter 14?

IF YOU FINISH BEFORE TIME IS CALLED, YOU MAY CHECK YOUR WORK ON THIS SECTION ONLY. DO NOT TURN TO ANY OTHER SECTION IN THE TEST.

SECTION FIVE

Time—30 Minutes   For each of the following questions, choose the best answer and darken the
39 Questions   corresponding oval on the answer sheet.

Directions: The following sentences test your knowledge of grammar, usage, diction (choice of words), and idiom. Some sentences are correct.
No sentence contains more than one error.
You will find that the error, if there is one, is underlined and lettered. Elements of the sentence that are not underlined will not be changed. In choosing answers, follow the requirements of standard written English.
If there is an error, select the <u>one underlined part</u> that must be changed to make the sentence correct, and fill in the corresponding oval on your answer sheet.
If there is no error, fill in answer oval (E).

1. Before <u>the advent of</u> modern surgical techniques,
              A
   <u>bleeding patients</u> with leeches <u>were considered</u>
         B   C
   therapeutically <u>effective</u>. <u>No error</u>
                       D   E

2. The <u>recent</u> establishment of "Crime Busters,"offi-
         A
   cially sanctioned neighborhood block-watching

   groups, <u>has</u> <u>dramatic</u> improved relations <u>between</u>
            B   C   D
   citizens and police. <u>No error</u>
                            E

3. The masterpiece auctioned so <u>successfully</u> today
                                    A
   depicts a Biblical scene in <u>which</u> the king is on his
                                 B
   throne <u>with</u> his counselors <u>respectively</u> standing
            C   D
   below. <u>No error</u>
              E

4. <u>During</u> the election campaign, the major political
     A
   parties <u>have agreement</u> that minorities must
            B
   <u>be given</u> the opportunity <u>to advance</u> in society.
     C   D
   <u>No error</u>
     E

5. Most of the delegates <u>which</u> attended the conven-
                            A
   tion <u>felt</u> the resolution was <u>too strongly</u> worded,
         B   C
   and the majority voted <u>against</u> it. <u>No error</u>
                            D   E

6. <u>Lost in the forest</u> on a cold night,
     A
   <u>the hunters built</u> a fire <u>to keep themselves</u> warm
     B   C
   and <u>to frighten away</u> the wolves. <u>No error</u>
         D   E

GO ON TO THE NEXT PAGE

7. The effort to <u>create appropriate</u> theatrical effects
                        A

    <u>often result</u> in settings that cannot be <u>effective</u>
         B   C

    without an imaginative <u>lighting</u> crew. <u>No error</u>
                                  D   E

8. Every one of the shops in the town <u>were closed</u> on
                                              A

    Thursday <u>because</u> of the <u>ten-inch</u> rainfall that
                 B   C

    <u>had fallen</u> during the day. <u>No error</u>
         D   E

9. <u>According to</u> the directions on the package, the
       A

    contents <u>are</u> intended for external use <u>only</u>, and
                 B   C

    <u>should not hardly</u> be swallowed, even in small
              D

    quantities. <u>No error</u>
                      E

10. Mr. Webster's paper is <u>highly imaginary</u> and
                                 A

    <u>very creative</u>, <u>but</u> seems to be <u>lacking in</u> cogency.
          B   C   D

    <u>No error</u>
        E

11. The late president's <u>numerous</u> memoirs now
                              A

    <u>about to be</u> published <u>promises</u> to be of special
         B   C

    <u>historical</u> interest. <u>No error</u>
         D   E

12. The point <u>on issue</u> was whether the dock workers,
                   A

    <u>who</u> were <u>an extremely</u> vocal group,
       B   C

    <u>would decide to</u> return to work. <u>No error</u>
              D   E

13. <u>Raising</u> living costs, <u>together</u> with escalating taxes,
       A   B

    <u>have</u> proved to be a burden for <u>everyone</u>. <u>No error</u>
       C   D   E

14. A number of <u>harried</u> department store employees
                     A

    <u>were congregating</u> <u>around</u> the water cooler
              B   C

    <u>to compare and discuss</u> their grievances. <u>No error</u>
              D   E

GO ON TO THE NEXT PAGE

Directions: The following sentences test correctness and effectiveness of expression. In choosing answers, follow the requirements of standard written English; that is, pay attention to grammar, choice of words, sentence construction, and punctuation.

In each of the following sentences, part of the sentence or the entire sentence is underlined. Beneath each sentence you will find five ways of phrasing the underlined part. Choice (A) repeats the original; the other four are different.

Choose the answer that best expresses the meaning of the original sentence. If you think the original is better than any of the alternatives, choose it; otherwise, choose one of the others. Your choice should produce the most effective sentence—clear and precise, without awkwardness or ambiguity.

15. In *War and Peace*, Tolstoy presented his theories on history, and <u>illustrated them</u> with a slanted account of actual historical events.

    (A) illustrated them
    (B) also illustrating them
    (C) he also was illustrating these ideas
    (D) then illustrated the theories also
    (E) then he went about illustrating them

16. In the United States, an increasing number of commuters <u>that believe their families to be</u> immune from the perils of city life.

    (A) that believe their families to be
    (B) that believe their families are
    (C) believes their families are
    (D) who believe their families to be
    (E) believe their families to be

17. <u>Developed by a scientific team at his university</u>, the president informed the reporters that the new process would facilitate the diagnosis of certain congenital diseases.

    (A) Developed by a scientific team at his university
    (B) Having been developed by a scientific team at his university
    (C) Speaking of the discovery made by a scientific team at his university
    (D) Describing the development of a scientific team at his university
    (E) As it had been developed by a scientific team at his university

18. One ecological rule of thumb states that there is opportunity for the accumulation of underground water reservoirs <u>but in regions where vegetation remains undisturbed</u>.

    (A) but in regions where vegetation remains undisturbed
    (B) unless vegetation being left undisturbed in some regions
    (C) only where undisturbed vegetation is in regions
    (D) only in regions where vegetation remains undisturbed
    (E) except for vegetation remaining undisturbed in some regions

19. The Equal Rights Amendment to Islandia's constitution is dying a lingering political death, <u>many dedicated groups and individuals have attempted</u> to prevent its demise.

    (A) many dedicated groups and individuals have attempted
    (B) although many dedicated groups and individuals have attempted
    (C) many dedicated groups and persons has attempted
    (D) despite many dedications of groups and individuals to attempt
    (E) also, many dedicated groups and individuals have attempted

GO ON TO THE NEXT PAGE

20. The ancient Chinese were convinced that air was composed of two kinds of particles, <u>one inactive and one active, the latter of which they called yin and which we today call oxygen</u>.

    (A) one inactive and one active, the latter of which they called yin and which we today call oxygen

    (B) an inactive and an active one called yin, now known as oxygen

    (C) an inactive type and the active type they called yin we now know to be oxygen

    (D) inactive and active; while they called the active type yin, today we call it oxygen

    (E) contrasting the inactive type with the active ones they named yin and we call oxygen

21. Developing a suitable environment for house plants <u>is in many ways like when you are managing</u> soil fertilization for city parks.

    (A) is in many ways like when you are managing

    (B) is in many ways similar to when you are managing

    (C) in many ways is on a par with managing your

    (D) is in many ways similar to the managing of

    (E) is in many ways like managing

22. Most students would get better grades if <u>writing were to be studied by them</u>.

    (A) writing were to be studied by them

    (B) they studied writing

    (C) writing was studied by them

    (D) they would have studied writing

    (E) they were to have studied writing

23. <u>If they do not go into bankruptcy</u>, the company will probably survive its recent setbacks.

    (A) If they do not go into bankruptcy

    (B) Unless bankruptcy cannot be avoided

    (C) If they can avoid bankruptcy

    (D) If bankruptcy will be avoided

    (E) Unless it goes bankrupt

24. Now that I have read the works of both Henry and William James, I am convinced that Henry is <u>the best psychologist and William the best writer</u>.

    (A) the best psychologist and William the best writer

    (B) a better psychologist, William is the best writer

    (C) the best as a psychologist, William the best as a writer

    (D) the best psychologist, William the better writer

    (E) the better psychologist and William the better writer

25. When he arrived at the hospital, the doctor found that <u>several emergency cases had been admitted before</u> he went on duty.

    (A) several emergency cases had been admitted before

    (B) there were several emergency cases admitted prior to

    (C) two emergency cases were being admitted before

    (D) a couple of emergency cases were admitted before

    (E) several emergency cases was admitted before

GO ON TO THE NEXT PAGE ⇨

26. The variety of Scandinavian health care services offered to residents at reduced cost <u>far exceeds low-cost health programs</u> available in the United States.

    (A) far exceeds low-cost health programs
    (B) far exceeds the number of low-cost health programs
    (C) tends to be greater than low-cost programs
    (D) far exceed the number of low-cost health programs
    (E) are greater than comparable low-cost health programs

27. The politician is benefiting from behavioral <u>research, there are new techniques for them</u> to utilize and new broadcasting methods to experiment with.

    (A) research, there are new techniques for them
    (B) research; there are new techniques for them
    (C) research; he has new techniques
    (D) research, there are new techniques for him
    (E) research; they have new techniques

28. <u>The poet Oscar Wilde was known for his aphoristic wit and brilliant conversation, he</u> wrote a number of memorable literary essays including "The Critic as Artist."

    (A) The poet Oscar Wilde was known for his aphoristic wit and brilliant conversation, he
    (B) The poet Oscar Wilde, known for his aphoristic wit and brilliant conversation; he
    (C) Known for his aphoristic wit and brilliant conversation, the poet Oscar Wilde
    (D) The poet Oscar Wilde was known for his aphoristic wit and brilliant conversation, however he
    (E) Oscar Wilde, the poet, known for his aphoristic wit and brilliant conversation, and he

29. According to Westin's book, <u>the typical Victorian family was more interested in maintaining the appearance of propriety than in</u> securing happiness for its individual members.

    (A) the typical Victorian family was more interested in maintaining the appearance of propriety than in
    (B) the appearance of propriety was more interesting to the typical Victorian family than
    (C) the typical Victorian family, more interested in maintaining the appearance of propriety than it was in
    (D) for a Victorian family it was typical that they would be more interested in maintaining the appearance of propriety than in
    (E) the typical Victorian family was more interested in the appearance of propriety than in

30. <u>Once an enclave of privileged white males, the Wodehouse Club's directors have</u> now decided to adopt a more inclusive membership policy.

    (A) Once an enclave of privileged white males, the Wodehouse Club's directors have
    (B) The directors of the Wodehouse Club, which was once an enclave of privileged white males, have
    (C) Though once an enclave of privileged white males, the Wodehouse Club's directors
    (D) Once an enclave of privileged white males, the Wodehouse Club's directors having
    (E) The directors of the enclave of privileged white males, the Wodehouse Club, has

GO ON TO THE NEXT PAGE

31. Supporters of the Eighteenth Amendment thought that banning alcohol would improve citizens' morals and enhance their quality of life by removing the temptation to drink; <u>national prohibition</u> ushered in thirteen years of bootlegging, speakeasies, and violent gangster crime.

    (A) national prohibition
    (B) in fact, national prohibition
    (C) furthermore, national prohibition
    (D) but national prohibition
    (E) consequently, national prohibition

32. Though multimedia presentations have their place in the school curriculum, it is ridiculous to claim, as some do, <u>that children learn as much from watching a one-hour video as a book.</u>

    (A) that children learn as much from watching a one-hour video as a book
    (B) that children will learn as much from watching a one-hour video as they did from a book
    (C) that children learn as much from watching a one-hour video as they do from reading a book
    (D) that a one-hour video teaches more to children than book-reading
    (E) that children watching a one-hour video learn as much as reading a book

33. Finland's national epic, the *Kalevala*, <u>based on an oral tradition that</u> the Balto-Finnish people preserved for some 2,500 years despite the upheavals of history and the pressures of foreign domination.

    (A) based on an oral tradition that
    (B) being based on an oral tradition that
    (C) is based on an oral tradition; this
    (D) basing itself on an oral tradition which
    (E) is based on an oral tradition that

34. The island of Santa Ynez was once a playground for wealthy American tourists; in recent years, however, civil unrest and a series of natural disasters <u>have made it so that it is not nearly as appealing</u> as a vacation spot.

    (A) have made it so that it is not nearly as appealing
    (B) are causing it to be made less appealing
    (C) greatly reducing its appeal
    (D) have greatly lessened its appeal
    (E) have not nearly made it as appealing

GO ON TO THE NEXT PAGE

Directions: The passage below is an early draft of an essay. Parts of the passage need to be rewritten.

Read the passage, and answer the questions that follow. Some questions are about individual sentences or parts of sentences; in these questions, you are asked to select the choice which will improve sentence structure and word choice. Other questions refer to parts of the essay or the entire essay and ask you to consider the organization and development of the essay. You should follow the conventions of standard written English in answering the questions. After you have chosen your answer, fill in the corresponding oval on your answer sheet.

Questions 35–39 are based on the following essay, which is a response to an assignment to write about an economic issue facing the United States.

(1) *Last year, my social studies class attended a talk given by a young woman who worked in a factory in Central America making shirts for a popular U.S. retail chain.* (2) *The working conditions she described were horrific.* (3) *She spoke of being forced to work 14-hour days and even longer on weekends.* (4) *The supervisors often hit her and the other women, most of whom were teenagers, to get them to work faster.* (5) *They gave them contaminated water to drink and were only allowed to go to the bathroom twice a day.* (6) *She urged us to boycott the retail chain and to inform consumers about the conditions in their factories.*

(7) *A group of us decided to meet with a representative of the chain and we would discuss our concerns and would announce our plans to boycott.* (8) *The representative said that low wages were necessary to keep costs down.* (9) *And she claimed a boycott would never work because it would be impossible to stop people from shopping at such a popular store.* (10) *"Nobody is going to listen to a bunch of teenagers," she said.* (11) *We decided to prove her wrong.*

(12) *First, we calculated that the workers' wages accounted for less than one percent of the price people paid for the shirts in the United States.* (13) *We argued that if the chain were willing to make slightly lower profits, it could afford to pay the workers more without raising prices.* (14) *And when we began informing people about the conditions under which the shirts they bought were made, they were horrified.* (15) *Many were agreeing to shop there no longer, they even wrote letters to the president of the chain in which he was urged to do something about the conditions in the factories.* (16) *Even local politicians got involved.* (17) *The winner of that year's City Council election pledged to change the condi-*

tions in the factories or shut the store down once and for all. (18) *Finally, with business almost at a standstill, the store agreed to consumers' demands.*

35. In context, which is the best version of the underlined portion of sentence 5 (reproduced below)?

    They gave them contaminated water to drink and were only allowed to go to the bathroom twice a day.

    (A) (As it is now)
    (B) and were only allowing them to go
    (C) and only allowed them to go
    (D) and they were only given permission to go
    (E) and were allowed to only go

36. In context, which of the following best replaces the word "their" in sentence 6 (reproduced below)?

    She urged us to boycott the retail chain and to inform consumers about the conditions in their factories.

    (A) the consumers'
    (B) its
    (C) the workers'
    (D) the company's
    (E) the students'

GO ON TO THE NEXT PAGE

37. Which of the following versions of the underlined portion of sentence 7 (reproduced below) is best?

    A group of us decided to meet with a representative of the chain __and we would discuss our concerns and would announce__ our plans to boycott.

    (A) (As it is now)
    (B) to discuss our concerns and announce
    (C) for the purpose of discussing our concerns and announcing
    (D) where we would discuss our concerns and announce
    (E) with whom we would be discussing our concerns and to whom we would announce

38. Which of the following would be the best replacement for the word "And" at the beginning of sentence 9 (reproduced below)?

    And she claimed a boycott would never work because it would be impossible to stop people from shopping at such a popular store.

    (A) Moreover,
    (B) Rather,
    (C) However,
    (D) Even so,
    (E) Instead,

39. In context, which of the following is the best way to revise the underlined portion of sentence 15 (reproduced below)?

    __Many were agreeing to shop there no longer, they even wrote letters to the president of the chain in which he was urged__ to do something about the conditions in the factories.

    (A) (As it is now)
    (B) Many agreed to no longer shop there and even writing letters to the president of the chain to urge him
    (C) Agreeing to shop there no longer, many even wrote letters to the president of the chain urging him
    (D) Many agreed to no longer shop there and also to urge the president of the chain by writing letters in which they asked him
    (E) Shopping there no longer, many agreed to write letters to the president of the chain to urge him

ANSWER KEY ON FOLLOWING PAGE

Practice Test One: **Answer Key**

SECTION ONE

1. A	9. A	17. D
2. B	10. E	18. D
3. A	11. B	19. A
4. C	12. A	20. B
5. E	13. D	21. C
6. C	14. C	22. D
7. B	15. A	23. A
8. C	16. E	24. C

SECTION TWO

1. D	8. D	15. E
2. B	9. A	16. E
3. B	10. E	17. B
4. B	11. E	18. A
5. C	12. B	
6. B	13. A	
7. A	14. C	

SECTION THREE

25. B	33 B	41. C
26. D	34. A	42. E
27. C	35. C	43. A
28. C	36. A	44. C
29. C	37. C	45. C
30. D	38. C	46. A
31. D	39. D	47. C
32. C	40. A	48. E

SECTION FOUR

19. E	31. 1,296
20. B	32. $\frac{5}{24}$ or .208
21. D	33. 9
22. D	34. 36
23. C	35. 45
24. A	36. 5
25. A	37. 48
26. B	38. $\frac{49}{4}$ or 12.25
27. E	
28. B	
29. 5	
30. 1	

SECTION FIVE

1. C	14. E	27. C
2. C	15. A	28. C
3. D	16. E	29. A
4. B	17. C	30. B
5. A	18. D	31. B
6. E	19. B	32. C
7. B	20. A	33. E
8. A	21. E	34. D
9. D	22. B	35. C
10. A	23. E	36. D
11. C	24. E	37. B
12. A	25. A	38. A
13. A	26. B	39. C

Answers and Explanations

SECTION ONE

1. A

The clue word "While" tells you that this sentence has a contrast. You need a word that will contrast with *familiar*. (A) *surprising* matches this prediction.

2. B

For this straight-ahead sentence, you need a choice with either two positive words or two negative words. The chairman would either *support* the decision because it *reinforced* worthwhile ideals, or *bemoan* the decision because it *went against* worthwhile ideals. Only choice (B) fits the bill with two negative words, *lamented* and *repudiation*.

3. A

Since Balanchine worked "within a classical context," he must have done something different in order to "challenge convention." You can predict that he used "traditional idioms" in new ways. *Novel*, choice (A), matches this prediction.

4. C

Start with the second part of the sentence. One brother is "quiet," the other "brash." Look for a word that goes with "brash" to fit the second blank, and a word that means *not alike* for the first blank. Choice (C), *dissimilar . . audacious*, does the trick.

5. E

The most important phrase in the sentence is "Prior to." Before America entered the war, Wilson couldn't maintain the *involvement* (A) or *belligerence* (B) of the United States, and (C) and (D) just don't make sense. (E) *neutrality* accurately represents the prewar status.

6. C

Start with the first blank of this contrasting sentence. The movie star's ex was bitter, so you need a word that goes with bitter, like *hateful* (A) or *malicious* (C). This bitter

memoir is a "betrayal" of their past, so you need a positive word for the second blank. *Intimacy*, choice (C), matches the prediction.

7. B

The clue word "whereas" tells you that this is a contrasting sentence, so you need a choice with contrasting words. Only choice (B), *original . . derivative*, provides the needed contrast.

Manifest Destiny Passages

8. C

The author uses the phrase "Manifest Destiny" in the second sentence. Immediately following this, she goes on to say "Americans believed that it was their mission to claim all the land from the Atlantic to the Pacific." This is the implied definition of "Manifest Destiny." You need a choice that talks about the expansion of America from east to west, and (C) fits the bill. Watch out for (A)—Americans may have desired to settle the west, but they saw "Manifest Destiny" as a mission, not just a desire. In pursuing their "Manifest Destiny," 19th century Americans operated on a prejudice but this prejudice isn't a definition of "Manifest Destiny" (D).

9. A

The context here is, "Fueled by fears of English alliances with Mexico, the aftermath of two economic depressions, and a desire to expand the slave trade, Americans, *egged on* by the politicians of the time, pushed westward . . ." A good prediction is "strongly encouraged," and that matches (A).

10. E

The author of Passage 1 approves of "Manifest Destiny" and says that despite the prejudices of 19th century Americans, the goal was just. The author of Passage 2 says that the pursuit of "Manifest Destiny" had tragic consequences—the loss of Native American culture and the ruin of the wilderness. He would most likely respond to author 1 by re-iterating his alternative point of view (E). In any case he would not have a positive response, like (B) and (C). (A) is too extreme—there's no indication that the author of Passage 1 is naive.

11. B

When answering questions about what both authors would agree with, be careful of trap answers that express the opinion of only one of the authors, and eliminate those choices that don't express the opinion of both authors. (A) only fits with Passage 1, while (C) and (D) are mentioned only in Passage 2. (E) talks about the inevitability of Manifest Destiny, which is not mentioned in either passage. (B), however, fits with both passages—it's mentioned in the third sentence of Passage 1, and the second sentence of Passage 2.

Music History Passage

This passage, which focuses on the effect of societal currents on women's participation in music, is somewhat dense, so you should read through it fairly quickly to get the gist, noting important themes in each paragraph as you go.

Paragraph one gives an overview of the social and political climate of the first half of the nineteenth century and the effect of this climate on the middle class, particularly with regard to music. In paragraph two, the author explains that, despite the increased access to music that the middle class enjoyed at this time, women were still excluded from participation in many musical activities. Paragraph three explains that negative opinions about women and music can be traced to eighteenth-century notions. Rousseau and Campe are quoted in this paragraph. Paragraph four continues the idea that women were restricted from full participation in the musical world and cites the example of Clara Schumann. Paragraph five outlines the accomplishments of Clara Schumann and introduces the idea of the "art song."

12. A

In the first paragraph, we learn that women's involvement with music was thought to enhance their marriageability, enhance their families' social status and help in child-rearing. This is best characterized by choice (A), since all of these forms of participation are consistent with women's traditional family roles.

13. D

Reread the second paragraph, including the cited lines. If you have trouble rephrasing an answer, test each of the choices. It's most reasonable to infer that, since women at this time needed men's support and advice, they must have conformed to society's expectations. None of the other choices is supported by the passage.

14. C

As we saw in the overview of the passage, paragraph three focuses on the influence of eighteenth-century opinions of women. Choice (C) explains that these beliefs were long-standing, which is supported by the information in this paragraph.

15. A

Reread the lines surrounding the cited word for this vocabulary-in-context question. What word could you substitute for "sensibility"? "Ability" would work, and choice (A), *aptitude*, does the trick. Choice (E), *knowledge*, is incorrect since the following sentence talks about the acquisition of musical knowledge as a distraction from women's duties.

16. E

Rereading the quote from Campe, you see that his focus is on the idea that music distracts women from their duties as wives, housekeepers, and mothers. This idea is paraphrased in choice (E).

17. D

The fourth paragraph focuses on society's negative view of women who performed music publicly or composed music. The topic of Clara Schumann is raised in this context, and the author's discussion of "societal censure" and "internal conflicts" lead us to believe that Schumann's lack of confidence was a product of society's views. This idea is paraphrased in choice (D).

18. D

Take the choices one by one, looking for evidence to support them in the passage. Paragraph one explicitly outlines the advantages of having a musically educated daughter (marriage, social status, enhanced mothering abilities), so choice (A) is wrong. Paragraph two tells us that women could be forbidden to play publicly, publish music, or accept fees, so (B) is out. Paragraph three is about eighteenth-century views of women, which was the intellectual source of nineteenth-century beliefs, knocking (C) out of the running. Choice (E) is negated by the information in the first paragraph about the burgeoning music business. Choice (D), Schumann's influence on general attitudes about women in music, is not mentioned, and it's correct.

Evolution Passage

This science passage is fairly straightforward and doesn't contain much scientific jargon, so you should be able to skim through it, taking note of the structure of the passage and its general themes.

Paragraph one introduces the concept of evolution as a process of gradual improvement whereby competition among species leads to the survival of superior species. Paragraph two introduces Darwin and his "wedges" model of interspecies competition, citing clams and brachiopods as examples. Paragraph three outlines Gould and Calloway's research into clams and brachiopods, which contradicts Darwin's theories. Paragraph four describes the theory of Gould and Calloway, which claims that environmental change is more important than competition in the survival of species. Paragraph five explores the implications for the status of Homo sapiens under Gould and Calloway's evolutionary scenario.

19. A

The general focus of the passage is on Gould and Calloway's conclusions about clams and brachiopods and the impact of their work on Darwin's theory of evolution. Choice (A) paraphrases this idea, and is correct. Choice (C) is too harsh, choice (D) is too specific, and choices (B) and (E) are just off-base.

20. B

The cited line shows the author poking a bit of fun at the human race's desire to see itself as superior to other species. Choice (B) gets to the heart of the quote, explaining that scientists might want to see their own species as the most advanced.

21. C

Darwin's "wedges" model, as described in the second paragraph, shows nature as a surface covered with thousands of sharp wedges jostling for the same space. These wedges represent competing species, choice (C).

22. D

The third paragraph focuses on Gould and Calloway's evidence about clams and brachiopods, asserting that the two species never competed for the same turf, and that the decline of brachiopods seems to have been caused by an environmental impact. Choices (A) and (C) are too strong;

choice (B) directly contradicts the passage; choice (E) is supported, but it's not the reason that the evidence is presented. Choice (D) correctly summarizes the author's reasons for presenting the evidence.

23. A

Read the entire sentence. A comet is directly referred to as a possible cause for the decline of brachiopods, choice (A). All the other choices are unsubstantiated or beyond the scope of the passage.

24. C

The final paragraph focuses on the status of humans in light of Gould and Calloway's new theories about evolution, and the author would most likely agree with choice (C). All the other choices are outside the scope of the author's possible conclusions, based on the information in the passage.

SECTION TWO

1. D

The hundredths' digit is the second digit after the decimal point, which, in this case, is 8.

2. B

Check out each of the choices. You can stop at choice (B), since $4x + 5x$ equals $9x$, not $9x^2$.

3. B

To simplify the equation, begin by doing the same thing to both sides. Multiply both sides by 3, and you get $2x = 90$, so $x = \dfrac{90}{2} = 45$, which is your answer.

4. B

The circle represents 100 percent of the household expenses. We need the region that represents rent, $33\frac{1}{3}$ percent of the whole. Since $33\frac{1}{3}$ is one-third of 100, you can eyeball the graph and find the region that represents one-third of the circle, region B.

5. C

Draw a diagram representing the rectangle divided into two squares. Since squares have equal sides and each square has an area of 25, each side of a square must be 5. Add 5 + 5 for the short sides of the rectangle, and 10 + 10 for the long sides, and you get your answer, 30.

6. B

Start by using the average rate formula to calculate the distance that John drove. Distance = Rate × Time. Distance = 48 miles per hour × 2.25 hours, so the distance is 108 miles. For John to drive the same distance in 2 hours, set up the equation: 108 (distance traveled = Rate × 2 (number of hours)). Your answer is 54, choice (B).

7. A

In order to solve for x, replace x in the equation with its value, $\sqrt{7}$. You get $(\sqrt{7} + 1)(\sqrt{7} - 1)$. Use FOIL (first, outer, inner, last) and you get $7 - \sqrt{7} + \sqrt{7} - 1$. The square roots of 7 cancel each other out, and you have $7 - 1 = 6$, choice (A).

8. D

First, let's convert from percent to fractions by dividing $66\frac{2}{3}$ by 100. You get $x = \frac{2}{3}y$. You can then solve for y by multiplying both sides by $\frac{3}{2}$, and your result is $\frac{3}{2}x = y$. You can then change back to percents by multiplying by 100 and find that y is 150 percent of x, choice (D).

9. A

Start by finding the least common multiple of 4, 6, and 10. It's 60. You can then check each of the choices to see if it's a factor of 60. Choice (A), 8, is the correct answer since it's not a factor of 60.

10. E

You may have been able to pick out the right answer without doing the calculation by realizing that the final sum is just $\frac{1}{64}$ shy of 1, or $\frac{63}{64}$. Otherwise, you would begin by finding the least common denominator for all the fractions, which is 64, and add them up. 63 is your final numerator.

11. E

Start with what you know about the shaded square. Since its area is 3, each side must be $\sqrt{3}$. The two vertical sides of the square each form a leg of a 30-60-90 right triangle, making the short legs 1 each and the longer legs 2 each. The top of the square is also $\sqrt{3}$, so the other legs of the upper equilateral triangle are also $\sqrt{3}$. Therefore, each side of the large equilateral triangle is $2 + \sqrt{3}$. Multiply by three and you get $6 + 3\sqrt{3}$, choice (E).

12. B

In order to add these square roots, you need to simplify them. $\sqrt{48}$ simplifies to $\sqrt{16} \times \sqrt{3}$, or $4\sqrt{3}$. $\sqrt{12}$ simplifies to $\sqrt{4} \times \sqrt{3}$, or $2\sqrt{3}$. So you now have $4\sqrt{3} + 2\sqrt{3} + \sqrt{3} = (4 + 2 + 1)\sqrt{3} = 7\sqrt{3}$, choice (B).

If you hate simplifying square roots, you could instead guesstimate your way to the answer (but you still have to know that $\sqrt{3}$ is close to 1.7). For instance, $\sqrt{48}$ is slightly less than 7, $\sqrt{12}$ is a bit more than 3, and $\sqrt{3}$ is slightly less than 2, so a good guesstimate for $\sqrt{48} + \sqrt{12} + \sqrt{3}$ is around $7 + 3 + 2$, or about 12. Of the answer choices, only (B), $7\sqrt{3} \approx 7 \times 1.7 \approx 12$, comes even close.

13. A

Set up an equation, replacing x and y in the symbol definition with the numbers and variables in the question stem: $3^2 + \frac{4}{2} = 5^2 + \frac{n}{2}$. Now solve for n: $11 = 25 + \frac{n}{2}$, so $11 - 25 = \frac{n}{2}$. Thus $n = 2(-14) = -28$, choice (A).

14. C

Average × Number of items = Sum. We know the average, 4, and the number of items, 3, and $4 \times 3 = 12$. If the sum of the three *distinct positive* integers is 12, the greatest possible value of one number can't be 11 (D) or 12 (E). 9 (D) works, which means the other numbers in the average are 2 and 1. You can check your work by averaging 9, 2, and 1, and sure enough, you get 4.

15. E

Since this is a right triangle, you can use the Pythagorean theorem to find the length of the second leg: $a^2 + b^2 = c^2$. Your equation will look like this: $(x + 2)^2 + b^2 = (x + 3)^2$.

Multiplying out both sides, you get $x^2 + 4x + 4 + b^2 = x^2 + 6x + 9$. To isolate b^2 on the left side, subtract $x^2 + 4x + 4$ from both sides, leaving $b^2 = 2x + 5$. Your answer for the value of b, then, is the square root of $2x + 5$, choice (E).

16. E

For remainder questions like this one, begin by picking a number for n. Since the remainder when n is divided by 9 is 7, pick any multiple of 9 and add 7. The easiest multiple is 9, so $9 + 7 = 16$. Plug 16 into the question and see what happens. $5 \times 16 = 80$; $80 \div 9 = 8$ remainder 8. Bingo! It's choice (E).

17. B

You may want to do a quick sketch to set this one up. Be sure as well to read the question carefully. Box A contains 4 black marbles and 1 white marble, for a ratio of 4:1. Box B contains 4 black marbles and 3 white marbles, for a ratio of 4:3. You want to move the minimum number of marbles from Box A to Box B, so start with 1 *black* marble (since Box A has the higher ratio of black to white marbles). You're left with 3:1 in Box A, and 5:3 in Box B. No luck, so move another marble. After a second black marble is moved, you're left with 2:1 in Box A and 6:3 in Box B. 2:1 and 6:3 are the same ratio, so choice (B), 2 marbles moved, is the correct answer.

18. A

Since r is cubed, if its value is multiplied by $\frac{1}{2}$, the value of V must be multiplied by $\frac{1}{8}$. To prove this, pick a number for r. If $r = 2$, $r^3 = 8$; $2 \times \frac{1}{2} = 1$, and $1^3 = 1$, which is $\frac{1}{8}$ of 8. Choice (A) is correct.

SECTION THREE

25. B

The key words here are "pollution" and "environmental benefits." You need a word that explains that the negative pollution may offset the benefits of the cars. Only choice (B), *outweigh*, matches this prediction.

26. D

The key word "but" tells you that this is a contrasting sentence. Look for a positive word for the first blank, like *impressed* (A) or *fired* (D). Note that the word "fired" could seem negative in a job context, but here it's positive, because the popular imagination was "set on fire." *Disputed*, a negative word, provides the contrast you need for the second blank, making choice (D) correct.

27. C

This question tests your vocabulary. Look among the choices for a word that goes with "starve." *Emaciated* (C) means extremely thin, and is the correct answer.

28. C

"Despite" is the key word that tips you off that this is a contrasting sentence. Look for a choice that provides two contrasting words. Only choice (C) gives you the contrast that you need, since *interaction* is positive, and *enmity* is negative.

29. C

This contrasting sentence is a little confusing because of the word "not." Rephrasing the sentence, "downsizing" is "becoming a permanent feature," so downsizing is probably not temporary. *Ephemeral*, choice (C), matches this prediction and is correct.

30. D

This is a long sentence, so focus first on the second part. Rephrasing, you see that patriarchy dominates because political and social forces do something with it. This must be a positive word, like "support." You can eliminate choices (A) and (C). Looking back at the whole sentence, you see that if these "social forces" are what's supporting patriarchy, patriarchy must not be a natural instinct for humans. *Instinctive* (D) matches this prediction and is correct.

31. D

For function questions like this one, put yourself in the author's shoes—why would she write such a sentence? The author starts with this question to let you know what the topic of the passage (A). She could have done it the conventional way; something like: "Scientists couldn't decide whether platypuses and echidnas were mammals or reptiles." Instead, she chose a more dramatic beginning—asking the same question that the scientists she discusses were asking.

32. C

When you back up a couple of lines from the discussion of eyes and ears, you see the phrase "For example." So what are the eyes and ears examples of? "These animals have some things in common with reptiles and some things in common with mammals." That fits (A) pretty well. Watch out for choice (B). It looks reasonable (it's about the differences between the two types of animals), but it doesn't quite work, since the author doesn't make such a definitive statement.

Blue-Star Woman Passage

This fiction passage tells the story of a Native American woman's struggle for identity as she tries to reconcile her lost culture with the laws of the country in which she lives. Read through the passage, focusing on the themes of names and laws that are repeated in the text.

33. B

The author's focus is on Blue-Star Woman and the effect of a changing world on her identity. Only choice (B) accurately describes the purpose of this personal story. All of the other choices are too abstract or outside the scope.

34. A

In the cited lines, Blue-Star Woman is compared to the ground squirrel, a creature living close to nature. The author has probably chosen this simile in order to reinforce the connection between her character and the natural world, choice (A).

35. C

Since the landowner's attitude toward Blue-Star Woman's occupation of his land is described as "easy," we can assume that she is allowed to stay there. *Permission* (C) conveys this idea. Choices (A) and (E) are negative words, and (B) and (D) don't work in this context.

36. A

In the second paragraph, the formal nature of the white man's law is contrasted with Blue-Star Woman's more emotional view of what is right. While the law of the land requires proof of tribal membership, the "law of heart" allows a person a piece of earth by virtue of her existence. This is paraphrased in choice (A).

37. C

You may need to carefully reread the third paragraph to get this one right. In lines 30–40, the official requires Blue-Star Woman to name her parents, which goes against her belief that the names of the dead shouldn't be spoken. This point, choice (C), is the key juxtaposition. Choice (A) might have been tempting, but earlier in the paragraph the author explains that pronouncing one's own name is no longer forbidden.

38. C

As we see throughout the passage, Blue-Star Woman's name is a symbol of her identity and culture. By stating that her name seems meaningless, she implies that her culture and customs are also losing their meaning.

39. D

This is an old-fashioned expression that means dating (D). If you weren't sure of the meaning, the context is a help, and you can always eliminate clearly wrong answers. For example, the author doesn't tell you how Rowan and Miss Ashley spent all their time (A). Be wary of extreme language in answer choices like *all*. This is a trap for those test takers who read "stepping out" too literally. Also, although you know they have been dating for a year, you don't know whether the author thinks that's too long.

40. A

Prior to this sentence, you read about how quiet Miss Ashley was, and how Rowan did most of the talking. You can infer that he likes quiet women who let him talk (A). (D) might be tempting, since Rowan did discuss business, but this is not very in keeping with the rest of the passage. (Rowan doesn't seem to have such progressive views.) Although (E) might also seem tempting at first, since Rowan spun dreams about the future, the author doesn't tell you if Miss Ashley shared these dreams.

The Black Leaders Pair

You're presented with a pair of passages, both excerpted from the writings of American black leaders. You should begin by reading through the first passage and answering the questions that pertain to it, questions 41–43. You can then read the second passage and attack the rest of the questions. Passage 1 is from the writings of Booker T.

Washington. It outlines Washington's views on the means by which black Americans could win individual and political rights, focusing on his belief that "slow but sure influences" and "natural, slow growth" are most likely to be successful.

41. C

Washington first refers to Southern whites in the first paragraph, in which he declares his belief that political rights will eventually be granted to blacks, once whites no longer feel forced to do so. This sentiment is echoed in choice (C). None of the other choices can be substantiated.

42. E

In lines 26–29, Washington states his beliefs about the reasons that the Atlanta officials invited him to speak at the Exposition. He viewed his selection as a reward for "merit in the Negro race" and not solely a reflection of his own talent or status, choice (E).

43. A

Reread the whole sentence surrounding the cited words. The "slow but sure influences" proceed from accomplishments such as the possession of property and good character, which is a paraphrase of choice (A).

44. C

Passage 2 contrasts sharply with the first passage, as Du Bois accuses Washington of representing "the old attitude of adjustment and submission." Du Bois advocates a more proactive approach and condemns Washington's methods, claiming that they have caused more harm than good.

Reread lines 10–16 in Passage 2. In the latter part of the sentence, Du Bois explains that, historically, races that have allowed themselves to surrender respect have been seen by their oppressors as unworthy of civilization. Du Bois cites this historical context to highlight the status of black people, showing that submission is not the way to win respect. Choice (C) is a good paraphrase of this idea.

45. C

This question might seem a little tricky, but if you reread the surrounding lines, it should become clearer. In lines 25–29 Du Bois describes the "palm-branch," Washington's policy of asking black people to give up certain rights. In lines 27–34, Du Bois outlines the negative consequences of this policy, a policy with which he clearly does not

agree. Thus, we can see that his reference to the "palm-branch," usually a metaphor for a gesture of peace, is ironic, and his tone critical, as described in choice (C). Other negative-sounding choices may have been tempting, but he is certainly not *distanced* (A), *mournful* (B), *surprised* (D) or *apathetic* (E).

46. A

As you may remember from question 43, Washington believed that whites would eventually grant blacks rights without any undue pressure, due to the essential goodness of human nature. Du Bois has a much more cynical attitude (which he justifies in his passage), and he would surely view Washington's view of human nature as excessively naive, choice (A). None of the other choices can be inferred from what we know of Du Bois's views.

47. C

It's hard to imagine that these two authors would agree on anything! Choice (C), however, seems to be the most reasonable assumption, since Washington speaks about the need for patience and Du Bois about the need for meaningful action. (A), the use of force, is not discussed by either writer. (B) vaguely contradicts Washington's feelings about the inclination of whites to reward the accomplishments of blacks. (D) and (E) aren't supported by either passage.

48. E

None of the other choices is specific enough to reflect the content of these two passages.

SECTION FOUR

19. E

Don't be intimidated by the number of variables in this question. Take one step at a time, keeping in mind that sometimes the data that are most helpful to use first are provided last—in this case, the first useful piece of information is the fact that $z = 4$:

Use $z = 4$ to determine y:

$y = 5z$

$y = 5(4)$

$y = 20$

Now use $y = 20$ to solve for x:

$x - y = 6$

$x - 20 = 6$

$x = 26$

20. B

Translate bit by bit:

"The sum of $9a$ and the square root of $2b$" means $9a + \sqrt{2b}$; "is equal to" means $=$; and "the square of the sum of $3a$ and $3b$" means $(3a + 3b)^2$.

21. D

If one pound serves 9 children and there are 15 children, then we need $\frac{15}{9}$ or 1.67 pounds to feed the children. If one pound serves 7 adults, and we have 60 adults, then we need $\frac{60}{7}$ or 8.57 pounds to feed the adults. So, in total we need $1.67 + 8.57$ or 10.24 pounds to feed all 75 people, which rounds up to 11 pounds.

22. D

The trickiest part of this question is realizing that 3^{-3} is the same as $\frac{1}{3^3}$, so

$3^{-3} + \left(\frac{1}{3}\right)^3 = \frac{1}{3^3} + \frac{1^3}{3^3} = \frac{1}{27} + \frac{1}{27} = \frac{2}{27}$

23. C

Replace every x in the expression with $\frac{1}{2}$ and then evaluate:

$\frac{2}{x} + \frac{2}{(x-1)} = \frac{2}{(\frac{1}{2})} + \frac{2}{((\frac{1}{2})-1)} = 4 + \left(\frac{2}{[-\frac{1}{2}]}\right) =$

$4 + (-4) = 0$

24. A

If $.2J = 1,500$, then $J = \frac{1,500}{.2} = 7,500$, and $.15J = .15(7,500) = 1,125$. Another road to the answer is to realize that because 15 is $\frac{3}{4}$ of 20, 15% of J must be $\frac{3}{4}$ of 20% of J, and $\frac{3}{4}(1,500) = 1,125$.

25. A

All of the answer choices are perfect squares, but all the ones other than (A) have other factors besides themselves, their square roots, and 1. To consider just some examples: (B) has 27 as a factor; (C) has 25 and 50; (D) has 72; (E) has 25. (A) is the only one that fits the criteria of the question, its only factors being 49, 7, and 1. Why? Only (A) is the square of a prime number.

26. B

Pick numbers. All of the choices, except (B), can be ruled out by squaring the first few integers. $1^2 = 1$; $5^2 = 25$; $6^2 = 36$; $7^2 = 49$. Nothing squared ends in 3.

27. E

Raise each of the three terms in the expression to the fourth power:

$(-3x^5y^4)^4 = (-3)^4[(x^5)^4][(y^4)^4] = 81x^{20}y^{16}$

28. B

Cross-multiply each choice. You will find that (A), (C), (D), and (E) are equivalent to $jm = kl$. Only (B) cross-multiplies to $jk = ml$.

29. 5

The intersection of sets is their overlap. $A = \{1, 2, 3, 4, 5, 6, 7, 8, 9, 0\}$ and $B = \{\text{even numbers}\}$. The overlap of these sets is $\{2, 4, 6, 8, 0\}$, which contains five elements.

30. 1

Radical equations follow the same rules as other equations; just remember that the solution to radical equations often entails squaring both sides:

$\sqrt{2-x} - 1 = 0$

$\sqrt{2-x} = 1$

$(\sqrt{2-x})^2 = (1)^2$

$2 - x = 1$

$1 = x$

31. 1,296

You just need to do some quick calculations. $8 \times 9 = 72$. Half of 72 is 36, and 36 squared is 1,296, your answer.

32. $\frac{5}{24}$ or .208

Use the average formula.

Average $= \dfrac{\text{Sum}}{\text{Number of elements}}$. The sum equals

$\dfrac{1}{4} + \dfrac{1}{6} = \dfrac{6}{24} + \dfrac{4}{24} = \dfrac{10}{24}$, so the average is half that, or $\dfrac{5}{24}$.

33. 9

Begin by picking a number for *A*. *A* can only be 4 or 9, since the unit digit of *A* + *A* equals 8. Start with 4: you get 4 + 4 = 8 in the ones column. In the tens column, plug in 4 for *A*. What number could you plug in for *B* so that you have the same number for both *B*s? That doesn't seem to work, so let's try 9; 9 + 9 = 18, so you carry a 1. In the tens column, 9, plus the 1 you carried, plus what would give you the same number for both *B*s? In fact, any digit except for 0 and 9 could be *B*. So, 9 is the correct answer.

34. 36

Start by finding the measure of ∠*BAC*. Since ∠*CAE* is 73 degrees, and *BAE* is 90 degrees, you can subtract 90 − 73 = 17 to get the degree measure of ∠*BAC*. ∠*BAD* is 53 degrees, so subtract again: 53 − 17 = 36, your answer.

35. 45

We know that the circumference is 9π, and since the circumference formula is 2π*r*, the radius is 4.5. Each short side of the rectangle is 4.5 × 2 = 9. Each long side is 4.5 × 3 = 13.5. Add the sides: 13.5 + 13.5 + 9 + 9 = 45.

36. 5

Start by figuring out how many cookies were eaten. Nuala started with 64, and 9 were left: 64 − 9 = 55. You need to pick a number of guests, a number greater than 9. Pick 11, since it's a factor of 55. If 11 guests ate 5 cookies each, you would be left with 9 cookies, which makes 5 the correct answer.

37. 48

The easiest way to solve this problem is to realize that a large box, at $5, costs $3 more than a small box, at $2. If all 150 of the boxes sold were small boxes, the total would have been $300, but the actual total, $444, is $144 more than that. Divide $144 by $3, and you will see that 48 of the boxes must have been large.

38. $\frac{49}{4}$ or 12.25

Begin by picking numbers for the sides of the rectangle. You could have 1 for the short sides and 6 for the long sides, giving you an area of 6. Picking 2 for the short sides and 5 for the long gives you an area of 10. Picking 3 for the short sides and 4 for the long sides gives you area 12. Did you notice that, the closer the numbers get, the larger the resulting area? Therefore, two numbers that are the same, 3.5 and 3.5 will give you the largest possible area, 12.25. Remember that squares fall under the category of rectangles, so it's OK to have a rectangle with equal sides. And it's handy to know that squares have the highest area-to-perimeter ratios of all rectangles.

SECTION FIVE

1. **C**

Bleeding, the gerund, is the subject of the verb *to be considered*, so you need to change the sentence to read *bleeding . . . was considered*.

2. **C**

The verb *improved* needs to be modified by an adverb. Change *dramatic* to *dramatically*.

3. **D**

This sentence has a word choice problem. *Respectively* is used when you consider one or more members of a group separately. In this case, the author is probably looking for the word *respectfully*, since the counselors are standing below the king's throne, showing their respect.

4. **B**

The second clause in this sentence lacks a verb. You could change *have agreement* to *have reached an agreement* or *have agreed*.

5. **A**

Have you ever heard "people aren't whiches" in your English class? That old grammar saying applies here: the delegates are people, so the sentence requires *who* instead of *which*.

6. E

This sentence contains no error.

7. B

The effort is the subject of the verb *to result*, and since *effort* is singular, the verb should be changed to *results*.

8. A

Every one is the subject of the verb *to be closed*. *Every one* takes the singular form of the verb, so it should read *was closed*.

9. D

Should not hardly just sounds wrong. There's no need for the word *hardly*, so you should omit it.

10. A

This question focuses on word choice. *Imaginary* refers to something that is not real, and the paper in question is surely real. *Imaginative* is a better choice here.

11. C

The *memoirs* are the subject of the verb *to promise*. Since *memoirs* are plural, you need the singular form, *promise*.

12. A

The point on issue just sounds wrong. The correct idiom is *point at issue*.

13. A

Raising is a form of the active verb "to raise." Since no one is performing an action, the passive verb "to rise" works better here to describe *rising living costs*.

14. E

This sentence contains no error.

15. A

The original sentence is best.

16. E

Choices (A), (B), and (D) contain *that* or *who*. These words seem to introduce an additional clause that never appears. Choice (E) uses the correct verb form *believe* and is correct.

17. C

Ask yourself: what was developed? As it stands, the sentence tells us that the president himself was developed by a scientific team (a scary thought!). Only choice (C) corrects the problem by providing a phrase that logically modifies *the president*.

18. D

The second part of the sentence describes regions that have certain characteristics. *Only* is the correct linking word to set those regions apart. Choice (C) doesn't make sense, so (D) is correct.

19. B

Choice (B) most clearly shows the connection between the first part of the sentence, the lingering political death, and the second part, the attempts of groups and individuals to prevent this demise. A conjunction like *although* is needed to show contrast and to link the two clauses.

20. A

This is a complex sentence, but the original sentence is best.

21. E

Choice (E) is the most clear and concise, omitting the unnecessary *when you are* from the original sentence.

22. B

Choices (A) and (C) use the passive voice, which is awkward. Choices (D) and (E) use incorrect forms of the conditional. (B) is the clearest choice.

23. E

The company is singular, so the use of the pronoun *they* in choices (A) and (C) is incorrect. Choices (B) and (D) awkwardly use the passive voice. (E) is the most clear and concise choice.

24. E

When comparing two people, *better* should be used instead of *best*. Only choice (E) does this correctly.

25. A

The original sentence is best.

26. B

The original sentence compares *the variety . . . of services* with *low-cost programs*, which doesn't make much sense. Choices (B) and (D) clarify the sentence by inserting *the number of*, and making a more appropriate comparison. However, choice (D) uses the wrong verb form, making choice (B) the best choice.

27. C

Choices (B), (C), and (E) all correctly use a semicolon to join the two independent clauses. Only choice (C), however, makes sense of the sentence by using *he* to refer to the politician.

28. C

(C) is the only choice which corrects this run-on sentence in a logical way: *Known for his aphoristic wit and brilliant conversation* introduces Oscar Wilde; the rest of the sentence provides additional information about him. (B) contains a fragment, (D) is a run-on which presents an illogical contrast between Wilde's wit and his writing, and (E) is extremely garbled.

29. A

The sentence is correct: *Maintaining* and *securing* are in the proper parallel form (both gerunds). (B) is convoluted and slightly alters the meaning of the sentence. (C) is a fragment. (D) is verbose and tangled. (E) has sacrificed correct parallel structure for the sake of brevity, comparing *the appearance* (a noun) to *securing* (a gerund).

30. B

The sentence contains a misplaced modifier: *Once an enclave of privileged white males* refers to *the Wodehouse Club*, not to its *directors*. Choice (B) correctly places the modifying phrase right next to the thing it's describing. (C) and (D) do not correct the misplaced modifier, and (D) is a fragment. (E) is poorly worded, and the verb has does not agree with the subject, *directors*.

31. B

What actually occurred when alcohol was banned turned out to be the opposite of what the prohibitionists had envisioned. Drinking continued (illegally) and crime actually increased. Therefore, you're looking for words that will express this ironic contrast between the idea and the reality. *In fact* is the best choice. (D) is wrong because although *but* expresses a contrast, it also creates a fragment (*but* must follow a comma, not a semicolon). (A), (C), and (E) fail to express the logical contrast between the two halves of the sentence.

32. C

What is being compared here? You can't compare an action (*watching* a video) to an object (*a book*)—it's not logical and it violates the rules of parallelism. (C) corrects the sentence by putting the two activities in parallel form. (B) fails to fix the parallelism problem, and it introduces strange and unnecessary changes in verb tense. (D) is awkwardly phrased (would you say "book-reading"?), and (E) also fails to fix the parallelism problem, creating a somewhat confusing comparison.

33. E

To correct this sentence fragment, all you need to do is insert the helping verb *is* before the participle based. *Based*, *being based*, and *basing* are all verb forms that cannot stand on their own as a sentence's main verb.

34. D

The underlined portion of the sentence is wordy and awkward. (D) expresses the same thought in a clearer, more concise way. (B) and (E) are just as convoluted as the original sentence, and (C) is a fragment.

35. C

They, the subject of the sentence, refers to the supervisors, while *them* refers to the workers. You need to change the sentence to clarify the fact that the supervisors only allowed the workers to go to the bathroom twice a day. Choice (C) clears things up: *They* (the supervisors) *only allowed them* (the workers) *to go*.

36. D

This question asks you to clear up the excessive use of pronouns in the paragraph. Choice (D), *the company's*, makes the most sense, since the factories belong to the company.

37. B

As it stands, the verb tenses in this sentence are confusing. Choice (B) makes the sentence clearer by eliminating the use of *would*.

38. A

When you reread the surrounding lines, you will see that sentence 9 provides additional information, but does not set up a contrast to earlier information. Only *moreover* (A) conveys this, since the linking words in all the other choices set up a contrast.

39. C

The original sentence misuses the passive voice and incorrectly joins independent clauses with a comma. Choice (C) clarifies the sentence by creating a dependent clause and using the correct active form of the verb "to write."

Chapter Seven: **Practice Test Two**

HOW TO TAKE THIS PRACTICE TEST

Before taking this practice test, find a quiet room where you can work uninterrupted for two and a half hours. Make sure you have a comfortable desk, your calculator, and several No. 2 pencils. Use the answer sheet to record your answers. Once you start, don't stop until you've finished. Remember—you can review any questions within a section, but you may not jump from one section to another.

PSAT Practice Test Two
Answer Sheet

Remove (or photocopy) this answer sheet and use it to complete the practice test. See the answer key following the test when finished. The "Compute Your Score" section at the end of Section Two will show you how to find your score.

Start with number 1 for each section. If a section has fewer questions than answer spaces, leave the extra spaces blank.

SECTION 1

1. Ⓐ Ⓑ Ⓒ Ⓓ Ⓔ	7. Ⓐ Ⓑ Ⓒ Ⓓ Ⓔ	13. Ⓐ Ⓑ Ⓒ Ⓓ Ⓔ	19. Ⓐ Ⓑ Ⓒ Ⓓ Ⓔ
2. Ⓐ Ⓑ Ⓒ Ⓓ Ⓔ	8. Ⓐ Ⓑ Ⓒ Ⓓ Ⓔ	14. Ⓐ Ⓑ Ⓒ Ⓓ Ⓔ	20. Ⓐ Ⓑ Ⓒ Ⓓ Ⓔ
3. Ⓐ Ⓑ Ⓒ Ⓓ Ⓔ	9. Ⓐ Ⓑ Ⓒ Ⓓ Ⓔ	15. Ⓐ Ⓑ Ⓒ Ⓓ Ⓔ	21. Ⓐ Ⓑ Ⓒ Ⓓ Ⓔ
4. Ⓐ Ⓑ Ⓒ Ⓓ Ⓔ	10. Ⓐ Ⓑ Ⓒ Ⓓ Ⓔ	16. Ⓐ Ⓑ Ⓒ Ⓓ Ⓔ	22. Ⓐ Ⓑ Ⓒ Ⓓ Ⓔ
5. Ⓐ Ⓑ Ⓒ Ⓓ Ⓔ	11. Ⓐ Ⓑ Ⓒ Ⓓ Ⓔ	17. Ⓐ Ⓑ Ⓒ Ⓓ Ⓔ	23. Ⓐ Ⓑ Ⓒ Ⓓ Ⓔ
6. Ⓐ Ⓑ Ⓒ Ⓓ Ⓔ	12. Ⓐ Ⓑ Ⓒ Ⓓ Ⓔ	18. Ⓐ Ⓑ Ⓒ Ⓓ Ⓔ	24. Ⓐ Ⓑ Ⓒ Ⓓ Ⓔ

☐ # right in Section 1

☐ # wrong in Section 1

SECTION 2

1. Ⓐ Ⓑ Ⓒ Ⓓ Ⓔ	6. Ⓐ Ⓑ Ⓒ Ⓓ Ⓔ	11. Ⓐ Ⓑ Ⓒ Ⓓ Ⓔ	16. Ⓐ Ⓑ Ⓒ Ⓓ Ⓔ
2. Ⓐ Ⓑ Ⓒ Ⓓ Ⓔ	7. Ⓐ Ⓑ Ⓒ Ⓓ Ⓔ	12. Ⓐ Ⓑ Ⓒ Ⓓ Ⓔ	17. Ⓐ Ⓑ Ⓒ Ⓓ Ⓔ
3. Ⓐ Ⓑ Ⓒ Ⓓ Ⓔ	8. Ⓐ Ⓑ Ⓒ Ⓓ Ⓔ	13. Ⓐ Ⓑ Ⓒ Ⓓ Ⓔ	18. Ⓐ Ⓑ Ⓒ Ⓓ Ⓔ
4. Ⓐ Ⓑ Ⓒ Ⓓ Ⓔ	9. Ⓐ Ⓑ Ⓒ Ⓓ Ⓔ	14. Ⓐ Ⓑ Ⓒ Ⓓ Ⓔ	
5. Ⓐ Ⓑ Ⓒ Ⓓ Ⓔ	10. Ⓐ Ⓑ Ⓒ Ⓓ Ⓔ	15. Ⓐ Ⓑ Ⓒ Ⓓ Ⓔ	

☐ # right in Section 2

☐ # wrong in Section 2

SECTION 3

25. Ⓐ Ⓑ Ⓒ Ⓓ Ⓔ	31. Ⓐ Ⓑ Ⓒ Ⓓ Ⓔ	37. Ⓐ Ⓑ Ⓒ Ⓓ Ⓔ	43. Ⓐ Ⓑ Ⓒ Ⓓ Ⓔ
26. Ⓐ Ⓑ Ⓒ Ⓓ Ⓔ	32. Ⓐ Ⓑ Ⓒ Ⓓ Ⓔ	38. Ⓐ Ⓑ Ⓒ Ⓓ Ⓔ	44. Ⓐ Ⓑ Ⓒ Ⓓ Ⓔ
27. Ⓐ Ⓑ Ⓒ Ⓓ Ⓔ	33. Ⓐ Ⓑ Ⓒ Ⓓ Ⓔ	39. Ⓐ Ⓑ Ⓒ Ⓓ Ⓔ	45. Ⓐ Ⓑ Ⓒ Ⓓ Ⓔ
28. Ⓐ Ⓑ Ⓒ Ⓓ Ⓔ	34. Ⓐ Ⓑ Ⓒ Ⓓ Ⓔ	40. Ⓐ Ⓑ Ⓒ Ⓓ Ⓔ	46. Ⓐ Ⓑ Ⓒ Ⓓ Ⓔ
29. Ⓐ Ⓑ Ⓒ Ⓓ Ⓔ	35. Ⓐ Ⓑ Ⓒ Ⓓ Ⓔ	41. Ⓐ Ⓑ Ⓒ Ⓓ Ⓔ	47. Ⓐ Ⓑ Ⓒ Ⓓ Ⓔ
30. Ⓐ Ⓑ Ⓒ Ⓓ Ⓔ	36. Ⓐ Ⓑ Ⓒ Ⓓ Ⓔ	42. Ⓐ Ⓑ Ⓒ Ⓓ Ⓔ	48. Ⓐ Ⓑ Ⓒ Ⓓ Ⓔ

☐ # right in Section 3

☐ # wrong in Section 3

KAPLAN
Test Prep and Admissions

Practice Test Two

SECTION ONE

Time—25 Minutes
24 Questions

For each of the following questions, choose the best answer and darken the corresponding oval on the answer sheet.

Select the lettered word or set of words that best completes the sentence.

Example:

Today's small, portable computers contrast markedly with the earliest electronic computers, which were ----.

(A) effective
(B) invented
(C) useful
(D) destructive
(E) enormous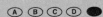

1. A drill sergeant ---- new recruits to be tractable and to ---- his orders.

(A) presumes . . conform to
(B) encourages . . look at
(C) expects . . comply with
(D) trains . . apply for
(E) compels . . retreat from

2. In spite of its ---- climate, the Sonoran Desert ---- many forms of plant and animal life.

(A) arid . . supports
(B) extreme . . uproots
(C) harsh . . destroys
(D) temperate . . rejects
(E) changing . . retains

3. During the Han Dynasty in China, manual work was respected by all; even noblemen felt that they could engage in it without ----.

(A) difficulty
(B) training
(C) remuneration
(D) discomfort
(E) dishonor

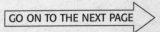

4. Until recently, modern historians have tended to attribute great influence to individual heroes, whereas now, many historians recognize the importance of social climate and ---- action.

   (A) collaborative
   (B) geographic
   (C) deliberate
   (D) subjective
   (E) ulterior

5. Although critics consider the author's first novel both original and ----, her publishers are apprehensive about its ---- appeal.

   (A) moving . . emotional
   (B) suspenseful . . vital
   (C) obscure . . lasting
   (D) sophisticated . . popular
   (E) entertaining . . obsolete

GO ON TO THE NEXT PAGE

Answer the questions below based on the information in the accompanying passages.

Questions 6–9 are based on the following passages.

Passage 1

Music is the perfect medium for the expression of political points of view. In fact, the motivational songs of repressed peoples have been sung in streets, at music halls, and around campfires for
(5) centuries. In America in particular, there is an honored history of musicians speaking for the people and bringing to light political problems largely disregarded by the rest of the mass media. Woody Guthrie, a stellar creator of socially con-
(10) scious music, serves as an excellent example. Some musicians, those of little heart, fear that taking a strong stand will cost them precious listeners. In fact, outspoken assertive musical artists like Guthrie tend to have the most loyal fans.

Passage 2

I listen to music to escape the troubles of my daily life. If I'm in the mood for social crises and political opinion, I'll go to the editorial section of the daily paper. Musicians should play music, not
(5) dabble in politics as a hobby. After all, what insights can a musician offer that cannot be more fully explored by professional journalists and reporters? No one expects a novice to sit down at a piano and produce beautiful music. Likewise, I
(10) don't expect someone who has spent his life on stage and in practice rooms to produce a political analysis of any great depth.

6. In Passage 1, "medium" (line 1) most nearly means

   (A) middle
   (B) fair
   (C) average
   (D) instrument
   (E) clairvoyant

7. The phrase "those of little heart" (line 11) in the Passage 1 serves to emphasize

   (A) the author's disdain for musicians who suppress their political beliefs
   (B) a political musician's loss of loyal listeners
   (C) the author's negative opinion many music listeners
   (D) the difficulty of writing effective political-protest music
   (E) Woody Guthrie's importance in American musical history

8. For the author of Passage 2, musicians who express political views are

   (A) artists who use their music in the best way possible
   (B) people who should run for political office
   (C) artists who bore all of their listeners
   (D) not interested in music as an escape
   (E) people who toy with serious topics outside of their specialty

9. The authors of the passages disagree about the

   (A) legal right of musicians to compose music with a political message
   (B) talent of Woody Guthrie
   (C) importance of political analysis
   (D) validity of political commentary in music
   (E) loyalty of Guthrie's fans

GO ON TO THE NEXT PAGE

Questions 10–14 are based on the following passage.

The following passage presents a scientific discussion of the human ability to use language.

It is the use of language that sets apart humans from the animals. Language is what enables us to reveal our conscious selves, to trans-mit knowledge to each other and to succeeding
(5) generations, to discuss and debate ideas, and to build and maintain the framework of civilization. Though research has been done and claims have been made that intelligent animals such as chim-panzees can learn to understand human language
(10) in a limited way, the evidence seems to indicate that true language is exclusively the province of humans.

Is a human born with the innate capacity for language, or is language a complex form of behav-
(15) ior that one learns as a child? The linguist Noam Chomsky has argued that humans possess innate structures in the brain that govern language acqui-sition; in other words, our brains are not unlike computers preprogrammed with the ability to
(20) learn how to use language creatively. Behavioral psychologists, on the other hand, see language as nothing more than "verbal behavior" that a child learns through experience.

Although this question is still unanswered, it
(25) is clear from the work of neuroscientists that once a human possesses language, certain structures and areas of the brain do control its use. Language tends to reside in only one hemisphere of the brain. Which hemisphere this is, the right or the
(30) left, is related to the "handedness" of a person: right-handers, for example, usually process lan-guage on the left-hand side of the brain. Neuroscientists have further determined that lan-guage is not localized to one specific area within
(35) the hemisphere. Rather, activities such as speaking and understanding written words seem to be han-dled by different areas.

Much of this information comes from studies of people who have suffered injuries to specific
(40) parts of the brain. Nineteenth-century scientist Pierre Paul Broca, for example, discovered the spe-cific region of the brain that controls the flow of words from brain to mouth: he did the autopsy of a brain-damaged patient who had been incapable
(45) of speaking for over twenty years and found the lesion in the brain tissue that had caused the problem. The area of the brain that enables us to comprehend speech was located by Broca's con-temporary Carl Wernicke in a similar way.

(50) A modern technique known as PET (positron emission tomography) scanning has made the study of language processing possible in normal subjects. Using PET, scientists are able to "see" how normal people think by monitoring the
(55) brain's use of oxygen during mental activity. The part of the brain that lights up in a PET scan of a person hearing words has been shown to be com-pletely different from the spot that lights up when the person speaks. In addition, it seems that even
(60) verbs and nouns are handled by different areas. Exactly why the various components of language should be distributed across the brain in this way remains, however, the subject of speculation.

10. The author's statement about what "language" entails (lines 2–6) is made primarily by using

(A) quotations

(B) scientific data

(C) generalizations

(D) analogies

(E) inferences

GO ON TO THE NEXT PAGE

11. The question in the second paragraph chiefly serves to

    (A) present a scientific dilemma that has been resolved

    (B) suggest that there are some questions not being addressed by scientists

    (C) summarize an issue that is the subject of continued debate

    (D) outline the position of the author

    (E) introduce a topic that will be discussed for the rest of the passage

12. The author mentions computers in the second paragraph primarily to illustrate the

    (A) way humans learn language through experience

    (B) importance of computer use to a child's language acquisition

    (C) progress in understanding language made using computer models

    (D) inability of computers to use language creatively

    (E) possibility that humans are born knowing how to use language

13. The best evidence that the brain processes speaking and hearing words in different areas is provided by the

    (A) studies of Pierre Paul Broca

    (B) experiments on chimpanzees

    (C) results of PET scans

    (D) observations of children learning language

    (E) studies of Carl Wernicke

14. The author discusses the work of Broca and Wernicke in the fourth paragraph to illustrate the

    (A) method by which early discoveries were made about the brain and language

    (B) imprecision of the techniques of nineteenth-century scientists

    (C) extent to which the localization of speech in the brain is understood

    (D) study of language processing in the brain of normal patients

    (E) range of early neuroscientific ideas about where language is processed in the brain

GO ON TO THE NEXT PAGE

Questions 15–24 are based on the following passage.

*In this passage, an essayist and author of children's stories
recalls being captivated by the sight of a young circus
rider rehearsing.*

After the lions had returned to their cages,
creeping angrily through the chutes, a little bunch
of us drifted away and into an open doorway
nearby, where we stood for a while in semidark-
(5) ness, watching a big brown circus horse go
harumphing around the practice ring. The long
rein, or tape, by which his trainer guided her
charge counterclockwise in his dull career formed
the radius of their private circle, of which she was
(10) the revolving center. The great size and meekness
of the horse, the repetitious exercise, the heat of
the afternoon, all exerted a hypnotic charm.

Behind me I heard someone say, "Excuse me,
please," in a low voice. She was halfway into the
(15) building when I turned and saw her—a girl of six-
teen or seventeen. In most respects she was like
any of two or three dozen showgirls you
encounter if you wander about the winter quarters
of Mr. John Ringling North's circus, in Sarasota.
(20) But her grave face and the naturalness of her
manner gave her a sort of quick distinction and
brought a new note into the gloomy octagonal
building. As soon as she had squeezed through the
crowd, she spoke a word or two to the older
(25) woman, whom I took to be her mother, stepped to
the ring, and waited while the horse coasted to a
stop in front of her. She gave the animal a couple
of affectionate swipes on his enormous neck and
then swung herself aboard. The horse immediately
(30) resumed his rocking canter, the woman goading
him on, chanting something that sounded like
"Hop! Hop!"

In attempting to recapture this mild spectacle,
I am merely acting as recording secretary for one
(35) of the oldest of societies—the society of those
who, at one time or another, have surrendered,
without even a show of resistance, to the bedazzle-
ment of a circus rider. It is not easy to communicate anything of this nature. The circus comes as

(40) close to being the world in microcosm as anything
I know; in a way, it puts all the rest of show business in the shade. Its magic is universal and complex. Out of its wild disorder comes order; from
its rank smell rises the good aroma of courage and
(45) daring; out of its preliminary shabbiness comes
the final splendor. And buried in the familiar
boasts of its advance agents lies the modesty of
most of its people. For me the circus is at its best
before it has been put together. In short, a man
(50) has to catch the circus unawares to experience its
full impact and share its gaudy dream.

The ten-minute ride the girl took achieved—
as far as I was concerned, who wasn't looking for
it, and quite unbeknownst to her, who wasn't even
(55) striving for it—the thing that is sought by per-
formers everywhere: a means of improving a shining ten minutes in the diligent way all serious
artists seize free moments to hone the blade of
their talent. Her brief tour included only elemen-
(60) tary postures and tricks, perhaps because they
were all she was capable of, perhaps because her
warmup at this hour was unscheduled and the
ring was not rigged for a real practice session. She
swung herself off and on the horse several times,
(65) gripping his mane. She did a few knee-stands—or
whatever they are called—dropping to her knees
and quickly bouncing back up on her feet again.
Most of the time she simply rode in a standing
position, well aft on the beast, her hands hanging
(70) easily at her sides, her head erect, her straw-col-
ored ponytail lightly brushing her shoulders, the
blood of exertion showing faintly through the tan
of her skin. Twice she managed a one-foot
stance—a sort of ballet pose, with arms out-
(75) stretched.

The richness of the scene was in its plainness,
its natural condition—of horse, of ring, of girl,
even to the girl's bare feet that gripped the bare
back of her proud and ridiculous mount. The
(80) enchantment grew not out of anything that happened or was performed but out of something that
seemed to go round and around and around with
the girl, attending her, a steady gleam in the shape
of a circle—a ring of ambition, of happiness,

GO ON TO THE NEXT PAGE ⟶

(85) of youth. (And the positive pleasures of equilibrium under difficulties.) In a week or two, all would be changed, all (or almost all) lost: the girl would wear makeup, the horse would wear gold, the ring would be painted, the bark would be clean for the
(90) feet of the horse, the girl's feet would be clean for the slippers that she'd wear. All, all would be lost.

15. In the first paragraph, the author describes the horse as

    (A) spirited and energetic
    (B) fierce and threatening
    (C) good-natured but unpredictable
    (D) old and frightened
    (E) huge but submissive

16. The word "charge" in line 8 most nearly means

    (A) a definite quantity of electricity
    (B) an accusation of blame
    (C) something under supervision
    (D) a formal requirement
    (E) a round of ammunition

17. In lines 16–23, the author's first description of the circus showgirl is intended to convey the idea that she

    (A) was bothered by the heat of the day
    (B) tried hard to fit in with the other showgirls
    (C) was obviously more talented than her peers
    (D) wished to entertain the spectators
    (E) resembled her peers yet stood apart from them

18. In lines 38–39, the author comments that "It is not easy to communicate anything of this nature" in order to

    (A) emphasize that he is describing an uncommon experience
    (B) admit the inadequacy of his powers as a writer
    (C) stress that the emotional reaction he is describing is complex and elusive
    (D) point out that people don't like to admit how attractive the circus is
    (E) confess that he envied the circus rider's prowess

19. The author mentions the boasts of circus advance agents (line 47) to provide evidence of the

    (A) problems that beset those who spend their lives in the circus
    (B) pressures driving the girl rider to succeed
    (C) ways in which circus employees regularly deceive the public
    (D) contrasts and paradoxes that make the circus a world in miniature
    (E) author's disillusionment with show business in general

20. The author indicates that, as she rode around the ring, the girl was

    (A) concentrating on simple tricks
    (B) receiving instructions from her mother
    (C) distracted by the crowd of onlookers
    (D) irritated by the horse's behavior
    (E) rehearsing for the evening's performance

GO ON TO THE NEXT PAGE

21. In paragraph 4, the author suggests that the girl can be called a "serious artist" because of her

    (A) physical grace and acrobatic talent
    (B) devotion to improving her skills
    (C) unusual rapport with the horse
    (D) ability to do a lot of tricks in a short time
    (E) meticulous attention to detail

22. In lines 65–66, the author adds the phrase "or whatever they are called" primarily to emphasize

    (A) his inability to remember what he knew as a child
    (B) his interest in the girl's attitude toward her work rather than her technical skill
    (C) the unimportance of the practice session in comparison to an actual circus performance
    (D) his ignorance of even the simplest acrobatic maneuvers
    (E) the girl's inability to perform correctly a particular maneuver

23. By mentioning the "plainness" of the scene in line 76, the author underscores the point that

    (A) the life of a circus performer is often dangerous and difficult
    (B) circus audiences fail to appreciate the hard work that showriders must do
    (C) the girl riding the horse was unaware of the onlookers
    (D) horse and rider would appear more glamorous during an actual performance
    (E) something other than the physical setting made the experience special

24. In the last paragraph of the passage, the author uses the phrase, "a ring of ambition, of happiness, of youth" to reflect

    (A) the gold rings on the girl's fingers
    (B) the ring of the circus stage
    (C) the ringing sound of the circus music
    (D) his desire to get married
    (E) the shape of the horse's stirrups

IF YOU FINISH BEFORE TIME IS CALLED, YOU MAY CHECK YOUR WORK ON THIS SECTION ONLY. DO NOT TURN TO ANY OTHER SECTION IN THE TEST. **STOP**

SECTION TWO

Time—25 Minutes
18 Questions

Solve each of the following problems, decide which is the best answer choice, and darken the corresponding oval on the answer sheet.

Notes:

(1)   Calculator use is permitted.

(2)   All numbers used are real numbers.

(3)   Figures are provided for some problems. All figures are drawn to scale and lie in a plane UNLESS otherwise indicated.

Information

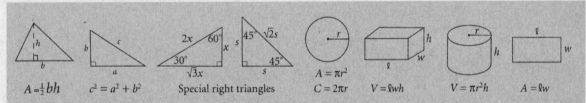

$A = \frac{1}{2}bh$ $c^2 = a^2 + b^2$ Special right triangles $A = \pi r^2$ $C = 2\pi r$ $V = \ell wh$ $V = \pi r^2 h$ $A = \ell w$

The sum of the degree measures of the angles of a triangle is 180.
The number of degrees of arc in a circle is 360.
A straight angle has a degree measure of 180.

1. If $r = 8$, then $(r + 4)^2 =$

    (A)   24
    (B)   64
    (C)   68
    (D)   80
    (E)   144

2. A stationery store ordered a shipment of 800 erasers and sold 360 of them. What percent of the shipment did it sell?

    (A) 3.6%
    (B) 4.5%
    (C) 18%
    (D) 36%
    (E) 45%

GO ON TO THE NEXT PAGE

STUDENT ENROLLMENT AT
MIDVILLE HIGH SCHOOL

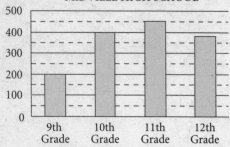

3. According to the bar graph above, the total number of students enrolled at Midville High School is approximately

(A) 1,325

(B) 1,375

(C) 1,400

(D) 1,425

(E) 1,500

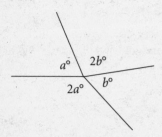

4. In the figure above, what is the value of $a + b$?

(A)   90

(B) 120

(C) 150

(D) 180

(E) 240

5. Josephine types 12 words every 20 seconds. At this rate, how many words does she type every 2 minutes?

(A) 18

(B) 20

(C) 36

(D) 42

(E) 72

6. Which of the following is an expression for "12 greater than the square root of the product of 10 and a"?

(A) $12 + \sqrt{10a}$

(B) $12 + \sqrt{10 + a}$

(C) $12\sqrt{10a}$

(D) $12 + 10\sqrt{a}$

(E) $\sqrt{10a + 12}$

7. The sum of the odd integers between 8 and 26 is how much greater than the sum of the even integers between 5 and 23?

(A) 18

(B) 19

(C) 21

(D) 27

(E) 33

GO ON TO THE NEXT PAGE

8. If $\dfrac{\frac{1}{a}}{\frac{1}{9}} = 3$, what is the value of a?

   (A) 1
   (B) 3
   (C) 9
   (D) 18
   (E) 27

9. The total cost of 5 books is $70. If the average (arithmetic mean) cost of 2 of the books is $15, what is the total cost of the remaining 3 books?

   (A) $40
   (B) $45
   (C) $50
   (D) $55
   (E) $60

Note: Figure not drawn to scale.

10. In the figure above, if $AC = 2CD$, $AC = 10$, and $BD = 9$, what is the length of BC?

    (A) 1
    (B) 3
    (C) 4
    (D) 6
    (E) 8

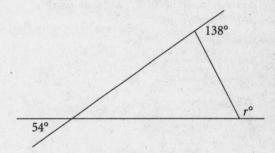

Note: Figure not drawn to scale.

11. In the triangle above, the sides have been extended as shown. What is the value of r?

    (A) 34
    (B) 42
    (C) 74
    (D) 84
    (E) 96

12. If a number is divisible by the first six positive even integers, the number must be divisible by all of the following EXCEPT

    (A) 18
    (B) 20
    (C) 24
    (D) 30
    (E) 40

13. If two points on a certain line in a coordinate plane have coordinates $(2, 6)$ and $(4, 9)$, what is the slope of the line?

    (A) $\dfrac{3}{4}$

    (B) $\dfrac{5}{4}$

    (C) $\dfrac{3}{2}$

    (D) 2

    (E) 3

GO ON TO THE NEXT PAGE

14. If $rs < 0$, which of the following statements CANNOT be true?

    (A) $r < 0$

    (B) $r > 0$

    (C) $r - s = 0$

    (D) $r + s = 0$

    (E) $r + s = 1$

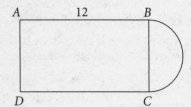

Note: Figure not drawn to scale.

15. The figure above is composed of a rectangle and a semicircle. If the area of the rectangle is 48, what is the area of the semicircle?

    (A) π

    (B) 2π

    (C) 4π

    (D) 8π

    (E) 12π

16. If $x^2 + 4x - 12 = 0$, which of the following is a possible value for x?

    (A) -6

    (B) -4

    (C) -2

    (D) 4

    (E) 6

17. If $a \, \circledast \, b$ is defined for all positive integers a and b by the equation $a \, \circledast \, b = a(b - a)$, then $4 \, \circledast \, (3 \, \circledast \, 5) =$

    (A)   2

    (B)   6

    (C)   8

    (D) 22

    (E) 28

18. In a crate of 56 oranges and apples, the ratio of the number of oranges to the number of apples is 4:3. After n apples and n oranges are removed, the ratio of the number of oranges to the number of apples is 3:2. What is the value of n?

    (A)   2

    (B)   5

    (C)   7

    (D)   8

    (E) 12

SECTION THREE

Time—25 Minutes   For each of the following questions, choose the best answer and darken the
24 Questions   corresponding oval on the answer sheet.

Select the lettered word or set of words that best completes the sentence.

Example:

Today's small, portable computers contrast markedly with the earliest electronic computers, which were ----.

(A) effective

(B) invented

(C) useful

(D) destructive

(E) enormous

25. Highly influenced by Frank Lloyd Wright's principles of design, the architect E. Fay Jones has built homes reputed to equal and even ---- Wright's successes at building in harmony with natural surroundings.

(A) echo

(B) question

(C) reconstruct

(D) surpass

(E) revise

26. Trumpets, including Pacific conch-shell trumpets, African ivory trumpets, orchestral valve trumpets, and tubas, comprise one of the most ---- categories of wind instruments.

(A) excessive

(B) discordant

(C) coherent

(D) absolute

(E) diverse

27. Weighing over seventy tons, *Brachiosaurus* was ---- creature, yet its brain was quite ----.

(A) an intelligent . . enormous

(B) a gargantuan . . small

(C) a minute . . tiny

(D) a prodigious . . fossilized

(E) an extinct . . extant

28. The ---- nature of the platypus makes it difficult to sight, even in the ---- space of a zoological exhibit.

(A) elusive . . confined

(B) crafty . . massive

(C) amiable . . inhabited

(D) playful . . structured

(E) slothful . . open

29. The original American colonies were ---- entities, each having its own government, maintaining its own militia, and functioning ----.

(A) dependent . . competitively

(B) distinct . . autonomously

(C) independent . . devotedly

(D) prosperous . . austerely

(E) united . . expressively

GO ON TO THE NEXT PAGE

30. Kudzu, a vine ---- to Japan, was introduced in the United States in 1876 and is now widely grown in the South.

    (A) segregated

    (B) unaccustomed

    (C) relative

    (D) contiguous

    (E) indigenous

31. By most contemporary European accounts, Tsar Peter the Great of Russia was ----, towering over others of his generation both physically and intellectually.

    (A) an egotist

    (B) an archetype

    (C) a celebrity

    (D) a titan

    (E) a sage

32. During the late 1860s, Emily Dickinson became increasingly ----, generally shunning personal contact with those outside her family circle.

    (A) conciliatory

    (B) reclusive

    (C) intemperate

    (D) meticulous

    (E) garrulous

GO ON TO THE NEXT PAGE

Answer the questions below based on the information in the accompanying passages.

Questions 33–34 are based on the following passage.

Recent research indicates that the Malagasy people of Madagascar likely originated in Indonesia, some 3,700 miles to the east of Madagascar in the Indian Ocean. Although there have never been any
(5) archaeological finds on the island that point unequivocally to Indonesia, linguistic and cultural evidence strongly supports this theory. Malagasy, for example, is a Malayo-Polynesian language that strikingly overlaps with Ma'anyan, a tongue spo-
(10) ken in Kalimantan in southeastern Indonesia. This linguistic lineage has cultural parallels such as rice cultivation, the cult of ancestors, and the widespread use of outrigger canoes which have a strong Indonesian resonance.

33. According to the passage, some of the strongest evidence for the claim that the settlers of Madagascar originated in Indonesia is to be found in

(A) the location of Indonesia 3,700 miles to the east in the Indian Ocean

(B) archaeological finds of outrigger canoes in Madagascar

(C) the linguistic overlap between Malagasy and a language spoken in Kalimantan

(D) the cultural overlap reflected in housing styles of the two regions

(E) references to Indonesian islands in the poetry of Madagascar

34. As used in the passage, "resonance" (line 14) most nearly means

(A) reverberation

(B) evidence

(C) consequence

(D) timbre

(E) character

GO ON TO THE NEXT PAGE

KAPLAN
Test Prep and Admissions

Questions 35–36 refer to the following passage.

Mammalian predator territories are dynamic rather than static spaces, constantly shifting over time in accordance with several factors, such as the population size of prey species and the
(5) dynamics between different predatory species. This complex interplay was dramatically illustrated at Yellowstone National Park, where the reintroduction of wolves (*Canis lupus*) in 1995 after half a century's absence reshaped the ecosystem within
(10) two years. The new arrivals had a major impact on the Yellowstone coyotes (*Canis latrans*), who were suddenly demoted to the position of second-ranking predator. The coyote population was cut in half, with a corresponding increase in rodents,
(15) while elk were forced to become far more vigilant.

35. The author's cites the introduction of wolves at Yellowstone primarily to

(A) stress that the territories of predators are continually changing in response to various factors

(B) emphasize that wolves are a more dominant predator than coyotes

(C) reinforce the claim that, once a predator has marked out a territory, it will maintain that area at any cost

(D) illustrate the influence of the population size of prey species on predator territories

(E) argue that human intervention in ecosystems can have unforeseen consequences

36. Which of the following statements, taken with the information in the paragraph, would best explain the cited increase in the rodent population of Yellowstone?

(A) Rodents were introduced into the park well before 1995.

(B) The rodent population has not increased in other national parks.

(C) Rodents are common prey for coyotes, but not for wolves.

(D) The population of elk has decreased substantially.

(E) Other species have increased even more dramatically.

GO ON TO THE NEXT PAGE ⇒

Questions 37–48 are based on the following passages.

The passages below are drawn from two articles that discuss the recent restoration of the ceiling of the Sistine Chapel.

Passage 1

One shudders to contemplate Michelangelo's reaction if he were to gaze up today at the famous frescoes* he painted on the ceiling of the Sistine Chapel over four centuries ago. A practical man,
(5) he would no doubt be unsurprised by the effects of time and environment on his masterpiece. He would be philosophical about the damage wrought by mineral salts left behind when rainwater leaked through the roof. The layers of dirt and
(10) soot from coal braziers that heated the chapel and from candles and incense burned during religious functions would—prior to their removal during restoration—likely have been taken in stride as well. But he would be appalled at the ravages
(15) inflicted on his work by the recent restorers.

The Vatican restoration team reveled in inducing a jarringly colorful transformation in the frescoes with their special cleaning solvents and computerized analysis equipment. But this effect was
(20) not, as they claim, achieved merely by removing the dirt and animal glue (employed by earlier restorers to revive muted colors) from the frescoes; they removed Michelangelo's final touches as well. Gone from the ceiling is the quality of suppressed anger
(25) and thunderous pessimism so often commented on by admiring scholars. That quality was not an artifact of grime, not a misleading monochrome imposed on the ceiling by time, for Michelangelo himself applied a veil of glaze to the frescoes to
(30) darken them after he had deemed his work too bright. The master would have felt compelled to add a few more layers of glaze had the ceiling radiated forth as it does now. The solvents of the restorers, in addition to stripping away the shadows, reacted
(35) chemically with Michelangelo's pigments to produce hues the painter never beheld.

Of course, the restorers left open an avenue for the reversal of their own progress towards color and brightness. Since the layers of animal
(40) glue are no longer there to serve as protection, the atmospheric pollutants from the city of Rome gained direct access to the frescoes. Significant darkening was already noticed in some of the restored work a mere four years after it was com-
(45) pleted. It remains to be seen whether the measure introduced to arrest this process—an extensive climate-control system—will itself have any long-term effect on the chapel's ceiling.

fresco: a style of painting on plaster using water-based pigments.

Passage 2

The question lingers long after one contrasts the areas of the Sistine Chapel's ceiling still shackled by grime with the colorful splendor of the frescoes that have been cleaned: how could
(5) Michelangelo's masterpiece have been allowed to fall into such ruin? The amount of responsibility shouldered in restoring such a work is daunting to even the most ambitious of experts, naturally, but this does not explain the inaction. Rather, we had
(10) come to believe from centuries of habituation to the darkness of the ceiling that Michelangelo had actually desired it to be part of the effect. The courageous work of the restorers has wiped away not only the dirt but also—painfully for those in
(15) certain circles—cherished myths as well.

The armament of the restorer has expanded in recent decades beyond artistic sensibility and historical knowledge. A chemist on the Vatican restoration team identified the composition of the
(20) layers covering Michelangelo's original colors. Since there was a stratum of dirt between the painting and the first layer of glaze, it was clear that several decades had elapsed between the completion of the ceiling and the application of the
(25) glaze. This justified the use of cleaning solvents that would lift off all but that final layer of dirt, which was kept for the sake of protection of the frescoes. The particular solvent employed, AB 57, was chosen because of the overall neutral action of
(30) its two chemicals on pigments: one temporarily tones them down, but the other livens them up to the same degree. Thus the colors that emerged

GO ON TO THE NEXT PAGE

from the shadows are truly what Michelangelo intended to be seen.

(35)   One member of the team asserted that the cleaning brought to light a painting that can be considered "the equivalent of a treatise, not written but painted, on the art of fresco painting." The luminous figures are without doubt the work of a

(40) master craftsman who executed typical Renaissance painting techniques to perfection. This is the source of the difficulty critics have with the restoration: the ceiling of the Sistine Chapel no longer seems to be the fruit of the wayward genius,

(45) defiant of Renaissance fresco-painting protocol, that Michelangelo was thought to be. They balk at the fact that the painter seems, like a vagabond given a good scrubbing, to be a complete stranger, rational and traditional and devoid of fearfulness

(50) and anger. But the veil that led to the misperceptions of Michelangelo has now been lifted, and we may better acquaint ourselves with him.

37. The word "philosophical" in Passage 1, line 7 is best interpreted to mean

(A) overwhelmed

(B) knowledgeable

(C) abstract

(D) unruffled

(E) pensive

38. The author of Passage 1 implies in the first paragraph that the deterioration of Michelangelo's frescoes

(A) has not resulted in an appreciable difference in their visual impact

(B) could have been prevented if the chapel were not kept in use

(C) was not abated by the misguided efforts of the restorers

(D) should have been accepted as an unfortunate but natural process

(E) was considered inevitable and irreversible at the time they were painted

39. In the second paragraph of Passage 1, the author creates a sense of irony by juxtaposing which two of the following elements?

(A) appreciation of the removal of grime from the ceiling versus sadness over the change of color

(B) description of the restorers' technical equipment versus description of Michelangelo's antiquated painting technique

(C) the claim that the color came from removing the dirt and glue versus the claim that glue had never been used

(D) the assertion that Michelangelo's glaze had been removed versus the assertion that the colors had been chemically enhanced

(E) the restorers' attitude towards brightly colored frescoes versus Michelangelo's attitude towards brightly colored frescoes

GO ON TO THE NEXT PAGE ⟹

40. In Passage 1, line 46, the word "arrest" most nearly means

   (A) attract
   (B) detain
   (C) capture
   (D) retard
   (E) contain

41. The author of Passage 2 apparently thinks that the "amount of responsibility" (line 6) involved in restoring the ceiling of the Sistine Chapel

   (A) was the reason that restorers allowed the masterpiece to deteriorate
   (B) reflects the fact that the frescoes are the greatest work of the Renaissance period
   (C) was not by itself a strong enough deterrent to have stopped restorers
   (D) protected the ceiling from premature efforts at restoration in the past
   (E) kept all but the finest restorers from attempting to work on the ceiling

42. The author of Passage 2 uses the evidence of the "stratum of dirt between the painting and the first layer of glaze" (lines 21–22) to establish that

   (A) good care had not been taken of the frescoes from the beginning
   (B) science has replaced art history as the driving force behind art restoration
   (C) the first layer of glaze was not part of the original masterpiece
   (D) it took an extremely long period of time to complete the whole work
   (E) the work of the Vatican chemist was extremely accurate

43. The quotation from a member of the restoration team (Passage 2, lines 37–38) suggests that he viewed the chapel ceiling as

   (A) a more educational experience than reading a book
   (B) a valuable source of information about fresco-painting techniques
   (C) a work that could have served as a model for other fresco painters
   (D) a repository of lost literature as well as an artistic masterpiece
   (E) the only good surviving example of a Renaissance fresco

44. It can be inferred from Michelangelo's reputation for being "defiant of Renaissance fresco-painting protocol" (Passage 2, line 45) that

   (A) his work was considered inferior by other Renaissance artists
   (B) he was a fiercely independent and individualistic thinker
   (C) historical conceptions of the artist have overestimated his negative traits
   (D) darkening of colors to produce a gloomy effect was not common practice
   (E) the restoration has jeopardized his position in history as a great artist

45. The reference to "a vagabond given a good scrubbing" (Passage 2, lines 47–48) serves to

   (A) give an idea of the simplicity of the cleaning operation
   (B) explain the disconcerting effect of the colorful frescoes on some critics
   (C) provide some biographical information about the painter
   (D) indicate that the cleaning of the chapel ceiling should not alter the artist's image
   (E) show that no art historian has ever really understood Michelangelo

GO ON TO THE NEXT PAGE

46. The authors of Passages 1 and 2 disagree primarily on which aspect of the painting on the ceiling of the Sistine Chapel?

    (A) whether the former darkened quality was to any degree intentional

    (B) the reason that the restoration of the painting was so long delayed

    (C) the specific techniques the restorers should have used

    (D) whether or not the frescoes were originally done in color

    (E) the extent of the damage that was caused by the grime

47. Which statement best expresses the objection that the author of Passage 2 would make about Passage 1's argument regarding the painting's "suppressed anger and thunderous pessimism" (lines 24–25)?

    (A) It makes little sense because the essential elements of the painting were not changed during the restoration.

    (B) It is weak because the painting has been the subject of many different and often contradictory interpretations.

    (C) It summarizes the long-held ideas that the restoration has proved to be erroneous.

    (D) It is unfounded because the restored painting does not exhibit the quality discussed.

    (E) It distorts the actual views of past art historical experts.

48. How would the author of Passage 1 respond to the fact mentioned in Passage 2 that a layer of dirt was kept "for the sake of protection of the frescoes" (lines 27–28)?

    (A) The protection clearly was not as effective as the restorers had hoped.

    (B) Nothing will be able to protect the frescoes now that the animal glue has been removed.

    (C) Chemical agents left in the dirt are continuing to cause damage to the ceiling.

    (D) The dirt layer will allow the painting to retain its dark and angry quality.

    (E) The restorers really kept the final layer of dirt in a futile attempt to pacify their critics.

SECTION FOUR

Time—25 Minutes   Solve each of the following problems, decide which is the best answer choice, and
   20 Questions   darken the corresponding oval on the answer sheet.

Notes:

(1)   Calculator use is permitted.

(2)   All numbers used are real numbers.

(3)   Figures are provided for some problems. All figures are drawn to scale and lie in a plane UNLESS
   otherwise indicated.

Information

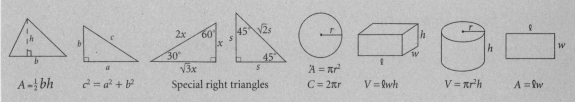

$A = \frac{1}{2}bh$ $c^2 = a^2 + b^2$ Special right triangles $A = \pi r^2$ $V = \ell wh$ $V = \pi r^2 h$ $A = \ell w$
   $C = 2\pi r$

The sum of the degree measures of the angles of a triangle is 180.
The number of degrees of arc in a circle is 360.
A straight angle has a degree measure of 180.

19.   When Mr. Schafer arrived at the grocery store,
   there were 8 cases of soda left on the shelf. One
   case contained 11 cans of soda, and each of the
   others contained 6. If Mr. Schafer bought all 8
   cases, how many cans of soda did he purchase at
   this store?

   (A) 53

   (B) 54

   (C) 57

   (D) 59

   (E) 65

20. A, B, and C are consecutive points on a line. The
   length of $\overline{AB}$ is 10, and the length of $\overline{BC}$ is 16
   more than the length of $\overline{AB}$. What is the length of
   $\overline{AC}$?

   (A) 26

   (B) 36

   (C) 46

   (D) 56

   (E) 66

21.   If $x + 5 = a$, then $3x + 15 =$

   (A) $a + 5$

   (B) $a + 15$

   (C) $3a$

   (D) $3a + 5$

   (E) $3a + 15$

GO ON TO THE NEXT PAGE

22. If the sum of the areas of the regions is 7, what is the average (arithmetic mean) of the areas of the two regions?

    (A) 0

    (B) $\frac{7}{2}$

    (C) $\frac{7}{4}$

    (D) 7

    (E) 14

23. Which of the following is equal to (3×10^3) + (3×10^4)?

    (A) 33×10

    (B) 33×10^3

    (C) 33×10^4

    (D) 3×10^7

    (E) 6×10^7

24. If $0 \leq x \leq 6$ and $-2 \leq y \leq 5$, which of the following gives the set of all possible values for xy?

    (A) $xy = 2$

    (B) $0 \leq xy \leq 30$

    (C) $-2 \leq xy \leq 11$

    (D) $-2 \leq xy \leq 30$

    (E) $-12 \leq xy \leq 30$

25. If the area of the square in the figure above is 25 and the perimeter of each of the 2 triangles is 21, what is the perimeter of the entire figure?

    (A) 30

    (B) 38

    (C) 42

    (D) 48

    (E) 80

26. When the sum of a set of numbers is divided by the average (arithmetic mean) of these numbers, the result is j. What does j represent?

    (A) half of the sum of the numbers in the set

    (B) the average of the numbers in the set

    (C) the sum of the numbers in the set

    (D) half of the average of the numbers in the set

    (E) the quantity of numbers in the set

GO ON TO THE NEXT PAGE

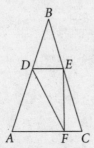

Note: Figure not drawn to scale.

27. In the figure above, $AB = BC$ and $DE = EF = DF$. If the measure of $\angle ABC$ is 50 degrees and the measure of $\angle BDE$ is 70 degrees, what is the degree measure of $\angle DFA$?

(A) 50
(B) 55
(C) 60
(D) 65
(E) 70

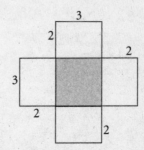

28. In the figure above, the shaded region and each of the four unshaded regions are rectangles. If a point on the figure is chosen at random, what is the probability that point is in the shaded region?

(A) $\dfrac{1}{9}$

(B) $\dfrac{3}{14}$

(C) $\dfrac{3}{11}$

(D) $\dfrac{3}{8}$

(E) $\dfrac{3}{7}$

GO ON TO THE NEXT PAGE

DIRECTIONS FOR STUDENT-PRODUCED RESPONSE QUESTIONS

For each of the questions below (29–38), solve the problem and indicate your answer by darkening the ovals in the special grid. For example:

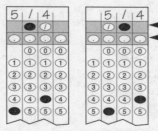

Answer: 1.25 or $\frac{5}{4}$ or 5/4

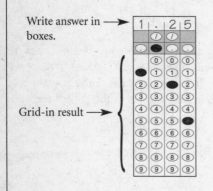

Write answer in boxes.

Grid-in result

Either position is correct.

Fraction line
Decimal point

You may start your answers in any column, space permitting. Columns not needed should be left blank.

- It is recommended, though not required, that you write your answer in the boxes at the top of the columns. However, you will receive credit only for darkening the ovals correctly.

- Grid only one answer to a question, even though some problems have more than one correct answer.

- Darken no more than one oval in a column.

- No answers are negative.

- Mixed numbers cannot be gridded. For example: the number $1\frac{1}{4}$ must be gridded as 1.25 or 5/4.

  (If $\boxed{1\,|\,1\,|\,/\,|\,4}$ is gridded, it will be interpreted as $\frac{11}{4}$ not $1\frac{1}{4}$.)

- Decimal Accuracy: Decimal answers must be entered as accurately as possible. For example, if you obtain an answer such as 0.1666..., you should record the result as .166 or .167. **Less accurate values such as .16 or .17 are not acceptable.**

Acceptable ways to grid $\frac{1}{6}$ = .1666...

29. The height of a particular species of tree is directly proportional to the average yearly rainfall where it grows. If a tree that lives in an area with an average yearly rainfall of 200 centimeters is 30 meters tall, how tall, in meters, is a tree that lives in an area with an average yearly rainfall of 10 centimeters?

30. A scientist begins an experiment with 50 bacteria in a petri dish. If the population doubles every 2 days, the number of bacteria in the dish can be expressed as $(50)2^{\frac{t}{2}}$, where t is the number of days that have passed since the start of the experiment. How many bacteria will be in the petri dish at the end of the sixth day of the experiment?

31. If $6y = 12$ and $x - 2y = 3$, what is the value of x?

32. Bill bought 3 books at $14.50 each. If the tax was already included in the cost, how much change did he receive from a $50 bill? (Disregard the $ sign when gridding your answer.)

33. A rectangular floor 56 inches by 60 inches is to be completely covered with non-overlapping rectangular tiles, each 6 inches by 8 inches. How many tiles are needed to cover the floor?

34. If $4^{n+1} = 64$, then $n^3 =$

35. If the ratio of a to b is 3 to 4 and the ratio of a to c is 2 to 5, what is the ratio of b to c?

36. If 3 coins are tossed simultaneously, what is the probability of getting exactly 2 tails?

37. What is the least positive integer j such that $84j$ is a perfect square?

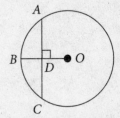

Note: Figure not drawn to scale.

38. In the figure above, AC has length 6 and is perpendicular to OB. If the circle has center O and radius 5, what is the length of BD?

SECTION FIVE

Time—30 Minutes   For each of the following questions, choose the best answer and darken the
39 Questions   corresponding oval on the answer sheet.

Directions: The following sentences test your knowledge of grammar, usage, diction (choice of words), and idioms.
Some sentences are correct.
No sentence contains more than one error.
You will find that the error, if there is one, is underlined and lettered. Elements of the sentence that are not under-
lined will not be changed. In choosing answers, follow the requirements of standard written English.
If there is an error, select the <u>one underlined part</u> that must be changed to make the sentence correct, and fill in
the corresponding oval on your answer sheet.
If there is no error, fill in answer oval (E).

1. The first female aviator <u>to cross</u> the English
                              A
    Channel, Harriet Quimby <u>flown</u> <u>by monoplane</u>
                               B   C
    from Dover, England, to Hardelot, France, <u>in</u>
                                                D
    1912. <u>No error</u>
            E

2. The reproductive behavior of sea horses <u>is notable</u>
                                              A
    <u>in respect of</u> the male, <u>who,</u> <u>instead of</u> the female,
         B   C   D
    carries the fertilized eggs. <u>No error</u>
                                      E

3. Early <u>experience</u> of racial discrimination <u>made</u> an
              A   B
    <u>indelible</u> <u>impression for</u> the late Supreme Court
         C   D
    Justice Thurgood Marshall. <u>No error</u>
                                   E

4. More journalists <u>as</u> you would suspect are <u>secretly</u>
                      A   B
    writing plays or novels, <u>which</u> they hope someday
                              C
    <u>to have published</u>. <u>No error</u>
         D   E

5. <u>As long ago as</u> the twelfth century, French
        A
    alchemists <u>have</u> perfected techniques <u>for refining</u>
                B   C
    precious metals <u>from</u> other ores. <u>No error</u>
                      D   E

6. Galileo begged Rome's indulgence for his
    <u>support of</u> a Copernican system <u>in which</u> the
        A   B
    Earth circled the sun <u>instead of</u> <u>occupied</u> a central
                           C   D
    position in the universe. <u>No error</u>
                                 E

GO ON TO THE NEXT PAGE

7. <u>Squandering</u> his inheritance, the prodigal son
A

   <u>felt no compunction</u> in <u>wasting</u> his <u>father's</u> hard-
   B   C   D

   earned fortune. <u>No error</u>
   E

8. Although the piano <u>as we know it today</u> did
A

   not exist in his time, Bach <u>was writing</u>
   B

   many pieces <u>that are</u> now frequently played
   C

   <u>on that instrument</u>. <u>No error</u>
   D   E

9. The chemist Sir Humphrey Davy was a friend

   <u>of the poet</u> William Wordsworth; <u>he</u> <u>would visit</u>
   A   B   C

   with several other guests <u>at</u> a tiny cottage in the
   D

   English Lake District. <u>No error</u>
   E

10. <u>Grading</u> research papers <u>over the years</u>, the profes-
    A   B

    sor became expert <u>at recognizing</u> submissions that
    C

    <u>have been plagiarized</u> or inadequately document-
    D

    ed. <u>No error</u>
    E

11. <u>During</u> the military coup, the deposed prime min-
    A

    ister's property was <u>put up</u> for sale without <u>him</u>
    B   C

    <u>having</u> any opportunity to object. <u>No error</u>
    D   E

12. The primary difference <u>between</u> the two
    A

    positions advertised <u>is</u> <u>that</u> one is exciting;
    B   C

    <u>the other, boring</u>. <u>No error</u>
    D   E

13. <u>To conserve calories</u>, to promote digestion,
    A

    <u>or so that they are</u> less vulnerable to predators,
    B

    wild animals <u>rest</u> during <u>many of</u> their waking
    C   D

    hours. <u>No error</u>
    E

14. <u>It</u> did not occur to the interviewer <u>to ask</u> either
    A   B

    the job applicant <u>nor</u> his reference <u>whether</u> the
    C   D

    applicant had completed the project he initiated.

    <u>No error</u>
    E

GO ON TO THE NEXT PAGE

Directions: The following sentences test correctness and effectiveness of expression. In choosing answers, follow the requirements of standard written English; that is, pay attention to grammar, choice of words, sentence construction, and punctuation.

In each of the following sentences, part of the sentence or the entire sentence is underlined. Beneath each sentence you will find five ways of phrasing the underlined part. Choice (A) repeats the original; the other four are different.

Choose the answer that best expresses the meaning of the original sentence. If you think the original is better than any of the alternatives, choose it; otherwise, choose one of the others. Your choice should produce the most effective sentence—clear and precise, without awkwardness or ambiguity.

15. James's ambition was <u>not only to study but also mastering</u> the craft of journalism.

    (A) not only to study but also mastering
    (B) not only studying but to try and master
    (C) not studying only, but also mastering
    (D) not only to study but also to master
    (E) to study and as well to master

16. The Islandian government, under pressure to satisfy the needs of consumers, <u>and loosening its</u> control of the economy.

    (A) and loosening its
    (B) by loosening its
    (C) is loosening their
    (D) but loosening their
    (E) is loosening its

17. To the surprise of the school's staff, the new freshman class at Ridgewood High <u>being larger than last year's</u>.

    (A) being larger than last year's
    (B) is large, more so than last year
    (C) which is larger than the one last year
    (D) is larger than last year's
    (E) by far larger than the last

18. Night shift workers lead a strange life, working while the rest of us are sleeping, <u>then sleeping</u> while the rest of us are working.

    (A) then sleeping
    (B) after which they sleep
    (C) then they sleep
    (D) until they go to sleep
    (E) but soon they are sleeping

19. <u>The young couple eventually returned to the grassy spot where they had left their sandwiches, strolling hand-in-hand.</u>

    (A) The young couple eventually returned to the grassy spot where they had left their sandwiches, strolling hand-in-hand.
    (B) Eventually, the young couple returned to the grassy spot where they had left their sandwiches, strolling hand-in-hand.
    (C) Strolling hand-in-hand, the grassy spot where they had left their sandwiches was returned to by the young couple.
    (D) The young couple, returning to the grassy spot where they had left their sandwiches, while strolling hand-in-hand.
    (E) Strolling hand-in-hand, the young couple eventually returned to the grassy spot where they had left their sandwiches.

GO ON TO THE NEXT PAGE ▷

20. <u>Amelia Earhart was born in Kansas the first person to fly from Hawaii to California.</u>

    (A) Amelia Earhart was born in Kansas the first person to fly from Hawaii to California.

    (B) Amelia Earhart being the first person to fly from Hawaii to California and was born in Kansas.

    (C) Being the first person to fly from Hawaii to California, Amelia Earhart was born in Kansas.

    (D) Amelia Earhart was the first person to fly from Hawaii to California and was born in Kansas.

    (E) Amelia Earhart, who was born in Kansas, was the first person to fly from Hawaii to California.

21. Samuel Johnson's Dictionary, published in 1755, <u>was neither the first in English nor the largest</u>, but its quotations illustrating definitions made it the best for many decades.

    (A) was neither the first in English nor the largest

    (B) neither was it the first in English nor the largest

    (C) neither was the first in English nor the largest

    (D) neither was the first in English, and it was not the largest either

    (E) was neither the first in English, nor was it the largest

22. In the Middle Ages, when astronomical phenomena were poorly understood, <u>the comets that seemed to portend</u> military conflicts or other social crises.

    (A) the comets that seemed to portend

    (B) the comets seeming to portend

    (C) the comets seemed to portend

    (D) the comets apparently portending

    (E) and when the comets seemed to portend

23. Unusual numbers of playwrights and artists <u>flourishing in the England of Shakespeare's time</u>, and the Italy of Michelangelo's day, when cultural conditions were particularly conducive to creativity.

    (A) flourishing in the England of Shakespeare's time

    (B) by flourishing in the England of Shakespeare's time

    (C) while flourishing in Shakespeare's England

    (D) flourished in the England of Shakespeare's time

    (E) having flourished in Shakespeare's England

24. During World War I, United States Army psychologists administered a forerunner of today's I.Q. tests, <u>where it had directions that</u> were given orally in acoustically-poor and crowded rooms.

    (A) where it had directions that

    (B) whereby there were directions that

    (C) whose directions

    (D) and for it they had directions which

    (E) and it had directions which

GO ON TO THE NEXT PAGE

25. A dispute arose between Rimland and Heartland over the eastern provinces from which twenty years before a great many people <u>had emigrated</u>.

 (A) had emigrated
 (B) emigrated
 (C) had immigrated
 (D) immigrated
 (E) migrated

26. In an effort to sound like an expert, <u>the director's speech which was riddled with esoteric references</u> and specialized terms.

 (A) the director's speech which was riddled with esoteric references
 (B) the director's speech was riddled with esoteric references
 (C) the director delivered a speech riddled with esoteric references
 (D) his speech which was riddled with esoteric references
 (E) the speech of the director was riddled with esoteric references

27. <u>If the construction strike has not occurred</u>, the contractor would have had no difficulty in finishing the renovation of the restaurant on time.

 (A) If the construction strike has not occurred
 (B) If the construction strike would not have occurred
 (C) Had the construction strike not of occurred
 (D) Had it not been that the construction strike had occurred
 (E) Had it not been for the construction strike

28. In retrospect, one can see the folly of trying to unite a region containing some four hundred distinct ethnic groups, <u>each with its own language, laws, and traditions</u>.

 (A) each with its own language, laws, and traditions
 (B) each of them has its own language, laws, and traditions
 (C) each with their own language, laws, and traditions
 (D) and each of them having its own language, laws, and traditions
 (E) when they each have their own language, laws, and traditions

29. Proponents of campaign finance reform point out that people who make large donations to politicians expect to be rewarded with special favors <u>and gaining easy access</u> to the corridors of power.

 (A) and gaining easy access
 (B) and they gain easy access
 (C) and easy access
 (D) as well as gaining easy access
 (E) and to be rewarded with easy access

30. <u>Had Churchill sent planes to defend Coventry</u> from the German air raid, the Nazis would have realized that their secret code had been broken by the Allies.

 (A) Had Churchill sent planes to defend Coventry
 (B) If Churchill would have sent planes to defend Coventry
 (C) Churchill having sent planes to defend Coventry
 (D) If Churchill sent planes to defend Coventry
 (E) Churchill, by sending planes to Coventry to defend it

GO ON TO THE NEXT PAGE

31. Television shows such as *M*A*S*H* and *All in the Family* took months or even years to build a large audience, most new series today never get that chance.

    (A) Television shows such as *M*A*S*H* and *All in the Family* took

    (B) Although television shows such as *M*A*S*H* and *All in the Family* took

    (C) With television shows such as *M*A*S*H* and *All in the Family* taking

    (D) Such television shows as *M*A*S*H* and *All in the Family* took

    (E) When television shows such as *M*A*S*H* and *All in the Family* took

32. Returning to her home town after a twenty-year absence, the desperate poverty Savka saw there shocked and saddened her.

    (A) the desperate poverty Savka saw there shocked and saddened her

    (B) the desperate poverty Savka saw there was shocking and also sad to her

    (C) Savka, shocked and saddened by the desperate poverty she saw there

    (D) Savka was shocked and saddened by the desperate poverty she saw there

    (E) was a desperate poverty that shocked and saddened Savka

33. The brochure for the writing camp promises that by the time you leave the camp, you complete an entire manuscript.

    (A) complete an entire manuscript

    (B) would complete an entire manuscript

    (C) will have completed an entire manuscript

    (D) have complete an entire manuscript

    (E) had completed an entire manuscript

34. When the electrochemists Stanley Pons and Martin Fleischmann declared in 1989 that they had achieved cold fusion; scientists around the world tried to duplicate the process, they were not successful.

    (A) cold fusion; scientists around the world tried to duplicate the process, they were not successful

    (B) cold fusion then scientists around the world tried to duplicate the process only without succeeding

    (C) cold fusion, consequently scientists around the world, without success, tried to duplicate the process

    (D) cold fusion, scientists around the world tried without success to duplicate the process

    (E) cold fusion; however, scientists around the world tried to duplicate the process, without success

GO ON TO THE NEXT PAGE

Directions: The passage below is an early draft of an essay. Parts of the passage need to be rewritten.

Read the passage, and answer the questions that follow. Some questions are about individual sentences or parts of sentences; in these questions, you are asked to select the choice which will improve sentence structure and word choice. Other questions refer to parts of the essay or the entire essay and ask you to consider the organization and development of the essay. You should follow the conventions of standard written English in answering the questions. After you have chosen your answer, fill in the corresponding oval on your answer sheet.

Questions 35–39 are based on the following passage.

(1) *Last summer I was fortunate enough to be able to spend a month in France.* (2) *It was the most exciting time of my life.* (3) *I stayed with a family in Montpellier, who were in the south of France.* (4) *It was very different from my life back in the United States.* (5) *Every morning we bought fresh bread from the bakery and had coffee in a bowl instead of a cup.* (6) *The milk came in bottles fresh from the dairy.*

(7) *Back home in Winnetka, Illinois, I wouldn't think anything of taking a ten-minute shower every day, or even twice a day in the summer.* (8) *In Montpellier, we only showered once every two days and were using far less water.* (9) *First you turn the water on to get wet, then turn it off and soap yourself up, then you turned it on again to rinse off, so the water is only on for about maybe two minutes.* (10) *And it was pretty hot there in the summer, I'd never taken showers in cold water before!* (11) *I couldn't imagine what it was like in the winter.* (12) *I also noticed that although the family had a car, they hardly ever used it.* (13) *The father took the bus to work in the morning and the mother rode her bicycle when doing errands.* (14) *Since the family wasn't poor, they were well-off, I realized that gas is much more expensive in France than in the U.S.* (15) *I realized that as Americans, we can afford to take long showers and drive everywhere because we pay much less for energy.* (16) *Living in Montpellier and seeing how frugally people lived there, I get angry thinking of the resources wasted in the U.S.* (17) *When I came home, I was much more energy conscious.* (18) *I didn't drink coffee out of a bowl anymore, but I started riding my bike to school and turning the thermostat down at night.*

35. In context, which of the following is the best way to revise sentence 3 (reproduced below)?

    I stayed with a family in Montpellier, who were in the south of France.

    (A) I stayed with a family in Montpellier, who were living in the south of France.

    (B) I stayed with a family in Montpellier, which is in the south of France.

    (C) In the south of France in Montpellier were living the family that I stayed with.

    (D) The south of France in Montpellier is where I stayed with a family.

    (E) I stayed in the south of France in Montpellier where lived a family.

36. Which of the following sentences, if added after sentence 6, would best link the first paragraph with the rest of the essay?

    (A) These differences were superficial, however; I was soon to discover other, more important ones.

    (B) How I longed for my familiar existence back in the United States!

    (C) I was not prepared for the culture shock I experienced.

    (D) But I didn't let such minor inconveniences ruin my overseas experience.

    (E) Although it took a while, eventually I got used to the new way of doing things.

GO ON TO THE NEXT PAGE ⟹

37. In context, which of the following versions of sentence 8 (reproduced below) is best?

    In Montpellier, we only showered once every two days and were using far less water.

    (A) Showering only once every two days, Montpellier was where I used far less water.

    (B) Showering only once every two days and using far less water were things we did in Montpellier.

    (C) In Montpellier, we only showered once every two days and used far less water.

    (D) In Montpellier, where once every two days was when we showered, a lot less water was used.

    (E) In Montpellier, we were only showering once every two days and using far less water.

38. Which of the following best replaces the word "*And*" at the beginning of sentence 10 (reproduced below)?

    And it was pretty hot there in the summer, I'd never taken showers in cold water before!

    (A) But

    (B) Although

    (C) Yet

    (D) When

    (E) Which

39. In context, which is the best version of the underlined portion of sentence 14 (reproduced below)?

    Since the family wasn't poor, they were well-off, I realized that gas is much more expensive in France than in the U.S.

    (A) The family not being poor, they were well-off

    (B) Well-off, not poor, being the family

    (C) Since the family was well-off, they were not poor

    (D) The family wasn't poor but well-off

    (E) Since the family was well-off rather than poor

IF YOU FINISH BEFORE TIME IS CALLED, YOU MAY CHECK YOUR WORK ON THIS SECTION ONLY. DO NOT TURN TO ANY OTHER SECTION IN THE TEST.

STOP

Practice Test Two: **Answer Key**

SECTION ONE

1. C	10. C	19. D
2. A	11. C	20. A
3. E	12. E	21. B
4. A	13. C	22. B
5. D	14. A	23. E
6. D	15. E	24. B
7. A	16. C	
8. E	17. E	
9. D	18. C	

SECTION TWO

1. E	8. B	15. B
2. E	9. A	16. A
3. D	10. C	17. C
4. B	11. E	18. D
5. E	12. A	
6. A	13. C	
7. D	14. C	

SECTION THREE

25. D	34. E	43. B
26. E	35. A	44. D
27. B	36. C	45. B
28. A	37. D	46. A
29. B	38. D	47. C
30. E	39. E	48. A
31. D	40. D	
32. B	41. C	
33. C	42. C	

SECTION FOUR

19. A	30. 400
20. B	31. 7
21. C	32. 6.5 or $\frac{13}{2}$
22. B	33. 70
23. B	34. 8
24. E	35. $\frac{8}{15}$ or .533
25. C	36. $\frac{3}{8}$ or .375
26. E	37. 21
27. D	38. 1
28. C	
29. 1.5 or $\frac{3}{2}$	

SECTION FIVE

1. B	14. C	27. E
2. B	15. D	28. A
3. D	16. E	29. C
4. A	17. D	30. A
5. B	18. A	31. B
6. D	19. E	32. D
7. E	20. E	33. C
8. B	21. A	34. D
9. B	22. C	35. B
10. D	23. D	36. A
11. C	24. C	37. C
12. D	25. A	38. B
13. B	26. C	39. E

Answers and Explanations

SECTION ONE

1. C

Take this straight-ahead sentence one blank at a time. The second blank may be the easier of the two to predict. A drill sergeant naturally would want new recruits to *follow* his orders. The only answer choice that matches this prediction is (C), *complies with*. Checking out the first words confirms that this answer choice works.

2. A

This contrasting sentence refers to the Sonoran desert, so you'd expect the climate to be *harsh* or *arid*, but in spite of this, that the desert could *sustain* many life forms. Choice (A) matches this prediction.

3. E

In sentences with a semicolon, you should refer to the other part of the sentence (the part that doesn't have a blank space) to find the clue. Here you're told in the first part of the sentence that manual work is *respected by all*; thus you could predict that even noblemen could engage in it without *dishonor*.

4. A

In this contrasting sentence, you can expect the missing word to counter the concept of *individual* heroes discussed in the first part of the sentence. *Collaborative* (A) matches this prediction.

5. D

In this two-blank contrasting sentence, it's probably easier to begin with the second blank. Although critics clearly like the book, the publishers are likely to be worried about its popular appeal, which is exactly what (D) gives you. And the first word, *sophisticated*, is a positive adjective, which is what we expect as well.

6. D

The sentence reads, "Music is the perfect medium for the expression of political points of view." Music is a *way* for people to express political opinions—*way* and *method* are good predictions, which fits well with (D), *instrument*. Note that *instrument* here has nothing to do with musical instruments, it means something more like *tool*. All the other choices are common meanings of *medium* that don't fit here.

7. A

This author supports musicians who express political views. The sentence in question is about musicians that are afraid to be political: "Some musicians, those of little heart, fear that taking a strong stand will cost them precious listeners." So, "those of little heart" is an insult; the writer is saying they lack courage (A). (B) is out, since the author says that listeners are actually more loyal to political musicians. The quote in question refers to musicians, not fans (C). The author never addresses the difficulty of writing political music (D). (E) is off base, because the phrase in question refers to non-political musicians, and Guthrie is described as just the opposite.

8. E

The author of Passage 2 does not like to see politics mixed with music. "Musicians should play music, not dabble in politics as a hobby." So, musicians who deal in political issues are dabblers (E). (A) is the viewpoint of author 1, not author 2. (B) is out of scope, since the idea of musicians running for office does not come up in either paragraph. (C) might be tempting, but is too extreme. The author might find political music boring, but he never says that all listeners find it boring. (D) is too extreme. The author says that he listens to music to escape, but doesn't imply that political musicians *never* write music that helps listeners escape their troubles.

9. D

Author 1 thinks that political music is great, while author 2 thinks that musicians should stick to music, and not dabble in politics. This point of disagreement is summed up by (D). Author 2 thinks that it's not a good idea for musicians to mess around with politics, but never implies that it's illegal (A). (B) and (D) are out of scope, since author 2 never mentions Guthrie or his fans—remember that author 2 doesn't like political music, but that doesn't mean that those musicians are untalented. (C) is a distortion; author 2 enjoys political analysis—he just thinks it should be left to professionals.

Language Ability Passage

This science passage shouldn't present too many difficulties for the reader who knows better than to get bogged down in the wealth of information presented in a typical science passage. When you first read the passage, instead of trying to take it all in, you should work on just getting a general sense of the structure of the passage and the broad themes under discussion.

The first paragraph introduces the main idea of the passage, which is that language separates humans from animals. The second paragraph mentions Chomsky's theory that humans are hardwired to acquire language. The third paragraph discusses the areas in the brain where language is processed. Paragraph four looks at how scientists originally came to know what they do about the way the brain processes language, and the final paragraph mentions a promising new investigative tool for brain-language research. If you can glean that from reading the passage, you're more than ready to attack the questions.

10. C

This is a line reference question, so reread the sentence in question. It's easy to see that the author here is not using *quotations* (A) or *scientific data* (B). Nor is she using *analogies* (D) or *inferences* (E). Phrases such as "to discuss and debate ideas" are *generalizations* (C).

11. C

The question that begins paragraph two serves to introduce and summarize the debate that is discussed in the rest of the paragraph. (A), (B), and (D) are wrong, and (E) is wrong because the topic shifts in the middle of the next paragraph.

12. E

The author mentions computers in his discussion of Chomsky's theory that our brains, like computers, are hardwired to acquire language. Choice (E) paraphrases Chomsky's theory.

13. C

You should have suspected that this information is found in the latter part of the passage, and if you scan there for the words "speak" and "hear" you'll find them in the sentence that begins on line 55, which discusses PET scans (C).

14. A

Scan for the reference to Broca and Wernicke in the fourth paragraph and reread this portion to figure out its relevance to the passage. As the passage notes, much of the information about the brain's acquisition of language comes from their studies. In other words, the author discusses the work of Broca and Wernicke to illustrate the method by which early discoveries were made about the brain and language (A).

Circus Rider Passage

This passage can be tough slogging through because the prose is very florid and rich in descriptive detail. Because this is a narrative passage, you should just try to concentrate on the author's attitude towards the subject of his reminiscence, in this case a young circus performer practicing her equestrian act. Clearly the author was extremely moved by the young showgirl's performance, particularly by her seriousness and dedication to her craft. Once you figure that out, you are ready to proceed to the questions.

15. E

In this specific question, you'll have to scan the first paragraph for the author's description of the horse. There you'll read of its "great size and meekness." The correct answer, *huge but submissive* (E), is a direct paraphrase of this.

16. C

This is a vocabulary-in-context question, so reread the sentence and predict the meaning of *charge* here, much as you would in a Sentence Completion. "The trainer guided her *charge*"—clearly here the charge refers to the horse and is a secondary definition of *charge*, which can mean "something under supervision."

17. E

Reread the lines before you try to answer the question. There you'll find that the showgirl is in "most respects" like the others, but that "her manner" distinguished her from them; in other words, she resembled her peers but stood apart from them (E). Avoid answer choices that are too strongly worded, such as (C).

18. C

Read before and after this line to get a sense of the context. You should get a sense that the sentence exists to stress that the author is trying to convey a feeling that is difficult to describe, which is what (C) says.

19. D

The sentence in question contrasts the boasts of the advance agents with the modesty of most circus workers. Choices (A), (B), (C), and (E) simply don't make sense in reference to this sentence. (D), with its mention of "contrasts," does make sense.

20. A

Reread the description of the showgirl's performance in the ring, located in the fourth paragraph. There it notes that "her brief tour included only elementary postures and tricks"; in other words, she was concentrating on simple tricks (A).

21. B

Scan for a reference to "serious artist"—it's mentioned in lines 57–58, where the girl reminds the author of the "way all serious artists seize free minutes to hone the blade of their talent." In other words, the girl is a serious artist because of her devotion to improving her skills (B).

22. B

Stay close to the broad theme of the passage. Here the author is not so much interested in giving a play-by-play of the girl's technical skills as in describing her dedication to her craft. For this question it may have been easier to find evidence to eliminate all the wrong answer choices. Any time you can find four wrong answers, you've found the right answer.

23. E

Again, reread the lines in question and stay close to the broad theme of the passage. The physical setting was plain, but the scene was elevated by the girl's performance and her obvious devotion to her craft. Again, even if (E) didn't pop out at you, you should have been able to eliminate the wrong answer choices by seeing that they either contradicted, or were never mentioned in, the passage.

24. B

Reread the last paragraph if you are unsure of the answer. The author is talking about the ring, or stage where the girl is performing. The "ring of ambition" is reflected by the ring of the circus stage.

SECTION TWO

1. E

Just substitute 8 for r in the equation. $(8 + 4)^2 = (12)^2 = 144$.

2. E

Percent $= \dfrac{\text{Part}}{\text{Whole}} \times 100\%$. Here the percent is $\dfrac{360}{800} \times 100\% = 45\%$.

3. D

Refer to the scale and translate the bars into numbers; 9th grade is 200, 10th grade is 400, 11th is 450, and 12th is about 380, so together they add up to $200 + 400 + 450 + 380 = 1,430$, which is closest to (D).

4. B

Since all the angles together add up to 360°, you know that $3a + 3b = 360$. Divide both sides of the equation by 3 and you get $a + b = 120$.

5. E

Take this rate problem one step at a time. If Josephine types 12 words in 20 seconds, then she types 36 words in 60 seconds or 1 minute; thus she types twice that, or 72 words, in 2 minutes.

6. A

Translate the English into math. For instance, "12 greater than" means you add 12 to the expression, and "the square root of the product of 10 and a" would translate as $\sqrt{10a}$, so the entire expression would translate to $12 + \sqrt{10a}$.

7. D

There is a shortcut to the correct answer, but always remember that it's better to be careful than wrong. The odd integers between 8 and 26 start at 9 and go to 25, and there are 9 integers in all. The even integers between 5 and 23 start at 6 and go to 22, and once again there are 9 integers in all. Note that each integer in the first set is 3 more than the corresponding integer in the second set. Thus the difference between the sums should be $3 \times 9 = 27$.

8. B

Begin by simplifying the fraction:

$\dfrac{\frac{1}{a}}{\frac{1}{9}} = \frac{1}{a} \div \frac{1}{9} = \frac{1}{a} \times \frac{9}{1} = \frac{9}{a}$. Thus $\frac{9}{a} = \frac{3}{1}$. Cross-multiply

and you get $3a = 9$, so $a = 3$.

9. A

If the average cost of two of the books is $15, the total cost of the two books is $30, which means that the total cost of the three remaining books is $70 − $30 = $40.

10. C

Note that the figure is not drawn to scale, so even though the points look evenly spaced, they're not. Label the lengths you're given and see what comes of it. For instance, you're told that $AC = 10$, and that it's twice the length of CD, so $CD = 5$. $BD = 9$, and since BD is composed of BC and CD, $CD = 9 − 5 = 4$.

11. E

To figure out the value of r, begin by filling in the angle measures for the triangle. For instance, the angle vertical to the 54° angle is also 54°, and the angle complimentary to the 138° angle has a degree measure of $180° − 138° = 42°$. Now that you know two of the angles in the triangle, you can calculate the angle measure of the third angle (which we'll call x): $x + 54 + 42 = 180$, so $x = 84$. The angle measure we're looking for is complementary to this angle, so $84 + r = 180$. Thus, $r = 96$.

12. A

First list out the first six positive integers: 2, 4, 6, 8, 10, and 12. It would be helpful to figure out the least common multiple of these integers, which is most easily accomplished by figuring out the prime factorization of each; 2 is prime; $4 = 2 \times 2$; $6 = 2 \times 3$; $8 = 2 \times 2 \times 2$; $10 = 2 \times 5$; $12 = 2 \times 2 \times 3$. So the smallest integer that would incor-

porate all of the necessary prime factors (i.e., the least common multiple) would be $2 \times 2 \times 2 \times 3 \times 5 = 120$. All of the answer choices can be divided into 120 except for 18, which contains an extra 3 among its prime factors.

13. C

Here you just have to know that slope is equal to $\dfrac{\text{rise}}{\text{run}}$, or, in mathematical terms, $\dfrac{y_2 - y_1}{x_2 - x_1}$. So here the slope equals $\dfrac{9 - 6}{4 - 2} = \dfrac{3}{2}$.

14. C

If $rs < 0$, then either r is negative and s is positive, or s is negative and r is positive. So clearly (A) and (B) can be eliminated. You could try to pick numbers to eliminate other answer choices. For instance, if $r = −1$ and $s = 1$, then (D) is true, and if $r = −1$ and $s = 2$, then (E) is true. Moreover, (C) *cannot* be true, because if $r − s = 0$, then $r = s$, which we know cannot be the case.

15. B

If the area of the rectangle is 48, then BC, which is the diameter of the semicircle, must be 4, because the area of a rectangle equals *length* × *width*. So the radius of the semicircle is half the diameter, or 2, and the area of the semicircle is $\frac{1}{2}(\pi r^2) = \frac{1}{2}[\pi(2)^2] = \frac{1}{2}(4\pi) = 2\pi$.

16. A

Use reverse FOIL to factor the quadratic equation.
$x^2 + 4x − 12 = (x + 6)(x − 2)$, so $(x + 6)(x − 2) = 0$.
Now set the terms in the parentheses to equal 0 in order to find the possible values for x; $(x + 6) = 0$ or $(x − 2) = 0$, so x is either −6 or 2.

17. C

Don't be freaked out by symbol questions. Just plug the numbers into the right-hand side of the symbol equation. Here you have a two-step symbol problem, so as with any equation you should begin inside the parentheses. $3 \circ 5 = 3(5 − 3) = 3 \times 2 = 6$. So now you are looking for $4 \circ 6$, which is $4(6 − 4) = 4 \times 2 = 8$.

18. D

Begin by applying your knowledge of ratios to the numbers you are given. Here you are told that the *before* ratio is 4:3, so the *before* ratio total is $4 + 3 = 7$. But the actual *before* total number of oranges and apples is 56, which is 8×7, so that means there are $8 \times 4 = 32$ oranges and $8 \times 3 = 24$ apples. Now you can backsolve to get the correct answer. We'll start with (C): If 7 apples and 7 oranges are removed, you'd be left with 25 oranges and 17 apples. $\frac{25}{17} \neq \frac{3}{2}$, but it's close, so let's try the next closest number, $n = 8$ (D). If 8 apples and 8 oranges are removed, you'd be left with 24 oranges and 16 apples. $\frac{24}{16} = \frac{3}{2}$, so (D) is the correct answer.

SECTION THREE

25. D

The key phrase here is "to equal and even—Wright's successes." So we are looking for a word that means *more than equal*. Choice (D), *surpass*, works nicely.

26. E

We are looking for a word that covers the wide variety of trumpets described in this sentence. Look for a word that means "varied" among the answer choices. Choice (E), *diverse*, works best here.

27. B

"Weighing over seventy tons" leads us to predict a word like *large* or *gigantic* for the first blank. The word "yet" sets up a contrast for the second blank. We want a word like *small* or *tiny* for the second blank. Only (B), *gargantuan*, and (D), *prodigious*, work for the first blank. Of these two options, only choice (B), *small*, works for the second blank. So (B) is correct.

28. A

Take this two-blank sentence one word at a time. Here it might be easier to begin with the first blank. You're looking for a word that works with "difficult to sight" in the first blank. *Elusive* (A) and *crafty* (B) are the only choices that work. Now predict a word for the second blank to choose between (A) and (B). We're looking for a word that sets up a contrast with "difficult to sight." Choice (A), *confined*, works here.

29. B

The key phrase here is "each having its own government, maintaining its own militia . . . " So, we want to choose words that describe the colonies as independent and autonomous. Both *distinct* (B) and *independent* (C) work for the first blank. Choice (B) is the correct answer, since putting *autonomously* in the second blank is consistent with the flow of the sentence.

30. E

Since kudzu was "introduced" to the United States in 1876, it must have flourished in Japan prior to then. So we are looking for a choice that is consistent with this idea. *Indigenous* means "native to a specific area or region," so (E) is correct.

31. D

We are looking for an answer choice that is consistent with the phrase "towering over others of his generation both physically and intellectually." A choice that connotes largeness is what we're looking for here. So choice (D), *a titan*, is right on the money.

32. B

Look for an answer that is consistent with "shunning personal contact with those outside her family circle." Choice (B), *reclusive*, is just what we're looking for.

Malagasy People

33. C

The passage states that there is "linguistic and cultural evidence" to support the theory. (C) cites the linguistic evidence that the Malagasy language is similar to a language spoke in Indonesia. The author mentions the geographical relationship of Indonesia to Madagascar, but the passage does not use this relationship as evidence for the claim that Indonesians settled Madagascar (A). (B) is directly contradicted by the passage, which explicitly states that there have been no archaeological finds that point unequivocally to Indonesia. (D) and (E) are out of scope, since the passage never refers to housing styles or poetry.

34. E

The author argues that rice cultivation, ancestor worship, and outrigger canoes are cultural evidence of a connection with Indonesia. So, a good prediction for the word "resonance" would be *origin*, or *style*. (E) fits well with these predictions. (A) and (D) are related to common meanings of resonance, but are too literal to work here, since there is no reference to sounds. The resonance is *used* as *evidence*, but the word resonance doesn't *mean* evidence (B). (C) doesn't fit at all in the sentence.

Predator Territories

35. A

The author writes "this complex interplay was dramatically illustrated…." So, what is the interplay? The first sentence says "mammalian predator territories … constantly [shift] over time." This is nicely summed up by (A). Although the wolves did push the coyotes down the food chain, this answer choice doesn't show the primary purpose of the Yellowstone example. (C) is the opposite of the main idea of the passage. Although the passage states in the first sentence that predator territories are affected by the size of prey populations, the Yellowstone example instead shows that one predator can affect the territory of another (D). (E) is out of the scope of the passage, since you don't know whether the consequence was unforeseen.

36. C

The author notes that "the coyote population was cut in half, with a corresponding increase in rodents…." Why would a decrease in coyotes lead to an increase in rodents? (C) provides an explanation; if the coyotes ate the rodents (but the wolves didn't), then a decrease in coyotes would likely lead to an increase in rodents. (A), (B), (D), and (E) all mention factors that cannot directly explain an increase in rodents.

The Sistine Chapel Pair

Here we have a pair of passages written by authors who have diametrically opposed points of view about the recent restoration of the Sistine Chapel. The author of Passage 1 goes after the restoration team with all the ammunition he's got. After spending a paragraph making the point that Michelangelo himself would have been appalled at the effects of the cleaning, the author goes on to assert that the cleaning process removed an essential artistic element of the frescoes. This element—of anger and pessimism—was, according to the author, not the result of centuries of dirt but was rather put there by the master himself. To add insult to injury, the restorers removed protective layers of glue in the process. After reading the first passage, you're ready answer questions 36–39.

Now it's time to focus on Passage 2, which counters the attack of Passage 1 by claiming that the dark, forbidding quality of the frescoes was not, as the author of Passage 1 argues, an effect intended by Michelangelo, but just dirt. The problem, according to Passage 2, is that people had gotten so used to how the frescoes looked before they were cleaned that the cleaning has wiped away "cherished myths" about Michelangelo as well as grime. According to the author, the process has revealed Michelangelo to be a master Renaissance craftsman. This, he states, is why people like the author of Passage 1 don't like what was done; they are used to seeing Michelangelo as a "wayward genius" rather than a great but conventional artist.

37. D

The point of this paragraph is that Michelangelo would not be bothered by the damage done by time and nature to the Sistine Chapel, but he would be upset by what the restorers did. In this vein, being "philosophical about the damage" wrought by rain means being "unruffled" by it, so (D) is correct.

38. D

The author of Passage 1 is not unhappy with the deterioration of the frescoes over time; he's unhappy with the restoration. The inference he wants the reader to make in the first paragraph is that if Michelangelo would have accepted the deterioration as unfortunate but natural, we should have accepted it also (D). (A) is wrong because the author of Passage 1 says that Michelangelo would be able to perceive the effect of time and the environment on the frescoes. (B) is wrong because there still would have been water damage, even if the Chapel were not kept in use. (C) is tricky: it's something the author implies, but not in the first paragraph. (E) is another close choice; it's wrong because we don't know for sure what Michelangelo thought about the deterioration of his frescoes when he was painting them. All we know is that the author thinks Michelangelo wouldn't be bothered by the damage if he saw it now.

39. E

The choices for this question are rather long, but if even just one of the two "elements" in a choice didn't make sense, you could have eliminated it. For example, (A) is wrong because author 1 does not appreciate the removal of grime at all. (B) is out because Michelangelo's painting techniques—other than the final application of glaze—are not described, nor is the claim made or mentioned that glue was never used on the painting (C). The "elements" in (D) and (E) can all be found in the second paragraph. (D) is wrong, and (E) is correct because (E) points out the author's use of irony in emphasizing that Michelangelo disliked what the restorers revel in: bright colors.

40. D

For this vocabulary-in-context question, refer to the line in question. The climate control system will "arrest"—that is, "retard"—the process of darkening by pollution (D). The other words are synonyms of "arrest" as it is used in other contexts.

41. C

In the second sentence of Passage 2, the author says that the responsibility of restoring the Sistine Chapel is great but "does not explain" why the Chapel had been allowed to fall into disrepair. In other words, the responsibility was not a strong enough deterrent by itself (C) to have stopped restorers. This makes (A), (D), and (E) wrong and (C) correct. Neither author claims that the frescoes are "the greatest work of the Renaissance period" (B)—this is an extreme choice.

42. C

The author of Passage 2 says that the layer of dirt between the painting and the first layer of glaze shows that the first layer of glaze was put on the painting a long time after Michelangelo finished it (if the glaze had been put on right after he finished it, dirt would have had no time to accumulate). The author is establishing that the first layer of glaze was not put on by Michelangelo (C) and therefore was acceptable to remove. Choices (A), (D), and (E) miss the author's purpose here, which is to justify the removal of that first layer of glaze. (B) is too broad in scope.

43. B

The point of the quotation from the member of the restoration team is that the Sistine Chapel is such a good example of fresco painting that it can be regarded as a "valuable source of information about fresco-painting techniques" (B). (A) and (D) both distort the author's comparison of the painting to a treatise on fresco art. There is no evidence in the passage that either (C) or (E) is true.

44. D

The author of Passage 2 says that as a result of the restoration's brightening of the fresco colors, Michelangelo no longer seems to have been a "wayward genius, defiant of Renaissance fresco-painting protocol." The inference you are required to make is that since the brightening of colors made Michelangelo seem to be more conventional as a Renaissance artist, it must have been standard at the time to paint frescoes in bright colors. In other words, darkening colors intentionally was not common practice (D). (A) and (B) may be true, but there is no direct evidence in the passage to support them (Michelangelo could have painted differently from others and still have been considered superior at the time; he also didn't necessarily need to be a "fiercely independent and individualistic thinker" to be defiant of fresco-painting protocol). Being defiant of Renaissance fresco-painting protocol is not a negative trait, so (C) is out. As for (E), the author of Passage 2 still considers Michelangelo a great artist even though he may not be a "wayward genius."

45. B

The author of Passage 2 uses the image of the cleaned-up vagabond to explain the reason critics don't like the effects of the restoration: they no longer recognize their beloved artist without the dark anger and fearfulness. (B) is correct. (A) and (C) can be ruled out as completely irrelevant. (D) contradicts the author of Passage 2's belief that the artist's image has been altered—it is now more accurate. This does not mean, though, that every single art historian has been wrong about Michelangelo; we have no way of knowing whether this extreme statement is true or not, so (E) is out.

46. A

The heart of the controversy over the Sistine Chapel is the question of color brightness: was the darkening of the ceiling intentional or not? Author 1 says yes, while author 2 says no. (A) is correct. (D) may have stopped you for a second, but both authors acknowledge that the frescoes were originally done in color. The delay of restoration (B) is something only author 2 discusses. (C) is wrong because author 1 doesn't think the restorers should have used anything. (E) is out because the amount of damage done by the dirt is not a point of contention between the authors.

47. C

As we've established, author 1 thinks that the quality of suppressed anger and thunderous pessimism was intentional. Author 2 considers author 1's view to be nothing but a "cherished myth" that the restoration has proved to be false (C). (A) is wrong because author 2 delights in the fact that the essential element of brightness was changed during the restoration. (B) is out because we know nothing about "many different and contradictory interpretations" of the painting. (D) makes no sense as a rebuttal to Passage 1 since the heart of author 1's argument is that the restoration destroyed the painting's quality of anger and pessimism. Finally, (E) is wrong because the views of author 1 are representative of the views of past historical experts.

48. A

Author 1's opinion of the restorers' "protection" of the frescoes can be found in the final paragraph of Passage 1: the paintings are now being directly affected by pollution, he says. No doubt author 1 would say sarcastically that the protection of one layer of dirt was "not as effective as the restorers had hoped" (A). (B) is too extreme; author 1 may be skeptical about protection of the frescoes, but it's always possible that something can do the job. Evidence that author 1 would respond as in (C) or (E) cannot be found in Passage 1, and (D) contradicts author 1's argument.

SECTION FOUR

19. A

Mr. Schafer bought 1 case with 11 cans of soda and 7 cases with 6 cans of soda each, so he bought $1(11) + 7(6)$ or $11 + 42 = 53$ cans of soda.

20. B

Use $AB = 10$ to solve for BC:
$BC = 16 + AB$
$BC = 16 + 10$
$BC = 26$

Now use $AB = 10$ and $BC = 26$ to solve for AC:
$AC = AB + BC$
$AC = 10 + 26$
$AC = 36$

21. C

Notice that $3x + 15$ is equivalent to $3(x + 5)$. Since $x + 5$ is a, $3x + 15 = 3(x + 5) = 3a$.

22. B

If you are uncertain of how to solve a problem, think logically and eliminate unrealistic answer choices. This will increase your odds of guessing the correct answer. Use *sum of terms* $= 7$ to solve for average:

$$average = \frac{sum\ of\ terms}{number\ of\ terms}$$

$$average = \frac{7}{2}$$

23. B

$(3 \times 10^3) + (3 \times 10^4) = 3,000 + 30,000 = 33,000 = 33 \times 1,000 = 33 \times 10^3$.

24. E

Find the range of values for the product xy by multiplying the maximum and minimum values of each variable, in every combination:

xy could equal $(0)(-2) = 0$
xy could equal $(0)(5) = 0$
xy could equal $(6)(-2) = -12$
xy could equal $(6)(5) = 30$

So the smallest value of xy is -12 and the largest is 30.

25. C

If the area of the square is 25, each side is 5. Use this fact to identify the sum of the lengths of the other two sides of each triangles. If each triangle has a perimeter of 21, the other 2 sides must add up to $21 - 5 = 16$. What's more, each of the two vertical sides of the square is 5. So, the perimeter of the entire figure is $2(16) + 2(5) = 42$.

26. E

Translating word problems into written equations can help you figure out where to get started on complicated questions. Solve for j using the average formula:

$$\text{average} = \frac{\text{sum of terms}}{\text{number of terms}}$$

Now, express this as

$$\frac{\text{sum of terms}}{\text{average of terms}} = \text{number of terms} = j$$

27. D

Since $AB = BC$, the angles across from them must be equal

too. If $\angle ABC$ is 50 degrees, $\angle BAC$ and $\angle BCA =$

$\frac{(180 - 50)}{2} = 65$ degrees. Since $DE = EF = DF$, triangle

DEF is equilateral, with all angles measuring 60 degrees.

You are given that $\angle BDE = 70$, so you can solve: $\angle ADF =$

$180 - \angle BDE + \angle EDF) = 180 - (70 + 60) = 50$. Finally,

$\angle DFA = 180 - (\angle ADF + \angle DAF) = 180 - (50 + 65) = 65$.

28. C

As with all probability questions, the trick is to compare a
part with a whole. As soon as you can pinpoint the part—
the shaded region—in relation to the whole—the entire
figure—you can solve the problem.

Area of unshaded region $= 4 \times (2 \times 3) = 24$

Area of shaded region $= (3 \times 3) = 9$

Total area of figure $= 24 + 9 = 33$

$$\text{Probability} = \frac{\text{desired outcome}}{\text{possible outcomes}} = \frac{9}{33} = \frac{3}{11}$$

29. 1.5 or $\frac{3}{2}$

Find an equation to relate the height of the tree to the
yearly rainfall. Since height is directly proportional to rainfall, you can represent their relationship as $h = kr$, where h
is height, r is rainfall, and k is a constant. Use the given values to find k; then, use the equation to find the height of
the tree in the low-rainfall area:

$30 = k(200)$

$.15 = k$

$h = .15(10) = 1.5$ meters

30. 400

This problem conveniently provides an equation you can
use to find the answer:

$(50)2^{\frac{6}{2}} = (50)2^3 = 50(8) = 400$

(You could also calculate the number of bacteria 2, 4, and
6 days after the start of the experiment by doubling the
number each time, beginning with the initial population
of 50.)

31. 7

If $6y = 12$, then $y = 2$. So, $x - 2y = 3$ can be rewritten as
$x - 2(2) = 3$; $x - 4 = 3$, so x must equal 7.

32. 6.5 or $\frac{13}{2}$

Three books at $14.50 = 3(\$14.50) = \$43.50$. If Bill paid
with a \$50 bill, he would receive $\$50 - \$43.50 = \$6.50$ in
change.

33. 70

To determine the total number of tiles necessary to cover
the floor, figure out the total area of the floor and divide
that value by the total area of a single tile. So

$$\frac{\text{Total Area}}{\text{Tile Area}} = \frac{56 \times 60}{6 \times 8} = \frac{56 \times 60}{8 \times 6} = 7 \times 10 = 70 \text{ tiles}.$$

34. 8

Begin by solving for n. We know that $4^{n+1} = 64$; $64 = 4^3$. So $n + 1 = 3$, and $n = 2$. Thus, $n^3 = 2^3 = 8$.

35. $\frac{8}{15}$ or .533

If you are given two ratios with one term in common, in
this case a, you can compare ratios if you have the same
number of "a"s in each ratio. We're told that $a{:}b$ is 3:4,
and $a{:}c$ is 2:5. The least common multiple of 2 and 3 is 6,
so we need to double the first ratio, and triple the second
ratio. So $a{:}b$ can be rewritten as 6:8, and $a{:}c$ can be rewritten as 6:15. Now since we have the same number of "a"s
in each ratio, we can compare "b"s to "c"s.
The ratio of b to c is $\frac{8}{15}$ or .533.

36. $\frac{3}{8}$, or .375

We must determine how many different ways the 3 coins
could land, and then count the number of possibilities that

have exactly 2 coins tails-up. It's easiest to do this systematically on paper, using "H" for "Heads" and "T" for "Tails."

H-H-H	T-H-H
H-H-T	T-H-T
H-T-H	T-T-H
H-T-T	T-T-T

Be sure to find every combination. There are 8 possible outcomes, but only 3 of them have exactly 2 tails showing. (Remember: The combination with 3 tails up doesn't fit the description.) So the probability of getting exactly two tails is 3 out of 8, or $\frac{3}{8}$.

37. 21

Begin by finding the prime factorization of 84; $84 = 21 \times 4 = 7 \times 3 \times 2 \times 2$. Notice that 2×2 is a perfect square. In this case, the smallest perfect square will consist of three pairs of prime factors. So we need to multiply 84 by 7×3 or 21 to get the smallest perfect square. So $j = 21$.

38. 1

To find the length of *BD*, first find the length of *OD* and subtract that from the length of *BO*. To find the length of *OD*, look at the right triangle of *ADO*. Since the radius is 5, you know the hypotenuse, *AO*, is 5. Since *AC* has a length of 6, and it is bisected by *BO*, you know that *AD* has a length of 3. So *ADO* is a 3-4-5 right triangle, and the missing side *OD* must be of length 4. *BD* is a radius with a length of 5. So the length of $BD - OD = 5 - 4 = 1$.

SECTION FIVE

1. B

The use of the word *flown* isn't right. *Flown*, the past participle form of *fly*, can't be used as a main verb without a form of the verb *have*. What's needed here is the simple past form of *fly*, which is *flew*.

2. B

In respect of is incorrect The prepositional phrase is *with respect to*.

3. D

Does something make an *impression for* someone? No, it makes an *impression on* someone.

4. A

The correct comparative form is *more . . . than*, not *more . . . as*.

5. B

This sentence describes events prior to a time in the past, so instead of the present perfect *have perfected*, it should use the past perfect *had perfected*.

6. D

Instead of takes a participle: *Occupied* should be corrected to *occupying*.

7. E

This sentence contains no error. The verb forms are correct and the preposition *in* is used idiomatically with *compunction*.

8. B

The past participle—*was writing*—is used to describe an ongoing action contemporary with another action. In this case, the simple past tense, *wrote*, should be used.

9. B

He could refer to either *Davy* or *Wordsworth*; this pronoun has no clear antecedent.

10. D

To indicate that plagiarism or documentation came before both the recognition and the becoming expert, this sentence needs the past perfect tense: *had been plagiarized* or inadequately documented.

11. C

The gerund, not the pronoun, should be the object of the preposition *without*, and the pronoun *him* should be changed to the possessive *his*.

12. D

A semicolon is used to separate two independent clauses. The second half of the sentence should read something like "the other is boring."

13. B

Items in a list need to be parallel. The underlined portion should read something like "or to be less vulnerable to predators."

14. C

The construction *either . . . or* requires *or*, not *nor*.

15. D

This sentence contains a parallelism problem. The idea in this sentence is best expressed with the *not only . . . but also* formula. When this formula is used, the two items connected by it have to be in the same grammatical form. Since what are described are *ambitions*, it's idiomatic to use infinitives.

16. E

The original sentence doesn't have a verb, because an "-ing" word without a helping verb isn't a verb. Choices (C) and (E) supply verbs, but choice (C) introduces an incorrect pronoun. The pronoun must refer to *government*, which is singular. So, the pronoun must be *its*.

17. D

Again, the original sentence doesn't have a verb. Choices (B) and (D) supply the missing verb, but (B) makes other changes that introduce new mistakes.

18. A

The original sentence is best. This sentence describes a two-step process. It's a bit like a very short list. Therefore, both steps must be given in parallel forms. The first step is *working* (with no pronoun), so the second step should be simply *sleeping* (with no pronoun).

19. E

Strolling hand-in-hand is a modifying phrase that modifies the noun *couple*. Only (E) places the modifying phrase next to *couple*.

20. E

The original sentence is a run-on. Choice (E) provides the best fix, by introducing a subordinate clause.

21. A

The original sentence is the most clear and concise.

22. C

The original sentence has no independent clause. This problem is corrected by getting rid of *that*. Choices (B) and (D) have no independent clauses, either; they contain "-ing" forms of verbs that can't function as main verbs.

23. D

Only (D) corrects the problem with the sentence by turning *flourishing* into *flourished*—a main verb in the past tense.

24. C

Choice (C) most clearly shows the connection between the first clause of the sentence, which identifies a kind of test, and the second clause of the sentence, which asserts something about the directions of the test. *Whose directions* compactly states the relation between these clauses.

25. A

The original sentence is best. The past perfect tense is correct because it describes an action that occurred prior to the main action of the sentence, which is in the past tense (*arose*). Note that *emigrated*, not *immigrated*, is the correct word here: you *emigrate* from a place, and *immigrate* to a place.

26. C

Logically, the introductory phrase should refer to the director himself, not to his speech. Therefore, the correct answer has to begin with *the director*.

27. E

Only (E) formulates the conditional mood correctly.

28. A

The sentence is fine as it is. (B) is a run-on. (C) and (E) contain plural pronouns that don't agree with their singular antecedents, and (D) makes no sense grammatically.

29. C

The donors expect to be rewarded with two things: *special favors* and *easy access*. For the sake of parallelism, both these things should be expressed in the same grammatical form: adjective + noun. The other choices are wordy and lack parallel structure; (E) is also redundant.

30. A

The first clause of the sentence correctly sets up a condition which was not fulfilled: Churchill did not send planes to defend Coventry, and hence the Nazis did not realize the allies had broken their code. (A) is another way of saying *If Churchill had sent planes to defend Coventry*. (B) is gramatically unsound: "if he would have" is a very common error. Watch out for it! (C) and (E) are fragments, and (D) uses a wrong verb tense (*sent* for the past perfect *had sent*).

31. B

The conjunction *although* correctly expresses the contrast that is implied here: television shows were formerly given time to build up an audience, but now they are not. (A) and (D) are run-on sentences, and (C) and (E) are illogical.

32. D

The opening phrase describes Savka, but the way the sentence is phrased, it sounds as though *the desperate poverty* is returning home after a 20-year absence. You know the correct answer will begin with *Savka* to correct the misplaced modifier. (C) is a sentence fragment, so (D) is the correct answer.

33. C

The phrase *by the time you leave* is the clue to the sentence's meaning. Some time in the future you will leave the camp, but before that happens, you will complete a manuscript. To express this sequence of events clearly, you need to use the future perfect tense: *you will have completed*.

34. D

The sentence as it stands contains a fragment before the semicolon and a run-on after it. Choices (B), (C), and (E) are all awkward and ungrammatical.

35. B

The word *who* modifies a person not a place. Since the first clause in this sentence ends with a place, Montpellier, you need to modify this with the word *which*.

36. A

The second paragraph explores differences between French and American lifestyles that are more substantial than those outlined in the first paragraph. (Sentence 18 nicely encapsulates the difference between the two paragraphs with its reference to fleeting versus long-lasting changes.) Thus (A), which hints at the "more important" distinctions described in the second paragraph, is the best connection. (B) and (C) come out of nowhere: The writer is merely noting, not lamenting, certain cultural differences. (D) is illogical because the writer describes her time in France as "exciting." (E) isn't bad as a conclusion to the first paragraph, but it doesn't work as a tie-in to the second paragraph.

37. C

(C) fixes sentence 8's inconsistency in tense by employing the simple past of both verbs, which is correct in context. (A) contains a misplaced modifier: Montpellier cannot be modified by a clause beginning with *showering*. (B) contains an awkward and unnecessary shift to the passive voice. (D) is awkwardly worded and changes the meaning of the original sentence. (E) is consistent in tense but its use of the past continuous ("were . . . showering") instead of the simple past doesn't work in context.

38. B

From context, we know that the writer is trying to say that despite the summer heat, cold-water showers were a new and different experience. (B) makes this clear. (A) and (C), although they seem to provide the requisite sense of contrast, produce ungrammatical sentences. (D) and (E) make no sense and do not form grammatical sentences either.

39. E

(E) removes the sentence fragment that is the principal weakness in sentence 14. (A) and (C) create sentence fragments, (B) is awkwardly worded, and (D), by removing the conjunction *since*, creates a sentence fragment.

Chapter Eight: **Practice Test Three**

HOW TO TAKE THIS PRACTICE TEST

Before taking this practice test, find a quiet room where you can work uninterrupted for two and a half hours. Make sure you have a comfortable desk, your calculator, and several No. 2 pencils. Use the answer sheet to record your answers. Once you start, don't stop until you've finished. Remember—you can review any questions within a section, but you may not jump from one section to another.

PSAT Practice Test Three
Answer Sheet

Remove (or photocopy) this answer sheet and use it to complete the practice test. See the answer key following the test when finished. The "Compute Your Score" section at the end of Section Two will show you how to find your score.

Start with number 1 for each section. If a section has fewer questions than answer spaces, leave the extra spaces blank.

SECTION 1

1. (A) (B) (C) (D) (E)   7. (A) (B) (C) (D) (E)   13. (A) (B) (C) (D) (E)   19. (A) (B) (C) (D) (E)
2. (A) (B) (C) (D) (E)   8. (A) (B) (C) (D) (E)   14. (A) (B) (C) (D) (E)   20. (A) (B) (C) (D) (E)
3. (A) (B) (C) (D) (E)   9. (A) (B) (C) (D) (E)   15. (A) (B) (C) (D) (E)   21. (A) (B) (C) (D) (E)
4. (A) (B) (C) (D) (E)   10. (A) (B) (C) (D) (E)   16. (A) (B) (C) (D) (E)   22. (A) (B) (C) (D) (E)
5. (A) (B) (C) (D) (E)   11. (A) (B) (C) (D) (E)   17. (A) (B) (C) (D) (E)   23. (A) (B) (C) (D) (E)
6. (A) (B) (C) (D) (E)   12. (A) (B) (C) (D) (E)   18. (A) (B) (C) (D) (E)   24. (A) (B) (C) (D) (E)

right in Section 1

wrong in Section 1

SECTION 2

1. (A) (B) (C) (D) (E)   6. (A) (B) (C) (D) (E)   11. (A) (B) (C) (D) (E)   16. (A) (B) (C) (D) (E)
2. (A) (B) (C) (D) (E)   7. (A) (B) (C) (D) (E)   12. (A) (B) (C) (D) (E)   17. (A) (B) (C) (D) (E)
3. (A) (B) (C) (D) (E)   8. (A) (B) (C) (D) (E)   13. (A) (B) (C) (D) (E)   18. (A) (B) (C) (D) (E)
4. (A) (B) (C) (D) (E)   9. (A) (B) (C) (D) (E)   14. (A) (B) (C) (D) (E)
5. (A) (B) (C) (D) (E)   10. (A) (B) (C) (D) (E)   15. (A) (B) (C) (D) (E)

right in Section 2

wrong in Section 2

SECTION 3

25. (A) (B) (C) (D) (E)   31. (A) (B) (C) (D) (E)   37. (A) (B) (C) (D) (E)   43. (A) (B) (C) (D) (E)
26. (A) (B) (C) (D) (E)   32. (A) (B) (C) (D) (E)   38. (A) (B) (C) (D) (E)   44. (A) (B) (C) (D) (E)
27. (A) (B) (C) (D) (E)   33. (A) (B) (C) (D) (E)   39. (A) (B) (C) (D) (E)   45. (A) (B) (C) (D) (E)
28. (A) (B) (C) (D) (E)   34. (A) (B) (C) (D) (E)   40. (A) (B) (C) (D) (E)   46. (A) (B) (C) (D) (E)
29. (A) (B) (C) (D) (E)   35. (A) (B) (C) (D) (E)   41. (A) (B) (C) (D) (E)   47. (A) (B) (C) (D) (E)
30. (A) (B) (C) (D) (E)   36. (A) (B) (C) (D) (E)   42. (A) (B) (C) (D) (E)   48. (A) (B) (C) (D) (E)

right in Section 3

wrong in Section 3

KAPLAN
Test Prep and Admissions

SECTION 4

19. Ⓐ Ⓑ Ⓒ Ⓓ Ⓔ   24. Ⓐ Ⓑ Ⓒ Ⓓ Ⓔ   29. Ⓐ Ⓑ Ⓒ Ⓓ Ⓔ   34. Ⓐ Ⓑ Ⓒ Ⓓ Ⓔ
20. Ⓐ Ⓑ Ⓒ Ⓓ Ⓔ   25. Ⓐ Ⓑ Ⓒ Ⓓ Ⓔ   30. Ⓐ Ⓑ Ⓒ Ⓓ Ⓔ   35. Ⓐ Ⓑ Ⓒ Ⓓ Ⓔ
21. Ⓐ Ⓑ Ⓒ Ⓓ Ⓔ   26. Ⓐ Ⓑ Ⓒ Ⓓ Ⓔ   31. Ⓐ Ⓑ Ⓒ Ⓓ Ⓔ   36. Ⓐ Ⓑ Ⓒ Ⓓ Ⓔ
22. Ⓐ Ⓑ Ⓒ Ⓓ Ⓔ   27. Ⓐ Ⓑ Ⓒ Ⓓ Ⓔ   32. Ⓐ Ⓑ Ⓒ Ⓓ Ⓔ   37. Ⓐ Ⓑ Ⓒ Ⓓ Ⓔ
23. Ⓐ Ⓑ Ⓒ Ⓓ Ⓔ   28. Ⓐ Ⓑ Ⓒ Ⓓ Ⓔ   33. Ⓐ Ⓑ Ⓒ Ⓓ Ⓔ   38. Ⓐ Ⓑ Ⓒ Ⓓ Ⓔ

□ # right in Section 4

□ # wrong in Section 4

If Section 4 of your test book contains math questions that are not multiple choice, continue to item 29 below. Otherwise, continue to item 29 above.

29.   30.   31.   32.   33.

34.   35.   36.   37.   38.

SECTION 5

1. Ⓐ Ⓑ Ⓒ Ⓓ Ⓔ   11. Ⓐ Ⓑ Ⓒ Ⓓ Ⓔ   21. Ⓐ Ⓑ Ⓒ Ⓓ Ⓔ   31. Ⓐ Ⓑ Ⓒ Ⓓ Ⓔ
2. Ⓐ Ⓑ Ⓒ Ⓓ Ⓔ   12. Ⓐ Ⓑ Ⓒ Ⓓ Ⓔ   22. Ⓐ Ⓑ Ⓒ Ⓓ Ⓔ   32. Ⓐ Ⓑ Ⓒ Ⓓ Ⓔ
3. Ⓐ Ⓑ Ⓒ Ⓓ Ⓔ   13. Ⓐ Ⓑ Ⓒ Ⓓ Ⓔ   23. Ⓐ Ⓑ Ⓒ Ⓓ Ⓔ   33. Ⓐ Ⓑ Ⓒ Ⓓ Ⓔ
4. Ⓐ Ⓑ Ⓒ Ⓓ Ⓔ   14. Ⓐ Ⓑ Ⓒ Ⓓ Ⓔ   24. Ⓐ Ⓑ Ⓒ Ⓓ Ⓔ   34. Ⓐ Ⓑ Ⓒ Ⓓ Ⓔ
5. Ⓐ Ⓑ Ⓒ Ⓓ Ⓔ   15. Ⓐ Ⓑ Ⓒ Ⓓ Ⓔ   25. Ⓐ Ⓑ Ⓒ Ⓓ Ⓔ   35. Ⓐ Ⓑ Ⓒ Ⓓ Ⓔ
6. Ⓐ Ⓑ Ⓒ Ⓓ Ⓔ   16. Ⓐ Ⓑ Ⓒ Ⓓ Ⓔ   26. Ⓐ Ⓑ Ⓒ Ⓓ Ⓔ   36. Ⓐ Ⓑ Ⓒ Ⓓ Ⓔ
7. Ⓐ Ⓑ Ⓒ Ⓓ Ⓔ   17. Ⓐ Ⓑ Ⓒ Ⓓ Ⓔ   27. Ⓐ Ⓑ Ⓒ Ⓓ Ⓔ   37. Ⓐ Ⓑ Ⓒ Ⓓ Ⓔ
8. Ⓐ Ⓑ Ⓒ Ⓓ Ⓔ   18. Ⓐ Ⓑ Ⓒ Ⓓ Ⓔ   28. Ⓐ Ⓑ Ⓒ Ⓓ Ⓔ   38. Ⓐ Ⓑ Ⓒ Ⓓ Ⓔ
9. Ⓐ Ⓑ Ⓒ Ⓓ Ⓔ   19. Ⓐ Ⓑ Ⓒ Ⓓ Ⓔ   29. Ⓐ Ⓑ Ⓒ Ⓓ Ⓔ   39. Ⓐ Ⓑ Ⓒ Ⓓ Ⓔ
10. Ⓐ Ⓑ Ⓒ Ⓓ Ⓔ   20. Ⓐ Ⓑ Ⓒ Ⓓ Ⓔ   30. Ⓐ Ⓑ Ⓒ Ⓓ Ⓔ   40. Ⓐ Ⓑ Ⓒ Ⓓ Ⓔ

□ # right in Section 5

□ # wrong in Section 5

Practice Test Three

SECTION ONE

Time—25 Minutes
24 Questions

For each of the following questions, choose the best answer and darken the corresponding oval on the answer sheet.

Select the lettered word or set of words that best completes the sentence.

Example:

Today's small, portable computers contrast markedly with the earliest electronic computers, which were ----.

(A) effective
(B) invented
(C) useful
(D) destructive
(E) enormous

1. The artist's students admired his work so much that they often sacrificed their own sense of originality and simply ---- the work of their teacher.

(A) censured
(B) praised
(C) discussed
(D) emulated
(E) demeaned

2. After swimming in the ---- English Channel for several hours, the athlete's body temperature dropped dramatically, causing her to shiver uncontrollably.

(A) calm
(B) frigid
(C) turbulent
(D) balmy
(E) polluted

3. Only ---- dogs can be trained to assist the blind, since the dogs' unwavering ---- is essential to the personal safety of the blind person.

(A) tractable . . obedience
(B) docile . . negligence
(C) clever . . dexterity
(D) unseasoned . . restraint
(E) smart . . domestication

GO ON TO THE NEXT PAGE ⟩

4. In order to relieve the drought in the ---- valley region of the state, the governor ---- water-saving measures throughout the area.

   (A) populous . . recalled
   (B) sodden . . encouraged
   (C) depleted . . decried
   (D) parched . . rescinded
   (E) arid . . instituted

5. The majority of the models at the car show were boxy and awkward in design, making the new Phantom model appear particularly ----.

   (A) modern
   (B) swift
   (C) ungainly
   (D) sleek
   (E) burnished

6. Despite the ---- of a thunderstorm quickly approaching from the horizon, the farm workers were ---- in completing their work before seeking shelter indoors.

   (A) expectation . . negligent
   (B) menace . . dilatory
   (C) threat . . diligent
   (D) absence . . languid
   (E) forecast . . unfortunate

7. In *The Prince*, Machiavelli argues that a prince can scheme and plot to maintain his power as long as these ---- are hidden from the public.

   (A) digressions
   (B) condemnations
   (C) antagonisms
   (D) machinations
   (E) pronouncements

GO ON TO THE NEXT PAGE

Answer the questions below based on the information in the accompanying passages.

Questions 8–12 refer to the following passage.

The following article, adapted from a Popular Science magazine, explains a natural phenomenon known as the lunar eclipse.

Many people are aware of the beauty of a solar eclipse, but are surprised to learn that lunar eclipses are often just as spectacular, and are both more common and easier to observe. The filtering
(5) and refraction of light from the Earth's atmosphere during a lunar eclipse creates stunning color effects that range from dark brown to red, orange, and yellow. Each of these light shows is unique since they are the result of the amount of dust and
(10) cloud cover in the Earth's atmosphere at the time of the eclipse. While total solar eclipses last only for a few minutes and can be seen only in a small area of a few kilometers, total lunar eclipses can last for several hours and can be seen over much
(15) of the planet. In fact, the beauty and stability of lunar eclipses make them a favorite of both amateur and professional photographers.

Lunar eclipses generally occur two to three times a year, and are possible only when the Moon
(20) is in its full phase. When we see the Moon, we are actually seeing sunlight reflected off the surface of the Moon. When the Earth is positioned in between the Moon and the Sun, however, the Earth's shadow falls on the Moon, and a lunar
(25) eclipse occurs. To better understand this process, it's helpful to imagine the Earth's shadow on the Moon as a pair of nested cones, with the Earth at the apex of the cones, and the Moon at their bases. The outer, more diffuse cone of shadow is
(30) called the penumbral shadow, while the inner, darker cone is the umbral shadow. The type of lunar eclipse—total, partial, or penumbral—that occurs depends both on how much of the Moon passes through the Earth's shadow and through
(35) which part of the shadows it passes. A penumbral eclipse occurs when the Moon passes through the Earth's outer shadow. This type of eclipse is both brief and subtle, and frequently goes unobserved by all but astronomers and the most avid devo-

(40) tees. By contrast, total and partial eclipses occur when all or part, respectively, of the Moon passes through of the umbral shadow of the Earth. These eclipses are quite easy to see and are widely observed.

(45) Unlike solar eclipses lunar eclipses are safe to watch. Solar radiation at the intensity that occurs during an eclipse of the Sun can cause a form of retinal burns known as eclipse blindness. In fact, the only way to safely view a solar eclipse is by
(50) using specially-designed filters. However, since the Moon's light is dissipated, reflected sunlight, it is completely safe to watch a lunar eclipse without any special equipment, although a pair of binoculars can certainly help the viewer appreciate the
(55) splendor of this beautiful phenomenon.

8. The main purpose of the passage is to

    (A) contrast lunar and solar eclipses

    (B) discuss lunar eclipses

    (C) explain why solar and lunar eclipses occur

    (D) demonstrate the equipment needed to safely view a solar eclipse

    (E) argue that lunar eclipses are more beautiful than solar eclipses

9. In line 15 "stability" most nearly means

    (A) visibility

    (B) equilibrium

    (C) strength

    (D) duration

    (E) poise

GO ON TO THE NEXT PAGE

10. According to the author, a partial lunar eclipse occurs

    (A) when all of the Moon passes through the Earth's umbral shadow

    (B) two to three times a year

    (C) when only a part of the Moon passes through the Earth's umbral shadow

    (D) when a part of the Moon passes through only the Earth's penumbral shadow

    (E) when the Moon passes between the Sun and the Earth

11. The author implies that penumbral eclipses are

    (A) more common than partial or full lunar eclipses

    (B) the result of a "cone" of shadow cast by the Moon onto the Earth

    (C) longer-lasting than most solar eclipses

    (D) more difficult to observe than other types of lunar eclipses

    (E) visible within only a small area

12. According to the passage, it is safe to watch a lunar eclipse, unlike a solar eclipse, because

    (A) a lunar eclipse is more subtle and brief than a solar eclipse

    (B) a lunar eclipse lasts much longer than a solar eclipse

    (C) moonlight is less intense than sunlight

    (D) special filters can be employed to view a lunar eclipse

    (E) a lunar eclipse results from the Moon passing through the Earth's shadow

GO ON TO THE NEXT PAGE

Questions 13–14 refer to the following passage.

Many people are surprised to learn that the idea of a flying machine stretches all the way back to ancient Greece. Archimedes, who identified the principle of buoyancy more than 2,000 years ago,
(5) may also have conceived of a flying machine using this principle. Throughout the years, other scientists and philosophers, Roger Bacon and Albertus Magnus among them, advanced designs for flying machines based on buoyancy. It wasn't until 1783,
(10) however, that the principle was tested. In the late summer of that year Joseph and Etienne Montgolfier built a hot air balloon propelled by a manure-and-straw fire that safely held aloft a trio of farm animals for eight minutes.

13. The passage implies that the principle of buoyancy

   (A) is Archimedes's main contribution to science

   (B) was invented by the Montgolfier brothers

   (C) is important for the functioning of hot air balloons

   (D) confounded both Roger Bacon and Albertus Magnus

   (E) was first fully understood in 1783

14. In line 8, the word "advanced" most nearly means

   (A) offered

   (B) contemplated

   (C) proceeded

   (D) moved

   (E) progressed

Questions 15–18 refer to the following passages.

Passage 1

Although movies depend on a host of contributors, every worthwhile film ultimately reflects the vision of only one individual—the director, or *auteur*. Without an *auteur*, a film would be a hodge-
(5) podge of disjointed camera angles, erratic performances, and inappropriate dialogue—a confused muddle of dozens of opinions about what should and should not be occurring on the screen. Instead, the *auteur* takes this raw material and gives it shape,
(10) texture, and meaning. Just as an author creates a book or an artist creates a painting, it is the *auteur* who creates the film to which we respond.

Passage 2

Unlike a book or a painting, a film is a collaborative work. We might be drawn to the cinema because we want to see our favorite star, but we can also appreciate a wonderful score, a great
(5) screenplay, or beautiful camerawork. How often have we heard someone say, "I loved the story but I hated the acting," or "The costumes were interesting but the special effects were boring"? Any sensitive viewer responds not to a single artistic
(10) vision in a film, but to dozens of such visions. In fact, it may well be this rich synthesis of creativity that makes the art form so exciting.

15. With which of the following statements would the writer of Passage 1 most strongly disagree?

   (A) The director is the most important person in filmmaking.

   (B) Many kinds of artists contribute to the making of a movie.

   (C) A worthwhile work of art reflects the vision of a single person.

   (D) The main purpose of movies is to entertain.

   (E) Movies do not have authors in the same way that books do.

GO ON TO THE NEXT PAGE

16. Which statement best expresses the main idea of Passage 2?

    (A) Moviegoers are primarily drawn to films by the performances of actors.

    (B) Many contributors influence the viewer's experience of a film.

    (C) Viewers must be sensitive to identify the many contributions to a movie.

    (D) A person may enjoy one aspect of a movie, but find another aspect disappointing.

    (E) Books and films are fundamentally different art forms.

17. The author of Passage 2 would most likely regard the statement that "it is the *auteur* who creates the film to which we respond" (Passage 1, lines 11–12) as

    (A) a shameful omission

    (B) a sound argument

    (C) an unfortunate simplification

    (D) an unresolved hypothesis

    (E) a regrettable necessity

18. Both passages refer to "a painting," but they differ in that

    (A) Passage 1 distinguishes between a painting and a movie, but Passage 2 concentrates on the similarities between the two art forms.

    (B) Passage 1 attributes equal value to a painting and a movie, but Passage 2 states that a movie is usually more interesting.

    (C) Passage 1 asserts that a painting has an individual creator, but Passage 2 declares that a painting is a collaborative work.

    (D) Passage 1 compares the creation of a film to the creation of a painting, but Passage 2 draws a contrast between them.

    (E) Passage 1 says that viewers respond to a painting as a whole, but Passage 2 points out that a painting is made of individual components.

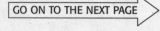

Questions 19–24 refer to the following passage.

The following is adapted from two excerpts from a 1926 diary of a resident of Moscow, Russia. At that time, Russia, as part of the Soviet Union, was ruled by a dictatorial government and was experiencing a severe economic depression.

Late afternoon, blustery and gray.

It has been many years since I have attended a performance of a play. My black fox fur is quite tattered, but I have spent the last two evenings
(5) before the fire mending it. Before the children were born, we went to the theater at least once a week. I wished later, during the upheaval, that we had not given it up. Once it was gone, truly gone, I missed it so.

(10) I did not expect to be this nervous. It's as if I've never been to a proper theater, and I can scarcely remember a time when I've so fussed over the state of my hair. I'm wondering if I will remember how to behave. In truth, the cause of my nervous
(15) condition is this feeling that the whole of Moscow has contrived to engage in a rebellious act. Will we be putting ourselves in danger tonight? It's hard to believe we will not. Perhaps only a handful of people will attend.

(20) *Later the same night, very cold.*

I certainly had no need to fret over the condition of my fox fur. Others even attended the performance with tattered bits of sweaters wrapped around their necks, but people were not judged
(25) for the state of their clothing. Triumph Square was abuzz with energy and anticipation. Once among the throng, all of my fears of punishment evaporated. Moscow was united tonight in support of its theater. The play was by Gogol and of course
(30) I've seen it many times, but never like this. The director was a man whose name I had almost forgotten, Vsevolod Meyerhold. The pace of the show was breathtaking. I found that I could scarcely keep up—it's very lucky I'm familiar with the
(35) script. The audience was quite bowled over. At the curtain call, much of the audience rose to their feet. The roar of the crowd was a mix of jeering

and applause. I was so overwhelmed with emotion, I found myself on my feet clapping loudly—
(40) until I realized that the figures on stage for the curtain call were only papier-mâché* dummies, rather than the actors from the performance. I even felt momentarily foolish for being taken in by the ruse. I wonder if this was why others in the
(45) crowd were scoffing, or if they were indeed unhappy with the entire production. I did not stop to ask anyone—the paper tomorrow morning will tell me. I rushed home, not bothered by the cold.

*a material made of paper pulp and glue

19. As used in the passage, "proper" (line 11) most nearly means

    (A) polite
    (B) correct
    (C) legitimate
    (D) adequate
    (E) moral

20. The author speculates that "Perhaps only a handful of people will attend" (lines 18–19) because she believes that

    (A) the citizens of Moscow have little interest in the theater
    (B) many people would be too afraid of punishment to attend
    (C) the audience will likely be unhappy with the entire production
    (D) people will be embarrassed to attend the theater in tattered clothes
    (E) the cold weather will deter many people coming

GO ON TO THE NEXT PAGE

21. In lines 21–22, the author notes that "I certainly had no need to fret over the condition of my fox fur" because

    (A) the author was among the most elegant of the attendees

    (B) the physical appearance of the play's attendees was immaterial

    (C) the author had successfully repaired the fur

    (D) the fur was less important than other aspects of her appearance

    (E) she would not be identified in such a large crowd

22. The pace of the play could be best described as

    (A) brisk

    (B) deliberate

    (C) unintelligible

    (D) typical

    (E) tedious

23. Based on the passage, which of the following best expresses the author's experience of the play?

    (A) She was scandalized by the appearance of the crowd.

    (B) She was angered by the papier-mâché dummies.

    (C) She was torn between appreciation and embarrassment.

    (D) She was confused by the pace of the scenes

    (E) She was elated to be in the theater again.

24. The change in the author's mood from afternoon to evening can best be described as a transition from

    (A) agitated to lethargic

    (B) jealous to confident

    (C) sorrowful to joyful

    (D) anxious to exhilarated

    (E) explosive to tranquil

IF YOU FINISH BEFORE TIME IS CALLED, YOU MAY CHECK YOUR WORK ON THIS SECTION ONLY. DO NOT TURN TO ANY OTHER SECTION IN THE TEST.   STOP

SECTION TWO

Time—25 Minutes
18 Questions

Solve each of the following problems, decide which is the best answer choice, and darken the corresponding oval on the answer sheet.

Notes:
(1)   Calculator use is permitted.
(2)   All numbers used are real numbers.
(3)   Figures are provided for some problems. All figures are drawn to scale and lie in a plane UNLESS otherwise indicated.

Information

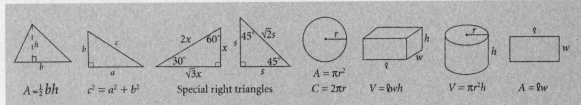

$A = \frac{1}{2}bh$ $c^2 = a^2 + b^2$ Special right triangles $A = \pi r^2$ $V = \ell wh$ $V = \pi r^2 h$ $A = \ell w$
                                                                        $C = 2\pi r$

The sum of the degree measures of the angles of a triangle is 180.
The number of degrees of arc in a circle is 360.
A straight angle has a degree measure of 180.

1. If $7x - 2 = 12x + 13$, then $6x =$

   (A) −18
   (B)   −5
   (C)   −3
   (D)   5
   (E)   18

2.

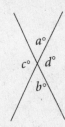

Two lines intersect as shown in the figure above. Which of the following could be false?

   (A) $2c = 2d$
   (B) $a + d = b + d$
   (C) $a - b = d - c$
   (D) $a + b = c + d$
   (E) $2(a + c) = 2(b + d)$

GO ON TO THE NEXT PAGE

3. In a certain bag, the only coins are 2 pennies, 1 nickel, 3 dimes, and 2 quarters. If one coin is drawn at random from the bag, what is the probability that the coin drawn is a dime?

(A) $\dfrac{1}{8}$

(B) $\dfrac{3}{8}$

(C) $\dfrac{1}{2}$

(D) $\dfrac{5}{8}$

(E) 1

4. The cost of a dozen pencils and 6 pens is $3.34. If 3 pencils cost $0.10, what is the cost of one pen, in cents?

(A) 36
(B) 42
(C) 49
(D) 53
(E) 59

5.

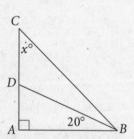

If $\overline{BD}$ bisects $\angle ABC$ in the figure above, what is the value of x?

(A) 40
(B) 50
(C) 60
(D) 70
(E) 80

6. If a is an odd integer and b is an even integer, which of the following must be odd?

(A) $2a + b$

(B) $3a + b$

(C) $2(a + b)$

(D) $\dfrac{b}{a}$

(E) $a + \dfrac{b}{2}$

7. If $x > 0$ and $x^{-3} = 8$, what is the value of x^2?

(A) $\dfrac{1}{4}$

(B) $\dfrac{1}{2}$

(C) 4

(D) 8

(E) 64

8.

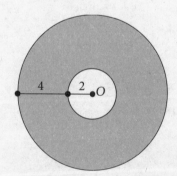

In the figure above, O is the center of both circles. What is the ratio of the shaded area to the unshaded area?

(A) 2:1
(B) 4:1
(C) 6:1
(D) 8:1
(E) 9:1

GO ON TO THE NEXT PAGE

9.

Composition of Football
Team by Grade Level

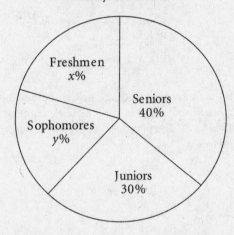

The graph above shows the composition by grade level of a high school football team. If the team has 60 players and there are exactly half as many freshmen as there are seniors, how many sophomores are on the team?

(A) 6
(B) 10
(C) 12
(D) 18
(E) 20

10.

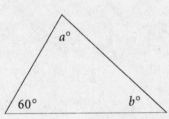

Note: Figure not drawn to scale.

If $a > 50°$, which of the following describes all possible values of b?

(A) $b < 70$
(B) $b > 70$
(C) $b = 70$
(D) $b \leq 70$
(E) $b \geq 70$

11. If $0.005 \leq x \leq 0.5$ and $0.25 \leq y \leq 25$, what is the maximum value of $\frac{x}{y}$?

(A) 0.0002
(B) 0.002
(C) 0.02
(D) 0.2
(E) 2

12.

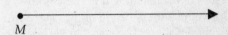

N and P are two points to the right of M on the number line above. If $2\overline{MN} = 5\overline{MP}$ what is the ratio of PN to MP?

(A) 2:5
(B) 2:3
(C) 3:2
(D) 5:2
(E) 5:7

GO ON TO THE NEXT PAGE

13.

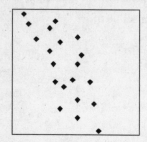

Which of the following is the best estimate for the slope of the line of best fit of the data shown in the scatterplot above? (Assume that the black bordered area is a square and that the scale of measurement is the same on every side.)

(A) −3

(B) $-\dfrac{1}{3}$

(C) $\dfrac{1}{3}$

(D) $\dfrac{2}{3}$

(E) 3

14. If $x = a - 5$ and $y = a + 1$, then $x - y =$

(A) −6

(B) −4

(C) 2

(D) 4

(E) 6

15.

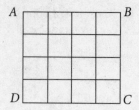

In the figure above, square $ABCD$ is divided into 16 small squares of equal size. The perimeter of $ABCD$ is 8. The perimeter of each of the small squares is

(A) $\dfrac{1}{4}$

(B) $\dfrac{1}{2}$

(C) 1

(D) 2

(E) 4

16. If $5x + 5y = 20$, what is the average (arithmetic mean) of x and y?

(A) 1

(B) 2

(C) 4

(D) 5

(E) 10

GO ON TO THE NEXT PAGE

17. If a, b, and c are positive integers and

$$a \triangle^{b}_{} c = \frac{b+c}{a} - \frac{a+c}{b} - \frac{a+b}{c}, \text{ then}$$

$$2 \triangle^{4}_{} 6 =$$

 (A) 2
 (B) 4
 (C) 8
 (D) 12
 (E) 18

18. Triangle DEF is an isosceles right triangle. The co-ordinates of point D are $(-2, 1)$ and the coordinates of point E are $(-2, 7)$. Which of the following could be the coordinates of point F?

 I. $(-8, 1)$
 II. $(4, 1)$
 III. $(4, 7)$

 (A) I only
 (B) II only
 (C) III only
 (D) II and III
 (E) I, II, and III

IF YOU FINISH BEFORE TIME IS CALLED, YOU MAY CHECK YOUR WORK ON
THIS SECTION ONLY. DO NOT TURN TO ANY OTHER SECTION IN THE TEST.   STOP

KAPLAN
Test Prep and Admissions

SECTION THREE

Time—25 Minutes   For each of the following questions, choose the best answer and darken the
24 Questions   corresponding oval on the answer sheet.

Select the lettered word or set of words that best completes the sentence.

Example:

Today's small, portable computers contrast markedly with the earliest electronic computers, which were ----.

(A) effective

(B) invented

(C) useful

(D) destructive

(E) enormous

25. Even though there was much curiosity about their personal lives, the celebrities of earlier times were able to maintain a degree of ---- that today's celebrities ----.

(A) privacy . . envy

(B) dignity . . regret

(C) significance . . mimic

(D) separation . . mock

(E) regard . . celebrate

26. Even in the most informal settings, Mrs. Davis always had the instinct to ---- and could not resist the urge to spread knowledge among her acquaintances.

(A) obscure

(B) evaluate

(C) educate

(D) speculate

(E) mediate

27. By frequently mentioning the titles of books he had read and quoting poems he had memorized, thus ---- his ----, John alienated many of his friends.

(A) enduring . . success

(B) delivering . . release

(C) praising . . conviction

(D) flaunting . . erudition

(E) degrading . . achievement

28. Legends often celebrate characters whose actions, such as robbing the rich to give to the poor or defying ---- authority, are perceived as ----.

(A) unjust . . unacceptable

(B) legitimate . . incredible

(C) impotent . . sufficient

(D) grandiose . . insurmountable

(E) corrupt . . commendable

GO ON TO THE NEXT PAGE

29. Many Swedish health experts claim that sitting in a hot sauna and then plunging into ice-cold water can have ---- effect that invigorates both the body and the spirit.

    (A) a tonic
    (B) an enfeebling
    (C) a delirious
    (D) an amorphous
    (E) a soothing

30. *Pamela: or Virtue Rewarded* by Samuel Richardson can be classified as ---- novel, since it takes the form of a series of letters.

    (A) a substantial
    (B) an epistolary
    (C) a popular
    (D) an auspicious
    (E) an eloquent

GO ON TO THE NEXT PAGE

Answer the questions below based on the information in the accompanying passages.

Questions 31–32 refer to the following passage.

Modern readers are often initially confused by the idea of honor held by the ancient Greeks. As described in the epic poem *The Iliad*, for example, honor can be attained in a tangible way, in the
(5) form of a reward for victory in battle. In that work, the transformation of the hero Achilles both illustrates this traditional conception and presages a more modern, less tangible connotation. Achilles feels himself gravely insulted and withdraws from
(10) the Trojan war when his war prize is confiscated by his confederate Agamemnon. Yet, when Agamemnon offers him an enormous reward for heroism later in the epic, Achilles refuses to accept it, protesting that material possessions cannot
(15) compensate for the friends lost in battle.

31. The word "gravely" in line 9 most nearly means

    (A) seriously
    (B) morbidly
    (C) impressively
    (D) catastrophically
    (E) gratuitously

32. Based on the passage, Achilles's conception of honor

    (A) came to exemplify the Homeric Greek ideal
    (B) was destroyed by Agamemnon's insult
    (C) was entirely based on heroism in battle
    (D) prompted a generous gift from Agamemnon
    (E) evolved to one more like a modern conception

GO ON TO THE NEXT PAGE

Questions 33–45 refer to the following passages.

The following passages discuss the use of dogs in law enforcement. Passage 1 is from an article that appeared in a Popular Science magazine. Passage 2 is adapted from a letter written by an expert in dog training that was published in a newspaper.

Passage 1

Although they are a relatively recent invention, canine (or K-9) units have gained widespread acceptance in police departments around the world. The use of dogs in police work has met
(5) with success for a number of reasons. First, dogs' phenomenal tracking instincts make them very valuable additions to searches, whether for suspects or missing persons. In addition, dogs' sense of smell makes searches more efficient than those
(10) carried out by humans alone. For example, while a crew of police officers might take a considerable amount of time to carefully search a large area for a suspect, a single police dog can make short work of the task. Furthermore, because odors can be
(15) detected in the dark and through the smallest crack under a door, a dog can work in dim areas and is undeterred by locks. Dogs can even apprehend suspects in a way that minimizes the chance of injury to the dogs, the suspects, and the dogs'
(20) handlers. Of course, all of these skills are not fully developed in the average canine—extensive training is needed to channel a dog's natural gifts to form an effective police dog.

The extraordinarily keen sense of smell that
(25) dogs possess—capable of perceiving even the faintest scent from a considerable distance—is the root of dogs' ability to track, which is the K-9 unit's more frequent assignment in police work. In exercising their sense of smell, dogs actually detect
(30) microscopic skin particles, known as skin rafts, that are continuously shed as people move through an environment. A tracking session begins with the introduction to the dog of a scent article, an item that bears the smell of the person
(35) being sought. A well-used item of clothing is ideal, but even something as far removed from a person as a clean cotton pad that has been exposed to the steering wheel in his or her car can suffice. K-9 dogs are trained to identify the odor from the

(40) scent article and then follow the trail of that scent. Although helpful at most times, dogs' tracking instincts and the needs of police work can come into conflict. An animal in the wild will gladly abandon the track of the person sought by police
(45) if the creature encounters another, fresher track. After all, why not pursue the prey that has passed by most recently? In a police investigation, however, it is essential that the dog stay focused on the trail of the original subject in spite of the myriad
(50) competing scents that the dog will encounter in a hunt through a crowded urban environment. Victory over a dog's instincts can only be achieved by extensive and continuing training.

Other forms of training are also vital for an
(55) effective K-9 unit. Seeing the muscled bodies and sharp teeth of a German Shepard striding alongside a police officer, many assume that the dog is likely to ferociously attack anyone who crosses its path. But in fact, the extensive process known as
(60) aggression training teaches the dogs to attack under only three circumstances: when commanded to do so by the handler, when the handler is attacked, and in order to protect the patrol car. Under other circumstances, the dogs are quite
(65) approachable and pose no threat to others. Rather than a dangerous weapon, then, a well-trained dog is thus best considered a highly selective tool.

GO ON TO THE NEXT PAGE

Passage 2

A puppy learns and grows at an extraordinary rate in their first two years of life; even a dog's capacity to learn later in life is shaped at this point. During no other period will such massive
(5) transformations in structure and capacity occur so quickly: a puppy grows from complete dependence into a dog capable of exploring its surroundings, obeying complicated commands, and even potentially surviving on its own. And, while dog
(10) owners the world over have long recognized a puppy's fundamental need for protection, nourishment, and nurturing, recent research has revealed that owners and trainers play a far larger role than simply providing physical shelter and
(15) sustenance during these first few years of a dog's life. Laboratory studies have demonstrated conclusively that puppies raised by attentive, stern owners or trainers in safe environments develop into better learners than do those raised in less secure
(20) environments with less attention and discipline.

While few would disagree that all young dogs deserve nurturing and protection during their formative years, such treatment is especially important for police dogs, which will be required
(25) to secure public safety and assist in crime prevention. Most state law enforcement agencies provide sufficient time while the dogs are still young and malleable to train their canine officers. These states also ensure postnatal health care for their
(30) law enforcement canines. In stark contrast, our state has failed to provide adequately for either of these vital measures, an unfortunate lapse in judgment that seriously compromises the quality of our police dogs.

(35) Our political leaders have shown a marked interest in the safety and welfare of our state, including concerns about the state's police dogs and the quality of our current canine officer training program. However, simply addressing the
(40) funding of our police dog training alone is not the solution to the emerging police dog problem. We must also consider the ages of dogs entering training. We must mandate that units train younger dogs, not the older, harder-to-teach

(45) canines that are now being recruited for training. We must recognize the truth of that old saw, "you can't teach an old dog new tricks;" a young dog is highly trainable and can serve as a valuable asset to our state police force.

33. The author of Passage 1 notes that a police dog "can work in dim areas and is undeterred by locks" (lines 16–17) to emphasize the fact that

(A) dogs are physically strong enough to overcome such obstacles

(B) extensive training prepares the dogs for such situations

(C) dogs work more quickly than their human counterparts

(D) a dark area allows the dogs to concentrate more fully on tracking

(E) dogs rely on their sense of smell rather than that of sight

34. As used in line 24 of Passage 1, "keen" most nearly means

(A) acute

(B) willing

(C) eager

(D) aggressive

(E) instinctual

35. Based on Passage 1, a clean cotton pad that has been exposed to the steering wheel of the subject of a hunt's car can serve as a scent article because

(A) the cotton pad is familiar to the tracking dog

(B) skin rafts were transferred from the wheel to the pad

(C) it trains a dog to ignore competing scents

(D) scent articles bear the smell of the person being tracked

(E) a dog's instincts compel it to follow the freshest trail

GO ON TO THE NEXT PAGE ⟩

36. The sentence in lines Passage 1, 46–47 ("After all,... recently?") serves primarily to

    (A) exemplify dogs' ability to focus on a single scent

    (B) emphasize the need for dogs to ignore competing scents

    (C) question the effectiveness of dogs' instincts

    (D) illustrate the skill of dogs' tracking abilities

    (E) clarify the purpose of dogs' instinctual behavior

37. In the final paragraph of Passage 1, the author distinguishes between

    (A) the importance of tools and weapons

    (B) dangerous and well-trained dogs

    (C) aggression training and tracking training

    (D) popular perception and reality

    (E) the quality of dog training and the age at which it begins

38. The author of Passage 2 argues that the care and training of young dogs

    (A) is less important than providing shelter and sustenance

    (B) refines dogs' natural tracking ability

    (C) has a great impact on dogs' later ability to learn

    (D) has only recently been recognized as important

    (E) will ensure a dogs' ability to survive on their own

39. In Passage 2, the phrase "these vital measures" (line 32) refers to

    (A) the nurturing and protection of young dogs

    (B) early training and postnatal care

    (C) dogs that are both young and malleable

    (D) tracking and aggression training

    (E) the training policies of the state in question and those of other states

40. As used in Passage 2, line 35, "marked" most nearly means

    (A) evident

    (B) satisfactory

    (C) indicated

    (D) stained

    (E) correct

41. The author of Passage 2 notes that "simply addressing the funding of our police dog training alone is not the solution to the emerging police dog problem" because

    (A) many politicians are insufficiently informed about the true cause of this problem

    (B) police dogs are best viewed as tools rather than weapons

    (C) it is also essential to change the age at which dogs are trained

    (D) the present quality of training is woefully inadequate

    (E) training programs should concentrate of tracking skills rather than aggression training

GO ON TO THE NEXT PAGE →

42. The authors of Passage 1 and Passage 2 would most likely both agree that

(A) training that occurs early in a police dog's life is most effective

(B) training must continue throughout a police dog's life

(C) tracking is the primary function of most police dogs

(D) training is essential to the development of an effective police dog

(E) politicians should work to ensure the success of K-9 programs

43. The author of Passage 2 would most likely agree with which of the following statements about lines 21–23 of Passage 1 ("extensive training...effective police dog").

(A) Such training is especially important to train police dogs to attack only under certain circumstances.

(B) The care and nurturing of young dogs is more important than police-work training.

(C) It is vital to instill both tracking and aggression skills.

(D) The primary function of such training is to refine a dog's natural tracking skills.

(E) Simply training extensively may not be sufficient to ensure the best possible police dog.

44. Passage 1 and Passage 2 differ in that

(A) Passage 1 takes a historical perspective, while Passage 2 takes a scientific perspective.

(B) Passage 1 describes a governmental policy, while Passage 2 explores the effects of that policy.

(C) Passage 1 presents a position, while Passage 2 argues against that position.

(D) Passage 1 seeks to inform, while Passage 2 seeks to persuade.

(E) Passage 1 is written for the general public, while Passage 2 is aimed at experts.

45. The author of Passage 2 most likely includes the well-known quote "you can't teach an old dog new tricks" in lines 46–47 because

(A) he likes to use clichés

(B) in this case, the cliché is really true

(C) readers will recognize the cliché

(D) he thinks it is funny

(E) he doesn't like old dogs

GO ON TO THE NEXT PAGE

Questions 46–48 refer to the following passage.

The rate of human speech is approximately 180 words per minute. Although we have long known that listeners can understand speech at a far faster rate (one of at least 400 words per minute), in the
(5) past it was difficult to accelerate a recording of speech without raising the pitch of the voice, creating the undesirable, if amusing, "chipmunk effect." However, digital time compression, a new technology, offers a solution. Instead of simply
(10) playing a recording more quickly on a cassette deck, this method uses a computer to shave off silences and prolonged segments of vowels. Recordings can thus be abbreviated considerably without sacrificing quality.

46. Which statement below is directly supported by evidence in the passage?

(A) Any abbreviation of a sound recording entails a loss of quality.

(B) Manipulating sound on a cassette deck is usually the most effective method of abbreviating recordings.

(C) The rate of human speech has not varied significantly over time.

(D) There is a difference between the typical rate of speech and that of speech comprehension.

(E) Digital time compression, while advantageous, may have unforeseen disadvantages.

47. The author regards the "chipmunk effect" (lines 7–8) as

(A) a useful but costly outcome

(B) a tragic but unavoidable outcome

(C) a comical but vital effect

(D) an unfortunate but unforeseen result

(E) an amusing but unwelcome consequence

48. The word "prolonged" in line 12 most nearly means

(A) unnecessary

(B) previous

(C) longer

(D) produced

(E) gigantic

IF YOU FINISH BEFORE TIME IS CALLED, YOU MAY CHECK YOUR WORK ON THIS SECTION ONLY. DO NOT TURN TO ANY OTHER SECTION IN THE TEST.

SECTION FOUR

Time—25 Minutes	Solve each of the following problems, decide which is the best answer choice, and
20 Questions	darken the corresponding oval on the answer sheet.

Notes:
(1)   Calculator use is permitted.
(2)   All numbers used are real numbers.
(3)   Figures are provided for some problems. All figures are drawn to scale and lie in a plane UNLESS
        otherwise indicated.

Information

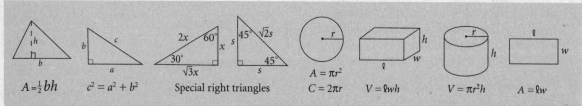

$A = \frac{1}{2}bh$ $c^2 = a^2 + b^2$ Special right triangles $A = \pi r^2$ $V = \ell wh$ $V = \pi r^2 h$ $A = \ell w$
                                                                      $C = 2\pi r$

The sum of the degree measures of the angles of a triangle is 180.
The number of degrees of arc in a circle is 360.
A straight angle has a degree measure of 180.

19. If $5a = 4$ and $\dfrac{b}{3} = 5$, then $ab =$

(A)   4
(B)   8
(C)   12
(D)   15
(E)   20

20.

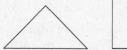

Figure I   Figure II   Figure III

In the figures above, Figure I is a triangle with
exactly two equal sides, Figure II is a square, and
Figure III is a regular hexagon. Which of the figures has more than three lines of symmetry?

(A) II only
(B) III only
(C) I and III
(D) II and III
(E) I, II, and III

GO ON TO THE NEXT PAGE

21. If $f(x) = 4^x - 5x$ what is the value of $f(2)$?

    (A) 3

    (B) 6

    (C) 10

    (D) 16

    (E) 18

22. If P is the set of all numbers between 0 and 10, inclusive, and Q is the set of all prime numbers, then the intersection of P and Q contains how many elements?

    (A) 0

    (B) 1

    (C) 2

    (D) 3

    (E) More than 3

23. The absolute value of a certain integer is greater than 7 and less than 12. Which of the following could NOT be the integer?

    (A) −11

    (B) −10

    (C) −8

    (D) 7

    (E) 8

24. A soccer team won X games, lost twice as many games as it won, and tied Y games. What fraction of the total number of games played was lost?

    (A) $\dfrac{2X}{X+Y}$

    (B) $\dfrac{2X}{3X+Y}$

    (C) $\dfrac{2X}{XY}$

    (D) $\dfrac{2X}{2X^2Y}$

    (E) $\dfrac{2X+Y}{X}$

25.

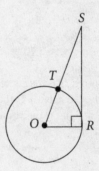

In the figure above, the radius of circle O is 6. If $ST = 4$, what is the length of $\overline{SR}$?

    (A) 6

    (B) $2\sqrt{13}$

    (C) 8

    (D) $2\sqrt{17}$

    (E) 10

GO ON TO THE NEXT PAGE

26. If $an \neq 0$, $\dfrac{a^{m+n}}{a^n} =$

    (A) a^m

    (B) a^{m+2n}

    (C) $\dfrac{1}{a^m}$

    (D) $-a^m$

    (E) a^{m+1}

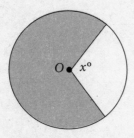

27. In the figure above, O is the center of the circle and the radius of the circle is 10. If the area of the shaded region is 70π, what is the value, in degrees, of x?

    (A) 98
    (B) 108
    (C) 144
    (D) 208
    (E) 252

28. How many three-digit integers greater than 500 contain only odd digits?

    (A) 25
    (B) 75
    (C) 125
    (D) 200
    (E) 250

GO ON TO THE NEXT PAGE

DIRECTIONS FOR STUDENT-PRODUCED RESPONSE QUESTIONS

For each of the questions below (29–38), solve the problem and indicate your answer by darkening the ovals in the special grid. For example:

Answer: 1.25 or $\frac{5}{4}$ or 5/4

Write answer in boxes. →

Grid-in result →

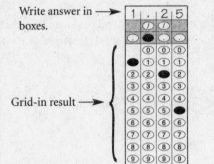
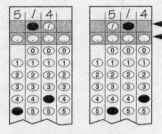

Either position is correct.

Fraction line
Decimal point

You may start your answers in any column, space permitting. Columns not needed should be left blank.

- It is recommended, though not required, that you write your answer in the boxes at the top of the columns. However, you will receive credit only for darkening the ovals correctly.

- Grid only one answer to a question, even though some problems have more than one correct answer.

- Darken no more than one oval in a column.

- No answers are negative.

- Mixed numbers cannot be gridded. For example: the number $1\frac{1}{4}$ must be gridded as 1.25 or 5/4.

(If $\boxed{1\,1\,/\,4}$ is gridded, it will be interpreted as $\frac{11}{4}$ not $1\frac{1}{4}$.)

- Decimal Accuracy: Decimal answers must be entered as accurately as possible. For example, if you obtain an answer such as 0.1666..., you should record the result as .166 or .167. **Less accurate values such as .16 or .17 are not acceptable.**

Acceptable ways to grid $\frac{1}{6}$ = .1666...

GO ON TO THE NEXT PAGE

KAPLAN
Test Prep and Admissions

29. Half a number is four more than one third of the number. What is the number?

30. What is the 499th term of the sequence $1, 2, 3, 4, 5, 1, 2, 3, 4, 5, 1, 2, \ldots \ldots$?

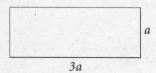

             $3a$

31. The figure above is a rectangle with area 48. What is the value of a?

32. If $m^2 - n^2 = 15$ and $m - n = 3$, what is the value of $m + n$?

33. If p is 20 percent of 140 and q is 25 percent of 56, what percent of p is q?

34. If $x > 0$ and $3\sqrt{x} - 7 = 20$, what is the value of x?

35. How many identical cubes, each with edges of 2 inches, can fit in a box that measures 18 inches by 10 inches by 8 inches?

36. If y varies directly as x^2, and $y = 8$ when $x = 2$, what is the value of y when $x = 1$?

37. The product of two consecutive positive integers is 29 more than their sum. What is the larger of the two integers?

38. If $a > 0$ and $b < 0$, and both a and b satisfy the equation $x^2 - 5x - 24 = 0$, what is the value of $a - b$?

IF YOU FINISH BEFORE TIME IS CALLED, YOU MAY CHECK YOUR WORK ON THIS SECTION ONLY. DO NOT TURN TO ANY OTHER SECTION IN THE TEST.

STOP

SECTION FIVE

Time—30 Minutes   For each of the following questions, choose the best answer and darken the
39 Questions   corresponding oval on the answer sheet.

Directions: The following sentences test your knowledge of grammar, usage, diction (choice of words), and idioms. Some sentences are correct.
No sentence contains more than one error.
You will find that the error, if there is one, is underlined and lettered. Elements of the sentence that are not underlined will not be changed. In choosing answers, follow the requirements of standard written English.
If there is an error, select the <u>one underlined part</u> that must be changed to make the sentence correct, and fill in the corresponding oval on your answer sheet.
If there is no error, fill in answer oval (E).

1. <u>Realizing that</u> the community opera company
      A

   <u>did not have</u> sufficient revenue to produce *La*
      B

   Traviata, <u>its perennial favorite,</u> <u>the board mem-</u>
                        C   D

   bers began to raise money for the performance.

   <u>No error</u>
      E

2. <u>One of the most</u> frequent types of injury that
      A

   baseball players <u>sustain is</u> a dislocated
                        B

   <u>shoulder, another</u> that occurs <u>nearly as</u> frequently
          C   D

   is a strained hamstring. <u>No error</u>
                                E

3. The hot-air balloonists <u>successfully traveled</u>
                                A

   around the world, but they refused to take full

   credit either for the technology <u>they invented</u> for
                                        B

   the flight <u>or for</u> their quick time, because they
                  C

   <u>had received</u> a good deal of help. <u>No error</u>
       D   E

4. <u>Although</u> she takes at least three singing lessons a
      A

   week, Mary is <u>almost as</u> poor a singer <u>as she is</u>
                      B   C

   a dancer. <u>No error</u>
      D   E

5. <u>Examining</u> their differences, the novelist's and the
      A

   reporter's <u>writing styles</u> are used <u>to portray</u> the
                  B   C

   same political situation in completely

   <u>different ways.</u> <u>No error</u>
       D   E

6. Many international vacationers <u>find</u> airplane rides
                                      A

   uncomfortable and <u>long, in</u> <u>other respects</u> they
                          B   C

   enjoy <u>traveling to</u> foreign countries. <u>No error</u>
            D   E

GO ON TO THE NEXT PAGE

7. The relationships between identical twins

   <u>have a particular</u> fascination <u>for</u> many people
        A   B

   <u>which</u> have maintained close relationships with
     C

   <u>their</u> own siblings. <u>No error</u>
     D   E

8. <u>Exaggerating</u> <u>their</u> nutritional importance,
      A   B

   <u>dieticians</u> overuse chocolate as an example of both
     C

   a <u>beneficial and a harmful</u> food. <u>No error</u>
            D   E

9. The social consequences of France's invasion of

   Russia in the nineteenth century <u>had perhaps</u>
                                  A

   <u>even more</u> of an impact on literature <u>than either</u>
     B   C

   politics <u>or relations</u> between nations. <u>No error</u>
          D   E

10. Sam <u>liked</u> to read <u>novels;</u> <u>of which</u> he found mys-
         A   B   C

    teries <u>especially</u> gripping. <u>No error</u>
         D   E

11. Many <u>pieces of</u> music <u>composed by</u> nineteenth-
          A   B

    century musicians in Europe, <u>in particular</u> reli-
                         C

    gious pieces, were <u>adaptations of</u> hymns sung in
                D

    church. <u>No error</u>
           E

12. <u>Trained to</u> tense her muscles and breathe from the
       A

    chest, <u>the dancer</u> had the <u>most difficulty</u> with
          B   C

    <u>yoga's</u> loose and full breathing methods. <u>No error</u>
     D   E

13. The <u>rapid spread</u> of infectious <u>diseases, frequently</u>
         A   B

    compounded in certain regions <u>because</u> the meth-
                         C

    ods for detection and prevention are not

    <u>well understood</u>. <u>No error</u>
       D   E

14. Suzanne Farrell, a retired New York City Ballet

    principal dancer <u>widely known</u> for her grace and
                 A

    elegance <u>onstage</u>, <u>conducts</u> the <u>upcoming</u> work-
           B   C   D

    shop. <u>No error</u>
         E

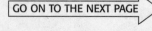
GO ON TO THE NEXT PAGE

Directions: The following sentences test correctness and effectiveness of expression. In choosing answers, follow the requirements of standard written English; that is, pay attention to grammar, choice of words, sentence construction, and punctuation.

In each of the following sentences, part of the sentence or the entire sentence is underlined. Beneath each sentence you will find five ways of phrasing the underlined part. Choice (A) repeats the original; the other four are different.

Choose the answer that best expresses the meaning of the original sentence. If you think the original is better than any of the alternatives, choose it; otherwise, choose one of the others. Your choice should produce the most effective sentence—clear and precise, without awkwardness or ambiguity.

15. This season the Raiders football games are mostly losses, <u>but those that do feature</u> considerable athletic performances.

    (A) but those that do feature
    (B) but they do feature
    (C) but that does feature
    (D) however featuring
    (E) however that does feature

16. Many of the students <u>studied relentless for passing</u> the test necessary to earn an A in the course.

    (A) studied relentless for passing
    (B) studied relentless to pass
    (C) studied to pass relentlessly
    (D) studied relentlessly for passing
    (E) studied relentlessly to pass

17. The violinist was overly excited at the beginning of the concert, <u>having shown admirable calm once the violin sonata got</u> underway.

    (A) having shown admirable calm once the violin sonata got
    (B) but he showed admirable calm once the violin sonata got
    (C) but showing admirable calm once the violin sonata got
    (D) once he showed admirable calm when the violin sonata got
    (E) however, he showed admirable calm when the violin sonata had been

18. The compositions of modern composers and their <u>predecessors, suggestive</u> of Bach's later work in that beat, instrumentation, and style combine to form a very rhythmic sound.

    (A) predecessors, suggestive
    (B) predecessors are suggesting
    (C) predecessors are suggestive
    (D) predecessors suggesting
    (E) predecessors, suggestions

19. Looking through the school's telescope on top of the science laboratory, <u>far above them a shooting star flew by</u>.

    (A) far above them a shooting star flew by
    (B) there was a shooting star flying above them
    (C) a shooting star flew by far above them
    (D) they saw a shooting star fly by far above them
    (E) they saw far above them a shooting star flew

20. The increase in available space has made it possible for our library to be entertaining <u>as well as educate</u>.

    (A) as well as educate
    (B) and being educational as well
    (C) as well as educational
    (D) and educates as well
    (E) as well as education

GO ON TO THE NEXT PAGE

21. In the mid to late 1500s, Queen Elizabeth I ascended the English throne and surprised much of English <u>society; she wanted</u> strong rule over her people and so did not marry.

    (A) society; she wanted
    (B) society, which allowed her to want
    (C) society, their idea was to want
    (D) society, and so she could want
    (E) society; in this way leading to the wanted

22. Whether there is truth to the assertion that there is extraterrestrial life in the universe remains unknown, <u>and somehow</u> many people have seen Unidentified Flying Objects (UFOs) in the sky.

    (A) and somehow
    (B) somehow
    (C) and that somehow
    (D) but somehow
    (E) that somehow

23. Home-team loyalty allows an athletic feat, no matter how many times previously accomplished, <u>to be proclaimed as staggering when attempted</u> and completed by a favorite athlete in a home game.

    (A) to be proclaimed as staggering when attempted
    (B) that is attempted as staggering to be proclaimed
    (C) to have been proclaimed as staggering when attempted
    (D) to be attempted as staggering when proclaimed
    (E) which once can proclaim as staggering when attempted

24. Nervous about change and new people, <u>the deterioration of the society was brought about by its apprehensive leaders</u>.

    (A) the deterioration of the society was brought about by its apprehensive leaders
    (B) the deterioration of the society has been brought about by its apprehensive leaders
    (C) the society was apprehensive its leaders caused to collapse
    (D) the apprehensive leaders of that society have brought about their collapse
    (E) the apprehensive leaders of that society brought about its collapse

25. Because women buy approximately 80 percent of the ties sold in the United States, <u>they are often displayed</u> near the perfume or women's clothing departments.

    (A) they are often displayed
    (B) they are often in display
    (C) ties are often displayed
    (D) ties are often being displayed
    (E) they can often be found at or

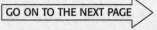

26. Laval, the first bishop of Quebec, exemplified aristocratic vigor and concern, <u>on account of his giving up his substantial inheritance to become an ecclesiastic</u> and to help shape Canadian politics and education.

    (A) on account of his giving up his substantial inheritance to become an ecclesiastic

    (B) since he gave up his substantial inheritance to become an ecclesiastic

    (C) since giving up his substantial inheritance to become an ecclesiastic

    (D) because of his having given up his substantial inheritance for the purpose of becoming an ecclesiastic

    (E) as a result of becoming an ecclesiastic through giving up his substantial inheritance

27. Even though the senators on the committee <u>were reluctant to schedule</u> a formal inquiry, they went on record as favoring one.

    (A) were reluctant to schedule

    (B) were reluctant as far as scheduling

    (C) were reluctant in scheduling

    (D) have been reluctant at scheduling

    (E) have had reluctance to schedule

28. Having read the works of Hemingway, Fitzgerald, and Steinbeck, <u>Hemingway is definitely overrated as a writer</u>.

    (A) Hemingway is definitely overrated as a writer

    (B) Hemingway has definitely been overrated as a writer

    (C) I am convinced that Hemingway is overrated as a writer

    (D) the writing abilities of Hemingway are overrated, I am convinced

    (E) I am convinced as a writer that Hemingway is overrated

29. Her eyes shining with tears, Aunt Helga told us over and over again how much she appreciated <u>us coming to her</u> ninetieth birthday party.

    (A) us coming to her

    (B) our coming to her

    (C) us having come to her

    (D) that we come to her

    (E) us for the fact of our coming to her

30. Many researchers contend that driving while talking on a cellular phone poses essentially the same risks <u>than if you drive</u> while intoxicated.

    (A) than if you drive

    (B) than to drive

    (C) as if one drives

    (D) as driving

    (E) as it does when driving

31. Before 1988, the corporation's board of directors included one hundred and fifty-three <u>members, none of the members were women</u>.

    (A) members, none of the members were women

    (B) members; and no women

    (C) members, none of them women

    (D) members, and of the members not one of them was a woman

    (E) members; none of them being women

GO ON TO THE NEXT PAGE

32. <u>The client was waiting for fifteen minutes when</u> the receptionist suddenly looked up from her work, noticed him, and informed him that his appointment had been canceled.

    (A) The client was waiting for fifteen minutes when

    (B) The client, having waited for fifteen minutes, when

    (C) Already the client was waiting for fifteen minutes when

    (D) When the client waited for fifteen minutes,

    (E) The client had been waiting for fifteen minutes when

33. <u>Because the polar ice caps are melting, therefore many</u> scientists and environmentalists fear that several small island nations will be completely covered by water in only a few decades.

    (A) Because the polar ice caps are melting, therefore many

    (B) Because the polar ice caps are melting, many

    (C) The polar ice caps are melting, therefore many

    (D) Because the polar ice caps are melting; many

    (E) The polar ice caps are melting; and many

34. One of the great literary artists of the nineteenth <u>century was Gustave Flaubert known for his obsession with the writer's craft</u>.

    (A) century was Gustave Flaubert known for his obsession with the writer's craft

    (B) century, Gustave Flaubert's obsession with the writer's craft was well known

    (C) century, Gustave Flaubert was known for his obsession with the writer's craft

    (D) century, Gustave Flaubert, known for his obsession with the writer's craft

    (E) century was Gustave Flaubert: known for his obsession with the writer's craft

GO ON TO THE NEXT PAGE ⟩

Directions: The passage below is an early draft of an essay. Parts of the passage need to be rewritten.

Read the passage, and answer the questions that follow. Some questions are about individual sentences or parts of sentences; in these questions, you are asked to select the choice which will improve sentence structure and word choice. Other questions refer to parts of the essay or the entire essay and ask you to consider the organization and development of the essay. You should follow the conventions of standard written English in answering the questions. After you have chosen your answer, fill in the corresponding oval on your answer sheet.

Questions 35–39 are based on the following passage.

(1) *One of the most important achievements after the American Revolution was the creation of the presidential office.* (2) *This was difficult because they feared popular leadership.* (3) *In the Founding Fathers' view, it was dangerous for the President to gain power from popularity.*

(4) *The Founders believed in the ignorance of the populace.* (5) *The office of the President needed to be independent of the popular will and the "common man."*

(6) *George Washington was a perfect example.* (7) *Just as the Founders wished, his heroics and regal bearing put him on a pedestal.* (8) *However, some of America's most famous presidents did not follow the Founders' ideals.* (9) *Andrew Jackson (nicknamed "Old Hickory") identified himself as a "common man" and used his popularity as a military hero to win the presidential election.* (10) *In other words, he makes the presidency what it is today: a popularity contest.*

(11) *Fourteen years later, Abraham Lincoln was virtually everything the Founders had not wanted in a leader.* (12) *He did not stand above popular opinion.* (13) *He courted public favor as "Honest Abe."* (14) *He had humble roots, a fact that he emphasized to gain public favor.* (15) *The Founders would have hated this.* (16) *But many people think that Lincoln was one of our best Presidents.* (17) *This suggests maybe they were wrong.*

35. Which of the following best replaces the word "they" in sentence 2 (reproduced below)?

   This was difficult because they feared popular leadership.

   (A) the revolutionaries
   (B) the complications
   (C) the Founding Fathers
   (D) the Presidents
   (E) the populace

36. In context, which of the following words are the most logical to insert at the beginning of sentence 5 (reproduced below)?

   The office of the President needed to be independent of the popular will and the "common man."

   (A) I have found that
   (B) On the other hand
   (C) And yet, for him
   (D) To them,
   (E) Resulting in,

37. In context, which is the best way to combine sentences 6 and 7 (reproduced below)?

   George Washington was a perfect example. Just as the Founders wished, his heroics and regal bearing put him on a pedestal.

   (A) (As it is now)
   (B) George Washington is a perfect example of what the Founders wanted although he was placed on a pedestal for his heroics and regal bearing.
   (C) Just like the Founders asked, George Washington's heroics and regal bearing put him on a pedestal.
   (D) George Washington is a perfect example of what the Founders wanted because his heroics and regal bearing put him on a pedestal.
   (E) George Washington is a perfect example of what they wanted, his heroics and regal bearing put him on a pedestal.

GO ON TO THE NEXT PAGE

38. In context, which of the following revisions is necessary in sentence 10 (reproduced below)?

    In other words, he makes the presidency what it is today: a popularity contest

    (A) Replace "he" with "Jackson"
    (B) Replace "the presidency" with "the President"
    (C) Replace "it is" with "it was"
    (D) Replace "makes" with "had made"
    (E) Replace "makes" with "made"

39. In context, which is the best way to combine sentences 16 and 17 (reproduced below)?

    But many people think that Lincoln was one of our best Presidents. This suggests maybe they were wrong.

    (A) They were wrong, many people suggested, thinking that Lincoln was one of our best Presidents.
    (B) Suggesting that they were wrong, many people think that Lincoln was one of our best Presidents.
    (C) But many people think that Lincoln was one of our best presidents, which suggests that maybe the Founders were wrong.
    (D) Furthermore, many people think that Lincoln was one of our best Presidents, suggesting that maybe the Founders were wrong.
    (E) Yet, maybe the Founders were wrong, many people think that Lincoln was one of our best Presidents.

IF YOU FINISH BEFORE TIME IS CALLED, YOU MAY CHECK YOUR WORK ON THIS SECTION ONLY. DO NOT TURN TO ANY OTHER SECTION IN THE TEST. STOP

ANSWER KEY ON FOLLOWING PAGE ⟶

Practice Test Three: **Answer Key**

SECTION ONE

1. D	9. D	17. C
2. B	10. C	18. D
3. A	11. D	19. C
4. E	12. C	20. B
5. D	13. C	21. B
6. C	14. A	22. A
7. D	15. E	23. E
8. B	16. B	24. D

SECTION TWO

1. A	8. D	15. D
2. D	9. A	16. B
3. B	10. A	17. A
4. C	11. E	18. E
5. B	12. C	
6. B	13. A	
7. A	14. A	

SECTION THREE

25. A	33. E	41. C
26. C	34. A	42. D
27. D	35. B	43. E
28. E	36. E	44. D
29. A	37. D	45. B
30. B	38. C	46. D
31. A	39. B	47. E
32. E	40. A	48. C

SECTION FOUR

19. C	31. 4
20. D	32. 5
21. B	33. 50
22. E	34. 81
23. D	35. 180
24. B	36. 2
25. C	37. 7
26. A	38. 11
27. B	
28. B	
29. 24	
30. 4	

SECTION FIVE

1. E	14. C	27. A
2. C	15. B	28. C
3. B	16. E	29. B
4. E	17. B	30. D
5. A	18. C	31. C
6. B	19. D	32. E
7. C	20. C	33. B
8. B	21. A	34. C
9. C	22. D	35. C
10. C	23. A	36. D
11. E	24. E	37. D
12. E	25. C	38. E
13. B	26. B	39. C

Answers and Explanations

SECTION ONE

1. D

Identify the tone of the sentence and select a word for the blank consistent with that tone. The students lost their sense of originality, so their paintings must have been similar to the teacher's. *Copied* is a good prediction. Choice (D) is a good match.

2. B

Don't overlook important clues in the sentence. Here, all the words could apply to the English Channel, but only one of them fits all the clues. If the athlete's body temperature dropped and she shivered uncontrollably, the English Channel must have been *very cold*. Choice (B) is a good match.

3. A

Be wary of half-right, half-wrong choices on two-blank Sentence Completion questions.

The first blank must describe dogs that would be good candidates for becoming seeing-eye dogs. Many choices might work here, such as *intelligent*, *friendly*, and *obedient*. The second blank is a little more specific, since it must be something that can be described as unwavering. *Attention* and *obedience* both fit. Notice also that the first blank is a precondition for the second blank. (Only a dog that is *blank* can be trained to be *blank*.) Choice (A) is it. *Tractable* dogs could be trained to show unwavering *obedience*.

4. E

Start with the second blank. If the valley region of the state needs to be relieved of drought, the governor must be *recommending* or *implementing* water-saving measures. The first blank should be a word that can describe a valley. Choice (E) works for both blanks.

5. D

Here (A) and (B) make some sense, but don't fit the clues as well as the correct answer. The Phantom must have looked very different from the other cars, since some quality in its appearance was highlighted those cars. The other cars looked awkward and boxy, so the Phantom must have looked quite *graceful*. Choice (D) is a good match. *Sleek* is the opposite of boxy and awkward.

6. C

Don't be tempted by a choice just because of a familiar context, like *forecast* and *thunderstorm*. *Despite* indicates that there is a contrast in this sentence. The contrast is between a fast-approaching thunderstorm and what the workers did before they went indoors. A good prediction would be *presence* for the first blank and *careful* for the second. In Choice (C), you get the contrast you need in the second blank. *Diligent* means *careful and conscientious effort.*

7. D

This sentence provides a definition; you need a word that refers to *plots and schemes*. Choice (D) is a good match.

Lunar Eclipses

The first paragraph introduces the passages topic—lunar eclipses. The author notes that, although lunar eclipses are less well-known that solar eclipses, they last longer, are more common, and are easier to observe. The second paragraph gets into details: lunar eclipses happen when the Earth comes in between the Sun and the Moon. Also they can be divided into three types: total, partial and penumbral. The final paragraph explains that, unlike solar eclipses, lunar eclipses can be directly observed. It's important to note that this passage is purely informational; the author of this passage doesn't express a particular point of view, except perhaps an implication that lunar eclipses deserve more attention.

8. B

The author discusses several things in the passage, all of which contribute to the general discussion of lunar eclipses. Sometimes the simplest answer is the correct one.

9. D

The author says that lunar eclipses are spectacular and that they last a long time. So, the "stability" of lunar eclipses refers to the fact that they last a long time, they don't disappear quickly like solar eclipses. (D) makes sense. The eclipses have a long duration.

10. C

The author discusses the types of lunar eclipses in paragraph 2, so go there for the answer. You learn that a partial eclipse occurs when a part of the Moon passes through part of the Earth's umbral shadow.

(A) is a distortion; it describes a total eclipse. (B) is a misused detail; it is the total number of *all types* of lunar eclipses per year.

11. D

It's difficult to make a prediction here, but you do know that the distinctions among penumbral, partial, and full eclipses appear only in paragraph 2. So, the correct answer will come from information in that paragraph. Choice (D) fits. They are "brief and subtle" and are often "unobserved by all but astronomers and the most avid devotees," while other lunar eclipses are "quite easy to see."

12. C

The issue of safety is discussed in paragraph 3. There you learn that "the Moon's light is dissipated, reflected sunlight." The light is not dangerous because it is not coming directly from the Sun, but is instead reflecting off of the Moon. Choice (C) is a good match.

Flying Machine Passage

13. C

The word "implies" should tip you off that you will need to put together clues from the passage. The passage concentrates on the principle of buoyancy in connection with flying machines, so search for an answer choice that establishes this connection. Choice (C) works. The passage states that the discovery of buoyancy led Archimedes and Bacon and Albertus Magnus to consider flying machines, and that the principle of these machines was tested by the hot air balloon.

14. A

Like Archimedes may have done, the other scientists *created* or *publicized* designs for flying machines. Choice (A) is a good match. It makes sense to say that the scientists *offered* designs.

Movie Passages

15. E

A writer would most strongly disagree with a statement that conflicts with his or her central argument. Read each statement to see if it agrees or disagrees with the author's central argument—that the director is the *auteur* of a film. Remember that you're looking for the choice with which the author would *disagree*. Author 2 would agree with choice (E), but it is the opposite of the thesis for Passage 1. Since you're looking for something with which author 1 would *disagree*, this is the correct answer.

16. B

In the first sentence, the author states that "a film is a collaborative work," and the rest of the passage emphasizes the importance of the individual contributions of the artists who create films. Choice (B) matches your prediction well.

17. C

The quote comes from author 1, who thinks that films solely represent the vision of the director. Author 2, however, writes that "any sensitive viewer responds not to a single artistic vision in a film, but to dozens of such visions." In other words, viewers respond to the input of many different contributors. Choice (C) makes sense. To say that people only respond to the director's vision is a *simplification*, since it ignores the influence of all the contributions that author 2 writes about.

18. D

Passage 1 says that an *auteur* creates a film in the same way that an artist creates a painting. Passage 2, on the other hand, says that a movie is not like a painting because film is a collaborative effort. Choice (D) is a good match.

Moscow 1926 Passage

19. C

The author is commenting on her own nervousness when she says "It's as if I've never been to a proper theater." Of course, she had been to the theater quite often before, a "proper theater" before the war. Here, "proper" means *the real deal*. Choice (C) fits well with your prediction.

20. B

The author describes the play as "a rebellious act," and asks "Will we be putting ourselves in danger tonight? It's hard to believe we will not." So, she thinks that fear of getting in trouble might keep people away. Choice (B) is a good match.

21. B

The author notes that some other attendees were even more tattered, "but people were not judged for the state of their clothing." In other words, other aspects of the event were more important than what people looked like. Choice (B) fits your prediction.

22. A

The author writes that "the pace of the show was breathtaking. I found that I could scarcely keep up." So, the pace must have been quite *fast*. Choice (A) is a good match.

23. E

Since there's a lot of information about the play, it's tough to put it all together to make a prediction. You can at least say confidently that she enjoyed the play, so look for a positive choice. Choice (E) fits. In the first entry, you learn that she used to go to the theater frequently, and later missed it. In the second entry, she's very excited to be at the play, so it makes sense to say that she's *elated to be in the theater again*.

24. D

Beware of half-right, half-wrong answers like (A).

In the afternoon, the author is quite nervous: "I did not expect to be this nervous." In the evening, she writes that "I was so overwhelmed with emotion, I found myself on my feet clapping." She seems to be delighted to see the play. Choice (D) fits well.

SECTION TWO

1. A

Most of your initial work here centers on finding x, but remember that you're asked to find $6x$.

$$7x - 2 = 12x + 13$$
$$-15 = 5x$$
$$-3 = x$$

Then solve for $6x$:

$$6x = 6(-3) = -18$$

2. D

You don't know the actual values of a, b, c, and d, but you don't need to. Focus on how the angles are related to one another.

(A) If two angles are vertical, then they are congruent. So c and d are congruent and $2c$ must be equal to $2d$.

(B) If two angles form a straight line, then they are supplementary angles and their sum is 180°. So $a + d = 180°$ and $b + d = 180°$.

(C) $a - b = 0$ and $d - c = 0$.

(D) This statement could be true—if any of the angles were right, for example—but does not have to be true. For example, if a is 60°, $a + b = 120°$ and $c + d = 240°$.

(E) $a + c = 180°$ and $b + d = 180°$. Multiplying each sum by 2 does not undo the equality of the two sums.

3. B

Insert data from the question into the probability formula:

$$\text{probability} = \frac{\text{number of desired outcomes}}{\text{number of possible outcomes}}$$

2 pennies
1 nickel
3 dimes
2 quarters
8 coins

Dimes as a fraction of all coins are $\frac{3}{8}$.

4. C

Some questions test your ability to translate a word problem into a math problem.

$$x = \text{cost of one pencil}$$
$$y = \text{cost of one pen}$$
$$12x + 6y = 3.34$$
$$3x = 0.10$$

Solve for x:

$$x = \frac{.10}{3}$$

Substitute the value of x into the first equation:

$$12\left(\frac{.10}{3}\right) + 6y = 3.34$$
$$.4 + 6y = 3.34$$
$$y = \$.49$$

5. B

Begin by thinking about the meaning of "$\overline{BD}$ bisects $\angle ABC$".

If $\angle ABD = 20$, $\angle CBD = 20$, so $\angle ABC = 40$.

The right angle at A, added to 40, is 130.

$180 - 130 = 50$.

6. B

Pick numbers. Say $a = 1$ and $b = 2$.

(A) $2(1) + (2) = 4$

(B) $3(1) + (2) = 5$; This is the correct answer.

(C) $2[(1) + (2)] = 6$

(D) $\frac{(2)}{(1)} = 2$

(E) $1 + \frac{(2)}{(2)} = 2$

7. A

Manage the problem in two steps. First isolate x; then square it.

Solve for x:

$$x^{-3} = 8$$
$$x^{\frac{1}{3}} = 8$$
$$x^3 = \frac{1}{8}$$
$$x = \frac{1}{2}$$

Then solve for x^2:

$$x^2 = \frac{1}{4}$$

8. D

Begin a ratio question by making sure you are clear about the parts being compared. In this case, you want the shaded area to the unshaded area.

Area of entire figure $= \pi r^2 = \pi(6)^2 = 36\pi$

Area of small unshaded circle $= \pi(2)^2 = 4\pi$

Area of shaded region $= 36\pi - 4\pi = 32\pi$

Shaded:Unshaded $= 32\pi{:}4\pi + 8{:}1$

9. A

Focus on how one piece of data sheds light on the next. You're asked for the number of sophomores, but the way to arrive at it is by first finding the number of freshmen.

Number of seniors $= 0.4 \times 60$ players $=$ 24 seniors

Number of freshman $= 0.5 \times$ seniors $=$ 12 freshman

Number of juniors $= 0.3 \times 60$ players $=$ 18 juniors
_____
54

Number of sophomores $= 60 - 54 = 6$ sophomores

10. A

In this question, you use an inequality to solve for the angles of a triangle. It's often helpful to write the inequality as an equality—an equation—until you solve the problem. Then, go back and incorporate the inequality.

Set a equal to 50°.

$$180° - (50° + 60°) = 70°$$

Since $a > 50°$, $b < 70°$.

11. E

To maximize the value of a fraction in which top and bottom are positive numbers, maximize the top and minimize the bottom.

$$\frac{\max x}{\min y} = \frac{0.5}{0.25} = 2$$

12. C

Draw and label points as you work through the solution. This will help you to visualize the relationships among the points.

Think of M as 0. Since $2\overline{MN} = 5\overline{MP}$, MN must be longer than MP. P will be located between M and N on the number line. If you divide the number line into units, $P = 2$, $N = 5$, so $2MN = 5MP$.

Now $PN = 3$, $MP = 2$, for a ratio of 3:2.

13. A

If you know that a line with a downward slant has a negative slope, you can immediately eliminate three choices.

Estimate the slope of a line drawn through the center of the points. It is closest to a line that drops down three units and over 1 unit, giving it a slope of −3.

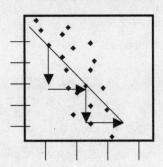

14. A

This question looks more complex than it actually is. Don't get sidetracked trying to solve for a. Once you substitute the given values of x and y, the as will cancel out.

$$x - y = (a - 5) - (a + 1)$$
$$= a - 5 - a - 1$$
$$= -6$$

15. D

Use data you're given about $ABCD$ to draw conclusions about the smaller squares. The perimeter of a square is 4 times the measure of a side, so each side of $ABCD$ must be 2 units long.

Each side is divided into 4 sections, so each section is $\frac{2}{4} = \frac{1}{2}$ unit.

Each section is a square, so the lengths of the sides are identical. The perimeter of the individual squares is

$$4 \times \frac{1}{2} \text{ unit} = 2 \text{ units.}$$

16. B

"The average of x and y" means $\frac{x + y}{2}$. Manipulate the equation into this form.

$$\frac{5x + 5y = 20}{5}$$
$$x + y = 4$$
$$\frac{x + y}{2} = \frac{4}{2} = 2$$

17. A

If the operation denoted by the symbol is complex—as it is here—the numbers to which you'll apply the symbolic operation have to be relatively simple.

$$2 \triangle 6 = \frac{4 + 6}{2} - \frac{2 + 6}{4} - \frac{2 + 4}{6} = 5 - 2 - 1 = 2$$

KAPLAN
Test Prep and Admissions

18. E

Probably the easiest way to answer this question is to draw a coordinate grid and locate each of the points. Although it might take a few moments to set up the grid, doing so will save you time in the long run.

In a 45-45-90 or isosceles right triangle, the legs are equal, and the hypotenuse is $\sqrt{2}$ times the length of a leg.

Test each point to see if it forms a 45-45-90 triangle. All three points could be the coordinates of point *F*.

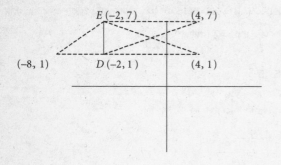

SECTION THREE

25. A

The sentence compares the past and present of an aspect of the lives of celebrities; the phrase "curiosity about their personal lives" tips you off that this aspect has to do with privacy, and the phrase "even though" indicates a contrast between what the public wanted and what the stars maintained. *Privacy* is a good prediction for the first blank. It's tough to make a prediction for the second blank, so look for a word that makes sense. Choice (A) fits well.

26. C

Mrs. Davis liked to "spread knowledge," so a good prediction for the first blank is *teach* or *inform*. Choice (C) is the best match.

27. D

Identify the positive or negative charge of a blank. Since John alienated his friends, the blanks must have a negative connotation. What has alienated John's friends? His habit of "mentioning titles of books he had read and quoting poems he had memorized." While it's tough to make an exact prediction, "*showing off* his *achievements*" is one possibility. Choice (D) fits well.

28. E

Start by predicting a possible answer for the blank you find easier to deal with. In this question, that may be the second blank. Since the characters are celebrated in legends, actions such as "robbing the rich to give to the poor" must be perceived as *admirable*. For the first blank, predict a word that makes "defying...authority" a good thing, for example, if that authority is *corrupt* or *unjust*. Choice (E) works well for both blanks.

29. A

When a question involves a straightforward definition, you can often use a word from the sentence as your prediction.

Plunging into ice-cold water doesn't sound like much fun, but the author writes that it can "invigorate" the body and spirit. In fact, *invigorating* would be a good prediction here. Choice (A) is a good match.

30. B

The only thing you know about the novel is that it is made up of letters. Look for a word that has this definition. Choice (B) fits. Even if you didn't know the definition of this uncommon term, you could probably eliminate the other choices, which contain more familiar words.

Greek Honor Passage

31. A

Since Achilles, withdrew from a war over an insult, he must have felt *very* insulted. Choice (A) fits.

32. E

Watch out for answer choices that are only partially correct. In a tough passage like this one, it's easy to get confused if you aren't clear on the author's main idea.

The paragraph says that Achilles's sense of honor changes. At the beginning, he is concerned with possessions won in battle. Later, however, Achilles thinks material possession can't make up for lost friends. The author also says that this is more attuned to a modern conception of honor. Choice (E) is a good match.

Canine Police

Passage 1

Passage 1 provides a general overview of police dogs. In paragraph 1, the author describes why the dogs are useful: they have "phenomenal tracking instincts," can search quickly, aren't deterred by darkness and locks, and can apprehend suspects in a way that minimizes the chance of injury. Paragraph 2 describes dogs' tracking abilities and how police use dogs for this purpose. It closes by noting that tracking success "can only be achieved only by extensive and continuing training." Paragraph 3 emphasizes the importance of aggression training, which trains a dog to attack only under specific circumstances.

Passage 2

Passage 2 presents an argument, although this is not apparent until the second paragraph. In paragraph 1, the author stresses the importance of the first two years of a dog's life. In paragraph 2, the author writes that early training is "especially important for police dogs." Unlike other states, the author's state doesn't provide such training. In paragraph 3, the author argues that politicians who are concerned with the quality of police dog training should consider not only its funding but also the age at which the dogs are trained.

33. E

The referenced sentence continues "because odors can be detected in the dark and through the smallest crack under a door." As long as a dog can use its sense of smell, it can search, unlike people who, relying primarily on their sense of sight, need light and unobstructed views. Choice (E) is a good match.

34. A

Carefully read the sentence in which the subject of the question appears. Here, "keen" applies to the sense of smell, not the dog, so you can rule out choices like (B) and (D). The dogs obviously have very *developed* sense of smell, so look for a choice that connotes this. Choice (A) is a good match.

35. B

The passage states that a scent article "bears the smell of the person being sought." The cotton pad, therefore, must pick up the person's scent from the steering wheel. Choice (B) fits. The passage states that skin rafts are what the dogs track. So, in order for the cotton pad to serve as a scent article, the skin rafts must have been transferred to the pad from the steering wheel.

36. E

The passage discusses the tendency of animals in the wild to abandon one trail for another, fresher one. The author indicates that this makes sense, because it allows the hunter to find a prey that "passed by most recently," and is therefore likely to be closer and easier to catch. Look for a choice that refers to this explanation of the dogs' behavior. Choice (E) is a good match.

37. D

When a question is limited to a specific part of the passage (like the last paragraph of Passage 1 here), watch out for choices that don't focus on the same section. In the final paragraph, the author writes that "many assume that the dog is likely to ferociously attack." The truth is that well-trained dogs attack only under specific circumstances. Choice (D) works. *Popular perception* refers to the perception of "many" who assume the dog will attack, while reality refers to true nature of the well-trained dogs.

38. C

The main idea of the first paragraph of Passage 2 is that "a dog's capacity to learn later in life is shaped" in the first two years of a puppy's life. Choice (C) is a good match.

39. B

Backtrack from the sentence in question. The previous sentence mentions "postnatal health care," while the *next* sentence back mentions "time while the dogs are still young…to train." These must be the "vital measures." Choice (B) is a good match.

40. A

What kind of interest have the politicians shown? They have "concerns about the state's police dogs and the quality of our current canine officer training programs." That sounds like a fairly *great* interest. Choice (A) works, and makes sense with the word "marked."

41. C

Right after the sentence in question, the author writes "We must also consider the ages of dogs entering training. We must mandate that units train younger dogs, not the older, harder-to-teach canines that are now being recruited for training." So, funding is not as important as the age of the dogs in training. Choice (C) is a good match.

42. D

For questions about paired passages, mentally summarize the author's main ideas in a single sentence before you attack the answer choices. For example, author 1 writes about the importance of training, and author 2 writes about the importance of early training. The overlap is training, so that's probably a good thing to look for as you look through the choices. Both authors would agree with Choice (D). Of course, author 2 would also note that the timing of the training is important, but he certainly wouldn't deny the importance of training.

43. E

Consider the main idea of the passages when a question asks to speculate about the reaction of one author to another. Author 2 agrees that training is important, but also feels that it must occur early in a dog's life. Choice (E) makes sense. Author 2 would state that the training must also take place at the right time in the dogs life.

44. D

There's not much to go on in the question stem, so dive right into the answer choices. Only choice (D) makes sense. Passage 1 provide lots of information about police dogs, while Passage 2 is intended to argue for a particular position, namely that police dogs should be trained earlier.

45. B

In order to find the correct answer, you need to read the text around the quote. The author specifically states, "we must recognize the truth of that old saw." That means, even though it is a cliché, it is true.

Chipmunk Effect Passage

46. D

There's no way to make a prediction here, so jump right into the answers. Choice (D) is a good match. The paragraph compares the rate of 180 words per minute for speaking versus the listening comprehension rate of 400 words per minute.

47. E

The author says that the "chipmunk effect" is "undesirable, if amusing." Looks for a choice that matches the sense of this pairing. Choice (E) is a good match.

48. C

Even if the answer seems obvious, you should refer to the context in which the word is used. The passage is discussing making recordings shorter, without making them faster, so you should look for a word that refers to length. Although the prolonged segments may be unnecessary, the meaning of prolonged in this sentence is longer.

SECTION FOUR

19. C

Focus on moving quickly but meticulously.

$$a = \frac{4}{5}$$

$$b = 15$$

$$ab = \frac{4}{5}(15) = 12$$

20. D

Think of a line of symmetry simply as a line that creates a mirror image on either side.

Figure I   Figure II   Figure III

21. B

Substitute 2 for x in the equation:

$f(2) = 4^2 - 5(2) = 16 - 10 = 6$

22. E

The intersection of sets is the set of common elements of the sets being intersected. Think of the intersection as the overlap of sets. The symbol for the intersection of sets is ∩.

To be in $P \cap Q$—that is, the intersection of P and Q—a number would have to be between 0 and 10, inclusive, and it would have to be prime. There are four such numbers: 2, 3, 5, 7.

23. D

All the integers from 7 to 12, exclusive, and all the integers from −7 to −12, exclusive, are possible values for the number in question. Only (D) doesn't fall into either one of these ranges.

24. B

Focus on this fraction:

$$\frac{\text{lost}}{\text{lost + won + tied}}$$

Lost = $2X$

Won = X

Tied = Y

$$\frac{\text{lost}}{\text{lost + won + tied}} = \frac{2X}{2X + X + Y} = \frac{2X}{3X + Y}$$

25. C

Be on the lookout for Pythagorean Triplets such as the 3-4-5 right triangle.

$OR = OT = 6$

$ST = 4$

$OS = 10$

So triangle ORS is a 3-4-5 right triangle in which the 3-4-5 ratio has been double to side lengths of 6, 8, and 10. Had you not noticed this, you could have solved for $\overline{SR}$ using the Pythagorean theorem:

$6^2 + x^2 = 10^2$

$36 + x^2 = 100$

$x^2 = 64$

$x = 8$

$SR = 8$

26. A

In this question, picking numbers is a great alternative to the algebra below.

$$\frac{a^{m+n}}{a^n} = \frac{a^m a^n}{a^n} = a^m$$

27. B

Knowing the radius of the circle, you can determine its area, and then its unshaded area. The ratio of the unshaded area to the total area is the same as the ratio of x to 360.

Area of circle = $\pi r^2 = 100\pi$

Area of shaded portion = 70π

Area of unshaded portion = $100\pi - 70\pi = 30\pi$

$$\frac{30\pi}{100\pi} = \frac{3}{10} = \frac{x}{360}$$

$10x = 1,080$

$x = 108$

28. B

Three-digit integers greater than 500 must be between 501 and 999. Eliminate groups that contain an even number of hundreds.

500s

~~600s~~

700s

~~800s~~

900s

Then eliminate groups that contain an even number of tens.

10s	~~20s~~	30s	~~40s~~	50s
~~60s~~	70s	~~80s~~	90s	

Finally, eliminate groups that contain an even number of ones.

1	~~2~~	3	4	5
~~6~~	7	~~8~~	9	

3 groups of hundreds × 5 groups of tens × 5 groups of ones = 75

29. 24

Some questions test your ability to translate words into math. Once you complete the translation, most of these questions become straightforward algebra.

$$\frac{1}{2}x = 4 + \frac{1}{3}x$$

$$\frac{x}{2} - \frac{x}{3} = 4$$

$$\frac{3x}{6} - \frac{2x}{6} = 4$$

$$\frac{3x - 2x}{6} = 4$$

$$\frac{x}{6} = 4$$

$$x = 24$$

30. 4

Look for a pattern.

Every 5th term is 5. So the 500th term is 5. One term before the 500th is then 4.

31. 4

Though several key formulas—such as area of a rectangle is length times width—are provided, know them ahead of time. You'll then move through related questions more quickly and confidently.

$$3a \times a = 48$$

$$a^2 = 16$$

$$a = 4$$

32. 5

This question illustrates the pay-off for recognizing certain classic factorables—such as the difference of two squares—on sight.

$$m^2 - n^2 = (m - n)(m + n) = 15$$

$$3(m + n) = 15$$

$$m + n = 5$$

33. 50

When percent questions take the form "...of a is b," put the "of" term on bottom and the "is" term on top. In this case, "...of p is q" becomes $\frac{q}{p}$.

$$p = .20(140) = 28$$

$$q = .25(56) = 14$$

$$\frac{q}{p} = \frac{14}{28} = .5 = 50\%$$

34. 81

Square both sides of an equation to get rid of a square root.

$$3\sqrt{x} - 7 = 20$$

$$3\sqrt{x} = 27$$

$$\sqrt{x} = 9$$

$$x = 3$$

35. 180

Notice that each dimension of one of the cubes fits evenly into each dimension of the box. Because of this, the answer to the question is simply the volume of the box divided by the volume of one of the cubes.

Volume of box: $18 \times 10 \times 8 = 1{,}440$ square inches

Volume of each cube: $2 \times 2 \times 2 = 8$ square inches

$1{,}440 \div 8 = 180$

36. 2

Don't let fancy wording intimidate you; this question only calls for a simple proportion and then some substitution.

"y varies directly with x^2" means $\frac{y}{x^2}$.

Substitute the given information:

$$\frac{8}{2^2} = \frac{y}{1^2}$$

$$\frac{8}{4} = \frac{y}{1}$$

$$4y = 8$$

$$y = 2$$

37. 7

The consecutive integers can be expressed as x and $x + 1$. So:

$$x(x + 1) = 29 + [x + (x + 1)]$$
$$x^2 + x = 29 + 2x + 1$$
$$x^2 - x - 30 = 0$$
$$(x - 6)(x + 5) = 0$$
$$x = -5 \text{ or } 6$$

The question states that x is a positive integer, so eliminate -5. If $x = 6$, $x + 1 = 7$.

38. 11

You're given $x^2 - 5x - 24 = 0$, which is a classic quadratic that you know how to factor. You're given that $a > 0$ and $b < 0$, which means simply that one root of the equation is positive and the other is negative. Finally, you're asked to identify the roots and then subtract the negative one from the positive one.

$$x^2 - 5x - 24 = 0$$
$$(x - 8)(x + 3) = 0$$
$$x = 8 \text{ or } -3$$
$$a > 0, \text{ so } a = 8$$
$$b < 0, \text{ so } b = -3$$
$$a - b = 8 - (-3) = 11$$

SECTION FIVE

1. E

The sentence is correct as written. (A) and (B) use the correct verb tenses. (C) clearly refers to *La Traviata* and the possessive pronoun "its" correctly refers to "the community opera company." (D) is the right subject to be modified by the long introductory clause.

2. C

This is an example of a run-on that uses a comma to connect two complete sentences. (C) should use a semicolon instead of a comma. (A) is idiomatically correct. In (B), the verbs *sustain* and *is* are correctly in the present tense. (D) correctly compares the frequencies of dislocated shoulders and strained hamstrings.

3. B

Look closely at the sequence of events. The technology was invented before the successful trip around the world. Therefore "they invented" should be in the past perfect ("they had invented"). In (A), the adverb "successfully" correctly modifies the verb "traveled." (C) is the second part of "either...or." (D) is correctly in the past perfect, as they received help before the successful travel.

4. E

Don't forget that 20% of identify errors questions are correct as written. The sentence is correct. (A) correctly sets up the contrast between Mary taking many singing lessons and being a poor singer. (B) and (C) correctly set up the comparison between Mary's singing and dancing. (D) is in the same form as "a singer" and thus a logical comparison.

5. A

The introductory phrase lacks a subject. Who is "examining their differences"? (A) should state who is examining the differences (for example, "If you examine"). (B) is plural because it refers to both the novelist's and the reporter's styles. The infinitive "to portray" (C) is used correctly. The adjective and noun pair "different ways" is correct.

6. B

When a comma divides two clauses, check whether they are both independent clauses. These are both independent clauses and therefore incorrectly written. The comma (B) should be a semicolon. (A) is correctly in the present tense. (C) establishes a correct comparison. (D) are idiomatically correct.

7. C

The sentence uses the relative pronoun "which" to refer to people. The correct pronoun is "who." (A) and (B) are idiomatically correct. (D) correctly refers to "many people."

8. B

The plural pronoun "their" would be correct if it referred to the plural noun "dieticians" but the nutritional importance of chocolate, not dieticians, is exaggerated. (B) should use the singular possessive pronoun "its." (A) is the correct form for this modifying phrase. (C) agrees with its verb "overuse." In (D), the adjectives "beneficial" and "harmful," although opposite in meaning, are used correctly.

9. C

The comparison between the impact of social consequences on literature and on politics or relations between nations must be parallel. They are two halves of the phrase "more impact on... than on...." (C) should read "than on either." In (D), the other parallel structure here—"either ... or"—is done correctly. (A) is correctly in the past tense. (B) correctly sets up the comparison.

10. C

There are two errors here. The relative pronoun *which* is incorrect. We can't substitute *novels* for *which* (try it: "he found the mysteries of novels especially gripping" doesn't catch the meaning). Also, the sentence uses a semicolon to connect a dependent and an independent clause. (C) solves both problems and forms a tighter sentence in which the semicolon is correct. The verb *liked* (A) correctly continues the past tense in *found*. (B) corrects the semicolon problem, but not the other. In (D), the adverb *especially* is used correctly to modify *gripping*.

11. E

This sentence is correct as written. (A) is idiomatically correct. (B) is correctly in the past tense. (C) correctly introduces the intervening phrase, and (D) uses the correct preposition.

12. E

This sentence is complicated, so take it one part at a time. (A) correctly refers to "the dancer." (B) is the correct noun to be placed directly after the introductory clause. (C) is idiomatically correct. (D) uses the possessive to refer to its "loose and full breathing methods."

13. B

As written, this sentence is a fragment, because there is no verb. (B) can be changed to "diseases is frequently," creating a full sentence. (A) and (D) are idiomatically correct. (C) correctly sets up a causal relationship.

14. C

The word "upcoming" indicates that the workshop is in the future, but the sentence is in the present tense. In (C), the verb "conducts" should be in the future tense ("will conduct"). (A) and (B) are idiomatically correct. (D) agrees with the noun "workshop."

15. B

The two main clauses of the sentence are not parallel. The subject of the two clauses should be the same, linked by the comparison word "but." The subject "football games" is parallel to the personal pronoun "they." (B) corrects this problem and correctly omits the relative pronoun "that." (D) removes the subject from the second clause altogether and also unnecessarily interchanges the transition words "however" and "but." (C) and (E) substitute the relative pronoun "that" for the correct personal pronoun "they."

16. E

The word "relentless" modifies the verb "studied" and so should be an adverb. (C), (D) and (E) correctly change "studied relentless" to "studied relentlessly." Only (E) changes "for passing" to the correct "to pass" (C) changes the meaning by making "relentlessly" modify the verb "pass" instead of "studied." (D) keeps "for passing," which is incorrect idiomatically. (B) doesn't address the original problem.

17. B

The verb tenses should reflect the fact that the second clause happened after the first clause. (B) and (E) correct the verb tense problem but only (B) is correct idiomatically. (E) incorrectly substitutes "had been" for "got." (C) incorrectly adds the gerund "showing." (D) changes the meaning by putting the word "once" in front, which should then lead to an example of the violinist's behavior.

18. C

This is a sentence fragment; there is no verb in an independent clause. The verb "add" in the second clause is made subordinate by the conjunction "that." Only (B) and (C) add the needed verb "are" and only (C) retains the meaning. (B) incorrectly states that the compositions themselves are actually suggesting. (D) and (E) don't correct the original problem.

19. D

There is no noun for the introductory clause to modify. "They" were looking through the school's telescope, so "they" needs to begin the second clause. (D) and (E) both do so but (E) incorrectly uses the past tense for "flew" ("they saw a star flew" should be "they saw a star fly"). (B) doesn't add a noun and (C) adds the wrong noun. The shooting star didn't look through the telescope.

20. C

The two phrases at the end of the sentence are not parallel: "entertaining" is an adjective; "educate" is a verb. The two phrases must either describe the library (adjective) or what the library does (verb). (C) correctly changes the verb "educate" to the adjective "educational" so that the library is entertaining and educational. (B) makes this change but adds "being" which is not parallel to "to be." (D) simply changes the plural verb "educate" to the singular verb "educates." (E) changes the verb "educate" to the noun "education."

21. A

The sentence is correct as it is—two independent clauses joined by a semicolon. (B) changes the sequence of events: the Queen wanted strong rule and so did not marry, not the other way around. (C) and (D) change the meaning from the Queen wanting strong rule to English society wanting strong rule. (C) also creates a run-on. (E) incorrectly forms a dependent clause after the semicolon.

22. D

The sentence sets up a contrast: we don't know if there is other life in the universe, but people have seen UFOs. We need a contrast transition word. Only (D) adds "but" and so is the correct answer. (C) keeps the transition word "and." (B) and (E) don't include a transition word.

23. A

This is a complicated sentence, but it is correct. Home-team loyalty (the sentence's first clause) allows all of the second clause to happen. (B) and (D) state that the feat was attempted as staggering instead of proclaimed as staggering. (C) illogically puts the second clause in the past tense. (E) is a sentence fragment.

24. E

The introductory phrase incorrectly modifies "the deterioration." The deterioration was not nervous, the leaders were. (D) and (E) correct the modification problem but only (E) uses the correct verb tense and pronoun. (D) incorrectly uses the past perfect tense and the pronoun "their," which would indicate the leaders' rather than society's collapse. (B) and (C) don't correct the modification problem.

25. C

Who's "they"? The ties or the women? From a common-sense perspective, of course, it has to be the ties. But "they" has an unclear antecedent, and to make this sentence correct you need to find a choice that makes it clear that the sentence is referring to the ties. Both (C) and (D) begin with the noun "ties" and are good places to start. Since you didn't identify any problem with the verb, (C), which maintains the original verb, looks like a good choice, and sure enough, when you check out (D), you see that it uses "being." Remember, be wary of any verb constructions that use "being." On the PSAT, they are often incorrect.

26. B

Choice (B) is the clearest and most concise choice. All the other choices use overly wordy and imprecise constructions.

27. A

The original sentence is best.

28. C

Having read the works describes the speaker, so you know that the correct answer will have *I* as the first word (the way the sentence is written, it sounds as though *Hemingway* read the works, because his name is placed directly after the modifying phrase). Only (C) and (E) begin with *I*, but (E) introduces yet another misplaced modifier (it says the speaker is a writer, not Hemingway).

29. B

The key to this question is realizing what Aunt Helga appreciates: it's not *us*, but our act of coming to her birthday party. *Our coming* correctly phrases this idea; *coming* is a gerund (a verb form that acts as a noun), and *our* is a possessive pronoun. *Us coming* is a common mistake; it's wrong because the pronoun *us* is not in the possessive form.

30. D

Idiomatically, *the same* should be followed by the preposition *as*, not *than*. There is also a problem of parallelism here: the two things being compared should be in the same grammatical form. Since *talking* is a gerund, the thing it's being compared to should also be a gerund: *driving*.

31. C

This run-on sentence is best corrected by choice (C), which is grammatically correct and doesn't include extra verbiage. (B) and (E) use the semicolon improperly, and (D) is wordy.

32. E

The sentence is unclear because it doesn't use the correct sequence of tenses. Since the client had already been waiting for fifteen minutes *before* the moment when the receptionist looked up, the first verb must be in the past perfect: *had been waiting.*

33. B

There is an error of subordination here: To express the causal relationship between melting ice caps and flooding of islands, you need only one conjunction: *because* or *therefore*. To have both is redundant. (Furthermore, the word *therefore* should be preceded by a semicolon, not a comma.)

34. C

This sentence fragment is best corrected by moving the verb *was* and inserting a comma after the introductory phrase describing Flaubert.

The Presidential Office Passage

35. C

There is no plural noun before "they" so we must read further. Sentence 3 states that the Founding Fathers considered it "dangerous" for the President to gain power from popularity. Therefore, it is the Founding Fathers who "feared popular leadership," and (C) is correct. (A) is out of scope; revolutionaries are never mentioned, just the Revolution itself. (B) is illogical; complications cannot fear anything. (D) and (E) pick up the wrong words from sentence 3.

36. D

Adding a phrase to the beginning of sentence 5 will probably set up its relationship to sentence 4. Sentence 5 makes a conclusion based on the Founders' idea in sentence 4. (D) refers to the Founders and shows that sentence 5 definitely follows from sentence 4. (A) uses the first person, although the author never refers to herself in the passage. (B) and (C) incorrectly set up a contrast between sentences 5 and 4. (C) also adds the pronoun "him," which doesn't clearly refer to anyone. (E) creates a sentence fragment.

37. D

We are given two short sentences and asked to combine them; we must determine their relationship to each other and the passage. Sentence 6 states that Washington is an example of the ideas in paragraph 2. Sentence 7 explains why he is a good example. (D) combines the sentences and adds the causal word "because." It also puts the first part of the sentence in present tense (he is an example) and changes "asked" to "wanted." (B) incorrectly uses the contrast transition word "although." (C) omits the idea that this is an example. (E) uses the ambiguous pronoun "they" instead of "the Founders" and also is a run-on.

38. E

This sentence confuses tenses. Andrew Jackson acted in the past to make the presidency what it is in the present. (E) correctly puts "makes" in the past tense. (A) is incorrect because "He" is not ambiguous; "he" clearly refers to Andrew Jackson. (B) is illogical; the President isn't a popularity contest, the presidency is. (C) and (D) make the wrong tense change. (C) puts what is happening in the present into the past tense. (D) changes to the past perfect tense, which would work only if a later action by Jackson was mentioned.

39. C

As written, the sentence states that "many people" may have been wrong. But the author's point is that the Founders may have been wrong. (C) corrects that problem and substitutes "the Founders" for the ambiguous pronoun "they." (A) and (B) change the meaning to say that the people actively suggested that the Founders were wrong. (D) uses the wrong transition word; it should be a word that indicates contrasts with sentence 15. (E) is a run-on sentence with a comma splice.

Chapter Nine: **Compute Your Score**

These scores are intended to give you an approximate idea of your performance. There is no way to determine your exact score for the following reasons.

- The New PSAT has not yet been released, so scoring criteria are not yet precise.
- Various statistical factors and formulas are taken into account on the real test.
- For each grade, the scaled score range changes from year to year.

The official score range for each section of the New PSAT will be 20–80. Taken together, the perfect total score becomes 240. The section scores correspond to the SAT score range of 200–800.

STEP 1: FIGURE OUT YOUR RAW SCORE FOR EACH PRACTICE TEST.

First, check your answers against the answer keys on the previous pages, and count up the number of right and the number of wrong answers for each section (except for Grid-ins, where you do not lose points for wrong answers). Remember, do not count questions left blank as wrong. Round up to the nearest whole number.

Practice Test One

	Number Right		Number Wrong			Raw Score

Critical Reading

Sections 1 & 3: ☐ − $\left(.25 \times \boxed{}\right)$ = ☐

Critical Reading Raw Score = ☐

Writing

Section 5: ☐ − $\left(.25 \times \boxed{}\right)$ = ☐

Writing Raw Score = ☐

Math

Section 2: ☐ − $\left(.25 \times \boxed{}\right)$ = ☐

Section 4A: ☐ − $\left(.25 \times \boxed{}\right)$ = ☐
(Questions 19–28)

Section 4B: ☐ = ☐
(Questions 29–38)
[No Wrong Answer Penalty]

Math Raw Score = ☐

Practice Test Two

	Number Right		Number Wrong		Raw Score

Critical Reading

Sections 1 & 3:   ☐   −   (.25 × ☐)   =   ☐

Critical Reading Raw Score   =   ☐

Writing

Section 5:   ☐   −   (.25 × ☐)   =   ☐

Writing Raw Score   =   ☐

Math

Section 2:   ☐   −   (.25 × ☐)   =   ☐

Section 4A: ☐   −   (.25 × ☐)   =   ☐
(Questions 19–28)

Section 4B: ☐   =   ☐
(Questions 29–38)
[No Wrong Answer Penalty]

Math Raw Score   =   ☐

Practice Test Three

	Number Right		Number Wrong			Raw Score
Critical Reading						
Sections 1 & 3:	☐	−	(.25 ×	☐	) =	☐
			Critical Reading Raw Score		=	☐
Writing						
Section 5:	☐	−	(.25 ×	☐	) =	☐
			Writing Raw Score		=	☐
Math						
Section 2:	☐	−	(.25 ×	☐	) =	☐
Section 4A: (Questions 19–28)	☐	−	(.25 ×	☐	) =	☐
Section 4B: (Questions 29–38) [No Wrong Answer Penalty]	☐				=	☐
			Math Raw Score		=	☐

STEP 2: CONVERT YOUR RAW SCORE TO A SCALED SCORE.

For each subject area in the practice test, convert your raw score to your scaled score using the table below.

RAW SCORE	SCALED SCORE*			RAW SCORE	SCALED SCORE*		
	Critical Reading	Math	Writing		Critical Reading	Math	Writing
48	80			20	53	58	57
47	80			19	52	57	56
46	79			18	51	55	55
45	78			17	50	53	53
44	77			16	49	51	52
43	76			15	48	50	50
42	75			14	47	49	49
41	74			13	46	48	47
40	73			12	44	47	46
39	72		80	11	43	46	44
38	71	80	80	10	42	45	43
37	70	80	79	9	41	44	42
36	69	78	78	8	40	42	41
35	68	76	77	7	39	41	40
34	67	74	76	6	38	40	39
33	66	73	74	5	36	39	38
32	65	72	73	4	35	38	36
31	64	71	72	3	34	36	34
30	63	70	70	2	33	35	32
29	62	69	69	1	32	34	30
28	61	68	68	0	30	32	29
27	60	66	67	−1	29	30	28
26	59	65	66	−2	28	28	26
25	58	64	64	−3	27	26	25
24	57	63	63	−4	26	24	24
23	56	62	62	−5	24	22	23
22	55	60	60	−6	22	21	21
21	54	59	59	−7	20	20	20

* unofficial scores; for guidance purposes only

| SECTION THREE: |

PSAT Study Aids

Appendix One: **SAT Essay Preview**

This appendix has nothing to do with your PSAT preparation. This appendix is only for the student who is using the PSAT to practice for the SAT or the student who plans to take the SAT next year. Is that you? If so, read on.

The PSAT does not have an essay, but starting this year the SAT does. You can consider this appendix your practice for the SAT's essay. (Of course our SAT book has lots more on the SAT essay, but we wanted to at least give you some advance warning in the PSAT book as well.)

The SAT Writing section is divided into two parts—an essay section and a multiple-choice section. The multiple-choice section is a lot like the PSAT's multiple-choice Writing section. The essay is totally different.

THE SAT ESSAY

For the essay portion of the test, your task is to write a short, *persuasive* essay on an assigned topic. The word *persuasive* is key. You can write the best essay ever on a meaningful experience or ways to become more involved in your community, but if you have not persuaded the reader to see things from a particular point of view, you won't earn a high score.

You are required to write about the topic you are given, but you don't need any specific knowledge to complete the SAT essay, and you do have a lot of freedom in what you actually write. Because the topic will be very broad in scope, you can write about what you know and are interested in.

Essay Directions

At the time of this printing, the College Board has stated that the directions for the essay will look like the following directions.

You will have 25 minutes to write your essay in your test booklet (two pages).

Directions: Consider carefully the following statement and the assignment below it.

> "The longer I live the more I see that I am never wrong about anything, and that all the pains I have so humbly taken to verify my notions have only wasted my time."
> -George Bernard Shaw

Assignment: Is a certain amount of arrogance a good human quality? In an essay, support your position by discussing an example (or examples) from literature, science and technology, the arts, current events, or your own experience or observation.

In an essay, support your position by discussing an example (or examples) from literature, science and technology, the arts, current events, or your own experience or observation.

Essay Scoring

The essays will be scored quickly and *holistically* by two readers. *Holistically* means your essay gets a single score—a number—that indicates its overall quality. This number takes into account a variety of essay characteristics, including organization and development of ideas, sentence structure, vocabulary, and grammar and usage. Thus, a highly persuasive and eloquent essay that has several run-ons or other minor errors could still earn a top score because of its overall effectiveness and impact.

Each reader will assign your essay a score ranging from a high of 6 to a low of 1. These two scores are added together to get a total score ranging from a high of 12 to a low of 2. The essay score accounts for one third of your final SAT Writing section score.

The following chart is a rubric that shows the main criteria that the graders use to score your essay.

THE ESSAY SCORING CHART

Score	Demonstrates	Organization	Language
6	clear and consistent competence, though it may have errors	is well organized and fully developed with supporting examples	displays consistent language facility, varied sentence structure, and range of vocabulary
5	reasonable competence, with occasional errors or lapses in quality	is generally organized and well developed with appropriate examples	displays language facility, with syntactic variety and a range of vocabulary
4	adequate competence with occasional errors and lapses in quality	is organized and adequately developed with examples	displays adequate but inconsistent language facility
3	developing competence, with weaknesses	inadequate organization or development	many errors in grammar or diction; little variety
2	some incompetence with one or more weaknesses	poor organization, thin development	frequent errors in grammar and diction; no variety
1	incompetence, with serious flaws	no organization, no development	severe grammar and diction errors obscure meaning

Here is what this means in plainer English:

6 Outstanding Essay

Convincingly and insightfully fulfills the writing assignment; ideas are well developed, clearly presented, and logically organized; superior command of vocabulary, grammar, style, and accepted conventions of writing; a few minor flaws may occur.

5 Solid Essay

Convincingly fulfills the writing assignment; ideas are adequately developed, clearly presented, and logically organized; strong command of vocabulary, grammar, style, and accepted conventions of writing; some minor flaws may occur.

4 Adequate Essay

Fulfills the writing assignment; ideas are adequately developed, presented, and organized; satisfactory command of vocabulary, grammar, style, and accepted conventions of writing; some flaws may occur.

3 Limited Essay

Doesn't adequately fulfill the writing assignment; lacks adequate development and organization of ideas; unsatisfactory command of vocabulary, grammar, style, and accepted conventions of writing; contains many flaws.

2 Flawed Essay

Doesn't fulfill the writing assignment; ideas are vague, poorly presented, and not logically organized; poor command of vocabulary, grammar, style, and accepted conventions of writing; contains numerous serious flaws.

1 Deficient Essay

Doesn't fulfill the writing assignment; ideas are extremely vague, very poorly presented, and not logically organized; extremely poor command of vocabulary, grammar, style, and accepted conventions of writing; is so seriously flawed that basic meaning is obscured.

ESSAY STRATEGIES

To help you achieve a high-scoring SAT essay, Kaplan has developed an SAT Essay-writing strategy called THINK-ORGANIZE-WRITE-FIX, otherwise known as TOWF. After you read your essay topic, you:

T HINK about the topic (2 minutes)
O RGANIZE your ideas (5 minutes)
W RITE your essay (15 minutes)
F IX any mistakes (3 minutes)

Here's our minute-by-minute rundown of the TOWF method.

Minutes 1–2: Think

This step takes two minutes. That leaves you 23 minutes to organize, write, and fix your essay. We suggest that you wait to write anything down during these two minutes and just brainstorm. There's plenty of time for writing later. But if it helps you to jot notes down while you think, than go for it.

Let's say that you get the following quote:

"A man walking down a crowded street noticed a dog lying by the side of the road that looked like it might be injured; but since everyone else just passed by, the man was satisfied to assume that the dog was fine. The next day he learned that the dog had been hit by a car and lay injured for two hours before a concerned man stopped and took it to the vet. The animal recovered, but the man never forgave himself for leaving it for someone else to help."

Narawhal Bherundi, *Autobiography*

Assignment: What is your view on individual responsibility in a situation in which many people could have reacted?

Then the assignment asks you to take a specific example from your personal experience, from current events, or from history, literature, or any other discipline and develop it to support your persuasive argument, using the quote as a guidepost.

Pick a Stance

In this essay, you must decide what your stance will be concerning individual responsibility. For example, if you believe that human beings do not have any obligation to help others, than you will want to build your argument around a particular story or experience explaining just that. Or you might believe that everyone is responsible for the welfare of others, even strangers, and thus, you would write to persuade the reader in that respect. What's important is that you take a position and state how you feel. It is not important what other people might think, just what you think, so avoid statements such as "some people feel …" or "a lot of people think …." Get the picture?

Choose Your Examples

Once you have picked your stance, you must choose examples that back up your argument. Think up two to three specific examples that you can write about intelligently and passionately. You could use an example from history, such as Mother Teresa and her life's work of helping others. You could use the scenario of a bystander witnessing a mugging. You could use an example from your life, like how you were stranded on the side of a road, and no one would stop to see if you needed help.

Use Specific Evidence

You've got to cite evidence to support your examples. When you are thinking of your examples, also think about one piece of evidence for each of them. Remember, arguing your point of view without having a good reason is not convincing and won't get you your highest essay score. For instance, you could site the many visits Mother Teresa made to impoverished countries as evidence for the before-mentioned example.

Minutes 3–7: Organize

This step takes up to five minutes. That may seem like a lot of time to spend before you write a single essay sentence. But taking a few minutes to organize your essay is definitely worth the time. If you take a few minutes to organize what you want to write, the essay will be a lot easier to write once you start it.

So you have your argument, your examples, and your evidence in your head. It's time to plan your essay. Use the scratch paper that is provided for you. Here is one way that your essay paragraphs could be organized:

First Paragraph

Clearly state your argument.

Briefly mention the evidence that you're going to cite in support of that argument.

Middle Paragraphs (2–3 paragraphs)

Explore and explain your evidence in detail. These paragraphs explain how the evidence supports the argument.

Last Paragraph

Briefly summarize your argument.

Let's try it out. We'll go with humans having an obligation to help others.

"A man walking down a crowded street noticed a dog lying by the side of the road that looked like it might be injured; but since everyone else just passed by, the man was satisfied to assume that the dog was fine. The next day he learned that the dog had been hit by a car and lay injured for two hours before a concerned man stopped and took it to the vet. The animal recovered, but the man never forgave himself for leaving it for someone else to help."

Narawhal Bherundi, *Autobiography*

Assignment: What is your view on individual responsibility in a situation in which many people could have reacted?

P1. Humans should take initiative to help/individual can have an effect.

P2. Shirking responsibility/sister stuck on side of road/no one stopped/had to make a dangerous walk.

P3. Personal experience/girl lost/walked her to class/made a new friend.

P4. Everyone has a responsibility to help, even if others don't.

Minutes 8–22: Write

The writing step of your essay should take about 15 minutes. That's plenty of time to write three to five solid paragraphs if you work from a prepared outline.

To write your strongest essay, follow your outline. You spent five minutes thinking about and organizing your essay, so stick to it! Don't panic and write from the opposing point-of-view. However, if you come up with the perfect example halfway through your essay, replace it in your outline, see how it works, then continue. But *try try try* not to erase and rewrite any big chunks of text. Trust yourself.

You also need to write clearly, write concisely, write complete sentences, and use proper grammar. If you use them on test day, your essay WILL be well written. But you only have 15 minutes. So write fast. Here is a quickly written essay (a draft version, you might say) about responsibility:

An individual can have a major effect on another individual or situation. In the example above, an individual save a dog's life. A group of people ignored the situation but an individual man actually did something. He stepped out of the mob mentality. Everyone else conformed to each other and walked by. This man stopped and saved the dog.

However, the primary man in the example did not do so. He conformed and walked by. He shirked his responsibility. This is like that one time my sister needed help and didn't get it. On her way home from college, she had car trouble and was stranded on the side of the road at night. Many cars passed by but no one stopped to see if they could give her a hand. After waiting for forever, she ended up having to walk to the nearest gas station two miles away, which is not safe for a young girl to do by herself. Here, no individual took responsibility to help her, and this refusal of responsibility could have led to more severe consequences.

On a lighter but related note, I had personal experience with individual responsibility. At the beginning of last year, I was walking to first period science class when I noticed a confused, nervous girl standing in the hallway. She looked like she was about to cry as everyone rushed past her. She was obviously lost, but no one who knew the way took responsibility to help her. I felt badly so approached her and asked if I could help. It turned out that she had just moved from another part of the country and knew no one at my high school. She couldn't find her science class, which turned out to be my science class, and was too shy to ask for help. I walked with her to science class, made a new friend, and took the responsibility to help someone.

At the end of the day, everyone has the responsibility not to conform in a situation in which many people can react. Each person should be the individual who takes action and helps. No one should assume that someone else will take responsibility, because maybe no one will.

Minutes 23–25: Fix

This step takes three minutes. It involves proofreading and fixing your essay. Hopefully, all you'll need to do is fix minor grammatical or spelling errors, change a few words here and there, and, maybe, add a sentence or two for clarity's sake.

If you spend the bulk of the 25 minutes thinking about, organizing, and writing the essay, the repair step should entail nothing more than putting the finishing touches on an already strong essay.

Here is our fixed up essay:

An individual can have a major effect on another individual or situation. In the example above, an individual <u>saved</u> a dog's life. A group of people ignored the <u>situation, but</u> an individual man actually did something. He stepped out of the mob mentality. Everyone else conformed to each other and walked by. This man stopped and saved the dog.

However, <u>the man</u> in the example did not do so. He conformed and walked by. He shirked his responsibility. <u>This relates to a situation that my sister experienced</u>. On her way home from college, she had car trouble and was stranded on the side of the road at night. Many cars passed <u>by, but</u> no one stopped to see if they could give her a hand. After waiting for <u>over an hour</u>, she ended up having to walk to the nearest gas station two miles away, which is not safe for a young girl to do by herself. Here, no individual took responsibility to help her, and this refusal of responsibility could have led to more severe consequences.

On a lighter but related note, I <u>had a personal</u> experience with individual responsibility. At the beginning of last year, I was walking to first period science class when I noticed a confused, nervous girl standing in the hallway. She looked like she was about to cry as everyone rushed past her. She was obviously lost, but no one who knew the way took responsibility to help her. I felt <u>badly for her, so I approached</u> her and asked if I could help. It turned out that she had just moved from another part of the country and knew no one at my high school. She couldn't find her science class, which turned out to be my science class, and was too shy to ask for help. I walked with her to science class, made a new friend, and took the responsibility to help someone.

At the end of the day, everyone has the responsibility not to conform in a situation in which many people can react. Each person should be the individual who takes action and helps. No one should assume that someone else will take responsibility, because maybe no one will.

SAMPLE ESSAYS AND GRADERS' COMMENTS

Here are three sample essays pertaining to the assignment below and how a SAT grader would probably grade them.

You will have 25 minutes to write your essay in your test booklet (two pages).

Directions: Consider carefully the following statement(s) and the assignment below it.

> "Don't flatter yourself that friendship authorizes you to say disagreeable things to your intimates. The nearer you come into relation with a person, the more necessary do tact and courtesy become. Except in cases of necessity, which are rare, leave your friend to learn unpleasant things from his enemies; they are ready enough to tell them."
>
> –Oliver Wendell Holmes,
> *The Autocrat of the Breakfast-Table*

> "A good friend can tell you what is the matter with you in a minute. He may not seem such a good friend after telling."
>
> –Arthur Brisbane, *The Book of Today*

Assignment: Should friends be honest with each other, even if a truthful comment could be hurtful? In an essay, support your position by discussing an example (or examples) from literature, science and technology, the arts, current events, or your own experience or observation.

Grade 6 Essay

One of the defining qualities of a good friendship is that both friends can be completely honest with each other. This does not mean that the two friends don't consider each others feelings or blurt out comments without thinking, but it does mean that each person can rely on the other to tell the truth, even if the truth can sometimes be awkward or hurtful.

My sister and I have always been close friends, even when we were younger. When my sister was in junior high school and I was in elementary school, she decided to get her hair permed because all of her friends were doing the same thing. Unfortunately, the treatment didn't work well on her hair and she ended up with a big, frizzy clump of curls that stuck out on the sides. Most of her friends didn't have the courage to tell her that it didn't look good. Instead, they just made fun of her behind her back. So it was up to me to tell her the truth. I was a bit scared to confront my older sister, because I knew that she would be upset. But I also knew that she would be more upset if no one dared to be honest with her. A few years earlier, we were in the opposite roles, and she had gently but firmly advised me against a choice that I later realized would have been embarrassing for me when I started school.

Although my sister was hurt when I told her that the perm didn't look good, she was more hurt to learn that some of her other friends had thought the same thing but hadn't said anything to her. She was angry with me at first for making a negative comment, but in the end she was glad I had told her so that she could go back to the hair stylist to fix the problem. Since my sister was very concerned about her appearance and personal style at that time in her life, she appreciated my honesty because it helped her get through a tough situation and our friendship grew stronger as a result of this experience.

In the years since this incident, my sister and I have both continued to be honest and upfront with each other, and we value this aspect of our relationship. After all, friendly honesty is far better than hostile honesty, so being a good friend involves telling the truth, no matter what the circumstances. Honesty truly is an essential component of a good friendship.

Grader's Comments: The author begins this essay with a clear statement based on the prompt, showing that she has clearly understood the topic. The remainder of the essay presents and develops an example to support her opinion. The example provided is relevant to multiple aspects of the prompt – the importance of honesty in friendship as well as the possibility that being honest can be difficult in certain situations.

The essay is well organized, with a clear narrative flow framed by a cohesive introduction and conclusion. The structure of the essay reflects that the author took time to plan before writing and carefully followed her plan as she composed her essay. Although the vocabulary used in the essay is not very sophisticated, the author's ideas are communicated effectively. Finally, there are few grammatical or spelling errors: "others" instead of "other's" in the first paragraph; a couple of sentences lacked commas in the second and third paragraphs. This author clearly managed her time effectively so that she could proofread her essay.

Grade 4 Essay

Being honest is part of being a good friend. However, their are times when you shouldn't be completely honest because what you say might hurt your friend's feelings.

For example, imagine that your best friend tells you his parents are getting divorced. He is obviously upset by this even though you know his parents haven't been getting along well because he constantly complained about their fights and even joked about hoping they'd get a divorce so he wouldn't have to listen to them anymore. In this situation, reminding your friend of his earlier comments or pointing out that his parents will be happier apart isn't the right thing to do because at a time like this you're friend doesn't need you to tell him the harsh truth, he needs you to by sympathetic and supportive. It's pretty likely that he'll hear all about the negative things from other people or even from his parents, so your job as his best friend is to try not to say or do anything unpleasant.

Another example could be if you're friend has bought something that she's really excited about. You might not agree that she's made a good choice or you might not like what she bought, but you don't need to spoil her enthusiasm by making a negative comment. Again, this is a time when you should keep quiet about your own opinion so that your friend can be happy.

There are certain situations when it's okay not to tell the complete truth to your friends. You should never lie to your friends, but an important part of being a good friend is knowing when to be totally honest and when to keep silent because a truthful comment could do more harm than good.

Grader's Comments: The author introduces his essay with a clear statement of his opinion, showing that he has understood the prompt. His two examples provide decent support for the topic, but the second example is vague and not well developed. The author would have a stronger essay if he expanded upon the prompt and provided additional details for the first example rather than trying to include a weak second example. Having a clear plan could help to accomplish this change in structure.

The essay is fairly well organized, with several keywords ("However," "For example," "Another example," "Again") that add structure to the author's argument. The weakest parts of this essay are some simplistic language and awkward sentences: in the second paragraph, the second sentence is long and wordy, and the third sentence is a run-on sentence and is very difficult to follow, so the author's meaning almost gets obscured by the effort it takes to decipher his thoughts. There are also a few usage/spelling errors: "their" instead of "they're" in the first paragraph; "you're" instead of "your" in the second and third paragraphs. The author needs to be more deliberate when writing the essay and needs to proofread to catch these spelling errors and prevent run-on sentences or awkward sentence structure.

Grade 2 Essay

No matter what, friends should tell each other the truth. That's the whole point of having friends, so you have some people around you that you can trust and talk to and that you know will tell you everything.

Friends can tell you negative things in a kind way so you can here the truth even if its not so good. Enemies tell you the same negative things in a mean way because their trying to hurt you. But friends can accomplish this in a nicer way.

Its important to know and learn the truth even if its about yourself or its something you don't want to face. You need honest friends to tell you the truth, because they do it out of love not hate like enemies.

Grader's Comments: This author starts strongly with a clear statement of her opinion, which is directly related to the topic of the prompt. However, the author continues with a series of generalizations, none of which are specific examples to support her opinion. She needs to spend more time planning her essay to make sure that she's got at least one strong example to include to support her argument.

This essay does not follow an organized structure, and it lacks good transitions and keywords. To improve this part of her writing, the author should make an outline during her planning stage and should focus on using several keywords while she writes, which will give her essay a stronger and clearer structure.

The author's language is simplistic and repetitive. The essay contains several grammatical and spelling errors: "that" twice instead of "whom/who" when referring to "people" in the first paragraph; "here" and "their" are misused for "hear" and "they're" in the second paragraph; "its" is misused numerous times for "it's" in the second and third paragraphs. The author should study the SAT grammar materials to improve this aspect of her writing and should also be sure to proofread to avoid careless errors.

Appendix Two: **Word Families**

❑ **Talkative**

garrulous
glib
loquacious
raconteur
verbose
voluble

❑ **Secret/Hidden**

abscond
alias
arcane
clandestine
covert
cryptic
enigma
furtive
incognito
inconspicuous
lurk
obscure
skulk
subterranean
surreptitious

❑ **Not Talkative**

concise
curt
laconic
pithy
reticent
succinct
taciturn

❑ **Praise**

accolade
adulation
commend
eulogize
exalt
extol
laud
lionize
plaudit
revere

❑ **Criticize/Scold**

admonish
berate
castigate
censure
chastise
defame
denigrate
disdain
disparage
excoriate
malign
obloquy
rail
rebuke
reproach
reprimand
reprove
revile
upbraid
vilify

❑ **Stubborn**

intractable
mulish
obdurate
obstinate
pertinacious
recalcitrant
refractory
tenacious

❑ **Lazy/Lacking Energy**

indolent
lackadaisical
laggard
languid
lassitude
lethargic
listless
loiter
phlegmatic
sluggard
somnolent
torpid

❑ **Cowardly**

craven
diffident
pusillanimous
timid
timorous

❑ **Inexperienced**

callow
fledgling
infantile
ingenuous
neophyte
novice
tyro

❑ **Obedient**

amenable
assent
compliant
deferential
docile
pliant
submissive
tractable

❑ **Haughty/Pretentious**

affected
aloof
bombastic
grandiloquent
grandiose
magniloquent
mannered
ostentatious
pontificate
supercilious

❑ **Friendly**

affable
amiable
amicable
bonhomie
convivial
gregarious

❑ **Lucky**

auspicious
fortuitous
opportune
serendipity

❑ **Soothe**

allay
alleviate
anodyne
assuage
liniment
mitigate
mollify
pacify
palliate
placate

❑ **Hostility/Hatred**

abhor
anathema
animosity
antagonism
antipathy
aversion
contentious
deplore
odious
rancor

❑ **Stupid**

buffoon
dolt
dupe
fatuous
imbecile
inane
insipid
obtuse
simpleton
vacuous
vapid

❑ **Subservient**

fawn
grovel
obsequious
servile
subjection
sycophant
toady

❑ **Argumentative**

adversarial
bellicose
belligerent
fractious
irascible
obstreperous
pugnacious
quibble

❑ **Cautious**

chary
circumspect
discretion
leery
prudent
wary

❑ **Impermanent**

ephemeral
evanescent
fleeting
transient
transitory

❑ **Ability/Intelligence**

acumen
adept
adroit
agile
astute
cogent
deft
dexterous
erudite
literate
lucidity
sagacious
trenchant

❑ **Kind/Generous**

altruistic
beneficent
benevolent
bestow
largess
liberal
magnanimous
munificent
philanthropic

Appendix Three: **Root List**

❑ A, AN—not, without

amoral, atrophy, asymmetrical, anarchy, anesthetic, anonymity, anomaly

❑ AB, A—from, away, apart

abnormal, abdicate, aberration, abhor, abject, abjure, ablution, abnegate, abortive, abrogate, abscond, absolve, abstemious, abstruse, annul, avert, aversion

❑ AC, ACR—sharp, sour

acid, acerbic, exacerbate, acute, acuity, acumen, acrid, acrimony

❑ AD, A—to, toward

adhere, adjacent, adjunct, admonish, adroit, adumbrate, advent, abet, accede, accretion, acquiesce, affluent, aggrandize, aggregate, alleviate, alliteration, allude, allure, ascribe, aspersion, aspire, assail, assonance, attest

❑ ALI, ALTR—another

alias, alienate, inalienable, altruism

❑ AM, AMI—love

amorous, amicable, amiable, amity

❑ AMBI, AMPHI—both

ambiguous, ambivalent, ambidextrous, amphibious

❑ AMBL, AMBUL—walk

amble, ambulatory, perambulator, somnambulist

❑ ANIM—mind, spirit, breath

animal, animosity, unanimous, magnanimous

❑ ANN, ENN—year

annual, annuity, superannuated, biennial, perennial

❑ ANTE, ANT—before

antecedent, antediluvian, antebellum, antepenultimate, anterior, antiquity, antiquated, anticipate

❑ ANTHROP—human

anthropology, anthropomorphic, misanthrope, philanthropy

❑ ANTI, ANT—against, opposite

antidote, antipathy, antithesis, antacid, antagonist, antonym

❑ AUD—hear

audio, audience, audition, auditory, audible

❑ AUTO—self

autobiography, autocrat, autonomous

❑ BELLI, BELL—war

belligerent, bellicose, antebellum, rebellion

❑ BENE, BEN—good

benevolent, benefactor, beneficent, benign

❑ BI—two

bicycle, bisect, bilateral, bilingual, biped

❑ BIBLIO—book

Bible, bibliography, bibliophile

❑ BIO—life
biography, biology, amphibious, symbiotic, macrobiotics

❑ BURS—money, purse
reimburse, disburse, bursar

❑ CAD, CAS, CID—happen, fall
accident, cadence, cascade, deciduous

❑ CAP, CIP—head
captain, decapitate, capitulate, precipitous, precipitate, recapitulate

❑ CARN—flesh
carnal, carnage, carnival, carnivorous, incarnate

❑ CAP, CAPT, CEPT, CIP—take, hold, seize
capable, capacious, captivate, deception, intercept, precept, inception, anticipate, emancipation, incipient, percipient

❑ CED, CESS—yield, go
cease, cessation, incessant, cede, precede, accede, recede, antecedent, intercede, secede, cession

❑ CHROM—color
chrome, chromatic, monochrome

❑ CHRON—time
chronology, chronic, anachronism

❑ CIDE—murder
suicide, homicide, infanticide, regicide, patricide

❑ CIRCUM—around
circumference, circumlocution, circumnavigate, circumscribe, circumspect, circumvent

❑ CLIN, CLIV—slope
incline, inclination, declivity, proclivity

❑ CLUD, CLUS, CLAUS, CLOIS—shut, close
conclude, reclusive, claustrophobia, cloister, preclude, occlude

❑ CO, COM, CON—with, together
coeducation, coagulate, coalesce, coerce, cogent, cognate, collateral, colloquial, colloquy, commensurate, commodious, compassion, compatriot, complacent, compliant, complicity, compunction, concerto, conciliatory, concord, concur, condone, conflagration, congeal, congenial, congenital, conglomerate, conjugal, conjure, conscientious, consecrate, consensus, consonant, constrained, contentious, contrite, contusion, convalescence, convene, convivial, convoke, convoluted, congress

❑ COGN, GNO—know
recognize, cognition, cognizance, incognito, diagnosis, agnostic, prognosis, gnostic, ignorant

❑ CONTRA—against
controversy, incontrovertible, contravene

❑ CORP—body
corpse, corporeal, corpulence

❑ COSMO, COSM—world
cosmopolitan, cosmos, microcosm, macrocosm

❑ CRAC, CRAT—rule, power
democracy, bureaucracy, theocracy, autocrat, aristocrat, technocrat

❑ CRED—trust, believe
incredible, credulous, credence

❑ CRESC, CRET—grow
crescent, crescendo, accretion

❑ CULP—blame, fault
culprit, culpable, inculpate, exculpate

❑ CURR, CURS—run
current, concur, cursory, precursor, incursion

DE—down, out, apart

depart, debase, debilitate, declivity, decry, deface, defamatory, defunct, delegate, delete, demarcation, demean, demur, deplete, deplore, depravity, deprecate, deride, derivative, desist, detest, devoid

DEC—ten, tenth

decade, decimal, decathlon, decimate

DEMO, DEM—people

democrat, demographics, demagogue, epidemic, pandemic, endemic

DI, DIURN—day

diary, quotidian, diurnal

DIA—across

diagonal, diatribe, diaphanous

DIC, DICT—speak

abdicate, diction, interdict, predict, indict, verdict

DIS, DIF, DI—not, apart, away

disaffected, disband, disbar, disburse, discern, discordant, discredit, discursive, disheveled, disparage, disparate, dispassionate, dispirit, dissemble, disseminate, dissension, dissipate, dissonant, dissuade, distend, differentiate, diffidence, diffuse, digress, divert

DOC, DOCT—teach

docile, doctrine, doctrinaire

DOL—pain

condolence, doleful, dolorous, indolent

DUC, DUCT—lead

seduce, induce, conduct, viaduct, induct

EGO—self

ego, egoist, egocentric

EN, EM—in, into

enter, entice, encumber, endemic, ensconce, enthrall, entreat, embellish, embezzle, embroil, empathy

ERR—wander

erratic, aberration, errant

EU—well, good

eulogy, euphemism, euphony, euphoria, eurythmics, euthanasia

EX, E—out, out of

exit, exacerbate, excerpt, excommunicate, exculpate, execrable, exhume, exonerate, exorbitant, exorcise, expatriate, expedient, expiate, expunge, expurgate, extenuate, extort, extremity, extricate, extrinsic, exult, evoke, evict, evince, elicit, egress, egregious

FAC, FIC, FECT, FY, FEA—make, do

factory, facility, benefactor, malefactor, fiction, fictive, beneficent, affect, confection, refectory, magnify, unify, rectify, vilify, feasible

FAL, FALS—deceive

infallible, fallacious, false

FERV—boil

fervent, fervid, effervescent

FID—faith, trust

confident, diffidence, perfidious, fidelity

FLU, FLUX—flow

fluent, affluent, confluence, effluvia, superfluous, flux

FORE—before

forecast, foreboding, forestall

FRAG, FRAC—break

fragment, fracture, diffract, fractious, refract

FUS—pour

profuse, infusion, effusive, diffuse

GEN—birth, class, kin

generation, congenital, homogeneous, heterogeneous, ingenious, engender, progenitor, progeny

❑ GRAD, GRESS—step

graduate, gradual, retrograde, centigrade, degrade, gradation, gradient, progress, congress, digress, transgress, ingress, egress

❑ GRAPH, GRAM—writing

biography, bibliography, epigraph, grammar, epigram

❑ GRAT—pleasing

grateful, gratitude, gratis, ingrate, congratulate, gratuitous, gratuity

❑ GRAV, GRIEV—heavy

grave, gravity, aggravate, grieve, aggrieve, grievous

❑ GREG—crowd, flock

segregate, gregarious, egregious, congregate, aggregate

❑ HABIT, HIBIT—have, hold

habit, cohabit, habitat, inhibit

❑ HAP—by chance

happen, haphazard, hapless, mishap

❑ HELIO, HELI—sun

heliocentric, heliotrope, aphelion, perihelion, helium

❑ HETERO—other

heterosexual, heterogeneous, heterodox

❑ HOL—whole

holocaust, catholic, holistic

❑ HOMO—same

homosexual, homogenize, homogeneous, homonym

❑ HOMO—man

homo sapiens, homicide, bonhomie

❑ HYDR—water

hydrant, hydrate, dehydration

❑ HYPER—too much, excess

hyperactive, hyperbole, hyperventilate

❑ HYPO—too little, under

hypodermic, hypothermia, hypochondria, hypothesis, hypothetical

❑ IN, IG, IL, IM, IR—not

incorrigible, indefatigable, indelible, indubitable, inept, inert, inexorable, insatiable, insentient, insolvent, insomnia, interminable, intractable, incessant, inextricable, infallible, infamy, innumerable, inoperable, insipid, intemperate, intrepid, inviolable, ignorant, ignominious, ignoble, illicit, illimitable, immaculate, immutable, impasse, impeccable, impecunious, impertinent, implacable, impotent, impregnable, improvident, impassioned, impervious, irregular

❑ IN, IL, IM, IR—in, on, into

invade, inaugurate, incandescent, incarcerate, incense, indenture, induct, ingratiate, introvert, incarnate, inception, incisive, infer, infusion, ingress, innate, inquest, inscribe, insinuate, inter, illustrate, imbue, immerse, implicate, irrigate, irritate

❑ INTER—between, among

intercede, intercept, interdiction, interject, interlocutor, interloper, intermediary, intermittent, interpolate, interpose, interregnum, interrogate, intersect, intervene

❑ INTRA, INTR—within

intrastate, intravenous, intramural, intrinsic

❑ IT, ITER—between, among

transit, itinerant, transitory, reiterate

❑ JECT, JET—throw

eject, interject, abject, trajectory, jettison

❑ JOUR—day

journal, adjourn, sojourn

❑ JUD—judge

judge, judicious, prejudice, adjudicate

❏ JUNCT, JUG—join
junction, adjunct, injunction, conjugal, subjugate

❏ JUR—swear, law
jury, abjure, adjure, conjure, perjure, jurisprudence

❏ LAT—side
lateral, collateral, unilateral, bilateral, quadrilateral

❏ LAV, LAU, LU—wash
lavatory, laundry, ablution, antediluvian

❏ LEG, LEC, LEX—read, speak
legible, lecture, lexicon

❏ LEV—light
elevate, levitate, levity, alleviate

❏ LIBER—free
liberty, liberal, libertarian, libertine

❏ LIG, LECT—choose, gather
eligible, elect, select

❏ LIG, LI, LY—bind
ligament, oblige, religion, liable, liaison, lien, ally

❏ LING, LANG—tongue
lingo, language, linguistics, bilingual

❏ LITER—letter
literate, alliteration, literal

❏ LITH—stone
monolith, lithograph, megalith

❏ LOQU, LOC, LOG—speech, thought
eloquent, loquacious, colloquial, colloquy, soliloquy, circumlocution, interlocutor, monologue, dialogue, eulogy, philology, neologism

❏ LUC, LUM—light
lucid, elucidate, pellucid, translucent, illuminate

❏ LUD, LUS—play
ludicrous, allude, delusion, allusion, illusory

❏ MACRO—great
macrocosm, macrobiotics

❏ MAG, MAJ, MAS, MAX—great
magnify, magnanimous, magnate, magnitude, majesty, master, maximum

❏ MAL—bad
malady, maladroit, malevolent, malodorous

❏ MAN—hand
manual, manuscript, emancipate, manifest, manumission

❏ MAR—sea
submarine, marine, maritime

❏ MATER, MATR—mother
maternal, matron, matrilineal

❏ MEDI—middle
intermediary, medieval, mediate

❏ MEGA—great
megaphone, megalomania, megaton, megalith

❏ MEM, MEN—remember
memory, memento, memorabilia, reminisce

❏ METER, METR, MENS—measure
meter, thermometer, perimeter, metronome, commensurate

❏ MICRO—small
microscope, microorganism, microcosm, microbe

❏ MIS—wrong, bad, hate
misunderstand, misanthrope, misapprehension, misconstrue, misnomer, mishap

❑ MIT, MISS—send
transmit, emit, missive

❑ MOLL—soft
mollify, emollient, mollusk

❑ MON, MONIT—warn
admonish, monitor, premonition

❑ MONO—one
monologue, monotonous, monogamy, monolith, monochrome

❑ MOR—custom, manner
moral, mores, morose

❑ MOR, MORT—dead
morbid, moribund, mortal, amortize

❑ MORPH—shape
amorphous, anthropomorphic, metamorphosis, morphology

❑ MOV, MOT, MOB, MOM—move
remove, motion, mobile, momentum, momentous

❑ MUT—change
mutate, mutability, immutable, commute

❑ NAT, NASC—born
native, nativity, natal, neonate, innate, cognate, nascent, renascent, renaissance

❑ NAU, NAV—ship, sailor
nautical, nauseous, navy, circumnavigate

❑ NEG—not, deny
negative, abnegate, renege

❑ NEO—new
neoclassical, neophyte, neologism, neonate

❑ NIHIL—none, nothing
annihilation, nihilism

❑ NOM, NYM—name
nominate, nomenclature, nominal, cognomen, misnomer, ignominious, antonym, homonym, pseudonym, synonym, anonymity

❑ NOX, NIC, NEC, NOC—harm
obnoxious, noxious, pernicious, internecine, innocuous

❑ NOV—new
novelty, innovation, novitiate

❑ NUMER—number
numeral, numerous, innumerable, enumerate

❑ OB—against
obstruct, obdurate, obfuscate, obnoxious, obsequious, obstinate, obstreperous, obtrusive

❑ OMNI—all
omnipresent, omnipotent, omniscient, omnivorous

❑ ONER—burden
onerous, exonerate

❑ OPER—work
operate, cooperate, inoperable

❑ PAC—peace
pacify, pacifist, pacific

❑ PALP—feel
palpable, palpitation

❑ PAN—all
panorama, panacea, panegyric, pandemic, panoply

❑ PATER, PATR—father
paternal, paternity, patriot, compatriot, expatriate, patrimony, patricide, patrician

❑ PATH, PASS—feel, suffer
sympathy, antipathy, empathy, apathy, pathos, impassioned

❑ PEC—money
pecuniary, impecunious, peculation

❑ PED, POD—foot
pedestrian, pediment, expedient, biped, quadruped, tripod

❑ PEL, PULS—drive
compel, compelling, expel, propel, compulsion

❑ PEN—almost
peninsula, penultimate, penumbra

❑ PEND, PENS—hang
depend, pendant, pendulous, compendium, suspense, propensity

❑ PER—through, by, for, throughout
perambulator, percipient, perfunctory, permeable, perspicacious, pertinacious, perturbation, perusal, perennial, peregrinate

❑ PER—against, destruction
perfidious, pernicious, perjure

❑ PERI—around
perimeter, periphery, perihelion, peripatetic

❑ PET—seek, go toward
petition, impetus, impetuous, petulant, centripetal

❑ PHIL—love
philosopher, philanderer, philanthropy, bibliophile, philology

❑ PHOB—fear
phobia, claustrophobia, xenophobia

❑ PHON—sound
phonograph, megaphone, euphony, phonetics, phonics

❑ PLAC—calm, please
placate, implacable, placid, complacent

❑ PON, POS—put, place
postpone, proponent, exponent, preposition, posit, interpose, juxtaposition, depose

❑ PORT—carry
portable, deportment, rapport

❑ POT—drink
potion, potable

❑ POT—power
potential, potent, impotent, potentate, omnipotence

❑ PRE—before
precede, precipitate, preclude, precocious, precursor, predilection, predisposition, preponderance, prepossessing, presage, prescient, prejudice, predict, premonition, preposition

❑ PRIM, PRI—first
prime, primary, primal, primeval, primordial, pristine

❑ PRO—ahead, forth
proceed, proclivity, procrastinator, profane, profuse, progenitor, progeny, prognosis, prologue, promontory, propel, proponent, propose, proscribe, protestation, provoke

❑ PROTO—first
prototype, protagonist, protocol

❑ PROX, PROP—near
approximate, propinquity, proximity

❑ PSEUDO—false
pseudoscientific, pseudonym

❑ PYR—fire
pyre, pyrotechnics, pyromania

❑ QUAD, QUAR, QUAT—four
quadrilateral, quadrant, quadruped, quarter, quarantine, quaternary

❑ QUES, QUER, QUIS, QUIR—question
quest, inquest, query, querulous, inquisitive, inquiry

❑ QUIE—quiet
disquiet, acquiesce, quiescent, requiem

❑ QUINT, QUIN—five
quintuplets, quintessence

❑ RADI, RAMI—branch
radius, radiate, radiant, eradicate, ramification

❑ RECT, REG—straight, rule
rectangle, rectitude, rectify, regular

❑ REG—king, rule
regal, regent, interregnum

❑ RETRO—backward
retrospective, retroactive, retrograde

❑ RID, RIS—laugh
ridiculous, deride, derision

❑ ROG—ask
interrogate, derogatory, abrogate, arrogate, arrogant

❑ RUD—rough, crude
rude, erudite, rudimentary

❑ RUPT—break
disrupt, interrupt, rupture

❑ SACR, SANCT—holy
sacred, sacrilege, consecrate, sanctify, sanction, sacrosanct

❑ SCRIB, SCRIPT, SCRIV—write
scribe, ascribe, circumscribe, inscribe, proscribe, script, manuscript, scrivener

❑ SE—apart, away
separate, segregate, secede, sedition

❑ SEC, SECT, SEG—cut
sector, dissect, bisect, intersect, segment, secant

❑ SED, SID—sit
sedate, sedentary, supersede, reside, residence, assiduous, insidious

❑ SEM—seed, sow
seminar, seminal, disseminate

❑ SEN—old
senior, senile, senescent

❑ SENT, SENS—feel, think
sentiment, nonsense, assent, sentient, consensus, sensual

❑ SEQU, SECU—follow
sequence, sequel, subsequent, obsequious, obsequy, non sequitur, consecutive

❑ SIM, SEM—similar, same
similar, verisimilitude, semblance, dissemble

❑ SIGN—mark, sign
signal, designation, assignation

❑ SIN—curve
sine curve, sinuous, insinuate

❑ SOL—sun
solar, parasol, solarium, solstice

❑ SOL—alone
solo, solitude, soliloquy, solipsism

❑ SOMN—sleep
insomnia, somnolent, somnambulist

❑ SON—sound
sonic, consonance, dissonance, assonance, sonorous, resonate

❏ SOPH—wisdom
philosopher, sophistry, sophisticated, sophomoric

❏ SPEC, SPIC—see, look
spectator, circumspect, retrospective, perspective, perspicacious, perspicuous

❏ SPER—hope
prosper, prosperous, despair, desperate

❏ SPERS, SPAR—scatter
disperse, sparse, aspersion, disparate

❏ SPIR—breathe
respire, inspire, spiritual, aspire, transpire

❏ STRICT, STRING—bind
strict, stricture, constrict, stringent, astringent

❏ STRUCT, STRU—build
structure, obstruct, construe

❏ SUB—under
subconscious, subjugate, subliminal, subpoena, subsequent, subterranean, subvert

❏ SUMM—highest
summit, summary, consummate

❏ SUPER, SUR—above
supervise, supercilious, supersede, superannuated, superfluous, insurmountable, surfeit

❏ SURGE, SURRECT—rise
surge, resurgent, insurgent, insurrection

❏ SYN, SYM—together
synthesis, sympathy, synonym, syncopation, synopsis, symposium, symbiosis

❏ TACIT, TIC—silent
tacit, taciturn, reticent

❏ TACT, TAG, TANG—touch
tact, tactile, contagious, tangent, tangential, tangible

❏ TEN, TIN, TAIN—hold, twist
detention, tenable, tenacious, pertinacious, retinue, retain

❏ TEND, TENS, TENT—stretch
intend, distend, tension, tensile, ostensible, contentious

❏ TERM—end
terminal, terminus, terminate, interminable

❏ TERR—earth, land
terrain, terrestrial, extraterrestrial, subterranean

❏ TEST—witness
testify, attest, testimonial, testament, detest, protestation

❏ THE—god
atheist, theology, apotheosis, theocracy

❏ THERM—heat
thermometer, thermal, thermonuclear, hypothermia

❏ TIM—fear, frightened
timid, intimidate, timorous

❏ TOP—place
topic, topography, utopia

❏ TORT—twist
distort, extort, tortuous

❏ TORP—stiff, numb
torpedo, torpid, torpor

❏ TOX—poison
toxic, toxin, intoxication

❏ TRACT—draw
tractor, intractable, protract

❑ TRANS—across, over, through, beyond

transport, transgress, transient, transitory, translucent, transmutation

❑ TREM, TREP—shake

tremble, tremor, tremulous, trepidation, intrepid

❑ TURB—shake

disturb, turbulent, perturbation

❑ UMBR—shadow

umbrella, umbrage, adumbrate, penumbra

❑ UNI, UN—one

unify, unilateral, unanimous

❑ URB—city

urban, suburban, urbane

❑ VAC—empty

vacant, evacuate, vacuous

❑ VAL, VAIL—value, strength

valid, valor, ambivalent, convalescence, avail, prevail, countervail

❑ VEN, VENT—come

convene, contravene, intervene, venue, convention, circumvent, advent, adventitious

❑ VER—true

verify, verity, verisimilitude, veracious, aver, verdict

❑ VERB—word

verbal, verbose, verbiage, verbatim

❑ VERT, VERS—turn

avert, convert, revert, incontrovertible, divert, subvert, versatile, aversion

❑ VICT, VINC—conquer

victory, conviction, evict, evince, invincible

❑ VID, VIS—see

evident, vision, visage, supervise

❑ VIL—base, mean

vile, vilify, revile

❑ VIV, VIT—life

vivid, vital, convivial, vivacious

❑ VOC, VOK, VOW—call, voice

vocal, equivocate, vociferous, convoke, evoke, invoke, avow

❑ VOL—wish

voluntary, malevolent, benevolent, volition

❑ VOLV, VOLUT—turn, roll

revolve, evolve, convoluted

❑ VOR—eat

devour, carnivore, omnivorous, voracious

Appendix Four: **Writing Skills**

PUNCTUATION REVIEW

Commas

1. Use commas to separate items in a series

If more than two items are listed in a series, they should be separated by commas. The final comma—the one that precedes the word "and"—may be omitted. An omitted final comma would not be considered an error on the PSAT.

Example: My recipe for buttermilk biscuits includes flour, baking soda, salt, shortening, and buttermilk.

ALSO RIGHT: My recipe for buttermilk biscuits includes flour, baking soda, salt, shortening and buttermilk.

Be watchful for commas placed **before** the first element of a series **or after** the last element.

WRONG: My recipe for chocolate cake includes, flour, baking soda, sugar, eggs, milk and chocolate.

WRONG: Flour, baking soda, sugar, eggs, milk and chocolate, are the ingredients in my chocolate cake.

2. Use commas to separate two or more adjectives before a noun

Example: I can't believe you sat through that long, dull movie three times in a row.

It is **incorrect** to place a comma **after** the last adjective in a series.

WRONG: The manatee is a blubbery, bewhiskered, creature.

3. Use commas to set off parenthetical clauses and phrases

If a phrase or clause is not necessary to the main idea expressed by a sentence, it should be set off by commas.

Example: Phillip, who never had any formal chef's training, bakes excellent cheesecake.

The main idea here is that Phillip bakes an excellent cheesecake. The intervening clause merely serves to further describe Phillip; it should therefore be enclosed in commas.

4. Use commas after introductory phrases

Example: Having watered his petunias every day during the drought, Harold was disappointed when his garden was destroyed by aphids.

Example: After the banquet, Harold and Melissa went dancing.

5. Use commas to separate independent clauses

Use a comma before a conjunction (*and*, *but*, *nor*, *yet*, etc.) that connects two independent clauses.

Example: Marta is good at basketball, but she's better at soccer.

Semicolons

Like commas, semicolons can be used to separate independent clauses. As we saw above, two related independent clauses that are connected by a conjunction such as *and*, *but*, *nor*, or *yet* should be punctuated by a comma. If the words *and*, *but*, *nor*, or *yet* aren't used, the clauses should be separated by a semicolon.

Example: Whooping cranes are an endangered species; there are only fifty of them alive today.

Example: Whooping cranes are an endangered species, and they are unlikely to survive if we continue to pollute their habitat.

Semicolons may also be used between independent clauses connected by words like *therefore*, *nevertheless*, and *moreover*. For more on this topic, see the section on "Sentence Structure" in this Appendix.

Colons

In Standard Written English, the colon is used only as a means of signaling that what follows is a list, definition, explanation, or restatement of what has gone before. A word or phrase such as *like the following*, *as follows*, *namely*, or *this* is often used along with the colon to make it clear that a list, summary, or explanation is coming up.

Example: This is what I found in her refrigerator: a moldy lime and a jar of peanut butter.

Example: Your instructions are as follows: Read the passage carefully, answer the questions, and turn over your answer sheet.

The Dash

The dash has two uses. One is to indicate an abrupt break in thought.

Example: The alligator, unlike the crocodile, will usually not attack humans—unless, that is, she feels that her young are in danger.

The dash can also be used to set off a parenthetical expression from the rest of the sentence.

Example: At 32° Fahrenheit—which is zero on the Celsius scale—water will freeze.

The Apostrophe

The apostrophe has two distinct functions. It is used with contracted verb forms to indicate that one or more letters have been eliminated:

Example: The **boy's** an expert at chess. (The boy is an expert at chess.)

Example: The **boy's** left for the day. (The boy has left for the day.)

The apostrophe is also used to indicate the possessive form of a noun.

Example: The **boy's** face was covered with mosquito bites after a day in the swamp.

GRAMMAR REVIEW

Subject-Verb Agreement

The form of a verb must match, or agree with, its subject in two ways: person and number.

1. Agreement of Person

When we talk about "person," we're talking about whether the subject and verb of a sentence show that the author is making a statement about himself (first person), the person he is speaking to (second person), or some other person, place, or thing (third person).

First Person Subjects: I, we.

Example: **I am** going to Paris. **We are** going to Rome.

Second Person Subject: you.

Example: **Are you** sure you weren't imagining that flying saucer?

Third Person Subjects: he, she, they, it, *and names of people, places, and things.*

Example: **He is driving** me crazy.

2. Agreement of Number

When we talk about number, we're talking about whether the subject and verb show that one thing is being discussed (singular) or that more than one thing is being discussed (plural).

HINT: Subjects and verbs must agree in number. Subjects and verbs that don't agree in number appear very frequently on the PSAT.

WRONG: The **children catches** the school bus every morning.

RIGHT: The **children catch** the school bus every morning.

Be especially careful of subject-verb agreement when the subject and verb are separated by a long string of words.

> WRONG: **Wild animals** in jungles all over the world **is** endangered.

> RIGHT: **Wild animals** in jungles all over the world **are** endangered.

Pronouns

A pronoun is a word that is used in place of a noun. The antecedent of a pronoun is the word to which the pronoun refers.

> Example: <u>Mary</u> was late for work because <u>she</u>
> ANTECEDENT   PRONOUN

> forgot to set the alarm.

Occasionally, an antecedent will appear in a sentence *after* the pronoun.

> Example: Because <u>he</u> sneezes so often, <u>Arthur</u>
>   PRONOUN   ANTECEDENT

> always thinks <u>he</u> might have the flu.
>   PRONOUN

1. Pronouns and Agreement

In clear, grammatical writing, a pronoun must clearly refer to, and agree with, its antecedent.

Number agreement of pronouns is more frequently tested on the PSAT than person agreement, although you may see a question that tests person agreement.

NUMBER AND PERSON

	Singular	Plural
First Person	I, me my, mine	we, us our, ours
Second Person	you your, yours	you your, yours
Third Person	he, him she, her it one his her, hers its one's	they, them their, theirs

Number Agreement

Pronouns must agree in number with their antecedents. A singular pronoun should stand in for a singular antecedent. A plural pronoun should stand in for a plural antecedent. Here's a typical PSAT pronoun error.

> WRONG: The bank turned Harry down when he applied for a loan because **their** credit department discovered that he didn't have a job.

What does the plural possessive *their* refer to? The singular noun *bank*. The singular possessive its is what we need here.

> RIGHT: The bank turned Harry down for a loan because **its** credit department discovered that he didn't have a job.

Person Agreement

Pronouns must agree with their antecedents in person too. A first-person pronoun should stand in for a first-person antecedent, and so on. One more thing to remember about which pronoun to use with which antecedent: Never use the relative pronoun *which* to refer to a human being. Use *who* or *whom* or *that*.

> WRONG: The woman **which** is standing at the piano is my sister.

> RIGHT: The woman **who** is standing at the piano is my sister.

2. Pronouns and Case

A more subtle type of pronoun problem is one in which the pronoun is in the wrong case. Look at the following chart:

	CASE	
	Subjective	**Objective**
First Person	I we	me us
Second Person	you	you
Third Person	he she it they one	him her it them one

Relative Pronouns   who   whom
                          that   that
                          which   which

When to Use Subjective Case Pronouns

Use the subjective case for the subject of a sentence.

Example: **She** is falling asleep.

WRONG: Nancy, Claire, and **me** are going to the ballet.

RIGHT: Nancy, Claire, and **I** are going to the ballet.

Use the subjective case after a linking verb like *to be*.

Example: It is **I**.

Use the subjective case in comparisons between the subject of verbs that are not stated, but understood.

Example: Gary is taller than **they** (are).

When to Use Objective Case Pronouns

Use the objective case for the object of a verb.

Example: I called **her**.

Use the objective case for the object of a preposition.

Example: I laughed at **him**.

Use the objective case after infinitives and gerunds.

Example: Asking **him** to go was a big mistake.

Example: To give **him** the scare of his life, we all jumped out of his closet.

Use the objective case in comparisons between objects of verbs that are not stated but understood.

Example: She calls you more than (she calls) **me**.

3. Who and Whom

Another thing you'll need to know is when to use the relative pronoun *who* (subjective case) and when to use the relative pronoun *whom* (objective case: *whom* goes with *him* and *them*). The following method is very helpful when you're deciding which one to use.

Example: Sylvester, (*who* or *whom*?) is afraid of the dark, sleeps with a Donald Duck night-light on.

Look only at the relative pronoun in its clause. Ignore the rest of the sentence.

(Who or whom?) is afraid of the dark.

Turn the clause into a question. Ask yourself:

Who or whom is afraid of the dark?

Answer the question with an ordinary personal pronoun.

He is.

If you've answered the question with a subjective case pronoun (as you have here), you need the subjective case who in the relative clause.

Sylvester, **who** is afraid of the dark, sleeps with a Donald Duck night-light on.

If you answer the question with an objective case pronoun, you need the objective case *whom* in the relative clause.

HINT: Try answering the question with he or him. Who goes with he (subjective case) and whom goes with him (objective case).

Sentence Structure

A **sentence** is a group of words that can stand alone because it expresses a complete thought. To express a complete thought, it must contain a subject, about which something is said, and a verb, which says something about the subject.

Example: Dogs bark.

Example: The explorers slept in yak-hide tents.

Example: Looking out of the window, John saw a flying saucer.

Every sentence consists of at least one clause. Many sentences contain more than one clause (and phrases, too).

A **clause** is a group of words that contains a subject and a verb. "Dogs bark," "The explorers slept in a yak-hide tent," and "John saw a flying saucer" are all clauses.

A **phrase** is a group of words that does not have both a subject and a verb. "Looking out of the window" is a phrase.

1. Sentence Fragments

On the PSAT, some of those innocent-looking groups of words beginning with capital letters and ending with periods are only masquerading as sentences. In reality, they're sentence fragments.

A sentence fragment is a group of words that seems to be a sentence but which is *grammatically* incomplete because it lacks a subject or a verb, **or** which is *logically* incomplete because other elements necessary for it to express a complete thought are missing.

WRONG: Eggs and fresh vegetables on sale at the farmers' market.

This is not a complete sentence because there's no verb to say something about the subject, *eggs and fresh vegetables*.

WRONG: Because Richard likes hippopotamuses.

Even though this contains a subject (Richard) and a verb (likes), it's not a complete sentence because it doesn't express a complete thought. We don't know what's true "*because* Richard likes hippopotamuses."

WRONG: Martha dreams about dinosaurs although.

This isn't a complete sentence because it doesn't express a complete thought. What makes Martha's dreaming about dinosaurs in need of qualification or explanation?

2. Run-On Sentences

Just as unacceptable as an incomplete sentence is a "too-complete" sentence, a run-on sentence.

A run-on sentence is actually two complete sentences stuck together either with just a comma or with no punctuation at all.

WRONG: The children had been playing in the park, they were covered with mud.

WRONG: The children had been playing in the park they were covered with mud.

There are a number of ways to fix this kind of problem. They all involve a punctuation mark or a connecting word that can properly connect two clauses.

Join the clauses with a semicolon.

RIGHT: The children had been playing in the park; they were covered with mud.

Join the clauses with a coordinating conjunction (*and, but, for, nor, or, so, yet*) and a comma.

RIGHT: The children had been playing in the park, and they were covered with mud.

Join the clauses with a subordinating conjunction (*after, although, if, since, while*).

RIGHT: Because the children had been playing in the park, they were covered with mud.

OR

RIGHT: The children were covered with mud because they had been playing in the park.

And, of course, the two halves of a run-on sentence can be written as two separate, complete sentences.

RIGHT: The children had been playing in the park. They were covered with mud.

Verbs

On the PSAT you'll find items that are wrong because a verb is in the wrong tense. To spot this kind of problem, you need to be familiar both with the way each tense is used **and** with the ways the tenses are used together. English has six tenses, and each has a simple form and a progressive form.

	Simple	Progressive
Present	I work	I am working
Past	I worked	I was working
Future	I will work	I will be working
Present Perfect	I have worked	I have been working
Past Perfect	I had worked	I had been working
Future Perfect	I will have worked	I will have been working

1. Using the Present Tense

Use the present tense to describe a state or action occurring in the present time.

Example: I **am** a student.

Example: They **are studying** the Holy Roman Empire.

Use the present tense to describe habitual action.

Example: They **eat** at Joe's Diner every night.

Example: My father never **drinks** coffee.

Use the present tense to describe things that are always true.

Example: The earth **is** round.

Example: Grass **is** green.

2. Using the Past Tense

Use the simple past tense to describe an event or state that took place at a specific time in the past and is now over and done with.

Example: Norman **broke** his toe when he tripped over his son's tricycle.

3. Using the Future Tense

Use the future tense for actions expected in the future.

Example: I **will call** you on Wednesday.

We often express future actions with the expression *to be going to*.

Example: I **am going to move** to another apartment soon.

4. Using the Present Perfect Tense

Use the present perfect tense for actions and states that started in the past and continue up to and into the present time.

Example: I **have been living** here for the last two years.

Use the present perfect for actions and states that happened a number of times in the past and may happen again in the future.

Example: I **have heard** that song several times on the radio.

Use the present perfect for something that happened at an unspecified time in the past.

Example: Anna **has seen** that movie already.

5. Using the Past Perfect Tense

The past perfect tense is used to represent past actions or states that were completed before other past actions or states. The more recent past event is expressed in the simple past, and the earlier past event is expressed in the past perfect.

Example: When I turned my computer on this morning, I realized that I **had exited** the program yesterday without saving my work.

6. Using the Future Perfect Tense

Use the future perfect tense for a future state or event that will take place before another future event.

Example: By the end of the week, I **will have worked** four hours of overtime.

7. Using the Proper Past Participle Form

If you use the present, past, or future perfect tense, make sure that you use the past participle and not the simple past tense.

WRONG: I have **swam** in that pool every day this week.

RIGHT: I have **swum** in that pool every day this week.

Irregular verbs have two different forms for simple past and past participle tenses. The following are some of the most common irregular verbs.

IRREGULAR VERBS

Infinitive	Simple Past	Past Participle
arise	arose	arisen
become	became	become
begin	began	begun
blow	blew	blown
break	broke	broken
come	came	come
do	did	done
draw	drew	drawn
drink	drank	drunk
drive	drove	driven
eat	ate	eaten
fall	fell	fallen
fly	flew	flown
freeze	froze	frozen
give	gave	given
grow	grew	grown
know	knew	known
ride	rode	ridden
rise	rose	risen
run	ran	run

see	saw	seen
shake	shook	shaken
shrink	shrank	shrunk
sing	sang	sung
speak	spoke	spoken
take	took	taken
throw	threw	thrown

Adjectives and Adverbs

On the PSAT, you may find an occasional item that's wrong because it uses an adjective where an adverb is called for, or vice versa.

An adjective modifies, or describes, a noun or pronoun.

Example: A woman in a **white** dress stood next to the **old** tree.

Example: The boat, **leaky** and **dirty**, hadn't been used in years.

An adverb modifies a verb, an adjective, or another adverb. Most, but not all, adverbs end in -*ly*. (Don't forget that some **adjectives**—*friendly*, *lovely*—also end in -*ly*.)

Example: The interviewer looked *approvingly* at the *neatly* dressed applicant.

Parallel Structure

On the PSAT, matching constructions must be expressed in parallel form. Make sure that when a sentence contains a **list** or makes a **comparison**, the items being listed or compared exhibit parallel structure.

1. Items in a List

WRONG: I love **skipping**, **jumping**, and **to play** tiddlywinks.

WRONG: I love **to skip**, **jump**, and **to play** tiddlywinks.

RIGHT: I love to **skip**, **jump**, and **play** tiddlywinks.

ALSO RIGHT: I love **to skip**, **to jump**, and **to play** tiddlywinks.

ALSO RIGHT: I love **skipping**, **jumping**, and **playing** tiddlywinks.

2. Items in a Comparison

Comparisons must do more than just exhibit parallel structure. Most faulty comparisons relate to the notion that you can't compare apples and oranges. You don't merely want comparisons to be grammatically similar; they must be logically similar as well.

WRONG: **To visualize** success is not the same as **achieving** it.

RIGHT: **To visualize** success is not the same as **to achieve** it.

ALSO RIGHT: **Visualizing** success is not the same as **achieving** it.

WRONG: **The rules of chess** are more complex than **checkers**.

RIGHT: **The rules of chess** are more complex than **those of checkers**.

ALSO RIGHT: **Chess** is more complex than **checkers**.

STYLE REVIEW

Pronouns and Reference

When we talk about pronouns and their antecedents, we say pronouns refer to or refer back to their antecedents. We noted earlier that pronouns must agree in person and number with their antecedents. But a different kind of pronoun reference problem exists when a pronoun either doesn't refer to any antecedent at all or doesn't refer clearly to one, and only one, antecedent.

Sometimes an incorrectly used pronoun has no antecedent.

POOR: Joe doesn't like what **they play** on this radio station.

Who are *they*? We can't tell, because there is no antecedent for *they*. On the PSAT, this sort of usage is an error.

RIGHT: Joe doesn't like what **the disc jockeys play** on this radio station.

Don't use pronouns without antecedents when doing so makes a sentence unclear. Sometimes a pronoun seems to have an antecedent until you look closely and see that the word that appears to be the antecedent is not a noun, but an adjective, a possessive form, or a verb. The antecedent of a pronoun must be a noun.

WRONG: When you are painting, make sure you don't get **it** on the floor.

RIGHT: When you are painting, make sure you don't get **paint** on the floor.

Other examples of pronoun reference problems:

WRONG: I've always been interested in astronomy and finally have decided to become **one**.

RIGHT: I've always been interested in astronomy and finally have decided to become an **astronomer**.

Don't use pronouns with remote references. A pronoun that is too far away from what it refers to is said to have a remote antecedent.

WRONG: Jane quit smoking and, as a result, temporarily put on a lot of weight. **It** was very bad for her health.

RIGHT: Jane quit smoking because **it** was very bad for her health, and, as a result, she temporarily gained a lot of weight.

Don't use pronouns with faulty broad reference. A pronoun with broad reference is one that refers to a whole idea instead of to a single noun.

WRONG: He built a fence to stop people from looking into his backyard. **That's** not easy.

RIGHT: He built a fence to stop people from looking into his backyard. **The fence was not easy to build**.

Redundancy

This type of style error is frequently tested on the PSAT. Words or phrases are redundant when they have basically the same meaning as something already stated in the sentence. Don't use two phrases when one is sufficient.

WRONG: The school was **established and founded** in 1906.

RIGHT: The school was **established** in 1906.

Relevance

Irrelevant asides, even when set off in parentheses, are to be avoided on the PSAT. Everything in the sentence should serve to get across the point in question. Something unrelated to that point should be cut.

POOR: No one can say for sure just how successful the new law will be in the fight against crime (just as no one can be sure whether he or she will ever be a victim of a crime).

BETTER: No one can say for sure just how successful the new law will be in the fight against crime.

Verbosity

Sometimes having extra words in a sentence results in a style problem. Conciseness is something that is valued on the PSAT.

WORDY: The supply of **musical instruments that are antique** is limited, so they become more valuable each year.

BETTER: The supply of **antique musical instruments** is limited, so they become more valuable each year.

WORDY: We **were in agreement with each other** that Max was an unsuspecting old fool.

BETTER: We **agreed** that Max was an unsuspecting old fool.

Commonly Misused Words

accept/except

Don't confuse the two. To *accept* means to receive or agree to something, whereas *except* is usually a preposition meaning excluding, although it can also mean to leave out.

WRONG: Can you **except** my apology?

RIGHT: Can you **accept** my apology?

affect/effect

These are easy to confuse. To *affect* means to have an *effect* on something. When the word is being used as a verb, the proper word to use is almost always *affect*; when it's being used as a noun, the proper word to use is almost always *effect*. (It should be noted that *effect* can also be a verb, meaning to bring about or cause to happen.)

WRONG: His affectations **effected** me to no good **affect**.

RIGHT: His affectations **affected** me to no good **effect**.

among/between

In most cases, you should use *between* for two items and *among* for more than two.

Example: The competition **between** Anne and Michael has grown more intense.

Example: He is always at his best **among** strangers.

But use common sense. Sometimes *among* is not appropriate.

Example: Plant the trees in the area **between** the road, the wall, and the fence.

amount/number

Amount should be used to refer to a uncountable quantity. *Number* should refer to a countable quantity.

Example: The **amount** of food he threw away would feed a substantial **number** of people.

as/like

Like is a preposition; it takes a noun object. *As*, when functioning as a conjunction, introduces a subordinate clause. Remember, a clause is a part of a sentence containing a subject and verb.

Example: He sings **like** an angel.

Example: He sings **as** an angel sings.

as . . . as . . .

The idiom is *as . . . as . . .*, **not** *as . . . than . . .*

WRONG: That suit is as expensive than this one.

RIGHT: That suit is as expensive as this one.

fewer/less

Use *fewer* before a plural noun; use less before a singular one.

Example: There are **fewer** apples on this tree than there were last year.

Example: He makes **less** money than she does.

neither . . . nor . . .

The correlative conjunction is *neither . . . nor . . .*, **not** *neither . . . or . . .*

Example: He is **neither** strong **nor** flexible.

Avoid the redundancy caused by using *nor* following a negative.

WRONG: Alice's departure was **not** noticed by Debby **nor** Sue.

RIGHT: Alice's departure was **not** noticed by Debby **or** Sue.

its/it's

Many people confuse *its* and *it's*. *Its* is possessive; *it's* is a contraction of *it is*:

Example: The cat licked **its** paws.

Example: **It's** raining cats and dogs.

their/they're/there

Many people confuse *their*, *there*, and *they're*. *Their* is possessive; *they're* is a contraction of *they are*:

Example: The girls rode **their** bikes home.

Example: **They're** training for the big race.

There has two uses: It can indicate place and it can be used as an expletive—a word that doesn't do anything in a sentence except delay the subject.

Example: Put the book over **there**.

Example: **There** will be fifteen runners competing for the prize.

Commonly Tested Idioms

Some phrases are wrong simply because that's just not the way we say it in English. This is especially true of preposition-verb word combinations. For instance,

WRONG: The fashion police **frowns at** wearing hats adorned with flowers.

RIGHT: The fashion police **frowns upon** wearing hats adorned with flowers.

The first sentence is only wrong because *frowns at* is not the correct idiomatic expression. Either your ear will recognize the correct idiom or it won't. Can you trust your ear on the following commonly tested idioms?

Commonly Tested Idioms

associate *with*

accuse *of*

apologize *for*

arrive *at*

believe *in*

believe *to be*

apologize *for*

attribute *to*

continue *to*

contrast *with*

credit *with*

decide *to*

define *as*

different *from*

discriminate *against*

distinguish *from*

dream *about/of*

forbid *to*

frown *upon*

object *to*

prohibit *from*

substitute *for*

target *at*

use *as*

view *as*

worry *about*

Appendix Five: **Word List**

A

ABANDON (n.)—total lack of inhibition

ABASE—to humble; disgrace

ABATE—decrease, reduce

ABDICATE—to give up a position, right, or power

ABERRATION—something different from the usual

ABET—to aid; act as accomplice

ABHOR—to loathe, detest

ABJECT—miserable, pitiful

ABOLITIONIST—one who opposes the practice of slavery

ABORTIVE—interrupted while incomplete

ABRIDGE—to condense, shorten

ABROGATE—to put an end to, abolish by authority

ABSCOND—to depart secretly

ABSOLVE—to forgive, free from blame

ABSTAIN—to choose not to do something

ACCOLADE—praise, distinction

ACCRUE—to accumulate, grow by additions

ACERBIC—bitter, sharp in taste or temper

ACME—highest point; summit

ACQUIESCE—to agree; comply quietly

ACRID—harsh, bitter

ACRIMONY—bitterness, animosity

ACUITY—sharpness

ACUMEN—sharpness of insight

ADAGE—old saying or proverb

ADAMANT—uncompromising, unyielding

> ### PSAT Emergency
> If you're short on time, you may want to just skim through these words to familiarize yourself with the type of vocabulary the PSAT often tests.

ADAPT—to accommodate; adjust

ADHERE—to cling or follow without deviation

ADJACENT—next to

ADMONISH—to caution or reprimand

ADROIT—skillful, accomplished, highly competent

ADULATION—high praise

ADUMBRATE—to sketch, outline in a shadowy way

ADVERSARIAL—antagonistic, competitive

AERIE—nook or nest built high in the air

AESTHETIC—pertaining to beauty or art

AFFABLE—friendly, easy to approach

AFFECTED (adj.)—pretentious, phony

AFFLUENT—rich, abundant

AFFRONT (n.)—personal offense, insult

AGENDA—plan, schedule

AGILE—well coordinated, nimble

AGITATION—commotion, excitement; uneasiness

AGRARIAN—relating to farming or rural matters

ALACRITY—cheerful willingness, eagerness; speed

ALIAS—assumed name

ALIENATED—distanced, estranged

ALLEGORY—symbolic representation

ALLEVIATE—to relieve, improve partially

ALLURE (v.)—to entice by charm; attract

ALLUSION—indirect reference

ALOOF—detached, indifferent

ALTRUISM—unselfish concern for others' welfare

AMBIGUOUS—uncertain; subject to multiple interpretations

AMBIVALENCE—attitude of uncertainty; conflicting emotions

AMELIORATE—to make better, improve

AMENABLE—agreeable, cooperative

AMEND—to improve or correct flaws in

AMENITY—pleasantness; something increasing comfort

AMIABLE—friendly, pleasant, likable

AMICABLE—friendly, agreeable

AMORAL—unprincipled, unethical

AMORPHOUS—having no definite form

AMPHIBIAN—creature equally at home on land or in water

AMPLE—abundant, plentiful

AMULET—ornament worn as a charm against evil spirits

ANACHRONISTIC—outdated

ANARCHY—absence of government or law; chaos

ANIMATION—enthusiasm, excitement

ANIMOSITY—hatred, hostility

ANNUL—to cancel, nullify, declare void, or make legally invalid

ANOMALY—irregularity or deviation from the norm

ANONYMITY—condition of having no name or an unknown name

ANTAGONIST—foe, opponent, adversary

ANTECEDENT (adj.)—coming before in place or time

ANTHOLOGY—collection of literary works

ANTIPATHY—dislike, hostility; extreme opposition or aversion

ANTIQUATED—outdated, obsolete

ANTIQUITY—ancient times; the quality of being old

ANTITHESIS—exact opposite or direct contrast

APATHY—lack of feeling or emotion

APHORISM—old saying or short, pithy statement

APOCRYPHAL—not genuine; fictional

APPEASE—to satisfy, placate, calm, pacify

APPROBATION—praise; official approval

APPROPRIATE (v.)—to take possession of

ARABLE—suitable for cultivation

ARBITRARY—depending solely on individual will; inconsistent

ARBOREAL—relating to trees; living in trees

ARCANE—secret, obscure, known only to a few

ARCHAIC—antiquated, from an earlier time; outdated

ARCHIPELAGO—large group of islands

ARDENT—passionate, enthusiastic, fervent

ARDUOUS—extremely difficult, laborious

ARID—extremely dry or deathly boring

ARSENAL—ammunition storehouse

ARTICULATE (adj.)—well spoken, expressing oneself clearly

ARTISAN—craftsperson; expert

ASCEND—to rise or climb

ASCETIC—self-denying, abstinent, austere

ASHEN—resembling ashes; pale

ASKEW—crooked, tilted

ASPERSION—false rumor, damaging report, slander

ASPIRE—to have great hopes; to aim at a goal

ASSAIL—to attack, assault

ASSIDUOUS—diligent, persistent, hard-working

ASSUAGE—to make less severe, ease, relieve

ASTRINGENT—harsh, severe, stern

ASTUTE—having good judgment

ATONE—to make amends for a wrong

ATROCIOUS—monstrous, shockingly bad

ATTAIN—to accomplish, gain

ATTENUATE—to make thin or slender; weaken

AUDACIOUS—bold, daring, fearless

AUDIBLE—capable of being heard

AUGMENT—to expand, extend

AUGUST—dignified, awe inspiring, venerable

AUSPICIOUS—having favorable prospects, promising

AUSTERE—stern, strict, unadorned

AUTHORITARIAN—extremely strict, bossy

AUTOCRAT—dictator

AVARICE—greed

AVENGE—to retaliate, take revenge for an injury or crime

AVER—to declare to be true, affirm

AVERSION—intense dislike

AVERT—to turn (something) away; prevent, hinder

AVIARY—large enclosure housing birds

AWRY—crooked, askew, amiss

B

BALEFUL—harmful

BALLAD—folk song, narrative poem

BALM—soothing, healing influence

BANAL—trite, overly common

BANE—something causing death, destruction, or ruin

BANTER—playful conversation

BASTION—fortification, stronghold

BAY (v.)—to bark, especially in a deep, prolonged way

BEGUILE—to deceive, mislead; charm

BEHEMOTH—huge creature

BELABOR—to insist repeatedly or harp on

BELIE—to misrepresent; expose as false

BELLIGERENT—hostile, tending to fight

BENEFACTOR—someone giving aid or money

BENEFICENT—kindly, charitable; doing good deeds; producing good effects

BENIGHTED—unenlightened

BENIGN—kindly, gentle, or harmless

BEQUEATH—to give or leave through a will; to hand down

BERATE—to scold harshly

BESEECH—to beg, plead, implore

BESTIAL—beastly, animal-like

BIAS—prejudice, slant

BIBLIOGRAPHY—list of books

BISECT—to cut into two (usually equal) parts

BLANCH—to pale; take the color out of

BLANDISH—to coax with flattery

BLASPHEMOUS—cursing, profane, irreverent

BLATANT—glaring, obvious, showy

BLIGHT (v.)—to afflict, destroy

BOISTEROUS—rowdy, loud, unrestrained

BOMBASTIC—using high-sounding but meaningless language

BOOR—crude person, one lacking manners or taste

BOTANIST—scientist who studies plants

BOVINE—cowlike; relating to cows

BRAZEN—bold, shameless, impudent; of or like brass

BROACH (v.)—to mention or suggest for the first time

BURGEON—to sprout or flourish

BURNISH—to polish, make smooth and bright

BUTTRESS (v.)—to reinforce or support

C

CACOPHONY—jarring, unpleasant noise

CAJOLE—to flatter, coax, persuade

CALLOUS—thick-skinned, insensitive

CALLOW—immature, lacking sophistication

CANDOR—honesty of expression

CANNY—smart; founded on common sense

CAPITULATE—to submit completely, surrender

CAPRICIOUS—impulsive, whimsical, without much thought

CARICATURE—exaggerated portrait, cartoon

CARTOGRAPHY—science or art of making maps

CASTIGATE—to punish, chastise, criticize severely

CATALYST—something causing change without being changed

CATHOLIC—universal; broad and comprehensive

CAUCUS—smaller group within an organization; a meeting of such a group

CAUSTIC—biting, sarcastic; able to burn

CEDE—to surrender possession of something

CENSORIOUS—severely critical

CESSATION—temporary or complete halt

CHAGRIN—shame, embarrassment, humiliation

CHAMPION (v.)—to defend or support

CHAOTIC—extremely disorderly

CHARLATAN—quack, fake

CHARY—watchful, cautious, extremely shy

CHASTISE—to punish, discipline, scold

CHIDE—to scold, express disapproval

CHROMATIC—relating to color

CIRCUITOUS—roundabout

CIRCUMFERENCE—boundary or distance around a circle or sphere

CIRCUMSCRIBE—to encircle; set limits on, confine

CIRCUMSPECT—cautious, wary

CITADEL—fortress or stronghold

CIVIL—polite; relating to citizens

CLAIRVOYANT (adj.)—having ESP, psychic

CLAMOR—to make a noisy outcry; a noisy outcry

CLANDESTINE—secretive

CLEMENCY—merciful leniency

CLOISTER (v.)—to confine, seclude

COALESCE—to grow together or cause to unite as one

CODDLE—to baby, treat indulgently

COERCE—to compel by force or intimidation

COGENT—logically forceful, compelling, convincing

COHERENT—intelligible, lucid, understandable

COLLATERAL—accompanying

COLLOQUIAL—characteristic of informal speech

COLLUSION—collaboration, complicity, conspiracy

COMMENSURATE—proportional

COMMODIOUS—roomy, spacious

COMMUNICABLE—transmittable

COMMUTE—to change a penalty to a less severe one

COMPENSATE—to repay or reimburse

COMPLACENT—self-satisfied, smug

COMPLEMENT—to complete, perfect

COMPLIANT—submissive and yielding

COMPLICITY—knowing partnership in wrongdoing

COMPUNCTION—feeling of uneasiness caused by guilt or regret

CONCAVE—curving inward

CONCEDE—to yield, admit

CONCILIATORY—overcoming distrust or hostility

CONCUR—to agree

CONDONE—to pardon or forgive; overlook, justify, or excuse a fault

CONDUIT—tube, pipe, or similar passage

CONFLAGRATION—big, destructive fire

CONFOUND—to baffle, perplex

CONGEAL—to become thick or solid, as a liquid freezing

CONGENIAL—similar in tastes and habits

CONGLOMERATE—collected group of varied things

CONJECTURE—speculation, prediction

CONSCIENTIOUS—governed by conscience; careful and thorough

CONSECRATE—to declare sacred; dedicate to a goal

CONSENSUS—unanimity, agreement of opinion or attitude

CONSOLATION—something providing comfort or solace for a loss or hardship

CONSOLIDATE—to combine, incorporate

CONSTRAINED—forced, compelled; confined, restrained

CONSTRUE—to explain or interpret

CONTENTIOUS—quarrelsome, disagreeable, belligerent

CONTINENCE—self-control, self-restraint

CONTRAVENE—to contradict, deny, act contrary to

CONTRITE—deeply sorrowful and repentant for a wrong

CONUNDRUM—riddle, puzzle or problem with no solution

CONVALESCENCE—gradual recovery after an illness

CONVENE—to meet, come together, assemble

CONVENTIONAL—typical, customary, commonplace

CONVEX—curved outward

CONVOLUTED—twisted, complicated, involved

COPIOUS—abundant, plentiful

CORROBORATE—to confirm, verify

COSMETIC (adj.)—relating to beauty; affecting the surface of something

COSMOPOLITAN—sophisticated, free from local prejudices

COTERIE—small group of persons with a similar purpose

COVERT—hidden; secret

COVET—to desire strongly something possessed by another

CRASS—crude, unrefined

CRAVEN—cowardly

CREDENCE—acceptance of something as true or real

CREDULOUS—gullible, trusting

CREED—statement of belief or principle

CRYPTIC—puzzling

CUISINE—characteristic style of cooking

CULMINATION—climax, final stage

CULPABLE—guilty, responsible for wrong

CUPIDITY—greed

CURMUDGEON—cranky person

CURSORY—hastily done, superficial

CURT—abrupt, blunt

CURTAIL—to shorten

CYNIC—person who distrusts the motives of others

D

DAUNT—to discourage, intimidate

DEARTH—lack, scarcity, insufficiency

DEBASE—to degrade or lower in quality or stature

DEBILITATE—to weaken, enfeeble

DEBUNK—to discredit, disprove

DECIDUOUS—falling off or shed seasonally; short-lived, temporary

DECORUM—proper behavior, etiquette

DECRY—to belittle, openly condemn

DEFACE—to mar the appearance of, vandalize

DEFAMATORY—slanderous, injurious to the reputation

DEFERENTIAL—respectful and polite in a submissive way

DEFLATION—decrease, depreciation

DEFUNCT—no longer existing, extinct

DELECTABLE—appetizing, delicious

DELEGATE (v.)—to give powers to another

DELETERIOUS—harmful, destructive, detrimental

DELUGE—flood

DEMAGOGUE—leader, rabble-rouser, usually using appeals to emotion or prejudice

DEMEAN—to degrade, humiliate, humble

DEMOGRAPHICS—data relating to study of human population

DEMOTE—to reduce to a lower grade or rank

DEMUR—to express doubts or objections

DENIGRATE—to slur someone's reputation

DEPLETE—to use up, exhaust

DEPLORE—to express or feel disapproval of; regret strongly

DEPLOY—to spread out strategically over an area

DEPRAVITY—sinfulness, moral corruption

DEPRECATE—to belittle, disparage

DEPRECIATE—to lose value gradually

DERIDE—to mock, ridicule, make fun of

DERIVATIVE—copied or adapted; not original

DESICCATE—to dry completely, dehydrate

DESIST—to stop doing something

DESPONDENT—feeling discouraged and dejected

DESPOT—tyrannical ruler

DESULTORY—at random, rambling, unmethodical

DETER—to discourage; prevent from happening

DEVIATE—to stray, wander

DEXTEROUS—skilled physically or mentally

DIALECT—regional style of speaking

DIAPHANOUS—allowing light to show through; delicate

DIATRIBE—bitter verbal attack

DICTUM—authoritative statement; popular saying

DIDACTIC—excessively instructive

DIFFIDENCE—shyness, lack of confidence

DIFFUSE—widely spread out

DIGRESS—to turn aside; to stray from the main point

DILAPIDATED—in disrepair, run down, neglected

DILATE—to enlarge, swell, extend

DILATORY—slow, tending to delay

DIPLOMACY—discretion, tact

DIRGE—funeral hymn

DISARRAY—clutter, disorder

DISBURSE—to pay out

DISCERN—to perceive something obscure

DISCONCERTING—bewildering, perplexing, slightly disturbing

DISCORDANT—harsh-sounding, badly out of tune

DISCREDIT—to dishonor or disgrace

DISCREPANCY—difference between

DISDAIN—to regard with scorn and contempt

DISGORGE—to vomit, discharge violently

DISHEVELED—untidy, disarranged, unkempt

DISPARAGE—to belittle, speak disrespectfully about

DISPARATE—dissimilar, different in kind

DISPASSIONATE—free from emotion; impartial, unbiased

DISPEL—to drive out or scatter

DISPENSE—to distribute, administer

DISPERSE—to break up, scatter

DISPIRIT—to dishearten, make dejected

DISREPUTE—disgrace, dishonor

DISSEMBLE—to pretend, disguise one's motives

DISSEMINATE—to spread far and wide

DISSIPATE—to scatter; to pursue pleasure to excess

DISSUADE—to persuade someone to alter original intentions

DISTRAUGHT—very worried and distressed

DITHER—to move or act confusedly or without clear purpose

DIURNAL—daily

DIVINE (v.)—to foretell or know by inspiration

DIVISIVE—creating disunity or conflict

DOCILE—tame, willing to be taught

DOCTRINAIRE—rigidly devoted to theories

DOGMATIC—rigidly fixed in opinion, opinionated

DOLEFUL—sad, mournful

DORMANT—at rest, inactive, in suspended animation

DOTING—excessively fond, loving to excess

DOUR—sullen and gloomy; stern and severe

DRIVEL—stupid talk; slobber

DROLL—amusing in a wry, subtle way

DULCET—pleasant sounding, soothing to the ear

DUPE—to deceive, trick; a fool or pawn

DUPLICITY—deception, dishonesty, double-dealing

DYSPEPTIC—suffering from indigestion; gloomy and irritable

E

EBB—to fade away, recede

EBULLIENT—exhilarated, full of enthusiasm and high spirits

ECLECTIC—selecting from various sources

ECSTATIC—joyful

EDICT—law, command, official public order

EDIFICE—building

EDIFY—to instruct morally and spiritually

EFFACE—to erase or make illegible

EFFERVESCENT—bubbly, lively

EFFIGY—stuffed doll; likeness of a person

EFFRONTERY—impudent boldness; audacity

EFFULGENT—brilliantly shining

EFFUSIVE—expressing emotion without restraint

EGOCENTRIC—acting as if things are centered around oneself

EGREGIOUS—conspicuously bad

ELATION—exhilaration, joy

ELEGY—mournful poem

ELICIT—to draw out, provoke

ELOQUENCE—fluent and effective speech

EMACIATED—skinny, scrawny, gaunt, especially from hunger

EMANCIPATE—to set free, liberate

EMBELLISH—to ornament; make attractive with decoration or details; add details to a statement

EMBEZZLE—to steal money in violation of a trust

EMINENT—celebrated, distinguished; outstanding, towering

EMOLLIENT—having soothing qualities, especially for skin

EMPATHY—identification with another's feelings

EMULATE—to copy, imitate

ENDEMIC—belonging to a particular area, inherent

ENERVATE—to weaken, sap strength from

ENGENDER—to produce, cause, bring about

ENIGMATIC—puzzling, inexplicable

ENJOIN—to urge, order, command; forbid or prohibit, as by judicial order

ENMITY—hostility, antagonism, ill-will

ENNUI—boredom, lack of interest and energy

ENORMITY—state of being gigantic or terrible

ENSCONCE—to settle comfortably into a place

ENTHRALL—to captivate, enchant, enslave

ENTREAT—to plead, beg

ENUNCIATE—to pronounce clearly

EPHEMERAL—momentary, transient, fleeting

EPICURE—person with refined taste in food and wine

EPIGRAM—short, witty saying or poem

EPILOGUE—concluding section of a literary work

EPITOME—representative of an entire group; summary

EQUANIMITY—calmness, composure

EQUINE—relating to horses

EQUIVOCAL—ambiguous, open to more than one interpretation

EQUIVOCATE—to use vague or ambiguous language intentionally

ERADICATE—to erase or wipe out

ERRANT—straying, mistaken, roving

ERUDITE—learned, scholarly

ESCHEW—to abstain from, avoid

ESOTERIC—understood by only a learned few

ESPOUSE—to support or advocate; to marry

ESTRANGE—to alienate, keep at a distance

ETHEREAL—not earthly, spiritual, delicate

EULOGY—high praise, often in a public speech

EUPHEMISM—use of an inoffensive word or phrase in place of a more distasteful one

EUPHONY—pleasant, harmonious sound

EUPHORIA—feeling of well-being or happiness

EVADE—to avoid, dodge

EVANESCENT—momentary, transitory, short-lived

EVICT—to put out or force out

EXACERBATE—to aggravate, intensify the bad qualities of

EXASPERATION—irritation

EXCERPT (n.)—selection from a book or play

EXCRUCIATING—agonizing, intensely painful

EXCULPATE—to clear of blame or fault, vindicate

EXECRABLE—utterly detestable, abhorrent

EXHILARATION—state of being energetic or filled with happiness

EXHORT—to urge or incite by strong appeals

EXONERATE—to clear of blame, absolve

EXORBITANT—extravagant, greater than reasonable

EXPEDIENT (adj.)—convenient, efficient, practical

EXPIATE—to atone for, make amends for

EXPLICIT—clearly defined, specific; forthright in expression

EXPONENT—one who champions or advocates

EXPOUND—to elaborate; to expand or increase

EXPUNGE—to erase, eliminate completely

EXPURGATE—to censor

EXTEMPORANEOUS—unrehearsed, on the spur of the moment

EXTENUATE—to lessen the seriousness, strength, or effect of

EXTOL—to praise

EXTRICATE—to free from, disentangle

EXTRINSIC—not inherent or essential, coming from without

EXUBERANT—lively, happy, and full of good spirits

EXUDE—to give off, ooze

EXULT—to rejoice

F

FABRICATE—to make or devise; construct

FACADE—face, front; mask, superficial appearance

FACILE—very easy

FALLACIOUS—wrong, unsound, illogical

FALLOW—uncultivated, unused

FANATICISM—extreme devotion to a cause

FARCICAL—absurd, ludicrous

FASTIDIOUS—careful with details

FATHOM (v.)—to measure the depth of, gauge

FATUOUS—stupid; foolishly self-satisfied

FAWN (v.)—to flatter excessively, seek the favor of

FAZE—to bother, upset, or disconcert

FECKLESS—ineffective, careless, irresponsible

FEIGN—to pretend, give a false impression; to invent falsely

FELICITOUS—suitable, appropriate; well-spoken

FELL (v.)—to chop, cut down

FERVID—passionate, intense, zealous

FETID—foul-smelling, putrid

FIASCO—disaster, utter failure

FIDELITY—loyalty

FINICKY—fussy, difficult to please

FLACCID—limp, flabby, weak

FLAGRANT—outrageous, shameless

FLAMBOYANT—flashy, garish; exciting, dazzling

FLAUNT—to show off

FLORA—plants

FLORID—gaudy, extremely ornate; ruddy, flushed

FLOUNDER—to falter, waver; to muddle, struggle

FLOUT—to treat contemptuously, scorn

FLUCTUATE—to alternate, waver

FOIBLE—minor weakness or character flaw

FOIL (v.)—to defeat, frustrate

FOMENT—to arouse or incite

FORD (v.)—to cross a body of water at a shallow place

FOREBODING—dark sense of evil to come

FORESTALL—to prevent, delay; anticipate

FORETHOUGHT—anticipation, foresight

FORGO—to go without, refrain from

FORLORN—dreary, deserted; unhappy; hopeless, despairing

FORSWEAR—to repudiate, renounce, disclaim, reject

FORTE—strong point, something a person does well

FORTUITOUS—happening by luck, fortunate

FOSTER—to nourish, cultivate, promote

FOUNDER (v.)—to fall helplessly; sink; fail

FRACAS—noisy dispute

FRACTIOUS—unruly, rebellious

FRAUDULENT—deceitful, dishonest, unethical

FRAUGHT—full of, accompanied by

FRENETIC—wildly frantic, frenzied, hectic

FULSOME—sickeningly excessive; repulsive

FUNEREAL—mournful, appropriate to a funeral

FURTIVE—secret, stealthy

G

GARGANTUAN—giant, tremendous

GARNER—to gather and store

GARRULOUS—very talkative

GAUNT—thin and bony

GENRE—type, class, category

GERMINATE—to begin to grow (as with a seed or idea)

GESTATION—growth process from conception to birth

GIBE—to make heckling, taunting remarks

GIRTH—distance around something

GLIB—fluent in an insincere manner; offhand, casual

GLUTTONY—eating and drinking to excess

GOAD—to prod or urge

GRANDILOQUENCE—pompous talk, fancy but meaningless language

GRANDIOSE—magnificent and imposing; exaggerated and pretentious

GRATIS—free, costing nothing

GRATUITOUS—free, voluntary; unnecessary and unjustified

GREGARIOUS—outgoing, sociable

GRIEVOUS—causing grief or sorrow; serious and distressing

GRIMACE—facial expression showing pain or disgust

GROVEL—to humble oneself in a demeaning way

GUILE—trickery, deception

GULLIBLE—easily deceived

GUSTATORY—relating to sense of taste

H

HABITAT—dwelling place

HACKNEYED—worn out by overuse

HAPLESS—unfortunate, having bad luck

HARBINGER—precursor, sign of something to come

HARDY—robust, vigorous

HAUGHTY—arrogant and condescending

HEDONISM—pursuit of pleasure as a goal

HEGEMONY—leadership, domination, usually by a country

HEINOUS—shocking, wicked, terrible

HEMORRHAGE—heavy bleeding; to bleed heavily

HETEROGENEOUS—composed of unlike parts, different, diverse

HEW—to cut with an ax

HIATUS—break, interruption, vacation

HOMAGE—public honor and respect

HOMOGENEOUS—composed of identical parts

HONE—to sharpen

HUSBAND (v.)—to farm; manage carefully and thriftily

HUTCH—pen or coop for animals; shack, shanty

HYGIENIC—clean, sanitary

HYPERBOLE—purposeful exaggeration for effect

HYPOCHONDRIA—unfounded belief that one is often ill

HYPOCRITE—person claiming beliefs or virtues he or she doesn't really possess

HYPOTHESIS—assumption subject to proof

I

ICONOCLAST—one who attacks traditional beliefs

IDEALISM—pursuit of noble goals

IDIOSYNCRASY—peculiarity of temperament, eccentricity

IGNOMINIOUS—disgraceful and dishonorable

ILLICIT—illegal, improper

ILLUSORY—unreal, deceptive

ILLUSTRIOUS—famous, renowned

IMMACULATE—spotless; free from error

IMMERSE—to bathe, dip; to engross, preoccupy

IMMUNE—exempt; protected from harm or disease; unresponsive to

IMMUTABLE—unchangeable, invariable

IMPAIR—to damage, injure

IMPASSE—blocked path, dilemma with no solution

IMPASSIVE—showing no emotion

IMPEACH—to charge with misdeeds in public office; accuse

IMPECCABLE—flawless, without fault

IMPECUNIOUS—poor, having no money

IMPEDIMENT—barrier, obstacle; speech disorder

IMPERIOUS—arrogantly self-assured, domineering, overbearing

IMPERTINENT—rude

IMPERVIOUS—impossible to penetrate; incapable of being affected

IMPETUOUS—quick to act without thinking

IMPLACABLE—inflexible, incapable of being pleased

IMPLICATE—to involve in a crime, incriminate

IMPLICIT—implied, not directly expressed

IMPORTUNE—to ask repeatedly, beg

IMPOTENT—powerless, ineffective, lacking strength

IMPOVERISH—to make poor or bankrupt

IMPRECATION—curse

IMPREGNABLE—totally safe from attack, able to resist defeat

IMPUDENT—arrogant, audacious

IMPUGN—to call into question, attack verbally

INANE—foolish, silly, lacking significance

INAUGURATE—to begin or start officially; to induct into office

INCANDESCENT—shining brightly

INCARCERATE—to put in jail; to confine

INCENDIARY—combustible, flammable, burning easily

INCENSE (v.)—to infuriate, enrage

INCEPTION—beginning

INCESSANT—continuous, never ceasing

INCHOATE—imperfectly formed or formulated

INCIPIENT—beginning to exist or appear; in an initial stage

INCISIVE—perceptive, penetrating

INCOGNITO—in disguise, concealing one's identity

INCONTROVERTIBLE—unquestionable, beyond dispute

INCORRIGIBLE—incapable of being corrected

INCREDULOUS—skeptical, doubtful

INCULCATE—to teach, impress in the mind

INDEFATIGABLE—never tired

INDELIBLE—permanent, not erasable

INDIGENOUS—native, occurring naturally in an area

INDIGENT—very poor

INDIGNANT—angry, incensed, offended

INDOLENT—habitually lazy, idle

INDOMITABLE—fearless, unconquerable

INDUBITABLE—unquestionable

INDUCE—to persuade; bring about

INEPT—clumsy, awkward

INERT—unable to move, tending to inactivity

INEVITABLE—certain, unavoidable

INEXORABLE—inflexible, unyielding

INFAMY—reputation for bad deeds

INFER—to conclude, deduce

INFINITESIMAL—extremely tiny

INFIRMITY—disease, ailment

INGENIOUS—original, clever, inventive

INGENUOUS—straightforward, open; naive and unsophisticated

INGRATE—ungrateful person

INGRATIATE—to bring oneself purposely into another's good graces

INHIBIT—to hold back, prevent, restrain

INIMICAL—hostile, unfriendly

INJUNCTION—command, order

INNATE—natural, inborn

INNOCUOUS—harmless; inoffensive

INNOVATE—to invent, modernize, revolutionize

INNUENDO—indirect and subtle criticism, insinuation

INSATIABLE—never satisfied

INSCRUTABLE—impossible to understand fully

INSIDIOUS—sly, treacherous, devious

INSINUATE—to suggest, say indirectly, imply

INSIPID—bland, lacking flavor; lacking excitement

INSOLENT—insulting and arrogant

INSTIGATE—to incite, urge, agitate

INSULAR—isolated, detached

INSURGENT (adj.)—rebellious, insubordinate

INSURRECTION—rebellion

INTEGRAL—central, indispensable

INTEGRITY—decency, honesty; wholeness

INTEMPERATE—not moderate

INTER—to bury

INTERLOPER—trespasser; meddler in others' affairs

INTERMITTENT—starting and stopping

INTERROGATE—to question formally

INTIMATION—clue, suggestion

INTRACTABLE—not easily managed

INTRANSIGENT—uncompromising, refusing to be reconciled

INTREPID—fearless

INTRINSIC—inherent, internal

INTROSPECTIVE—contemplating one's own thoughts and feelings

INTROVERT—someone given to self-analysis

INUNDATE—to cover with water; overwhelm

INURE—to harden; accustom; become used to

INVECTIVE—verbal abuse

INVETERATE—confirmed, long-standing, deeply rooted

INVIDIOUS—envious; obnoxious

INVINCIBLE—invulnerable, unbeatable

IOTA—very tiny amount

IRASCIBLE—easily angered

IRIDESCENT—showing many colors

ITINERANT—wandering from place to place, unsettled

ITINERARY—route of a traveler's journey

J

JADED—tired by excess or overuse; slightly cynical

JARGON—nonsensical talk; specialized language

JETTISON—to cast off, throw cargo overboard

JINGOISM—belligerent support of one's country

JOCULAR—jovial, playful, humorous

JUNCTURE—point where two things are joined

K

KERNEL—innermost, essential part; seed grain, often in a shell

KINETIC—relating to motion; characterized by movement

KNELL—sound of a funeral bell

KUDOS—fame, glory, honor

L

LABYRINTH—maze

LACHRYMOSE—tearful

LACKADAISICAL—idle, lazy; apathetic, indifferent

LACONIC—using few words

LAGGARD—dawdler, loafer, lazy person

LAMENT (v.)—to deplore, grieve

LAMPOON—to attack with satire, mock harshly

LANGUID—lacking energy, indifferent, slow

LARDER—place where food is stored

LARGESS—generosity; gift

LASSITUDE—lethargy, sluggishness

LATENT—present but hidden; potential

LAUDABLE—deserving of praise

LAXITY—carelessness

LEGERDEMAIN—trickery

LEGIBLE—readable

LENIENT—easygoing, permissive

LETHARGY—indifferent inactivity

LEVITATE—to rise in the air or cause to rise

LEVITY—humor, frivolity, gaiety

LEXICON—dictionary, list of words

LIBERAL—tolerant, broad-minded; generous, lavish

LIBERTINE—one without moral restraint

LICENTIOUS—immoral; unrestrained by society

LIMPID—clear, transparent

LIONIZE—to treat as a celebrity

LISSOME—easily flexed, limber, agile

LISTLESS—lacking energy and enthusiasm

LITERATE—able to read and write; well-read and educated

LITHE—moving and bending with ease; graceful

LIVID—discolored from a bruise; reddened with anger

LOITER—to stand around idly

LOQUACIOUS—talkative

LUCID—clear and easily understood

LUDICROUS—laughable, ridiculous

LUGUBRIOUS—sorrowful, mournful; dismal

LUMBER (v.)—to move slowly and awkwardly

LUMINOUS—bright, brilliant, glowing

LURID—harshly shocking, sensational; glowing

LUXURIANCE—elegance, lavishness

LYRICAL—suitable for poetry and song; expressing feeling

M

MAELSTROM—whirlpool; turmoil; agitated state of mind

MAGNANIMOUS—generous, noble in spirit

MAGNATE—powerful or influential person

MALADY—illness

MALAPROPISM—humorous misuse of a word

MALCONTENT—discontented person, one who holds a grudge

MALEFACTOR—evil-doer; culprit

MALEVOLENT—ill-willed; causing evil or harm to others

MALICE—animosity, spite, hatred

MALINGER—to evade responsibility by pretending to be ill

MANDATORY—necessary, required

MANNERED—artificial or stilted in character

MAR—to damage, deface; spoil

MARITIME—relating to the sea or sailing

MARTIAL—warlike, pertaining to the military

MARTINET—strict disciplinarian, one who rigidly follows rules

MARTYR—person dying for his or her beliefs

MAUDLIN—overly sentimental

MAWKISH—sickeningly sentimental

MEDIEVAL—relating to the Middle Ages (about A.D. 500–1500)

MELANCHOLY—sadness, depression

MENAGERIE—various animals kept together for exhibition

MENDACIOUS—dishonest

MENDICANT—beggar

MENTOR—experienced teacher and wise adviser

MERCURIAL—quick, shrewd, and unpredictable

MERETRICIOUS—gaudy, falsely attractive

MERITORIOUS—deserving reward or praise

METAMORPHOSIS—change, transformation

METAPHOR—figure of speech comparing two different things

METICULOUS—extremely careful, fastidious, painstaking

METTLE—courageousness; endurance

MILITATE—to operate against, work against

MISANTHROPE—person who hates human beings

MISCONSTRUE—to misunderstand, fail to discover

MISERLINESS—extreme stinginess

MISNOMER—an incorrect name or designation

MISSIVE—note or letter

MITIGATE—to soften, or make milder

MNEMONIC—relating to memory; designed to assist memory

MOLLIFY—to calm or make less severe

MOLT (v.)—to shed hair, skin, or an outer layer periodically

MONASTIC—extremely plain or secluded (as in a monastery)

MONOLOGUE—dramatic speech performed by one actor

MONTAGE—composite picture

MOOT—debatable; purely academic, deprived of practical significance

MORBID—gruesome; relating to disease; abnormally gloomy

MORIBUND—dying, decaying

MOROSE—gloomy, sullen, or surly

MORSEL—small bit of food

MOTE—small particle, speck

MOTLEY—many colored; composed of diverse parts

MOTTLE—to mark with spots

MUNDANE—worldly; commonplace

MUNIFICENT—generous

MUTABILITY—changeability

MYRIAD—immense number; multitude

N

NADIR—lowest point

NASCENT—starting to develop, coming into existence

NEBULOUS—vague, cloudy

NEOPHYTE—novice, beginner

NETTLE (v.)—to irritate

NICHE—recess in a wall; best position for something

NIHILISM—belief that existence and all traditional values are meaningless

NOCTURNAL—pertaining to night; active at night

NOISOME—stinking, putrid

NOMADIC—moving from place to place

NOMINAL—existing in name only; negligible

NOTORIETY—unfavorable fame

NOVICE—apprentice, beginner

NOVITIATE—state of being a beginner or novice

NOXIOUS—harmful, unwholesome

NUANCE—shade of meaning

NULLIFY—to make legally invalid; to counteract the effect of

O

OBDURATE—stubborn

OBFUSCATE—to confuse, obscure

OBLIQUE—indirect, evasive; misleading, devious

OBLIVIOUS—unaware, inattentive

OBSEQUIOUS—overly submissive, brownnosing

OBSOLETE—no longer in use

OBSTINATE—stubborn

OBSTREPEROUS—troublesome, boisterous, unruly

OBVIATE—to make unnecessary; to anticipate and prevent

OCCLUDE—to shut, block

ODIOUS—hateful, contemptible

OFFICIOUS—too helpful, meddlesome

OMINOUS—menacing, threatening, indicating misfortune

OMNISCIENT—having infinite knowledge, all-seeing

ONEROUS—burdensome

OPAQUE—impervious to light; difficult to understand

OPINE—to express an opinion

OPPORTUNE—appropriate, fitting

OPPROBRIOUS—disgraceful, contemptuous

OPULENCE—wealth

ORATION—lecture, formal speech

OSCILLATE—to move back and forth

OSSIFY—to turn to bone; to become rigid

OSTENTATIOUS—showy

OSTRACISM—exclusion, temporary banishment

OUSTER—expulsion, ejection

OVERWROUGHT—agitated, overdone

P

PACIFY—to restore calm, bring peace

PALATIAL—like a palace, magnificent

PALAVER—idle talk

PALL (n.)—covering that darkens or obscures; coffin

PALL (v.)—to lose strength or interest

PALLIATE—to make less serious, ease

PALLID—lacking color or liveliness

PALPABLE—obvious, real, tangible

PALTRY—pitifully small or worthless

PANACEA—cure-all

PANACHE—flamboyance, verve

PANDEMIC—spread over a whole area or country

PANEGYRIC—elaborate praise; formal hymn of praise

PANORAMA—broad view; comprehensive picture

PARADIGM—ideal example, model

PARADOX—contradiction, incongruity; dilemma, puzzle

PARAGON—model of excellence or perfection

PARAMOUNT—supreme, dominant, primary

PARAPHRASE—to reword, usually in simpler terms

PARASITE—person or animal that lives at another's expense

PARCH—to dry or shrivel

PARIAH—outcast

PARITY—equality

PAROCHIAL—of limited scope or outlook, provincial

PARODY—humorous imitation

PARRY—to ward off or deflect

PARSIMONY—stinginess

PARTISAN—strong supporter; biased in favor of

PASTICHE—piece of literature or music imitating other works

PATHOS—pity, compassion

PATRICIAN—aristocrat

PATRONIZE—to condescend to, disparage; to buy from

PAUCITY—scarcity, lack

PAUPER—very poor person

PEDAGOGUE—teacher

PEDANT—boring academic, nit-picker

PEDESTRIAN (adj.)—commonplace

PEER (n.)—contemporary, equal, match

PEERLESS—unequaled

PENCHANT—inclination

PENSIVE—thoughtful

PENURY—extreme poverty

PERENNIAL—present throughout the years; persistent

PERFIDIOUS—faithless, disloyal, untrustworthy

PERFUNCTORY—done in a routine way; indifferent

PERIPATETIC—moving from place to place

PERJURE—to tell a lie under oath

PERMEABLE—penetrable

PERNICIOUS—very harmful

PERPETUAL—endless, lasting

PERTINENT—applicable, appropriate

PERUSAL—close examination

PESTILENCE—epidemic, plague

PETULANCE—rudeness, peevishness

PHALANX—massed group of soldiers, people, or things

PHILANDERER—pursuer of casual love affairs

PHILANTHROPY—love of humanity; generosity to worthy causes

PHILISTINE—narrow-minded person, someone lacking appreciation for art or culture

PHLEGMATIC—calm in temperament; sluggish

PHOBIA—exaggerated, illogical fear

PIETY—devoutness

PILFER—to steal

PINNACLE—peak, highest point of development

PIQUE (n.)—fleeting feeling of hurt pride

PITHY—profound, substantial; concise, succinct, to the point

PLACATE—to soothe or pacify

PLACID—calm

PLAGIARIST—one who steals words or ideas

PLAINTIFF—injured person in a lawsuit

PLATITUDE—stale, overused expression

PLENITUDE—abundance, plenty

PLETHORA—excess, overabundance

PLIANT—pliable, yielding

PLUCKY—courageous, spunky

PLUMMET—to fall, plunge

PLY (v.)—to use diligently; to engage; to join together

POIGNANT—emotionally moving

POLEMIC—controversy, argument; verbal attack

POLYGLOT—speaker of many languages

PONTIFICATE—to speak in a pretentious manner

PORE (v.)—to study closely or meditatively

POROUS—full of holes, permeable to liquids

PORTENT—omen

POSTERITY—future generations; all of a person's descendants

POTABLE—drinkable

PRAGMATIC—practical; moved by facts rather than abstract ideals

PRATTLE (n.)—meaningless, foolish talk

PRECARIOUS—uncertain

PRECIPICE—edge, steep overhang

PRECIPITOUS—hasty, quickly, with too little caution

PRECLUDE—to rule out

PRECOCIOUS—unusually advanced at an early age

PRECURSOR—forerunner, predecessor

PREDILECTION—preference, liking

PREFACE (n.)—introduction to a book; introductory remarks to a speech

PREMEDITATE—to consider, plan beforehand

PREPOSSESSING—attractive, engaging, appealing

PREPOSTEROUS—absurd, illogical

PRESAGE—to foretell, indicate in advance

PRESCIENT—having foresight

PRESUMPTUOUS—rude, improperly bold

PRETEXT—excuse, pretended reason

PREVALENT—widespread

PREVARICATE—to lie, evade the truth

PRISTINE—untouched, uncorrupted

PRIVATION—lack of usual necessities or comforts

PROBITY—honesty, high-mindedness

PROCLIVITY—tendency, inclination

PROCRASTINATOR—one who continually and unjustifiably postpones

PRODIGAL (adj.)—wasteful, extravagant, lavish

PRODIGIOUS—vast, enormous, extraordinary

PROFICIENT—expert, skilled in a certain subject

PROFUSE—lavish, extravagant

PROGENITOR—originator, forefather, ancestor in a direct line

PROGENY—offspring, children

PROGNOSIS—prediction of disease outcome; any prediction

PROLIFIC—productive

PROLOGUE—introductory section of a literary work or play

PROMONTORY—piece of land or rock higher than its surroundings

PROMULGATE—to make known publicly

PROPENSITY—inclination, tendency

PROPITIOUS—favorable, advantageous

PROPONENT—advocate, defender, supporter

PROSAIC—relating to prose; dull, commonplace

PROSCRIBE—to condemn; to forbid, outlaw

PROSTRATE—lying face downward, lying flat on ground

PROTAGONIST—main character in a play or story, hero

PROTEAN—readily assuming different forms or characters

PROTOCOL—ceremony and manners observed by diplomats

PROVINCIAL—rustic, unsophisticated, limited in scope

PROWESS—bravery, skill

PROXIMITY—nearness

PRUDENT—careful, cautious

PRY—to intrude into; force open

PSEUDONYM—pen name; fictitious or borrowed name

PUERILE—childish, immature, silly

PUGNACIOUS—quarrelsome, eager and ready to fight

PULCHRITUDE—beauty

PUNCTILIOUS—careful in observing rules of behavior or ceremony

PUNGENT—strong or sharp in smell or taste

PUNITIVE—having to do with punishment

PURGE—to cleanse or free from impurities

Q

QUAGMIRE—marsh; difficult situation

QUANDARY—dilemma, difficulty

QUARANTINE—isolation period—originally of 40 days—to prevent spread of disease

QUELL—to crush or subdue

QUERULOUS—inclined to complain, irritable

QUIBBLE—to argue about insignificant and irrelevant details

QUIESCENCE—inactivity, stillness

QUINTESSENCE—most typical example; concentrated essence

QUIXOTIC—overly idealistic, impractical

QUOTIDIAN—occurring daily; commonplace

R

RACONTEUR—witty, skillful storyteller

RAIL (v.)—to scold with bitter or abusive language

RAMBLE—to roam, wander; to babble, digress

RAMIFICATION—an implication, outgrowth, or consequence

RANCOR—bitter hatred

RANT—to harangue, rave, forcefully scold

RAPPORT—relationship of trust and respect

RAPT—deeply absorbed

RAREFY—to make thinner, purer, or more refined

RASH (adj.)—careless, hasty, reckless

RAUCOUS—harsh sounding; boisterous

RAVAGE—to destroy, devastate

RAVENOUS—extremely hungry

RAZE—to tear down, demolish

REACTIONARY—marked by extreme conservatism, especially in politics

REBUFF (n.)—blunt rejection

REBUKE—to reprimand, scold

REBUT—to refute by evidence or argument

RECALCITRANT—resisting authority or control

RECANT—to retract a statement, opinion, etcetera

RECLUSIVE—shut off from the world

RECONDITE—relating to obscure learning; known to only a few

RECOUNT—to describe facts or events

REDRESS—relief from wrong or injury

REDUNDANCY—unnecessary repetition

REFRACT—to deflect sound or light

REFUGE—escape, shelter

REGIMEN—government rule; systematic plan

REJOINDER—response

RELINQUISH—to renounce or surrender something

RELISH (v.)—to enjoy greatly

REMUNERATION—pay or reward for work, trouble, etcetera

RENASCENT—reborn, coming into being again

RENEGADE—traitor, person abandoning a cause

RENEGE—to go back on one's word

RENOWN—fame, widespread acclaim

REPAST—meal or mealtime

REPEAL—to revoke or formally withdraw (often a law)

REPENTANT—apologetic, guilty, remorseful

REPLETE—abundantly supplied

REPOSE—relaxation, leisure

REPREHENSIBLE—blameworthy, disreputable

REPROACH—to find fault with; blame

REPROBATE—morally unprincipled person

REPROVE—to criticize or correct

REQUITE—to return or repay

RESCIND—to repeal, cancel

RESIDUE—remainder, leftover, remnant

RESILIENT—able to recover quickly after illness or bad luck; able to bounce back to shape

RESOLUTE—determined; with a clear purpose

RESPITE—interval of relief

RESPLENDENT—splendid, brilliant

RESTIVE—impatient, uneasy, restless

RETICENT—not speaking freely; reserved

RETORT (n.)—cutting response

RETROSPECTIVE—review of the past

REVELRY—boisterous festivity

REVERE—to worship, regard with awe

REVERT—to backslide, regress

REVILE—to criticize with harsh language, verbally abuse

RHETORIC—persuasive use of language

RIBALD—humorous in a vulgar way

RIDDLE (v.)—to make many holes in; permeate

RIFE—widespread, prevalent; abundant

RISQUÉ —bordering on being inappropriate or indecent

ROBUST—strong and healthy; hardy

ROSTRUM—stage for public speaking

ROTUND—round in shape; fat

RUE—to regret

RUMINATE—to contemplate, reflect upon

RUSTIC—rural

S

SACCHARINE—excessively sweet or sentimental

SAGACIOUS—shrewd

SALIENT—prominent or conspicuous

SALLOW—sickly yellow in color

SALUBRIOUS—healthful

SALUTATION—greeting

SANCTION (n.)—permission, support; law; penalty

SANCTUARY—haven, retreat

SANGUINE—ruddy; cheerfully optimistic

SARDONIC—cynical, scornfully mocking

SATIATE—to satisfy

SAUNTER—to amble; walk in a leisurely manner

SAVANT—learned person

SAVORY—agreeable in taste or smell

SCALE (v.)—to climb to the top of

SCINTILLA—trace amount

SCINTILLATE—to sparkle, flash

SCOFF—to deride, ridicule

SCORE (n.)—notation for a musical composition

SCORE (v.)—to make a notch or scratch

SCRUPULOUS—restrained; honest; careful and precise

SCRUTINY—careful observation

SCURRILOUS—vulgar, low, indecent

SECULAR—not specifically pertaining to religion

SEDENTARY—inactive, stationary; sluggish

SEMINAL—relating to the beginning or seeds of something

SENESCENT—aging, growing old

SENTIENT—aware, conscious, able to perceive

SEQUESTER—to remove or set apart; put into seclusion

SERAPHIC—angelic, pure, sublime

SERPENTINE—serpentlike; twisting, winding

SERVILE—submissive, obedient

SHARD—piece of broken glass or pottery

SHIRK—to avoid a task due to laziness or fear

SIMPER—to smirk, smile foolishly

SINECURE—well-paying job or office that requires little or no work

SINGE—to burn slightly, scorch

SINUOUS—winding; intricate, complex

SKEPTICAL—doubtful, questioning

SKULK—to move in a stealthy or cautious manner; sneak

SLIGHT—to treat as unimportant; insult

SLOTH—sluggishness, laziness

SLOUGH—to discard or shed

SLOVENLY—untidy, messy

SOBRIETY—seriousness

SODDEN—thoroughly soaked; saturated

SOJOURN—visit, stay

SOLACE—comfort in distress; consolation

SOLICITOUS—concerned, attentive; eager

SOLILOQUY—literary or dramatic speech by one character, not addressed to others

SOLUBLE—capable of being solved or dissolved

SOMBER—dark and gloomy; melancholy, dismal

SOMNOLENT—drowsy, sleepy; inducing sleep

SONOROUS—producing a full, rich sound

SOPHISTRY—deceptive reasoning or argumentation

SOPHOMORIC—immature and overconfident

SOPORIFIC—sleepy or tending to cause sleep

SORDID—filthy; contemptible and corrupt

SOVEREIGN—having supreme power

SPARTAN—austere, severe, grave; simple, bare

SPONTANEOUS—on the spur of the moment, impulsive

SPORADIC—infrequent, irregular

SPURIOUS—lacking authenticity; counterfeit, false

SPURN—to reject or refuse contemptuously; scorn

SQUALID—filthy; morally repulsive

SQUANDER—to waste

STACCATO—marked by abrupt, clear-cut sounds

STAID—self-restrained to the point of dullness

STAND (n.)—group of trees

STARK—bare, empty, vacant

STIFLE—to smother or suffocate; suppress

STIPEND—allowance; fixed amount of money paid regularly

STOCKADE—enclosed area forming defensive wall

STOIC—indifferent to or unaffected by emotions

STOLID—having or showing little emotion

STRIDENT—loud, harsh, unpleasantly noisy

STRINGENT—imposing severe, rigorous standards

STUPEFY—to dull the senses of; stun, astonish

STYMIE—to block or thwart

SUAVE—smoothly gracious or polite; blandly ingratiating

SUBJUGATE—to conquer, subdue; enslave

SUBLIME—awe-inspiring; of high spiritual or moral value

SUBLIMINAL—subconscious; imperceptible

SUBTERFUGE—trick or tactic used to avoid something

SUBTERRANEAN—hidden, secret; underground

SUBTLE—hard to detect or describe; perceptive

SUBVERT—to undermine or corrupt

SUCCINCT—terse, brief, concise

SUCCULENT—juicy; full of vitality or freshness

SUFFRAGIST—one who advocates extended voting rights

SULLEN—brooding, gloomy

SULLY—to soil, stain, tarnish, taint

SUPERCILIOUS—arrogant, haughty, overbearing, condescending

SUPERFICIAL—hasty; shallow and phony

SUPERFLUOUS—extra, more than necessary

SUPERSEDE—to take the place of; replace

SUPPLICANT—one who asks humbly and earnestly

SURFEIT—excessive amount

SURLY—rude and bad-tempered

SURMISE—to make an educated guess

SURMOUNT—to conquer, overcome

SURREPTITIOUS—characterized by secrecy

SUSCEPTIBLE—vulnerable, unprotected

SYBARITE—person devoted to pleasure and luxury

SYCOPHANT—self-serving flatterer, yes-man

SYLLABUS—outline of a course

SYMBIOSIS—cooperation, mutual helpfulness

SYNOPSIS—plot summary

SYNTHESIS—blend, combination

T

TACIT—silently understood or implied

TACITURN—uncommunicative, not inclined to speak much

TACTILE—relating to the sense of touch

TAINT—to spoil or infect; to stain honor

TALON—claw of an animal, especially a bird of prey

TANG—sharp flavor or odor

TANGENTIAL—digressing, diverting

TANGIBLE—able to be sensed, perceptible, measurable

TAWDRY—gaudy, cheap, showy

TEMPERANCE—restraint, self-control, moderation

TEMPERED—moderated, restrained

TEMPESTUOUS—stormy, raging, furious

TENABLE—defensible, reasonable

TENACIOUS—stubborn, holding firm

TENET—belief, doctrine

TENUOUS—weak, insubstantial

TEPID—lukewarm; showing little enthusiasm

TERSE—concise, brief, free of extra words

TESTAMENT—statement of belief; will

TETHER—to bind, tie

THEOCRACY—government by priests representing a god

THESAURUS—book of synonyms and antonyms

TIMOROUS—timid, shy, full of apprehension

TIRADE—long, violent speech; verbal assault

TOADY—flatterer, hanger-on, yes-man

TOME—book, usually large and academic

TORPID—lethargic; unable to move; dormant

TORTUOUS—having many twists and turns; highly complex

TOXIN—poison

TRACTABLE—obedient, yielding

TRANSCEND—to rise above, go beyond

TRANSIENT (adj.)—temporary, short-lived, fleeting

TRANSITORY—short-lived, existing only briefly

TRANSLUCENT—partially transparent

TRAVESTY—parody, exaggerated imitation, caricature

TREMULOUS—trembling, quivering; fearful, timid

TRENCHANT—acute, sharp, incisive; forceful, effective

TREPIDATION—fear and anxiety

TRIFLING—of slight worth, trivial, insignificant

TRITE—shallow, superficial

TROUPE—group of actors

TRUNCATE—to cut off, shorten by cutting

TUNDRA—treeless plain found in arctic or subarctic regions

TURGID—swollen, bloated

TURPITUDE—inherent vileness, foulness, depravity

TYRO—beginner, novice

U

UBIQUITOUS—being everywhere simultaneously

UMBRAGE—offense, resentment

UNADULTERATED—absolutely pure

UNANIMITY—state of total agreement or unity

UNCONSCIONABLE—unscrupulous; shockingly unfair or unjust

UNCTUOUS—greasy, oily; smug and falsely earnest

UNDULATING—moving in waves

UNEQUIVOCAL—absolute, certain

UNIFORM (adj.)—consistent and unchanging; identical

UNIMPEACHABLE—beyond question

UNSCRUPULOUS—dishonest

UPBRAID—to scold sharply

UPROARIOUS—loud and forceful

URBANE—courteous, refined, suave

USURP—to seize by force

USURY—practice of lending money at exorbitant rates

UTOPIA—perfect place

V

VACILLATE—to waver, show indecision

VAGRANT—person with no home and no means of support

VANQUISH—to conquer, defeat

VAPID—tasteless, dull

VARIEGATED—varied; marked with different colors

VAUNTED—boasted about, bragged about

VEHEMENT—strong, urgent

VENDETTA—prolonged feud marked by bitter hostility

VENERABLE—respected because of age

VENT (v.)—to express, say out loud

VERACITY—accuracy, truth

VERBATIM—word for word

VERBOSE—wordy

VERITY—truthfulness; belief viewed as true and enduring

VERMIN—small creatures offensive to humans

VERNACULAR—everyday language used by ordinary people; specialized language of a
profession

VERNAL—related to spring

VERSATILE—adaptable, all-purpose

VESTIGE—trace, remnant

VEX—to irritate, annoy; confuse, puzzle

VIABLE—workable, able to succeed or grow

VICARIOUS—enjoyed through imagined participation in another's experience

VIE—to compete, contend

VIGILANT—attentive, watchful

VILIFY—to slander, defame

VIM—energy, enthusiasm

VINDICATE—to clear of blame; support a claim

VINDICTIVE—spiteful, vengeful, unforgiving

VIRTUOSO—someone with masterly skill; expert musician

VIRULENT—extremely poisonous; malignant; hateful

VISCOUS—thick, syrupy, and sticky

VITRIOLIC—burning, caustic; sharp, bitter

VITUPERATE—to abuse verbally

VIVACIOUS—lively, spirited

VOCIFEROUS—loud, vocal, and noisy

VOLITION—free choice, free will; act of choosing

VOLUBLE—speaking much and easily, talkative; glib

VORACIOUS—having a great appetite

VULNERABLE—defenseless, unprotected; innocent, naive

W

WAIVE—to refrain from enforcing a rule; to give up a legal right

WAN—sickly pale

WANTON—undisciplined, unrestrained, reckless

WARY—careful, cautious

WHET—to sharpen, stimulate

WHIMSICAL—playful or fanciful idea

WRIT—written document, usually in law

WRY—amusing, ironic

X

XENOPHOBIA—fear or hatred of foreigners or strangers

Y

YOKE (v.)—to join together

Z

ZENITH—highest point, summit

ZEPHYR—gentle breeze

ZOOLOGIST—scientist who studies animals

Appendix Six: **Math in a Nutshell**

The math on the PSAT covers a lot of ground—from arithmetic to algebra to geometry.

Don't let yourself be intimidated. We've highlighted the 100 most important concepts that you'll need for PSAT Math and listed them in this chapter.

Use this list to remind yourself of the key areas you'll need to know. Do four concepts a day, and you'll be ready within a month. If a concept continually causes you trouble, circle it and refer back to it as you try to do the questions.

You've probably been taught most of these concepts in school already, so this list is a great way to refresh your memory.

NUMBER PROPERTIES

1. Number Categories

Integers are **whole numbers;** they include negative whole numbers and zero.

A **rational number** is a number that can be expressed as a **ratio of two integers. Irrational numbers** are real numbers—they have locations on the number line—but they **can't be expressed precisely as a fraction or decimal.** For the purposes of the PSAT, the most important **irrational numbers** are $\sqrt{2}$, $\sqrt{3}$, and π.

2. Adding/Subtracting Signed Numbers

To **add a positive and a negative,** first ignore the signs and find the positive difference between the number parts. Then attach the sign of the original number with the larger number part. For example, to add 23 and −34, first ignore the minus sign and find the positive difference between 23 and 34—that's 11. Then attach the sign of the number with the larger number part—in this case it's the minus sign from the −34. So, 23 + (−34) = −11.

Make **subtraction** situations simpler by turning them into addition. For example, you can think of −17 − (−21) as −17 + (+21).

To **add or subtract a string of positives and negatives,** first turn everything into addition. Then combine the positives and negatives so that the string is reduced to the sum of a single positive number and a single negative number.

3. Multiplying/Dividing Signed Numbers

To multiply and/or divide positives and negatives, treat the number parts as usual and **attach a minus sign if there were originally an odd number of negatives.** For example, to multiply −2, −3, and −5, first multiply the number parts: 2 × 3 × 5 = 30. Then go back and note that there were *three*—an *odd* number—negatives, so the product is negative: (−2) × (−3) × (−5) = −30.

4. PEMDAS

When performing multiple operations, remember to perform them in the right order: **PEMDAS,** which means **P**arentheses first, then **E**xponents, then **M**ultiplication and **D**ivision (left to right), and lastly **A**ddition and **S**ubtraction (left to right). In the expression $9 - 2 \times (5 - 3)^2 + 6 \div 3$, begin with the parentheses: $(5 - 3) = 2$. Then do the exponent: $2^2 = 4$. Now the expression is: $9 - 2 \times 4 + 6 \div 3$. Next do the multiplication and division to get: $9 - 8 + 2$, which equals 3. If you have difficulty remembering PEMDAS, use this sentence to recall it: **P**lease **E**xcuse **M**y **D**ear **A**unt **S**ally.

5. Counting Consecutive Integers

To count consecutive integers, **subtract the smallest from the largest and add 1.** To count the integers from 13 through 31, subtract: 31 − 13 = 18. Then add 1: 18 + 1 = 19.

NUMBER OPERATIONS AND CONCEPTS

6. Exponential Growth

If r is the ratio between consecutive terms, a_1 is the first term, a_n is the nth term, and S_n is the sum of the first n terms, then $a_n = a_1 r^{n-1}$ and $S_n = \dfrac{a_1 - a_1 r^n}{1 - r}$.

7. Union and Intersection of Sets

The things in a set are called elements or members. The union of Set A and Set B, sometimes expressed as $A \cup B$, is the set of elements that are in either or both of Set A and Set B. If Set $A = \{1, 2\}$ and Set $B = \{3, 4\}$, then $A \cup B = \{1, 2, 3, 4\}$. The intersection of Set A and Set B, sometimes expressed as $A \cap B$, is the set of elements common to both Set A and Set B. If Set $A = \{1, 2, 3\}$ and Set $B = \{3, 4, 5\}$, then $A \cap B = \{3\}$.

DIVISIBILITY

8. Factor/Multiple

The **factors** of integer n are the positive integers that divide into n with no remainder. The **multiples** of n are the integers that n divides into with no remainder. For example, 6 is a factor of 12, and 24 is a multiple of 12. 12 is both a factor and a multiple of itself, since $12 \times 1 = 12$ and $12 \div 1 = 12$.

9. Prime Factorization

To find the prime factorization of an integer, just keep breaking it up into factors until **all the factors are prime.** To find the prime factorization of 36, for example, you could begin by breaking it into 4×9: $36 = 4 \times 9 = 2 \times 2 \times 3 \times 3$.

10. Relative Primes

Relative primes are integers that have no common factor other than 1. To determine whether two integers are relative primes, break them both down to their prime factorizations. For example: $35 = 5 \times 7$, and $54 = 2 \times 3 \times 3 \times 3$. They have **no prime factors in common,** so 35 and 54 are relative primes.

11. Common Multiple

A common multiple is a number that is a multiple of two or more integers. You can always get a common multiple of two integers by **multiplying** them, but, unless the two numbers are relative primes, the product will not be the *least* common multiple. For example, to find a common multiple for 12 and 15, you could just multiply: $12 \times 15 = 180$.

To find the **least common multiple**, check out the **multiples of the larger integer** until you find one that's **also a multiple of the smaller.** To find the LCM of 12 and 15, begin by taking the multiples of 15: 15 is not divisible by 12; 30 is not; nor is 45. But the next multiple of 15, 60, *is* divisible by 12, so it's the LCM.

12. Greatest Common Factor (GCF)

To find the greatest common factor, break down both integers into their prime factorizations and multiply **all the prime factors they have in common.** $36 = 2 \times 2 \times 3 \times 3$, and $48 = 2 \times 2 \times 2 \times 2 \times 3$. What they have in common is two 2s and one 3, so the GCF is $2 \times 2 \times 3 = 12$.

13. Even/Odd

To predict whether a sum, difference, or product will be even or odd, just **take simple numbers like 1 and 2 and see what happens.** There are rules—"odd times even is even," for example—but there's no need to memorize them. What happens with one set of numbers generally happens with all similar sets.

14. Multiples of 2 and 4

An integer is divisible by 2 (even) if the **last digit is even.** An integer is divisible by 4 if the **last two digits form a multiple of 4.** The last digit of 562 is 2, which is even, so 562 is a multiple of 2. The last two digits form 62, which is *not* divisible by 4, so 562 is not a multiple of 4. The integer 512, however is divisible by four because the last two digits form 12, which is a multiple of 4.

15. Multiples of 3 and 9

An integer is divisible by 3 if the **sum of its digits is divisible by 3.** An integer is divisible by 9 if the **sum of its digits is divisible by 9.** The sum of the digits in 957 is 21, which is divisible by 3 but not by 9, so 957 is divisible by 3 but not by 9.

16. Multiples of 5 and 10

An integer is divisible by 5 if the **last digit is 5 or 0.** An integer is divisible by 10 if the **last digit is 0.** The last digit of 665 is 5, so 665 is a multiple of 5 but *not* a multiple of 10.

17. Remainders

The remainder is the **whole number left over after division.** 487 is 2 more than 485, which is a multiple of 5, so when 487 is divided by 5, the remainder will be 2.

FRACTIONS AND DECIMALS

18. Reducing Fractions

To reduce a fraction to lowest terms, **factor out and cancel** all factors the numerator and denominator have in common.

$$\frac{28}{36} = \frac{4 \times 7}{4 \times 9} = \frac{7}{9}$$

19. Adding/Subtracting Fractions

To add or subtract fractions, first find a **common denominator,** then add or subtract the numerators.

$$\frac{2}{15} + \frac{3}{10} = \frac{4}{30} + \frac{9}{30} = \frac{4+9}{30} = \frac{13}{30}$$

20. Multiplying Fractions

To multiply fractions, **multiply** the numerators and **multiply** the denominators.

$$\frac{1}{2} \div \frac{3}{5} = \frac{5 \times 3}{7 \times 4} = \frac{15}{28}$$

21. Dividing Fractions

To divide fractions, **invert** the second one and **multiply.**

$$\frac{1}{2} \div \frac{3}{5} = \frac{1}{2} \times \frac{5}{3} = \frac{1 \times 5}{2 \times 3} = \frac{5}{6}$$

22. Mixed Numbers and Improper Fractions

To convert a mixed number to an improper fraction, **multiply** the whole number part by the denominator, then **add** the numerator. The result is the new numerator (over the same denominator). To convert $7\frac{1}{3}$, first multiply 7 by 3, then add 1, to get the new numerator of 22. Put that over the same denominator, 3, to get $\frac{22}{3}$.

To convert an improper fraction to a mixed number, divide the denominator into the numerator to get a **whole number quotient with a remainder.** The quotient becomes the whole number part of the mixed number, and the remainder becomes the new numerator—with the same denominator. For example, to convert $\frac{108}{5}$, first divide 5 into 108, which yields 21 with a remainder of 3. Therefore, $\frac{108}{5} = 21\frac{3}{5}$.

23. Reciprocal

To find the reciprocal of a fraction, **switch the numerator and the denominator.** The reciprocal of $\frac{3}{7}$ is $\frac{7}{3}$. The reciprocal of 5 is $\frac{1}{5}$. The product of reciprocals is 1.

24. Comparing Fractions

One way to compare fractions is to **re-express them with a common denominator.** $\frac{3}{4} = \frac{21}{28}$ and $\frac{5}{7} = \frac{20}{28}$. $\frac{21}{28}$ is greater than $\frac{20}{28}$, so $\frac{3}{4}$ is greater than $\frac{5}{7}$. Another method is to **convert them both to decimals.** $\frac{3}{4}$ converts to .75 , and $\frac{5}{7}$ converts to approximately .714.

25. Converting Fractions and Decimals

To convert a fraction to a decimal, **divide the bottom into the top.** To convert $\frac{5}{8}$, divide 8 into 5, yielding .625.

To convert a decimal to a fraction, set the decimal over 1 and **multiply the numerator and denominator by 10** raised to the number of digits to the right of the decimal point.

To convert .625 to a fraction, you would multiply $\frac{.625}{1}$ by $\frac{10^3}{10^3}$ or $\frac{1000}{1000}$. Then simplify: $\frac{625}{1000} = \frac{5 \times 125}{8 \times 125} = \frac{5}{8}$.

26. Repeating Decimal

To find a particular digit in a repeating decimal, note the **number of digits in the cluster that repeats.** If there are 2 digits in that cluster, then every second digit is the same. If there are 3 digits in that cluster, then every third digit is the same. And so on. For example, the decimal equivalent of $\frac{1}{27}$ is .037037037..., which is best written $.\overline{037}$. There are 3 digits in the repeating cluster, so every third digit is the same: 7. To find the 50th digit, look for the multiple of 3 just less than 50—that's 48. The 48th digit is 7, and with the 49th digit the pattern repeats with 0. The 50th digit is 3.

27. Identifying the Parts and the Whole

The key to solving most fractions and percents story problems is to identify the part and the whole. Usually you'll find the **part** associated with the verb *is/are* and the **whole** associated with the word *of*. In the sentence, "Half of the boys are blonds," the whole is the boys ("*of the* boys"), and the part is the blonds ("*are* blonds").

PERCENTS

28. Percent Formula

Whether you need to find the part, the whole, or the percent, use the same formula:

Part = Percent × Whole

Example: What is 12 percent of 25?
Setup: Part = .12 × 25

Example: 15 is 3 percent of what number?
Setup: 15 = .03 × Whole

Example: 45 is what percent of 9?
Setup: 45 = Percent × 9

29. Percent Increase and Decrease

To increase a number by a percent, **add the percent to 100 percent,** convert to a decimal, and multiply. To increase 40 by 25 percent, add 25 percent to 100 percent, convert 125 percent to 1.25, and multiply by 40. 1.25 × 40 = 50.

30. Finding the Original Whole

To find the **original whole before a percent increase or decrease,** set up an equation. Think of the result of a 15 percent increase over *x* as 1.15*x*.

Example: After a 5 percent increase, the population was 59,346. What was the population before the increase?
Setup: 1.05*x* = 59,346

31. Combined Percent Increase and Decrease

To determine the combined effect of multiple percent increases and/or decreases, **start with 100 and see what happens.**

Example: A price went up 10 percent one year, and the new price went up 20 percent the next year. What was the combined percent increase?
Setup: First year: 100 + (10 percent of 100) = 110. Second year: 110 + (20 percent of 110) = 132. That's a combined 32 percent increase.

RATIOS, PROPORTIONS, AND RATES

32. Setting up a Ratio

To find a ratio, put the number associated with the word *of* on top and the quantity associated with the word *to* on the bottom and reduce. The ratio of 20 oranges to 12 apples is $\frac{20}{12}$, which reduces to $\frac{5}{3}$.

33. Part-to-Part Ratios and Part-to-Whole Ratios

If the parts add up to the whole, a part-to-part ratio can be turned into two part-to-whole ratios by putting **each number in the original ratio over the sum of the numbers.**

If the ratio of males to females is 1 to 2, then the males-to-people ratio is $\frac{1}{1+2} = \frac{1}{3}$ and the females-to-people ratio is $\frac{2}{1+2} = \frac{2}{3}$. In other words, $\frac{2}{3}$ of all the people are female.

34. Solving a Proportion

To solve a proportion, **cross multiply:**

$$\frac{x}{5} = \frac{3}{4}$$
$$4x = 3 \times 5$$
$$x = \frac{15}{4} = 3.75$$

35. Rate

To solve a rates problem, **use the units** to keep things straight.

Example: If snow is falling at the rate of one foot every four hours, how many inches of snow will fall in seven hours?

Setup:
$$\frac{1 \text{ foot}}{4 \text{ hours}} = \frac{x \text{ inches}}{7 \text{ hours}}$$
$$\frac{12 \text{ inches}}{4 \text{ hours}} = \frac{x \text{ inches}}{7 \text{ hours}}$$
$$4x = 12 \times 7$$
$$x = 21$$

36. Average Rate

Average rate is *not* simply the average of the rates.

$$\text{Average } A \text{ per } B = \frac{\text{Total } A}{\text{Total } B}$$
$$\text{Average Speed} = \frac{\text{Total distance}}{\text{Total time}}$$

To find the average speed for 120 miles at 40 mph and 120 miles at 60 mph, **don't just average the two speeds.** First figure out the total distance and the total time. The total distance is 120 + 120 = 240 miles. The times are two hours for the first leg and three hours for the second leg, or five hours total. The average speed, then, is $\frac{240}{5} = 48$ miles per hour.

AVERAGES

37. Average Formula

To find the average of a set of numbers, **add them up and divide by the number of numbers.**

$$\text{Average} = \frac{\text{Sum of the terms}}{\text{Number of terms}}$$

To find the average of the 5 numbers 12, 15, 23, 40, and 40, first add them: $12 + 15 + 23 + 40 + 40 = 130$. Then divide the sum by 5: $130 \div 5 = 26$.

38. Average of Evenly Spaced Numbers

To find the average of evenly spaced numbers, just **average the smallest and the largest.** The average of all the integers from 13 through 77 is the same as the average of 13 and 77:

$$\frac{13 + 77}{2} = \frac{90}{2} = 45$$

39. Using the Average to Find the Sum

$$\text{Sum} = (\text{Average}) \times (\text{Number of terms})$$

If the average of 10 numbers is 50, then they add up to 10×50, or 500.

40. Finding the Missing Number

To find a missing number when you're given the average, **use the sum.** If the average of 4 numbers is 7, then the sum of those 4 numbers is 4×7, or 28. Suppose that 3 of the numbers are 3, 5, and 8. These 3 numbers add up to 16 of that 28, which leaves 12 for the fourth number.

41. Median and Mode

The median of a set of numbers is the **value that falls in the middle of the set.** If you have 5 test scores, and they are 88, 86, 57, 94, and 73, you must first list the scores in increasing or decreasing order: 57, 73, 86, 88, 94.

The median is the middle number, or 86. If there is an even number of values in a set (6 test scores, for instance), simply take the average of the 2 middle numbers.

The mode of a set of numbers is the **value that appears most often.** If your test scores were 88, 57, 68, 85, 99, 93, 93, 84, and 81, the mode of the scores would be 93 because it appears more often than any other score. If there is a tie for the most common value in a set, the set has more than one mode.

POSSIBILITIES AND PROBABILITY

42. Counting the Possibilities

The fundamental counting principle: If there are *m* **ways** one event can happen and *n* **ways** a second event can happen, then there are *m* × *n* **ways** for the 2 events to happen. For example, with 5 shirts and 7 pairs of pants to choose from, you can have $5 \times 7 = 35$ different outfits.

43. Probability

$$\text{Probability} = \frac{\text{Favorable Outcomes}}{\text{Total Possible Outcomes}}$$

For example, if you have 12 shirts in a drawer and 9 of them are white, the probability of picking a white shirt at random is $\frac{9}{12} = \frac{3}{4}$. This probability can also be expressed as .75 or 75%.

POWERS AND ROOTS

44. Multiplying and Dividing Powers

To multiply powers with the same base, **add the exponents and keep the same base:**

$$x^3 \times x^4 = x^{3+4} = x^7$$

To divide powers with the same base, **subtract the exponents and keep the same base:**

$$y^{13} \div y^8 = y^{13-8} = y^5$$

45. Raising Powers to Powers

To raise a power to a power, **multiply the exponents:**

$$(x^3)^4 = x^{3 \times 4} = x^{12}$$

46. Simplifying Square Roots

To simplify a square root, **factor out the perfect squares** under the radical, unsquare them, and put the result in front.

$$\sqrt{12} = \sqrt{4 \times 3} = \sqrt{4} \times \sqrt{3} = 2\sqrt{3}$$

47. Adding and Subtracting Roots

You can add or subtract radical expressions **when the part under the radicals is the same:**

$$2\sqrt{3} + 3\sqrt{3} = 5\sqrt{3}$$

Don't try to add or subtract when the radical parts are different. There's not much you can do with an expression like:

$$3\sqrt{5} + 3\sqrt{7}$$

48. Multiplying and Dividing Roots

The product of square roots is equal to the **square root of the product:**

$$\sqrt{3} \times \sqrt{5} = \sqrt{3 \times 5} = \sqrt{15}$$

The quotient of square roots is equal to the **square root of the quotient:**

$$\frac{\sqrt{6}}{\sqrt{3}} = \sqrt{\frac{6}{3}} = \sqrt{2}$$

49. Negative Exponent and Rational Exponent

To find the value of a number raised to a negative exponent, simply rewrite the number, without the negative sign, as the bottom of a fraction with 1 as the numerator of the fraction: $3^{-2} = \frac{1}{3^2} = \frac{1}{9}$. If x is a positive number and a is a nonzero number, then $x^{\frac{1}{a}} = \sqrt[a]{x}$. So $4^{\frac{1}{2}} = \sqrt[2]{4} = 2$. If p and q are integers, then $x^{\frac{p}{q}} = \sqrt[q]{x^p}$. So $4^{\frac{3}{2}} = \sqrt[2]{4^3} = \sqrt{64} = 8$.

ABSOLUTE VALUE

50. Determining Absolute Value

The absolute value of a number is the distance of the number from zero on the number line. Because absolute value is a distance, it is always positive. The absolute value of 7 is 7; this is expressed $|7| = 7$. Similarly, the absolute value of −7 is 7: $|-7| = 7$. Every positive number is the absolute value of 2 numbers: itself and its negative.

ALGEBRAIC EXPRESSIONS

51. Evaluating an Expression

To evaluate an algebraic expression, **plug in** the given values for the unknowns and calculate according to **PEMDAS**. To find the value of $x^2 + 5x - 6$ when $x = -2$, plug in −2 for x: $(-2)^2 + 5(-2) - 6 = -12$.

52. Adding and Subtracting Monomials

To combine like terms, **keep the variable part unchanged while adding or subtracting the coefficients:**

$$2a + 3a = (2 + 3)a = 5a$$

53. Adding and Subtracting Polynomials

To add or subtract polynomials, **combine like terms.**

$$(3x^2 + 5x - 7) - (x^2 + 12) =$$
$$(3x^2 - x^2) + 5x + (-7 - 12) =$$
$$2x^2 + 5x - 19 =$$

54. Multiplying Monomials

To multiply monomials, **multiply the coefficients and the variables separately:**

$$2a \times 3a = (2 \times 3)(a \times a) = 6a^2$$

55. Multiplying Binomials—FOIL

To multiply binomials, use **FOIL.** To multiply $(x + 3)$ by $(x + 4)$, first multiply the **F**irst terms: $x \times x = x^2$. Next the **O**uter terms: $x \times 4 = 4x$. Then the **I**nner terms: $3 \times x = 3x$. And finally the **L**ast terms: $3 \times 4 = 12$. Then add and combine like terms:

$$x^2 + 4x + 3x + 12 = x^2 + 7x + 12$$

56. Multiplying Other Polynomials

FOIL works only when you want to multiply two binomials. If you want to multiply polynomials with more than two terms, make sure you **multiply each term in the first polynomial by each term in the second.**

$$(x^2 + 3x + 4)(x + 5) =$$
$$x^2(x + 5) + 3x(x + 5) + 4(x + 5) =$$
$$x^3 + 5x^2 + 3x^2 + 15x + 4x + 20 =$$
$$x^3 + 8x^2 + 19x + 20$$

After multiplying two polynomials together, the number of terms in your expression before simplifying should equal the number of terms in one polynomial multiplied by the number of terms in the second. In the example, you should have $3 \times 2 = 6$ terms in the product before you simplify like terms.

FACTORING
ALGEBRAIC EXPRESSIONS

57. Factoring out a Common Divisor

A factor common to all terms of a polynomial can be **factored out.** All three terms in the polynomial $3x^3 + 12x^2 - 6x$ contain a factor of $3x$. Pulling out the common factor yields $3x(x^2 + 4x - 2)$.

58. Factoring the Difference of Squares

One of the test maker's favorite factorables is the **difference of squares.**

$$a^2 - b^2 = (a - b)\ (a + b)$$

$x^2 - 9$, for example, factors to $(x - 3)(x + 3)$.

59. Factoring the Square of a Binomial

Recognize polynomials that are squares of binomials:

$$a^2 + 2ab + b^2 = (a + b)^2$$
$$a^2 - 2ab + b^2 = (a - b)^2$$

For example, $4x^2 + 12x + 9$ factors to $(2x + 3)^2$, and $n^2 - 10n + 25$ factors to $(n - 5)^2$.

60. Factoring Other Polynomials—FOIL in Reverse

To factor a quadratic expression, **think about what binomials you could use FOIL on to get that quadratic expression.** To factor $x^2 - 5x + 6$, think about what **F**irst terms will produce x^2, what **L**ast terms will produce $+6$, and what **O**uter and **I**nner terms will produce $-5x$. Some common sense—and a little trial and error—lead you to $(x - 2)(x - 3)$.

61. Simplifying an Algebraic Fraction

Simplifying an algebraic fraction is a lot like simplifying a numerical fraction. The general idea is to **find factors common to the numerator and denominator and cancel them.** Thus, simplifying an algebraic fraction begins with factoring.

For example, to simplify $\frac{x^2 - x - 12}{x^2 - 9}$, first factor the numerator and denominator:

$$\frac{x^2 - x - 12}{x^2 - 9} = \frac{(x-4)(x+3)}{(x-3)(x+3)}$$

Canceling $x + 3$ from the numerator and denominator leaves you with $\frac{x-4}{x-3}$.

SOLVING EQUATIONS

62. Solving a Linear Equation

To solve an equation, do whatever is necessary to both sides to **isolate the variable.** To solve the equation $5x - 12 = -2x + 9$, first get all the x's on one side by adding $2x$ to both sides: $7x - 12 = 9$. Then add 12 to both sides: $7x = 21$. Then divide both sides by 7: $x = 3$.

63. Solving "In Terms Of"

To solve an equation for one variable **in terms of** another means to **isolate the one variable on one side of the equation,** leaving an expression containing the other variable on the other side of the equation. To solve the equation $3x - 10y = -5x + 6y$ for x in terms of y, isolate x:

$$3x - 10y = -5x + 6y$$

$$3x + 5x = 6y + 10y$$

$$8x = 16y$$

$$x = 2y$$

64. Translating from English into Algebra

To translate from English into algebra, look for the key words and systematically turn phrases into algebraic expressions and sentences into equations. Be careful about order, especially when subtraction is called for.

Example: The charge for a phone call is r cents for the first 3 minutes and s cents for each minute thereafter. What is the cost, in cents, of a phone call lasting exactly t minutes? ($t > 3$)

Setup: The charge begins with r, and then something more is added, depending on the length of the call. The amount added is s times the number of minutes past 3 minutes. If the total number of minutes is t, then the number of minutes past 3 is $t - 3$. So the charge is $r + s(t - 3)$.

65. Solving a Quadratic Equation

To solve a quadratic equation, put it in the "$ax^2 + bx + c = 0$" form, **factor** the left side (if you can), and set each factor equal to 0 separately to get the two solutions. To solve $x^2 + 12 = 7x$, first rewrite it as $x^2 - 7x + 12 = 0$. Then factor the left side:

$$(x - 3)(x - 4) = 0$$

$$x - 3 = 0 \text{ or } x - 4 = 0$$

$$x = 3 \text{ or } 4$$

66. Solving a System of Equations

You can solve for 2 variables only if you have 2 distinct equations. 2 forms of the same equation will not be adequate. **Combine the equations** in such a way that **one of the variables cancels out.** To solve the 2 equations $4x + 3y = 8$ and $x + y = 3$, multiply both sides of the second equation by -3 to get: $-3x - 3y = -9$. Now add the 2 equations; the $3y$ and the $-3y$ cancel out, leaving: $x = -1$. Plug that back into either one of the original equations and you'll find that $y = 4$.

67. Solving an Inequality

To solve an inequality, do whatever is necessary to both sides to **isolate the variable.** Just remember that when you **multiply or divide both sides by a negative number,** you must **reverse the sign.** To solve $-5x + 7 < -3$, subtract 7 from both sides to get: $-5x < -10$. Now divide both sides by -5, remembering to reverse the sign: $x > 2$.

68. Radical Equations

A radical equation contains at least one radical expression. Solve radical equations by using standard rules of algebra. If $5\sqrt{x} - 2 = 13$, then $5\sqrt{x} = 15$ and $\sqrt{x} = 3$, so $x = 9$.

FUNCTIONS

69. Function Notation and Evaluation

Standard function notation is written $f(x)$ and read "f of 4." To evaluate the function $f(x) = 2x + 3$ for $f(4)$, replace x with 4 and simplify: $f(4) = 2(4) + 3 = 11$.

70. Direct and Inverse Variation

In direct variation, $y = kx$, where k is a nonzero constant. In direct variation, the variable y changes directly as x does. If a unit of Currency A is worth 2 units of Currency B, then $A = 2B$. If the number of units of B were to double, the number of units of A would double, and so on for halving, tripling, etc. In inverse variation, $xy = k$, where x and y are variables and k is a constant. A famous inverse relationship is $rate \times time = distance$, where distance is constant. Imagine having to cover a distance of 24 miles. If you were to travel at 12 miles per hour, you'd need 2 hours. But if you were to halve your rate, you would have to double your time. This is just another way of saying that rate and time vary inversely.

71. Domain and Range of a Function

The domain of a function is the set of values for which the function is defined. For example, the domain of $f(x) = \dfrac{1}{1 - x^2}$ is all values of x except 1 and -1, because for those values the denominator has a value of 0 and is

therefore undefined. The range of a function is the set of outputs or results of the function. For example, the range of $f(x) = x^2$ is all numbers greater than all or equal to zero, because x^2 cannot be negative.

COORDINATE GEOMETRY

72. Finding the Distance Between Two Points

To find the distance between points, **use the Pythagorean theorem** or **special right triangles.** The difference between the x's is one leg and the difference between the y's is the other.

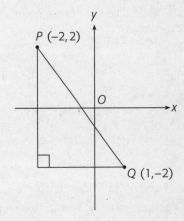

In the figure above, PQ is the hypotenuse of a 3-4-5 triangle, so $PQ = 5$.

You can also use the **distance formula:**

$$d = \sqrt{(x_1 - x_2)^2 + (y_1 - y_2)^2}$$

To find the distance between $R(3, 6)$ and $S(5, -2)$:

$$d = \sqrt{(3 - 5)^2 + [6 - (-2)^2]}$$

$$= \sqrt{(-2)^2 + (8)^2}$$

$$= \sqrt{68} = 2\sqrt{17}$$

73. Using Two Points to Find the Slope

$$\text{Slope} = \frac{\text{Change in } y}{\text{Change in } x} = \frac{\text{Rise}}{\text{Run}}$$

The slope of the line that contains the points $A(2, 3)$ and $B(0, -1)$ is:

$$\frac{y_A - y_B}{x_A - x_B} = \frac{3 - (-1)}{2 - 0} = \frac{4}{2} = 2$$

74. Using an Equation to Find the Slope

To find the slope of a line from an equation, put the equation into the **slope-intercept** form:

$$y = mx + b$$

The **slope is m**. To find the slope of the equation $3x + 2y = 4$, rearrange it:

$$3x + 2y = 4$$

$$2y = -3x + 4$$

$$y = -\frac{3}{2}x + 2$$

The slope is $-\frac{3}{2}$.

75. Using an Equation to Find an Intercept

To find the y-intercept, you can either put the equation into $y = mx + b$ (slope-intercept) form—in which case **b is the y-intercept**—or you can just **plug $x = 0$** into the equation and **solve for y**. To find the x-intercept, **plug $y = 0$** into the equation and **solve for x**.

LINES AND ANGLES

76. Intersecting Lines

When two lines intersect, **adjacent angles are supplementary and vertical angles are equal.**

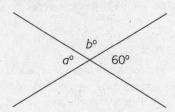

In the figure above, the angles marked $a°$ and $b°$ are adjacent and supplementary, so $a + b = 180$. Furthermore, the angles marked $a°$ and $60°$ are vertical and equal, so $a = 60$.

77. Parallel Lines and Transversals

A transversal across parallel lines forms **four equal acute angles and four equal obtuse angles.**

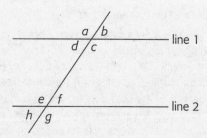

In the figure above, line 1 is parallel to line 2. Angles a, c, e, and g are obtuse, so they are all equal. Angles b, d, f, and h are acute, so they are all equal.

Furthermore, **any of the acute angles is supplementary to any of the obtuse angles.** Angles a and h are supplementary, as are b and e, c and f, and so on.

TRIANGLES—GENERAL

78. Interior and Exterior Angles of a Triangle

The 3 angles of any triangle **add up to 180 degrees.**

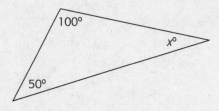

In the figure above, $x + 50 + 100 = 180$, so $x = 30$.

An exterior angle of a triangle is equal to the **sum of the remote interior angles.**

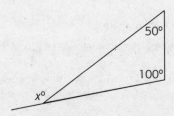

In the figure above, the exterior angle labeled $x°$ is equal to the sum of the remote angles: $x = 50 + 100 = 150$.

The 3 exterior angles of a triangle add up to 360 degrees.

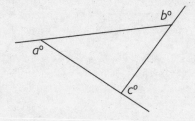

In the figure above, $a + b + c = 360$.

79. Similar Triangles

Similar triangles have the same shape: **corresponding angles are equal and corresponding sides are proportional.**

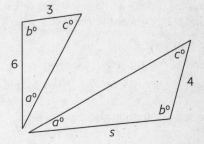

The triangles above are similar because they have the same angles. The 3 corresponds to the 4 and the 6 corresponds to the s.

$$\frac{3}{4} = \frac{6}{s}$$

$$3s = 24$$

$$s = 8$$

80. Area of a Triangle

$$\text{Area of Triangle} = \frac{1}{2}(\text{base})(\text{height})$$

The height is the perpendicular distance between the side that's chosen as the base and the opposite vertex.

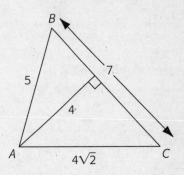

In the triangle above, 4 is the height when the 7 is chosen as the base.

$$\text{Area} = \frac{1}{2}bh = \frac{1}{2}(7)(4) = 14$$

81. Triangle Inequality Theorem

The length of one side of a triangle must be **greater than the difference and less than the sum** of the lengths of the other two sides. For example, if it is given that the length of one side is 3 and the length of another side is 7, then you know that the length of the third side must be greater than $7 - 3 = 4$ and less than $7 + 3 = 10$.

82. Isosceles and Equilateral Triangles

An isosceles triangle is a triangle that has **2 equal sides.** Not only are 2 sides equal, but the angles opposite the equal sides, called **base angles**, are also equal.

Equilateral triangles are triangles in which **all 3 sides are equal.** Since all the sides are equal, all the angles are also equal. All 3 angles in an equilateral triangle measure 60 degrees, regardless of the lengths of sides.

RIGHT TRIANGLES

83. Pythagorean Theorem

For all right triangles:

$$(\text{leg}_1)^2 + (\text{leg}_2)^2 = (\text{hypotenuse})^2$$

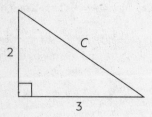

If one leg is 2 and the other leg is 3, then:

$$2^2 + 3^2 = c^2$$
$$c^2 = 4 + 9$$
$$c = \sqrt{13}$$

84. The 3-4-5 Triangle

If a right triangle's leg-to-leg ratio is 3:4, or if the leg-to-hypotenuse ratio is 3:5 or 4:5, it's a 3-4-5 triangle and you don't need to use the Pythagorean theorem to find the third side. Just figure out what multiple of 3-4-5 it is.

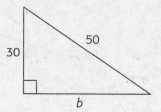

In the right triangle shown, one leg is 30 and the hypotenuse is 50. This is 10 times 3-4-5. The other leg is 40.

85. The 5-12-13 Triangle

If a right triangle's leg-to-leg ratio is 5:12, or if the leg-to-hypotenuse ratio is 5:13 or 12:13, then it's a 5-12-13 triangle and you don't need to use the Pythagorean theorem to find the third side. Just figure out what multiple of 5-12-13 it is.

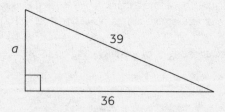

Here one leg is 36 and the hypotenuse is 39. This is 3 times 5-12-13. The other leg is 15.

86. The 30-60-90 Triangle

The sides of a 30-60-90 triangle are in a ratio of
$x : x\sqrt{3} : 2x$. You don't need the Pythagorean theorem.

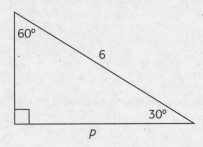

If the hypotenuse is 6, then the shorter leg is half that, or
3; and then the longer leg is equal to the short leg times
$\sqrt{3}$, or $3\sqrt{3}$.

87. The 45-45-90 Triangle

The sides of a 45-45-90 triangle are in a ratio of
$x : x : x\sqrt{2}$.

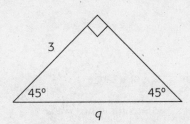

If one leg is 3, then the other leg is also 3, and the
hypotenuse is equal to a leg times $\sqrt{2}$, or $3\sqrt{2}$.

OTHER POLYGONS

88. Characteristics of a Rectangle

A rectangle is a **four-sided figure with four right angles.**
Opposite sides are equal. Diagonals are equal.

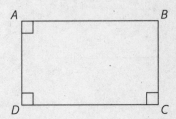

Quadrilateral *ABCD* above is shown to have three right
angles. The fourth angle therefore also measures 90
degrees, and *ABCD* is a rectangle. The perimeter of a rectangle is equal to the sum of the lengths of the four sides,
which is equivalent to 2(length + width).

Area of Rectangle = length × width

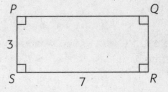

The area of a 7-by-3 rectangle is $7 \times 3 = 21$.

89. Characteristics of a Parallelogram

A parallelogram has **two pairs of parallel sides.** Opposite sides are equal. Opposite angles are equal. Consecutive angles add up to 180 degrees.

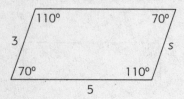

In the figure above, s is the length of the side opposite the 3, so $s = 3$.

Area of Parallelogram = base × height

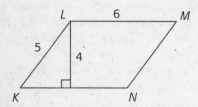

In parallelogram *KLMN* above, 4 is the height when *LM* or *KN* is used as the base. Base × height = 6 × 4 = 24.

90. Characteristics of a Square

A square is a **rectangle with four equal sides.**

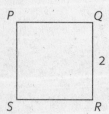

If *PQRS* is a square, all sides are the same length as *QR*. The perimeter of a square is equal to four times the length of one side.

Area of Square = (Side)^2

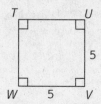

The square above, with sides of length 5, has an area of $5^2 = 25$.

91. Interior Angles of a Polygon

The **sum of the measures of the interior angles of a polygon = $(n - 2) \times 180$**, where n is the number of sides.

Sum of the Angles = $(n - 2) \times 180$

The eight angles of an octagon, for example, add up to $(8 - 2) \times 180 = 1{,}080$.

CIRCLES

92. Circumference of a Circle

Circumference = $2\pi r$

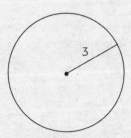

In the circle above, the radius is 3, and so the circumference is $2\pi(3) = 6\pi$.

93. Length of an Arc

An **arc** is a piece of the circumference. If n is the degree measure of the arc's central angle, then the formula is:

$$\text{Length of an Arc} = \left(\frac{n}{360}\right)(2\pi r)$$

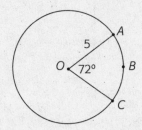

In the figure above, the radius is 5 and the measure of the central angle is 72 degrees. The arc length is $\frac{72}{360}$ or $\frac{1}{5}$ of the circumference:

$$\left(\frac{72}{360}\right)(2\pi)(5) = \left(\frac{1}{5}\right)(10\pi) = 2\pi$$

94. Area of a Circle

$$\text{Area of a Circle} = \pi r^2$$

The area of the circle is $\pi(4)^2 = 16\pi$.

95. Area of a Sector

A **sector** is a piece of the area of a circle. If n is the degree measure of the sector's central angle, then the formula is:

$$\text{Area of a Sector} = \left(\frac{n}{360}\right)(\pi r^2)$$

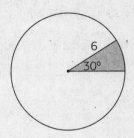

In the figure above, the radius is 6 and the measure of the sector's central angle is 30 degrees. The sector has $\frac{30}{360}$ or $\frac{1}{12}$ of the area of the circle:

$$\left(\frac{30}{360}\right)(\pi)(6^2) = \left(\frac{1}{12}\right)(36\pi) = 3\pi$$

96. Tangency

When a line is tangent to a circle, the radius of the circle is perpendicular to the line at the point of contact.

SOLIDS

97. Surface Area of a Rectangular Solid

The surface of a rectangular solid consists of three pairs of identical faces. To find the surface area, find the area of each face and add them up. If the length is l, the width is w, and the height is h, the formula is:

$$\text{Surface Area} = 2lw + 2wh + 2lh$$

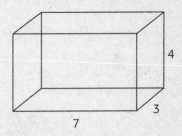

The surface area of the box above is:
$2 \times 7 \times 3 + 2 \times 3 \times 4 + 2 \times 7 \times 4 = 42 + 24 + 56 = 122$

98. Volume of a Rectangular Solid

Volume of a Rectangular Solid = *lwh*

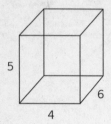

The volume of a 4-by-5-by-6 box is

$4 \times 5 \times 6 = 120$

A cube is a rectangular solid with length, width, and height all equal. If *e* is the length of an edge of a cube, the volume formula is:

Volume of a Cube = e^3

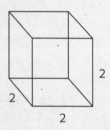

The volume of this cube is $2^3 = 8$.

99. Volume of a Cylinder

Volume of a Cylinder = $\pi r^2 h$

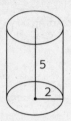

In the cylinder above, $r = 2$, $h = 5$, so:

Volume $= \pi(2^2)(5) = 20\pi$

100. Finding the Midpoint

The midpoint of two points on a line segment is the average of the *x*-coordinates of the endpoints and the average of the *y*-coordinates of the endpoints. If the endpoints are (x_1, y_1) and (x_2, y_2), the midpoint is $\left(\frac{x_1 + x_2}{2}, \frac{y_1 + y_2}{2}\right)$. The midpoint of (3, 5) and (9, 1) is $\left(\frac{3 + 9}{2}, \frac{5 + 1}{2}\right)$.

PSAT Vitals

PSAT VITALS

Take this with you to the test, or keep it in your wallet or purse for quick reference.

PSAT Basics

2 hours and 10 minutes long /5 sections /1 break

5 sections = 2 Math /2 Critical Reading /1 Writing

Top Score: 240 (80 $\times$ 3 sections)

PSAT Ground Rules

NOT allowed to jump back and forth between sections.

NOT allowed to return to earlier sections to change answers.

NOT allowed to spend more than the allotted time on any section.

ARE allowed to move around within a section.

ARE allowed to flip through your section at the beginning to see what type of questions are coming up.

Order of Difficulty

Questions Arranged Easiest > Hardest	Yes	No
All Math	Y	
Critical Reading: Sentence Completion	Y	
Critical Reading: Reading Comprehension		N
Writing		N

Basic Strategies

Educated Guessing

Always guess when you can eliminate one wrong answer choice.

Don't Answer Questions in Order.

When you run into questions that look tough, circle them in your test booklet and skip them. Go back and try again after you have answered the easier ones.

Writing

Three question types: Usage, Sentence Correction, Revision-in-Context.

One strategy works for all three types: Read and listen for error—Identify the error—Check answer choices.

Math

Answer all grid-ins. There is no penalty for guessing. The worst that can happen is that you get zero points on the questions you guessed on.

Remember the 5-Step Method (Estimate difficulty—Read question—Skip?—Look for fast approach—Guess.)

Critical Reading

Sentence Completion questions: Remember the 4-Step Method (Read—Predict—Select—Plug In)

Reading Comprehension questions: Remember the 5-Step Method (Read—Locate—Predict—Scan—Select)

Bring to Test

ID

Pencils

Calculator

Watch

Snacks